RANK AND TITLE
IN THE
OLD KINGDOM

RANK AND TITLE IN THE OLD KINGDOM

THE STRUCTURE OF THE EGYPTIAN ADMINISTRATION IN THE FIFTH AND SIXTH DYNASTIES

BY

Klaus Baer

THE UNIVERSITY OF CHICAGO PRESS

Library of Congress Catalog Number: 60–7231

THE UNIVERSITY OF CHICAGO PRESS, CHICAGO 37
Cambridge University Press, London, N.W.1, England
The University of Toronto Press, Toronto 5, Canada

Printed by THE UNIVERSITY OF CHICAGO PRESS,
Chicago, Illinois, U.S.A.

PREFACE

*

This book was originally written in the spring and summer of 1958 as a doctoral thesis in the Department of Oriental Languages and Civilizations of the University of Chicago. In preparing the manuscript for publication almost a year later, it seemed best to make no substantial changes, rather than to risk the possibility of considerable delay due to the pressure of other work. The material published in books and articles that did not reach Chicago until the late summer of 1958 has thus, in general, not been included. In any case, absolute completeness in collecting pertinent data is an unattainable goal; the writer hopes that material he has overlooked or that was published subsequent to completion of the manuscript will enable others to assess the likelihood of the conclusions presented here being correct.

The study is basically the presentation of a single argument, and it has been the author's aim to compose it in such a manner as to allow the reader to follow the steps by which the conclusions were reached. As a result, statements will be found in the earlier portions of the book which are rejected at a later stage in the discussion. This is particularly true of the datings assigned the tombs in chapter iii, which was written before the rest and is based only on archeological and other evidence not connected with the ranking systems of titles; it was intended to provide the basis for establishing the ranking sequences characteristic for different periods in the Old Kingdom, and its conclusions are necessarily tentative. The datings finally decided on are listed in the Appendix to chapter vi, which should always be consulted.

In order to keep the work within the limits of one volume, the presentation has been highly condensed, with most of the material being given in the form of abbreviated lists; much of the argument could only be outlined. The writer regrets that the result is a little difficult to follow in some cases but hopes that he has presented in each step of the discussion an adequate description of the procedure followed and at least brief references to all the material used. In view of the highly tabular nature of the presentation, it seemed unnecessary to add indexes, which would in most cases simply have repeated the lists and tables in a slightly altered form. It is hoped that the reader will not have too much trouble in finding references to specific examples or discussions of individual tombs.

It is a pleasure to acknowledge the aid and assistance the author has received from many sides, without which this work could never have been written. From Professor Selim Hassan, Hans Goedicke (then of Brown University), and Charles Nims, I obtained copies of unpublished texts. The authorities at the Boston Museum of Fine Arts, the Cairo Museum, the Chicago Museum of Natural History, and the museum of the Oriental Institute of the University of Chicago gave me access to unpublished objects in their collections. At the Boston Museum of Fine Arts, I was also given access to the photographs and records of their many seasons of excavation at Giza. Much help was also obtained from the photographic files of the Oriental Institute at Chicago, and I would like to acknowledge particularly the assistance I received there from the late Miss Jessie Abbot. The unpublished materials obtained from these sources enabled me to fill several serious lacunae in the presentation of this study.

During the years 1952–54, I had the privilege of studying in Egypt on a Fulbright grant under the supervision of Professor Ahmed Fakhry, who gave me full access to the materials excavated by the Project of Pyramid Studies, which he directed. It was at that time that my interest in studying the administration of Old Kingdom Egypt was aroused; and the use of the index of Old Kingdom names and titles that had been prepared under his supervision by Dorothy Eady helped me considerably when I began to collect material for this study. I regret that the book as it stands now has so little bearing on the many interesting problems raised by his finds.

I am grateful to Professors Anthes of Pennsylvania, Edel of Bonn, Helck of Hamburg and Dr. Henry Fischer of the Metropolitan Museum of Art and Dr. Smith of the Boston Museum of Fine Arts for their many helpful comments and suggestions.

Finally the writer owes a great debt of gratitude to the members of his advisory committee, Professors Wilson, Edgerton, and Seele and to the other members of the staff of the Oriental Institute with whom he was privileged to discuss the work and to whose advice this work owes whatever merit it may have. Without the facilities provided by the Oriental Institute library and the continual assistance from Miss Vindenäs and Mrs. Putzey, the librarians, this book would never, in the most literal sense of the term, have been written.

CONTENTS

*

LIST OF ABBREVIATIONS

*

ABU-BAKR, *Giza*	ABU-BAKR, ABDEL-MONEIM, *Excavations at Giza*. Cairo, 1953——.
AJA	*American Journal of Archaeology*. Baltimore (etc.), 1897——.
ASAE	*Annales du service des antiquités de l'Égypte*. Cairo, 1900——.
BMFA	*Bulletin of the Museum of Fine Arts*. Boston, 1903——.
BMMA	*The Bulletin of the Metropolitan Museum of Art, New York*. New York, 1905–42; New Series, 1942——.
Cairo, *CG*, 1–380	BORCHARDT, LUDWIG. *Statuen und Statuetten von Königen und Privatleuten*. Vol. I. ("Catalogue général des antiquités égyptiennes du museé du Caire," Vol. LIII.) Berlin, 1911. Quoted by number.
Cairo, *CG*, 1295–1541	BORCHARDT, LUDWIG. *Denkmäler des Alten Reiches*. Vol. I. ("Catalogue général des antiquités égyptiennes du musée du Caire," Vol. XCVII.) Berlin, 1937. Quoted by number. Nos. 1542–1808 are to be published in the projected second volume, which has not yet appeared.
CRAIBL	*Comptes-rendus de l'académie des inscriptions et belles-lettres*. Paris, 1857——.
FIFAO	*Fouilles de l'institut français d'archéologie orientale du Caire*. Rapports préliminaires. Cairo, 1924——.
GARDINER, *Onomastica*	GARDINER, A. H. *Ancient Egyptian Onomastica*. 3 vols. London, 1947.
HELCK, *Untersuchungen*	HELCK, WOLFGANG. *Untersuchungen zu den Beamtentiteln des ägyptischen Alten Reiches*. Glückstadt, 1954.

HESP	SMITH, W. S. *A History of Egyptian Sculpture and Painting in the Old Kingdom.* 2d ed. London, 1949.
Hieroglyphic Texts, I	SCOTT-MONCRIEFF, P. D. *Hieroglyphic Texts from Egyptian Stelae, etc., in the British Museum.* Vol. I. London, 1911.
Hieroglyphic Texts, VI	HALL, H. R. *Hieroglyphic Texts from Egyptian Stelae, etc., in the British Museum.* Vol. VI. London, 1922.
JAOS	*Journal of the American Oriental Society.* New Haven, 1849——.
JEA	*Journal of Egyptian Archaeology.* London, 1914——.
JNES	*Journal of Near Eastern Studies.* Chicago, 1942——.
LAAA	*Annals of Archaeology and Anthropology.* Liverpool, 1908–48.
LEPSIUS, *Denkmäler*	LEPSIUS, RICHARD. *Denkmäler aus Aegypten und Aethiopien.* 12 vols. Berlin, 1849–56.
———, *Erg.*	*Ergänzungsband.* Leipzig, 1913.
———, *Text*	*Text.* 5 vols. Leipzig, 1897–1913.
LUTZ, *Statues*	LUTZ, H. F. *Egyptian Statues and Statuettes in the Museum of Anthropology of the University of California.* Leipzig, 1930.
LUTZ, *Steles*	LUTZ, H. F. *Egyptian Tomb Steles and Offering Stones of the Museum of Anthropology and Ethnology of the University of California.* Leipzig, 1927.
MARIETTE, *Mastabas*	MARIETTE, AUGUSTE. *Les mastabas de l'Ancien Empire.* Paris, 1889. Quoted mostly by the letter and number of the tombs.
MDIAAK	*Mitteilungen des deutschen Instituts für ägyptische Altertumskunde in Kairo.* Wiesbaden, 1930——.
MIOF	*Mitteilungen des Instituts für Orientforschung.* Berlin, 1953——.
MMAFC	*Mémoires publiés par les membres de la mission archéologique française au Caire.* Cairo, 1884–1934.
Nachr. Gött.	*Nachrichten von der Gesellschaft der Wissenschaften zu Göttingen.* Since the Second World War the title has been changed to *Nachrichten der Akademie der Wissenschaften in Göttingen.*

PSBA	*Proceedings of the Society of Biblical Archaeology*. London, 1878–1918.
REISNER, *Giza*, I	REISNER, G. A. *A History of the Giza Necropolis*. Vol. I. Cambridge, Mass., 1942.
REISNER and SMITH, *Giza*, II	REISNER, G. A. and SMITH, W. S. *A History of the Giza Necropolis*. Vol. II. Cambridge, Mass., 1955.
SELIM HASSAN, *Giza*	SELIM HASSAN. *Excavations at Giza*. Vol. I, Oxford, 1932; Vols. II–VIII, Cairo, 1936–53.
Urkunden, I	SETHE, KURT H. *Urkunden des Alten Reichs*. 2d ed. Leipzig, 1932–33.
Wörterbuch	ERMAN, ADOLF and GRAPOW, HERMANN. *Wörterbuch der ägyptischen Sprache*. 6 vols., Leipzig, 1925–50.
WZKM	*Wiener Zeitschrift für die Kunde des Morgenlandes*. Vienna, 1887——.
ZÄS	*Zeitschrift für ägyptische Sprache und Altertumskunde*. Leipzig, 1863–1943. Berlin, 1954——.

I

INTRODUCTION

*

This study is an attempt to ascertain the relative rank of titles in use during the Fifth and Sixth Dynasties of the Egyptian Old Kingdom, and to draw some historical conclusions from the sequences of some of the better attested classes of titles. The writer's aim when beginning his researches was totally different: a sociological study of higher officialdom in the later Old Kingdom in the hope that some light would be cast upon the disintegration of the central authority and the rise of semiautonomous families in the provinces. In pursuing this problem, there was drawn up a reasonably complete index of names and titles of individuals known to have lived during the period being studied. It was the author's hope that a detailed study of these would enable him to establish family relationships among the higher officials. Unfortunately, it did not work out. A certain number of genealogies are, of course, well known and discussed in the pertinent literature; but any attempt to extend the amount of material was foredoomed to failure by the impossibility of determining whether two separate occurrences of a given name referred to the same person or not. The only result was a certain feeling of distrust towards a good many proposed genealogies, particularly in cases where the tombs of the persons involved do not form a closed group; the cases that seemed reliable are discussed in our list of sources in chapter iii, where the information is used for purposes of relative dating.

It became evident that some other kind of data must be brought to bear on the problem. After an equally futile attempt to use the names of servants occurring in a person's tomb as an aid toward identification, the writer's attention was drawn to the titles—and soon distracted from the problem originally envisaged to the subject of this work. The point of departure was some remarks made by Wolfgang Helck, which seemed to indicate the existence, at least during the later Old Kingdom, of a limited number of titles serving as rank indicators. If these could be determined, it might be easier to identify persons.* This also did not work out, but in the course of studying the titles, it seemed to the writer that their arrangement in the lines of text showed a considerable degree of consistency. In order to test this observation, which was reinforced in the writer's mind by statements of Margaret Murray and Alexandre Varille (which we shall discuss in greater detail below),† an attempt was made to conflate the titles in some of the larger tombs of the Fifth and Sixth Dynasties, beginning with *Ptḥ-ḥtp* [160],‡ his son and grandson [13] and [161] and the enormous mastaba of *Mrrw-kȝ* [197]. A reasonably consistent sequence of titles resulted. This seemed to be a good method for penetrating the structure of the administration of the later Old Kingdom, and the subject was accordingly changed. Helck's discussion is the best place to start.

In its barest outline, Helck's argument is the following. At the end of the Fourth Dynasty, the princes of the ruling dynasty came to be excluded from the administration of Egypt, but continued to hold the old *Machttitel* such as *jrj-pꜥt*, *ḥȝtj-ꜥ*, and *smr wꜥtj*, which thus developed into titles indicating a rank at court. Since the holders of these titles had power of command over other government officials, it became necessary to give at least the title *ḥȝtj-ꜥ* to the vizier, now no longer a member of the royal family. From such a procedure, the idea grew that the title itself possessed power. This belief in the magical power of titles led, at the end of the Fifth Dynasty, first to the resumption of archaic titles, and later to the acquisition on the part of higher officials of titles formerly reserved for princes. They were not desired simply as "honorary" titles but rather as an expression of the increasing *Eigenmächtigkeit* of the individual. The bureaucratic subordination of officials that obtained during the Fifth Dynasty was replaced by a system of rank based on these titles; in the Fifth Dynasty this system of rank had been restricted to the relatively few, mostly princely, bearers of such titles as were mentioned earlier in this paragraph. In the Sixth Dynasty this system came to be extended to the whole body of officials. The power of command was felt to depend on the possession of these titles; they thus became all-important while the designations of the actual offices sank to insignificance. Therefore, when *Wnj* [110] describes the mustering of troops for his campaign, he lists first these

* *Untersuchungen*, particularly the chapter "Hofrangordnung und Titelentwertung am Ende des Alten Reiches," see pp. 111–19. For complete bibliographical information see the Bibliography at the end of this book.

† Murray, *Index of Names and Titles of the Old Kingdom*, p. 1; Varille, *La Tombe de Ni-Ankh-Pepi à Zâouiyet el Mâyetîn*, p. 33.

‡ The numbers in brackets refer to the list of sources in chapter iii, where references will be found.

rank-titles (*ḥꜣtj-ꜥ*, *sḏꜣwtj bjtj*, and *ḥt-ꜥꜣt smr wꜥtj*) and only then the titles indicating offices (*ḥrj-tp*, *ḥqꜣ ḥt*, *smr jmj-rꜣ ꜥw*, *jmj-rꜣ ḥm-nṯr*, and *jmj-rꜣ gs-pr*). In the temple of Pepi II, officials are listed according to their titles of rank, not their functions; and from the overlapping of these, their order can be determined. In the course of the Sixth Dynasty, the number of these designations of rank is increased by such titles as *jmj-rꜣ Šmꜥ*, *jmj-rꜣ ḫntj-š*, and *ẖrj-tp nswt*, which had formerly indicated the execution of a practical function. This extension of the system of rank is characteristic for the late Old Kingdom. As lower echelon officials rapidly proceeded to annex the rank-indicators of their superiors, these titles rapidly lost their value, and eventually even the title of vizier could become such a rank-indicator on occasion; its bearer then owed obedience only to the king. However, the acquisition of these titles was not an automatic prerogative of specific offices, but was always a sign of personal success and favor with the king.

I began with this view of Helck's, to which I hope I have done justice. It soon became clear, or at least seemed so to me, that the system of rank was considerably more extensive, both in time and in range than Helck had supposed. As I shall attempt to show in the course of this study, each title had a specific rank throughout the Fifth and Sixth Dynasties, and the separation of titles into rank-indicators and function-indicators only complicates the issue.

That certain sequences of titles seem to recur regularly has been observed before. Thus Varille, in the passage already referred to above remarks:

> Les trois premiers titres ne sont pas effectifs mais honorifiques. Ils sont énumérés dans leur ordre d'importance décroissante comme on pourra le constater en comparant le *cursus honorum* de Ni-Ankh-Pepi avec les titulatures des fonctionnaires de la même époque. Tous les personnages qui se vantent d'avoir été [*ḥqꜣ ḥt*], [*smr wꜥtj*] et [*ẖrj-tp nswt*] énumèrent ces trois dignités dans le même ordre que Ni-Ankh-Pepi.

A similar observation was made by Constant de Wit in regard to the sequence *špss nswt*, *smr pr*.* I have made no attempt to collect such references with any degree of completeness. The two just given are the most recent ones that have come to my attention. One might suppose that some general principle underlies such observations. As far as I know, however, only one attempt has been made to elucidate it. In the passage already referred to, Margaret Murray states:

> On pls. 47–66 an attempt has been made to arrange the titles in their original order. . . . In this attempt . . . , the basis is the horizontal lines of

* "Enquête sur le titre de *śmr pr*," *Chronique d'Égypte*, XXXI, 89.

the inscription. When the inscription was first drawn up by the scribe, the list of titles must have been written in horizontal lines; but the artist, in arranging the list to fit into vertical columns, altered the relative position of many of the titles in order to bring the most important to the tops of the columns. In the horizontal lines of the inscriptions we often get a certain sequence of titles, the same titles being so divided up in the vertical columns as to read alternately from one column to another.

This method of analysis was not tested to any great extent by Margaret Murray, and many difficulties developed immediately. After mentioning a long list of possible reasons for this state of affairs, she finally is forced to confess, "but even then a certain percentage remains of which I can make little."

Evidently, the method proposed for arranging the titles is inadequate and rests on untenable assumptions, such as that the Egyptians of the Old Kingdom habitually wrote in horizontal lines; and the suggestion that the titles were arranged in horizontal order in vertical columns seems a bit weird. To my knowledge this is the only attempt to determine the original sequence of titles; if another was made it has escaped not only me but also Hermann Junker, who makes no reference to any such system in his monumental publication of his excavations at Giza.*

It seemed inherently likely that some such system of arranging titles could have existed; and there was obviously some truth to the observation that lines and columns of titles appeared to begin with high-ranking and conclude with low-ranking titles. Assuming then that within any given line of text, the titles were written in order from highest to lowest (and leaving out of consideration for the moment the exact meaning of "high" and "low" in this context), and assuming that this order represented some organized system larger than the individual line of text, it should be possible to conflate the titles occurring in a large tomb into some sort of consistent pattern. The success of this experiment with the large tombs already mentioned formed the starting point of our investigations.

From the beginning, titles of women were excluded from consideration in order to limit a subject that was rapidly threatening to exceed all reasonable bounds. Then it seemed best to make a distinction, not always made in dealing with Old Kingdom titles, between titles proper and epithets.† A title is a term indicating a specific office, function, or dignity; an epithet, though equally stereotyped in form, simply makes a general statement about a person equally applicable to a man in all

* The passage, *Giza*, XI, 129, indicates that Junker believes just the opposite of the point we intend to make. According to him the last title in a string is the most significant.

† Compare, for instance, the index of titles in Junker, *Giza*, XII, 166–76, where both classes are lumped together.

walks and stations in life. In doubtful cases only usage can decide the question: Is the phrase restricted in distribution or is it found indiscriminately? In practice, we have omitted the following classes of phrases as being epithets rather than titles:

1. All phrases beginning with *jmꜣḫw*.
2. All phrases beginning with *jmj-jb*.
3. *Jrr ḥzzt nb.f* and similar expressions.
4. All phrases beginning with *mrjj* and *mrr*.
5. All phrases beginning with *nb jmꜣḫ*.
6. *Sḫmḫ jb nb.f* and similar phrases.

In a few doubtful cases, an expression that seems rather to be an epithet than a title has been included. Where presented here in a group of titles it has been inclosed in parentheses.

As a general rule, the order of elements in a line of text seems to be title, epithet, and name; any of the three can be omitted, and it certainly would not be too difficult to find exceptions to the sequence, though it is valid in the overwhelming majority of cases.

We define a string of titles as a sequence of titles in the *same* line of text, not interrupted by an epithet, mention of a name or any other extraneous matter.

In chapter ii we shall attempt to document the following three propositions:

1. In tombs of the Fifth and Sixth Dynasties, the titles are arranged in a string so as to follow each other in descending order of rank. Conflation of the strings of titles within a tomb results in a reasonably consistent ranking chart. In tombs dating from the Fourth and very early Fifth Dynasties, however, this is only possible within such a wide margin of fluctuation that we must assume, for the time being, that no systematic attempt was made to record the titles in any order. An exception is found occasionally in the Fifth Dynasty, when a high-ranking title is repeated at the end of a string of titles just before the name of the owner of the tomb. This repetition, however, serves as its own warning. An example of this will be included in the discussion in chapter ii.

2. The sequence of titles in a tomb is based on a generally accepted system of ranking the titles in vogue at the time, and not on any other factor such as the order in which the bearer acquired the titles.

3. The differences in the system of ranking titles that appear when the ranking charts of tombs are compared with each other are, therefore, due to changes made from time to time in the system.

The bulk of this book will be devoted to illustrating these propositions and drawing historical conclusions from the data obtained in the process. Here we would like to discuss briefly the bearing of these statements on Helck's views.

In the first place, the distinction between rank-indicating and office-indicating titles disappears; all titles have a specific rank. Instead, we must revert to the concept, rejected by Helck, of honorary titles, or rather titles implying the execution of no specific, practical functions within the administrative machinery of Egypt. It would be rash to deny the existence of ceremonial functions that may have been attached to such titles and that may have been of great importance to the Egyptians of the Old Kingdom. The acquisition of a higher-ranking honorific would amount to a promotion of an official without necessarily changing his function. This is illustrated, for instance, by the career of *Nḫbw* [286] (see below, pp. 37–38).

I think it will be generally admitted that such titles as *jrj-pꜥt*, *ḥꜣtj-ꜥ*, and *smr wꜥtj* fall into the classification of honorifics, rank-indicators if the reader so desires, that no longer implied any practical duties. In many other cases, however, it would be almost impossible at the present stage of our knowledge to make a decision. In any case, the determination of the functions, if any, connected with a title is not one of the aims of this study, nor is it in any way essential to the discussion of the three points made above.

At the end of the Fourth Dynasty, when the princes came to be excluded from the active administration of the state, they naturally continued to hold titles indicating their high rank (not *Machttitel* but simply titles of highest rank) and whatever ceremonial functions they still fulfilled. It is only natural that the highest officials of the administration would be granted at least the lowest of these titles so as to guarantee them a rank higher than that of their subordinates.

I think it quite unnecessary to conclude from this that the Egyptians considered that power resided by some magical means in the title itself. It would be quite effective enough as a mere indicator of position and royal favor. It would lead us too far to enter into a discussion of the ancient Egyptian conception of magic; but leaving this difficult topic aside, we can state the point at issue as follows: Did the ancient Egyptians conceive power as being inherent in a title quite apart from the power of the king who granted it, or did the title obtain its effectiveness as a reflection of the king's favor and trust and as an indication that its bearers' official actions were, in theory at least, on royal command? I tend to favor the latter alternative.

In this context, I think that Helck overstresses the resumption of archaic titles in the later Fifth and Sixth Dynasties. The two concrete examples given are those of *Ḥtp-ḥr-n-Ptḥ* [358] and *Wr-nwnw* [117]. But these are exceptional cases even within the context of their times. The former recorded a most extraordinary accumulation of current, artificially archaized and genuinely archaic titles in his tomb; but the procedure is so unparalleled as to lead us to think that he was simply following a personal foible, particularly as a perusal of Helck's discussion shows that the majority of these titles can be converted into titles more current at the time by the application of simple de-archaizing rules, such as replacing *mḏḥ* by *jmj-rꜣ*. *Wr-nwnw* had peculiar titles that appear to have been connected with a ritual drama of the contending of Horus and Seth. They are quite unparalleled from the Old Kingdom; but I would not want to conclude from this that either the ritual or the titles connected therewith were a revival of archaic practices. In the case of more ordinary titles, Helck gives no specific instances. I do not want to enter into a detailed discussion here, as it is not very material to my thesis, but it seems to me that the absence of an unusual title which is documented from the Fourth and Sixth Dynasties from the tombs of officials of similar high rank in the Fifth might just as well be explained by poor documentation. Tombs of the Sixth Dynasty generally contained more titles and had more decorated wall spaces than those of the Fifth. The chances of survival are accordingly greater. The argument from silence seems dangerous in the Old Kingdom except when dealing with the commonest kind of title.

To return to the main point: I question the need for supposing the Egyptians of the later Old Kingdom to have regarded the titles as being endowed with a different kind of efficacy than was believed at an earlier time.

During the Sixth Dynasty, the use of high-ranking honorifics becomes much commoner than it had been. But does this indicate anything more than a progressive cheapening of titles as they gradually become prerogatives of office rather than distinctions awarded to a few? The phenomenon is hardly unknown in recent history. When a title such as *ḥꜣtj-ꜥ* is granted to officials under the vizier, the vizier himself must be granted a higher-ranking title such as *jrj-pꜥt*. The titles would then become cheapened, though this would not necessarily imply a change in their relative rank.

The Fifth Dynasty cannot then be contrasted with the Sixth as a period of bureaucratic subordination; the same principle of ranking titles was valid in both dynasties. Nor were the honorifics considered to be of greater importance during the Sixth Dynasty than titles indicating a practical function. It would, however, be of common occurrence that a person would be granted honorifics of higher rank than his functional title, and it is only natural that the higher-ranking title would be stated by preference. The only distinction, then, between the two groups of titles that Helck distinguishes in the biography of *Wnj* is that the first group was of higher rank, in general, than the second. The reader can check this by comparing them with the ranking chart of common titles that we have established for Period VI C (the time of *Wnj*) in chapter v. The courtiers' titles in the temple of Pepi II were also simply the highest titles the individuals held.

In the framework of our suppositions, Helck's statement that the system of ranking was extended during the Sixth Dynasty to titles that had formerly indicated offices can only be interpreted as indicating that the titles had lost functional significance; any decision in such matters involves a series of discussions that I intend to avoid. For this reason it has not seemed necessary to enter into any detailed discussion of the three major works dealing with Old Kingdom titles: Junker, *Giza*, Vols. I–XII; Pirenne, *Histoire des institutions et du droit privé de l'Ancienne Égypte*, Vols. I–III; and the bulk of Helck, *Untersuchungen zu den Beamtentiteln des ägyptischen Alten Reiches.* All these works are largely devoted to a study of the various branches of the administration of Egypt on the basis of the translated meanings of the titles, a subject of great importance, but not strictly germane to this study.

Before proceeding to the main points of this study, a few technical matters must be discussed. Our purpose here is not a philological discussion of either the meanings or the readings of names and titles. They have, therefore, been given in transliteration only, wherever possible, with readings chosen largely on the basis of general acceptance and their uncontroversial nature. The index in Junker, *Giza*, XII, 166–76 has been followed as a guide, but not slavishly. The system of transliteration is that used by Edel in his *Altägyptische Grammatik* and uses the following alphabet: *ꜣ j ꜥ w b p f m n r h ḥ ḫ ẖ z s š q k g t ṯ d ḏ*. This eliminates a few diacriticals that are not strictly necessary.

We now proceed to a discussion of our first point, that titles are written in a string in descending order of rank.

II
THE RANKING OF TITLES

*

First we must document the statement made at the conclusion of chapter i. If the titles in each string of titles on the walls of a tomb are written in order of rank, this implies, of course, that there was in the mind of the scribe responsible for decorating the walls of the tomb or the composition of the document a fixed sequence of titles, from which he made selections for each string he wrote. Conversely, it should be possible, by conflating the strings of titles found in a tomb, to obtain some approximation to the system of ranked titles underlying them. On the other hand, if the statement is wrong, and the titles are not arranged in the strings according to rank, an attempt to conflate the strings of titles, at least in the larger tombs that contain a great number of strings, should result in utter confusion. The impossibility of obtaining such a conflated ranking chart would effectively disprove our hypothesis.

The procedure to be followed is thus in principle quite simple. We collect all the strings of titles from a large tomb and attempt to conflate them; this process is repeated for as many tombs as possible. We have carried out this process for virtually all the tombs available to us that contained more than isolated titles; the coverage was reasonably complete for tombs and documents from the time of Khufu to the end of the Sixth Dynasty and rather sporadic outside these limits, since we tried, in general, only to include those whose dating was uncertain and might thus fit within the limits. The reasons for this selection will become evident later. The complete list of the sources so analyzed is given in the next chapter. It contains about 675 entries. Not all of them, of course, contained enough titles or enough strings to constitute very convincing evidence one way or the other; and it soon became evident that the ranking of titles in the Fourth Dynasty was sufficiently haphazard to restrict the validity of the ranking system to the Fifth Dynasty, though showing enough consistency to indicate that the system was already developing informally. Even so, enough tombs remained with long and numerous strings of titles that did lend themselves to conflation to prove the statement.

To avoid the risk of begging a question, it should be stressed here that we are using the term "ranking" only in the mathematical sense for the time being; we are implying only that the titles follow each other according to a fixed order, and "higher" and "lower" are used only to imply precedence or succession in that order. We hope to demonstrate later in this chapter that this ordering of titles did have the implications of rank in the social and administrative sense, but this is not a priori inherent in the existence of a system of ranking titles. Other explanations could also be possible.

The strings of titles on which the 675-odd ranking charts are based covered two reams of paper in small handwriting; the charts themselves ranged in length from two titles to several pages. It thus becomes impractical to present the complete material here. We will in this chapter give a few of the examples containing the largest number of strings. These carry the most conviction toward the proof of our statement and show the method as well as the difficulties encountered. They should suffice to demonstrate to the reader that there is considerable validity to the system of ranking titles; I hope that it will be taken on trust that the cases we could not present here also fit the system and present in the aggregate a body of material that comes as close to proof and the elimination of the possibility of coincidence as can be expected in a study dealing with a period as remote and poorly documented as the Old Kingdom of Egypt.

Ideally, the conflation of the strings of titles in a tomb would result in a simple sequence of titles, identical with the ranking scheme from which the strings are presumed to be extracts. In practice, we encounter several difficulties. The most exasperating one is due to the poor preservation or publication of a tomb; titles tended to be written near the tops of walls and thus were likely to be removed first when the tomb was destroyed. All too many editors neglect to indicate the line divisions in the texts on the walls of the tomb and copy the strings as a continuous text;* it is not uncommon to find publications giving only a haphazardly arranged list of the titles that occur in the tomb with no indication of their position, frequency, or combinations. In most cases, the result of such treatment is to render the tomb concerned totally useless for our purpose, but while this can be an irritation, it at least does not complicate our argument.

* This is largely responsible for those cases in which only a part of the titles actually preserved in a tomb could be utilized for this study. The author is not entirely guiltless on this count in the case of unpublished material on which he had the opportunity to take notes while in Egypt on a Fulbright grant.

Another difficulty is more of a nuisance. The selection of titles in the strings as preserved in a tomb is usually such that it becomes impossible to determine the relationship of every title to every other title; in order to arrange the titles in a single, straight sequence we must have such complete information. Usually we are faced with numerous occasions in which the relationship of two titles to a third can be determined, but not to each other. The ranking chart then shows a branching, which was certainly not present in the mind of the ancient outline draftsman but is simply the result of inadequate data. In most tombs there will be enough well preserved long strings of titles to enable us to arrange at least a very considerable proportion of the owner's titles in a single sequence, but there are some cases, particularly in tombs in which the false door and other parts that contained the longer strings of titles have been lost, where the best ranking chart that can be constructed is a rather uninformative tangle of branchings.

A more serious source of trouble is an error on the part of the ancient scribe. The number of titles in use during the Old Kingdom was immense; I would estimate the figure at almost two thousand. It is only to be expected that there would be some uncertainty in the mind of the scribe as to the ranking of the more unusual ones. One can legitimately question whether a relative ranking had ever been established within such groups as the *jmjw-rꜣ* of the numerous branches of the "treasury" (*šnwtj*, *prwj-ḥḏ*, *prwj-nb*, *jzwj ẖrj-ḫtm*, etc., etc.) or, if it had, whether the scribes could keep them straight. In any case, a certain amount of fluctuation does occur in these cases, to my mind remarkably little, but still bothersome. The examples presented later in this chapter will contain several specimens of such fluctuation. In almost all cases, it is within relatively narrow limits.

Another source of uncertainty in the scribe's mind would be, to anticipate our conclusions at the end of this chapter, a recent change in the official ranking of the titles concerned. We shall point out in chapter v one or two cases that could possibly be explained in this fashion. For all practical purposes, however, this seems to be a type of error that virtually never occurs.

Unfortunately the next type is all the more common. We would hardly be dealing with ancient Egypt, if the common, inexcusable mistake did not arise on numerous occasions to throw obstacles in the way of the student. In large tombs with numerous strings of titles they are relatively easy to detect; where a sequence is well documented in many strings, an isolated instance where the sequence differs is automatically suspect. In smaller tombs things are more difficult. Where a sequence of titles is documented one way in two strings and the other way in one, it is usually impossible to tell whether we are faced with a fluctuation due to uncertainty in the mind of the scribe or a plain mistake. Of course, if a sequence is attested only once, and a mistake was made in the composition of that particular string, there is no way in which we could detect, or even suspect it in most cases.

We shall now present the strings of titles and the ranking charts constructed therefrom for a few of the larger tombs. A few remarks will be necessary. The number in brackets preceding the name of the owner of the tomb refers to the list of sources in chapter iii, where the references will be found. We include both the titles of the owner and of his dependents in the relatively rare cases in which their titles are arranged in strings. Such dependents' strings will be preceded by an asterisk.

The following conventions are used in the ranking charts which follow the presentation of the strings of titles in each tomb:

A outranks B, which outranks C.

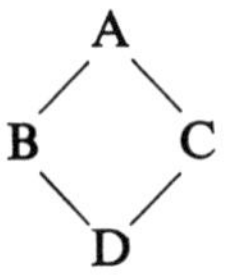

A outranks B and C. B and C both outrank D. The relationship of B to C could not be determined from the data in the tomb.

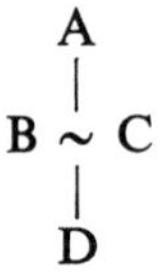

A outranks B and C, both of which outrank D. The ranking of B and C fluctuates in the preserved strings.

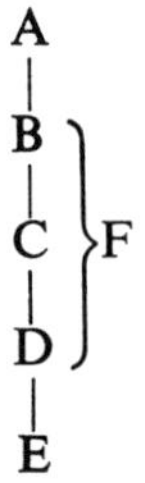

The ranking of F in terms of the established sequence A, B, C, D, E fluctuates from a position just outranking B to one just outranked by D.

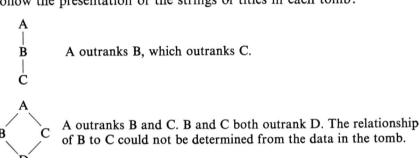

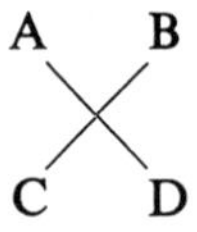

A outranks D; B outranks C. The crossing of the lines has no significance whatsoever and is imposed solely by the exigencies of space.

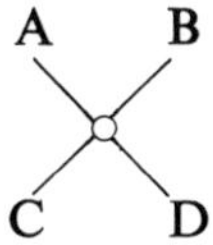

A outranks C and D; B also outranks C and D. The circle indicates that every title connected to it by a line from above outranks every title connected to it from below. The relative ranking of A and B, or C and D remains unknown.

We shall now begin our presentation with the titles in the tomb of *Mrrw-kꜣ*, who had more than any other individual in the Old Kingdom.

[197] *Mrrw-kꜣ* (the references are to the plate numbers in the Oriental Institute Publication):

7. *jmj-ḫt ḥm-nṯr, ḫntj-š Ḏd-swt Ttj*. (Possibly a later addition. Cf. [389A] in chap. iii.)
8. *ḥm-kꜣ, jrj-jz.*
23. *smr wꜥtj, ẖrj-ḥbt.*
27. *jmj-ḫt ḥm-kꜣ, zš qbḥ.*
    sḥḏ ḥm-kꜣ, zꜣb sḥḏ zs.
    sḥḏ ḥm-kꜣ, zꜣb jmj-rꜣ zš.
35. [. . .] *wrw, ḫrp nstj.*
    [. . .]*t, jmj-rꜣ pr nswt nb stp-zꜣ.*
37. *ḥqꜣ ḥt, zš ꜥ nswt n ḫft-ḥr.*
    ḥqꜣ ḥt, jmj-rꜣ zš ꜣḥt. (two times).
    ḥqꜣ ḥt, jmj-rꜣ zš mrt.
    ḥqꜣ ḥt, zꜣb jmj-rꜣ zš.
39. *ḥm-kꜣ, sḥḏ zꜣb jmj-rꜣ zš*. (sic!).*
    jmj-ḫt ḥm-kꜣ, zš qbḥ pr-ꜥꜣ.
51. *zš zꜣ* ([hieroglyph]), *ḥm-kꜣ*. (Only really well carved example of these two titles in a prominent place.)
57. *ḥm-kꜣ, sḥḏ zꜣb jmj-rꜣ zš*. (sic!).
59. *jrj-pꜥt, ḥꜣtj-ꜥ, ẖrj-ḥbt ḥrj-tp, jmꜣ-ꜥ, smr wꜥ[tj . . .].*
    [. . .], *ḥꜣtj-ꜥ, tꜣtj zꜣb ṯꜣtj, ẖrj-ḥbt ḥrj-tp, jmꜣ-ꜥ, smr wꜥtj,* [. . .] *Jnpw* [. . .].
62. *ẖrj-ḥbt ḥrj-tp, jmꜣ-ꜥ, smr wꜥtj* [. . .].
    ẖrj-ḥbt ḥrj-tp, jmꜣ-ꜥ, smr wꜥtj, wt Jnpw.
    jrj-pꜥt, ḥꜣtj-ꜥ, ẖrj-ḥbt ḥrj-tp, jmꜣ-ꜥ, smr wꜥtj, wt Jnpw.
    sḥḏ ḥm-nṯr, ḫntj-š Ḏd-swt-Ttj. (two times).
    jrj-pꜥt, ḥꜣtj-ꜥ, jmj-jz Nḫn, mnjw Nḫn, ḥrj-tp Nḫb, smr wꜥtj, wt Jnpw. (two times).
    tꜣtj zꜣb ṯꜣtj, jmj-rꜣ zš ꜥ nswt, jmj-rꜣ ḥwt-wrt 6, *jmj-rꜣ jzwj n ḫkr nswt, ḥrj-sštꜣ n wḏt-mdw nbt nt nswt.* (two times).
    ẖrj-ḥbt ḥrj-tp, jmꜣ-ꜥ, smr wꜥtj, wt Jnpw, ḥts Jnpw, smꜣ Jnpw, ḥrj wrw. (two times).
    sḏꜣwtj bjtj, smr wꜥtj, ẖrj-ḥbt, zš mḏꜣt ntr, ḫrp jꜣwt nbt nṯrt, ḥrj-sštꜣ n mdw nṯr. (two times).

* This, of course, stands for *sḥḏ ḥm-kꜣ, zꜣb jmj-rꜣ zš* as in pl. 27, and has been entered as such in the ranking chart. Here I have reproduced the text mechanically in the order in which it stands on the wall. The transposition has been studied by Fischer, and, as he writes me, is to be published in an article which has not yet (July, 1959) appeared.

smr wꜥtj, wt Jnpw, ꜥ ꜥntj, ꜥ ḥqꜣt, ḫrp nstj, ḫrp ḥwt Nt, jmj-rꜣ pr nswt nb stp-zꜣ, ḥrj-sštꜣ n mꜣꜣt wꜥ. (two times).
ḫrj-ḥbt, ḥrj-sštꜣ n pr dwꜣt, ꜥḏ-mr Dwꜣ-Ḥr-ḫntj-pt. (two times).

64. *sḥḏ ḥm-nṯr, ḫntj-š Ḏd-swt-*[*Ttj*].
[. . .], *tꜣtj zꜣb ṯꜣtj, jmj-rꜣ zš ꜥ nswt.*
[. . .]*ꜥ, smr wꜥtj, wt Jnpw.*
65. **ḫrj-ḥbt, zš mḏꜣt nṯr.*
69. *jrj-pꜥt, ḥꜣtj-ꜥ, ḫrj-ḥbt ḥrj-tp, jmꜣ-ꜥ, smr wꜥtj, wt Jnpw.* (two times).
ḫrj-ḥbt ḥrj-tp, jmꜣ-ꜥ, smr wꜥtj, wt Jnpw.
70. *jrj-pꜥt, ḥꜣtj-ꜥ, ḫrj-ḥbt ḥrj-tp,* [*jmꜣ*]*-ꜥ,* [. . .].
jrj-pꜥt, ḥꜣtj-ꜥ, ḫrj-ḥbt ḥrj-tp, smr wꜥtj, wt Jnpw.
72. *jrj-pꜥt, ḥꜣtj-ꜥ, tꜣtj zꜣb ṯꜣtj, jmj-rꜣ zš ꜥ nswt, ḫrj-ḥbt ḥrj-tp, jmꜣ-ꜥ, smr wꜥtj,* [. . .].
jrj-pꜥt, ḥꜣtj-ꜥ, tꜣtj zꜣb ṯꜣtj, jmj-rꜣ zš ꜥ nswt, ḫrj-ḥbt ḥrj-tp, jmꜣ-ꜥ, smr wꜥtj, [. . .] *Jnpw,* [. . .].
74. *jrj-pꜥt, ḥꜣtj-ꜥ, ḫrj-ḥbt ḥrj-tp, jmꜣ-ꜥ, smr wꜥtj, wt Jnpw.* (two times).
75+ *jrj-pꜥt, ḥꜣtj-ꜥ, tꜣtj zꜣb ṯꜣtj, jmj-rꜣ zš ꜥ nswt, ḫrj-ḥbt ḥrj-tp, jmꜣ-ꜥ, smr*
76. *wꜥtj, wt Jnpw, ḥts Jnpw, smꜣ Jnpw, ḥrj wrw, zš mḏꜣt nṯr, ḫrp jꜣwt nbt nṯrt, ḫrp nstj, ḫrp ḥwt Nt.* (two times).
jrj-pꜥt, ḥꜣtj-ꜥ, tꜣtj zꜣb ṯꜣtj, jmj-rꜣ zš ꜥ nswt, ḫrj-ḥbt ḥrj-tp, jmꜣ-ꜥ, smr wꜥtj, wt Jnpw, ḥts Jnpw, smꜣ Jnpw, ḥrj wrw.
78. *jrj-pꜥt, ḫrj-ḥbt ḥrj-tp, smr wꜥtj, zš mḏꜣt nṯr.*
[. . .], *ꜥ ꜥntj, ꜥ ḥqꜣt.*
83. **ḥm-kꜣ, zš zꜣ.* (seven times, but possibly two short columns rather than a string).
**ḥm-kꜣ, sḥḏ zꜣb sḥḏ zš.* (sic!).
85. **ḥm-kꜣ, zš zꜣ.* (eight times).
90. *jrj-pꜥt, ḫrj-ḥbt ḥrj-tp, smr wꜥtj.*
ḥꜣtj-ꜥ, smr wꜥtj, wt (?) *Jnpw, ḥts* (sc. *Jnpw*).
96. *jrj-pꜥt, ḫrj-ḥbt ḥrj-tp, zš mḏꜣt nṯr.*
jmꜣ-ꜥ, ḥts Jnpw, smr wꜥtj, wt Jnpw. (sic!).
ḥꜣtj-ꜥ, jmj-jz Nḫn, mnjw Nḫn, ḥrj-tp Nḫb.
100. *jrj-pꜥt, ḥꜣtj-ꜥ, jmj-jz Nḫn, mnjw Nḫn.*
[*st*]*m, ḫrp šnḏwt nbt, ꜥḏ-mr Dp, ḫrp m nṯrw.*
101. *jrj-pꜥt, jmꜣ-ꜥ, ḥts Jnpw, smr wꜥtj, ḫrj-ḥbt.*
tꜣtj zꜣb ṯꜣtj, jmj-rꜣ zš ꜥ nswt.
102. *ḫrj-ḥbt ḥrj-tp, smr wꜥtj, zš mḏꜣt nṯr, ḫrp jꜣwt nbt nṯrt.* (two times).
103. *tꜣtj zꜣb ṯꜣtj, ḫrj-ḥbt ḥrj-tp, jmꜣ-ꜥ, smr wꜥtj.*
ḥꜣtj-ꜥ, jmj-jz Nḫn, mnjw Nḫn, ḥrj-tp Nḫb.
106. [. . .] *jmꜣ-ꜥ, smr wꜥtj, ḥts Jnpw, wt Jnpw.*
107. *jrj-pꜥt, ḥꜣtj-ꜥ, ḫrj-ḥbt* [*ḥrj*]*-tp,* [. . .].
sḥḏ [*ḥm-nṯr*] *Ḏd-swt-*[*Ttj,* . . .]*ꜥ, smr wꜥtj, ḥts Jnpw, wt Jnpw, zš mḏꜣt nṯr, ḫrp jꜣwt nbt nṯrt.* (two times. The text given here has been composed from two parallel versions on symmetrical sides of a false door.)

113. *sḥḏ ḥm-nṯr, ḫntj-š Ḏd-sw-Ttj.*
ḫrj-ḥbt ḥrj-tp, smr wʿtj, zš mḏꜣt nṯr, ḫrp jꜣwt nbt nṯrt, ʿ ʿntj.
. . .]wt, ḫrp nstj, ḫrp ḥwt Nt, ʿꜣ Dwꜣw.
[ḥrj-sštꜣ n pr]-dwꜣt, wʿ wr ḥb.
116. **ḥm-kꜣ, zš zꜣ.*
128. **smr wʿtj, ḫrj-ḥbt.*
132. *ḫrj-ḥbt ḥrj-tp, smr wʿtj, zš mḏꜣt nṯr, ʿꜣ Dwꜣw,* [. . .].
jmꜣ-ʿ, ḥts Jnpw, wt Jnpw, [. . .].
tꜣtj zꜣb ṯꜣtj, jmj-[. . .].
stm, ḫrp šnḏwt nbt, [. . .].
sḏꜣwtj bjtj, smr wʿtj, ḥrj s[. . .].
jmj-rꜣ ḫkr nswt nb, jmj-rꜣ pr [. . .].
ḫrj-ḥbt, ḥrj-sštꜣ n [. . .].
133. *sḥḏ ḥm-nṯr, ḫntj-š* [*Ḏd-swt-Ttj*], *jrj-pʿt, ḥꜣtj-ʿ,* [. . .].
[. . .], *ḫrp jꜣwt nbt nṯrt, smsw snwt, ʿꜣ Dwꜣw,* [. . .].
[. . .], *ʿ ʿntj, ʿ hqꜣt, ḫrp nstj, ḫrp ḥwt Nt,* [. . .].
[. . .] *nswt, jmj-rꜣ zš ʿ nswt, jmj-rꜣ ḥwt-wrt* [6, . . .].
[. . .], *r P nb, ḫrp jbṯ Ḥr, wʿ wr ḥb,* [. . .].
135. *jrj-pʿt, ḫrj-ḥbt* [. . .].
137. *stm, ḫrp šnḏwt nbt,* [. . .].
143. *jrj-pʿt, ḥꜣtj-ʿ, smr wʿtj.*
ḥts Jnpw, wt Jnpw.
144. *jrj-pʿt, ḥꜣtj-ʿ, smr wʿtj, ḥts Jnpw, wt Jnpw.*
148. *sḥḏ ḥm-nṯr, ḫntj-š Ḏd-swt-Ttj, jrj-pʿt, ḥꜣtj-ʿ, ḫrj-ḥbt ḥrj-tp, jmꜣ-ʿ, smr wʿtj, ḥts Jnpw, wt Jnpw.* (two times).
jmꜣ-ʿ (sic! mistake for *ḥꜣtj-ʿ*?), *ḫrj-ḥbt ḥrj-tp, smr wʿtj, zš mḏꜣt nṯr, ḫrp jꜣwt nbt nṯrt.*
154. **ḫrj-ḥbt, ḥrj-sštꜣ n nswt m st nbt.*
156. **smr wʿtj, ḫrj-ḥbt.*
159. *sḥḏ ḥm-nṯr, ḫntj-š* [*Ḏd*]*swt-*[*Ttj*].
[. . .], *ḫrj-ḥbt ḥrj-tp, smr wʿtj, zš mḏꜣt nṯr, ḫrp jꜣwt nbt nṯrt.*
[. . .], *wt Jnpw, ḥrj wrw, ḫrp ḥwt Nt.*
[. . . , *tꜣtj zꜣb*] *ṯꜣtj, jmj-rꜣ kꜣt nbt nt nswt, jmj-rꜣ ḥt-wrt* 6.
[. . .], *ʿḏ-mr Dp, smsw snwt, ʿꜣ Dwꜣw, ḫrp m nṯrw.*
[. . .], *mdw Ḥp, r P nb, ḫrp jbṯ Ḥr.*
[. . . , *ʿḏ-mr*] *Dwꜣ-Ḥr-ḫntj-pt, ḥrj-sštꜣ n pr dwꜣt.*
[*ḥrj sšt*]*ꜣ n mdw nṯr.*
167. **sḥḏ ḥm-kꜣ, zꜣb sḥḏ zš.*
180. *sḥḏ ḥm-nṯr, ḫntj-š Ḏd-swt-Ttj.*
jrj-pʿt, ḫrj-ḥbt ḥrj-tp, zš mḏꜣt nṯr, ḫrp jꜣwt nbt nṯrt, ḫrp m nṯrw.
ḥꜣtj-ʿ, jmj-jz, mnjw Nḫn, ḥrj-tp Nḫb, jmj-rꜣ pr nswt nb stp-zꜣ.
jmꜣ-ʿ, smr wʿtj, ḥts Jnpw, wt Jnpw, ʿ ʿntj, ḫrp nstj.
tꜣtj zꜣb ṯꜣtj, jmj-rꜣ kꜣt nbt nt nswt, jmj-rꜣ ḥt-wrt 6.
stm, ḫrp šnḏwt nbt, ʿḏ-mr Dp, ʿḏ-mr Dwꜣ-Ḥr-ḫntj-pt.

182. *sḥḏ ḥm-nṯr, ḫntj-š* [*Ḏd-*]*swt-*[*Ttj*]. (two times).
[jrj-pꜥt, ẖrj-ḥbt] ḥrj-tp, zš mḏꜣt nṯr, ḫrp jꜣwt nbt nṯrt, ḫrp m nṯrw. (two times).
ḥꜣtj-ꜥ, jmj-jz, mnjw Nḫn, ḥrj-tp Nḫb, jmj-rꜣ pr nswt nb stp-zꜣ. (two times).
jmꜣ-ꜥ, smr wꜥtj, ḥts Jnpw, wt Jnpw, ꜥ ꜥntj, ḫrp nstj. (two times).
tꜣtj zꜣb ṯꜣtj, jmj-rꜣ kꜣt nbt nt nswt, jmj-rꜣ ḥt-wrt 6.
tꜣtj zꜣb ṯꜣtj, jmj-rꜣ kꜣt nbt nt nswt, jmj-rꜣ zš ꜥ nswt.
stm, ḫrp šnḏwt nbt, ꜥḏ-mr Dp, smsw snwt, ḫrp ḥwt Nt. (two times).
sḏꜣwtj bjtj, mdw Ḥp, r P nb, ḫrp jbṯ Ḥr. (two times).

183. *sḥḏ ḥm-nṯr, ḫntj-š* [*Ḏd-*]*swt-*[*Ttj*].
[. . .] *zš mḏꜣt nṯr, ḫrp jꜣwt nbt nṯrt, ḫrp m nṯrw.*
ḥꜣtj-ꜥ, jmj-jz, mnjw Nḫn, ḥrj-tp Nḫb, jmj-rꜣ pr nswt nb stp-zꜣ.
jmꜣ-ꜥ, smr wꜥtj, ḥts Jnpw, ꜥ ꜥntj, ḫrp nstj.
tꜣtj zꜣb ṯꜣtj, jmj-rꜣ kꜣt nbt nt nswt, jmj-rꜣ ḥt-wrt 6.
stm, ḫrp šnḏwt nbt, ꜥḏ-mr Dp, smsw snwt, ḫrp ḥwt Nt.

191. *ẖrj-ḥbt ḥrj-tp, smr wꜥtj.*

195. *ẖrj-ḥbt ḥrj-tp, jmꜣ-ꜥ, smr wꜥtj, wt Jnpw.* (two times).

198. [*tꜣtj*] *zꜣb ṯꜣtj, ẖrj-ḥbt ḥrj-tp, jmꜣ-ꜥ, smr wꜥtj, ḥts Jnpw, wt Jnpw.*
jrj-pꜥt, ḥꜣtj-ꜥ, tꜣtj zꜣb ṯꜣtj, ẖrj-ḥbt ḥrj-tp, smr wꜥtj. (two times).
[. . .], *jmꜣ-ꜥ, ḥts Jnpw,* [. . .].
jmꜣ-ꜥ, ḥts Jnpw, wt Jnpw, zš mḏꜣt nṯr.

201. *jrj-pꜥt, r P nb, sḏtj nswt, ḥꜣtj-ꜥ, wr ẖrj-ḥbt ḥrj-tp, tꜣtj zꜣb ṯꜣtj, stm, jmꜣ-ꜥ, smr wꜥtj, wt Jnpw, ḥts Jnpw, ꜥ ḥqꜣt, zš mḏꜣt nṯr, ḫrp jꜣwt nbt nṯrt.*
jrj-pꜥt, r P nb.
smr wꜥtj, ḫw-ꜥ, ḥqꜣ Bꜣt, ḫrp hꜣṯs km, ẖrj nws n Wꜣḏt, ḥrj-sštꜣ n pr dwꜣt.
ḥꜣtj-ꜥ, jmj-jz Nḫn, ḥrj-tp Nḫb, (*jmj-jb n nswt ḫntj jdbwj.fj*), *ḥrj-sštꜣ n mꜣꜣt wꜥ.*
wr ẖrj-ḥbt ḥrj-tp, jmꜣ-ꜥ, ꜥ ḥqꜣt, zš mḏꜣt ntr, ꜥ ꜥntj, ꜥꜣ Dwꜣw, ḫrp m nṯrw, ḫrp jꜣwt nbt nṯrt, ḫrp nstj, jmj-rꜣ ꜥḥ-nṯr Šmꜥ, smꜣ Ḥr, wr mꜣ.
stm, ḫrp snḏwt nbt, ꜥḏ-mr Dwꜣ-Ḥr-ḫntj-pt, ḫrp ḥwt Nt, ḫrp šmsw Ḥr, wr 5 *m pr Ḏḥwtj, jmj-rꜣ pr nswt nb stp-zꜣ, smꜣ Mn.*

203. *jrj-pꜥt, r P nb, sḏtj nswt.* (two times).
ḥꜣtj-ꜥ, wr ẖrj-ḥbt ḥrj-tp, stm, jmꜣ-ꜥ, smr wꜥtj, ḫw-ꜥ, ḥqꜣ Bꜣt. (two times).

204. *jrj-pꜥt, r P nb, sḏtj nswt, ḥꜣtj-ꜥ, wr ẖrj-ḥbt ḥrj-tp, tꜣtj zꜣb ṯꜣtj, stm, jmꜣ-ꜥ, smr wꜥtj, ꜥ ḥqꜣt, wt Jnpw, ḥts Jnpw, zš mḏꜣt nṯr, ḫrp jꜣwt nbt nṯrt.* (The same string as the first on pl. 201, on the opposite wall, but note that the three titles following *smr wꜥtj* were reversed accidentally.)

205. *jrj-pꜥt, r P nb.*
smr wꜥtj, ḫw-ꜥ, ḥqꜣ Bꜣt, ḫrp hꜣṯs km, ẖrj nws n Wꜣḏt, ḥrj-sštꜣ n pr dwꜣt.
ḥꜣtj-ꜥ, jmj-jz Nḫn, mnjw Nḫn, ḥrj-tp Nḫb, (*jmj-jb n nswt ḫntj jbdwj-fj*), *ḥrj-sštꜣ n mꜣꜣt wꜥ.*
wr ẖrj-ḥbt ḥrj-tp, jmꜣ-ꜥ, ꜥ ḥqꜣt, zš mḏꜣt ntr, ꜥ ꜥntj, ꜥꜣ Dwꜣw, ḫrp m nṯrw, ḫrp jꜣwt nbt nṯrt, ḫrp nstj, jmj-rꜣ ꜥḥ-nṯr Šmꜥ, smꜣ Ḥr, wr mꜣ.
stm, ḫrp snḏwt nbt, ꜥḏ-mr Dwꜣ-Ḥr-ḫntj-pt, ḫrp ḥwt Nt, ḫrp šmsw Ḥr, wr 5 *m pr Ḏḥwtj, jmj-rꜣ pr nswt nb stp-zꜣ, smꜣ Mn.*

206+ *jrj-pꜥt, r P nb, sḏtj nswt, ḥꜣtj-ꜥ, wr ẖrj-ḥbt ḥrj-tp, stm, jmꜣ-ꜥ, smr wꜥtj.*

207+ *jrj-pꜥt, ḥꜣtj-ꜥ, tꜣtj zꜣb ṯꜣtj, jmj-rꜣ zš ꜥ nswt, ẖrj-ḥbt ḥrj-tp, jmꜣ-ꜥ, smr*

208. *wꜥtj, wt Jnpw, ḥts Jnpw, zš mḏꜣt nṯr, ḫrp jꜣwt nbt nṯrt, ḫrp nstj, ḫrp ḥwt Nt, ẖrj-ḥbt, ḥrj-sštꜣ n pr dwꜣt.*
jrj-pꜥt, ḥꜣtj-ꜥ, ẖrj-ḥbt ḥrj-tp, jmꜣ-ꜥ, smr wꜥtj, wt Jnpw, zš mḏꜣt nṯr.
jrj-pꜥt, ḥꜣtj-ꜥ, tꜣtj zꜣb ṯꜣtj, jmj-rꜣ zš ꜥ nswt, ẖrj-ḥbt ḥrj-tp, jmꜣ-ꜥ, smr wꜥtj, wt Jnpw, ḥts Jnpw, smꜣ Jnpw, ḥrj wrw, zš mḏꜣt nṯr, ḫrp jꜣwt nbt nṯrt, ḫrp nstj, ḫrp ḥwt Nt.

210. *jrj-pꜥt, ḥꜣtj-ꜥ, tꜣtj zꜣb ṯꜣtj, ẖrj-ḥbt ḥrj-tp, jmꜣ-ꜥ, smr wꜥtj, wt Jnpw, ḥts Jnpw, ḥrj wrw, zš mḏꜣt nṯr, ḫrp jꜣwt nbt nṯrt, ḫrp nstj.*
jrj-pꜥt, ḥꜣtj-ꜥ, tꜣtj zꜣb ṯꜣtj, smr wꜥtj, ẖrj-ḥbt, zš mḏꜣt nṯr, ḫrp jꜣwt nbt nṯrt.
ꜥꜣ Dwꜣw, ḫrp m nṯrw.
ẖrj-ḥbt, ꜥḏ-mr Dwꜣ-ḥr-ḫntj-pt.
mdw Ḥzꜣt, smr wꜥtj.
jrj-pꜥt, ḥꜣtj-ꜥ, ẖrj-ḥbt ḥrj-tp, jmꜣ-ꜥ, smr wꜥtj, ḥts Jnpw, wt Jnpw, zš mḏꜣt nṯr, ḫrp jꜣwt nbt nṯrt, ḫrp nstj, ḫrp ḥwt Nt.
jrj-pꜥt, ḥꜣtj-ꜥ.
ḥrj-sštꜣ n pr dwꜣt, ḥm Bꜣw P, ḥm Bꜣw Nḫn. (Text altered.)

211. *jrj-pꜥt, ḥꜣtj-ꜥ, tꜣtj zꜣb ṯꜣtj, ẖrj-ḥbt ḥrj-tp, jmꜣ-ꜥ, smr wꜥtj.* (two times).
wt Jnpw, ḥts Jnpw, smꜣ Mn, ḥrj wrw, zš mḏꜣt nṯr, ḫrp jꜣwt nbt nṯrt. (two times).
ꜥ ꜥntj, ꜥ ḥqꜣt, ḫrp nstj, ḫrp ḥwt Nt, jmj-rꜣ pr nswt nb stp-zꜣ. (two times).
ẖrj-ḥbt, ḥrj-sštꜣ n pr dwꜣt, ḥrj-sštꜣ n mdw nṯr.
(jmj-jb n nswt ḫntj jdbwj.fj), jmj-rꜣ ddt pt qmꜣt tꜣ.

212. *[. . .], ꜥꜣ Dwꜣw, ḫrp m nṯrw, ḥrj-tp Nḫb.*
sḥḏ ḥm-nṯr Ḏd-swt-Ttj, jrj-pꜥt, jmꜣ-ꜥ, ḥts Jnpw, ꜥ ḥqꜣt, ḫrp nstj, ḫw-ꜥ, ḥqꜣ Bꜣt, ꜥ ꜥntj, ḫrp ḥwt Nt.
tꜣtj zꜣb ṯꜣtj, jmj-rꜣ zš ꜥ nswt, smr wꜥtj, ḥrj-sštꜣ n wḏꜥ-mdw n ḥt-wrt 6, *wḏ-mdw n srw.*
sḥḏ ḥm-nṯr Ḏd-swt-Ttj, ḥꜣtj-ꜥ, ẖrj-ḥbt ḥrj-tp, sḏꜣwtj bjtj, stm, ḫrp snḏwt nbt, ꜥḏ-mr Dp, ḫrp m nṯrw.
smr wꜥtj, wt Jnpw, ḥrj wrw, smsw snwt, jmj-jz, mnjw Nḫn, ḥrj-tp Nḫb, jmj-rꜣ wꜥbtj, ḥm Bꜣw Nḫn.
ẖrj-ḥbt, zš mḏꜣt nṯr, ḫrp jꜣwt nbt nṯrt.
ḥm Bꜣw P, jmj-rꜣ ḫkr nswt nbt, jmj-rꜣ [. . .].
stm, ḫrp šnḏwt nbt, smr wꜥtj, wt Jnpw, ḫrp jꜣwt nbt nṯrt.
[. . .] *nb, jmj-rꜣ pr-ꜥḥꜣ, jmj-rꜣ wꜥbtj.*
[. . .], *ḥts Jnpw, ḥrj-sštꜣ n mꜣꜣt wꜥ.*
[. . .] *špst nt pr-ꜥꜣ, ḥrj wpwt štꜣt pr-ꜥꜣ.*

213. *jrj-pꜥt, ḥꜣtj-ꜥ, ẖrj-ḥbt ḥrj-tp, jmꜣ-ꜥ, smr wꜥtj, ḥts Jnpw.*

217. *sḏꜣwtj bjtj, mdw Ḥp.*
stm, ḫrp šnḏwt nbt, ꜥḏ-mr Dpw.
ẖrj-ḥbt ḥrj-tp, zš mḏꜣt nṯr, ḫrp jꜣwt nbt nṯrt.
jmꜣ-ꜥ, smr wꜥtj, ẖrj-ḥbt, wr jdt.
stm, ḫrp snḏwt nbt, ḫrp jꜣwt nbt nṯrt.

jrj-pꜥt, ḥꜣtj-ꜥ, jmj-jz Nḫn, mnjw Nḫn.
ḫrj-ḥbt ḥrj-tp, zš mḏꜣt nṯr, ḫrp nstj.
ḫw-ꜥ, ḥqꜣ Bꜣt, ḫrp hꜣṯs km, jmj-rꜣ jpt nswt.
smsw snwt, wr mꜣ m prwj.
smr wꜥtj, jmj-rꜣ qbḥwj pr-ꜥꜣ.
ꜥ ꜥntj, ꜥꜣ Dwꜣw, ḫrp jꜣwt nbt nṯrt.

218. *ḫrj-ḥbt ḥrj-tp, zš mḏꜣt nṯr, ḫrp jꜣwt nbt nṯrt.*
ḥm-nṯr Ḥr jmj šnt, jmj-rꜣ pr nswt nb stp-zꜣ.
jmj-rꜣ swt špst pr-ꜥꜣ, jmj-rꜣ prwj-ḥḏ.
jmj-rꜣ šnwtj, jmj-rꜣ pr-pḫrt.
smr wꜥtj, wt Jnpw, ḥqꜣ Bꜣt, ḫrp hꜣṯs km.
jmꜣ-ꜥ, ꜥ ḥqꜣt, ꜥ ꜥntj, smꜣ Mn.
jmj-rꜣ ḥt-wrt 6, *jmj-rꜣ šnwtj.*
sḏꜣwtj bjtj, smr wꜥtj, r P nb.
jmj-rꜣ wꜥbtj, jmj-rꜣ prwj-nb.

219. *jrj-pꜥt, ḥꜣtj-ꜥ, tꜣtj zꜣb ṯꜣtj.*

Isolated titles have not been included in this listing. There are well over two hundred strings of titles in this tomb. From them Charts I, A–C have been constructed, using the conventions just given. The mastaba of *Mrrw-kꜣ* contains more strings of titles by far than any other tomb; many of them are quite rare. We can thus expect a greater number of mistakes and uncertainties than usual. The burial chamber in particular (pls. 201–11) contains a great number of titles not documented elsewhere in the mastaba; it also seems to have been decorated relatively carelessly, as is shown by the first strings on Plates 201 and 204, respectively. They were obviously intended to be identical, but being written on opposite walls, the beginning of one was opposite the end of the other. In the course of copying the text from one wall to the other, the scribe managed to reverse the order of three of the titles.

The reader will notice that in the case of a conflict, preference has regularly been given to the title sequences of the owner of the tomb and the relatively rare cases where a dependent's titles are written in a well carved string, carefully separated from the scene. Titles of servants that are squeezed in between figures of persons and objects are always more or less suspect. This explains why, for instance, the well documented sequence *ḥm-kꜣ, zš zꜣ* has only been given equal probability with the reverse, which is documented only once, but that in a case where the title is written large and not squeezed between figures of servants. (Cf. also n. 14 to the chart of *Mrrw-kꜣ*'s titles.)

Despite all the errors and fluctuations that are noted on the charts and in the footnotes, it is the writer's opinion that the great majority of the titles have a fixed position in the ranking scheme, and one that is repeated sufficiently frequently virtually to exclude any chance of coincidence. By its very size, this mastaba then is one of the best supports for our theory, even though the same size does increase the chance of errors.

CHART I A*

TITLES OF *MRRW-Kꜣ* [197] (UPPER HALF)

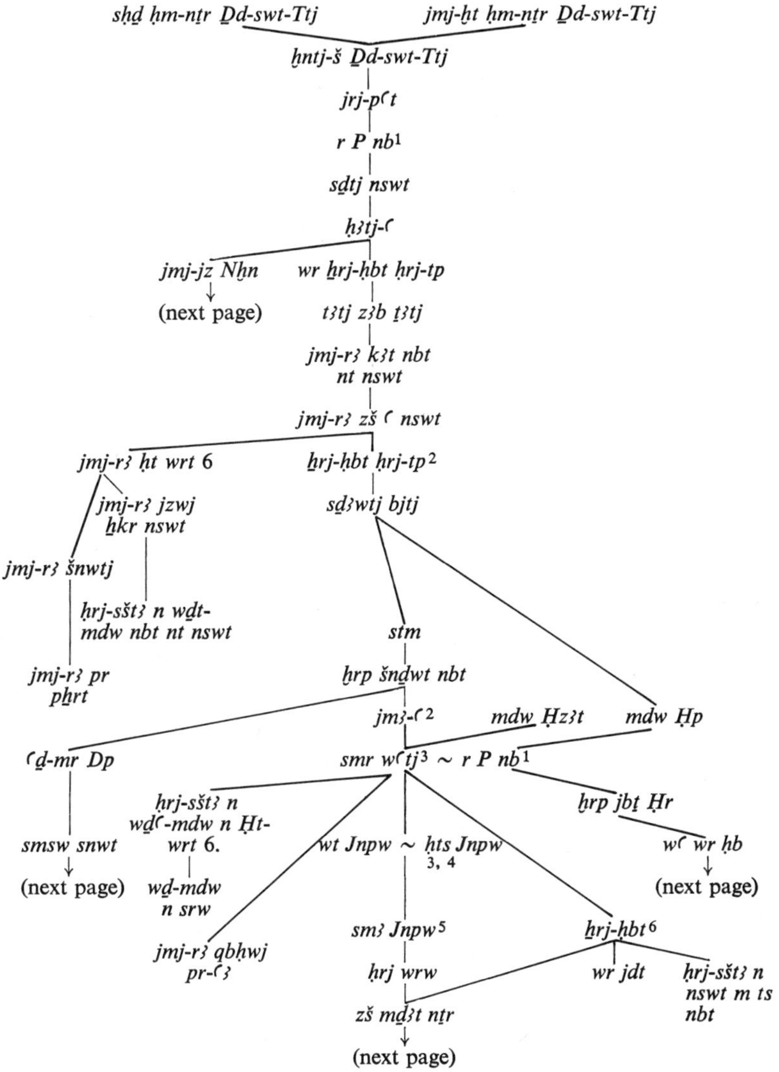

* For chart notes see p. 21.

CHART I B

TITLES OF *MRRW-Kꜣ* [197] (LOWER HALF)

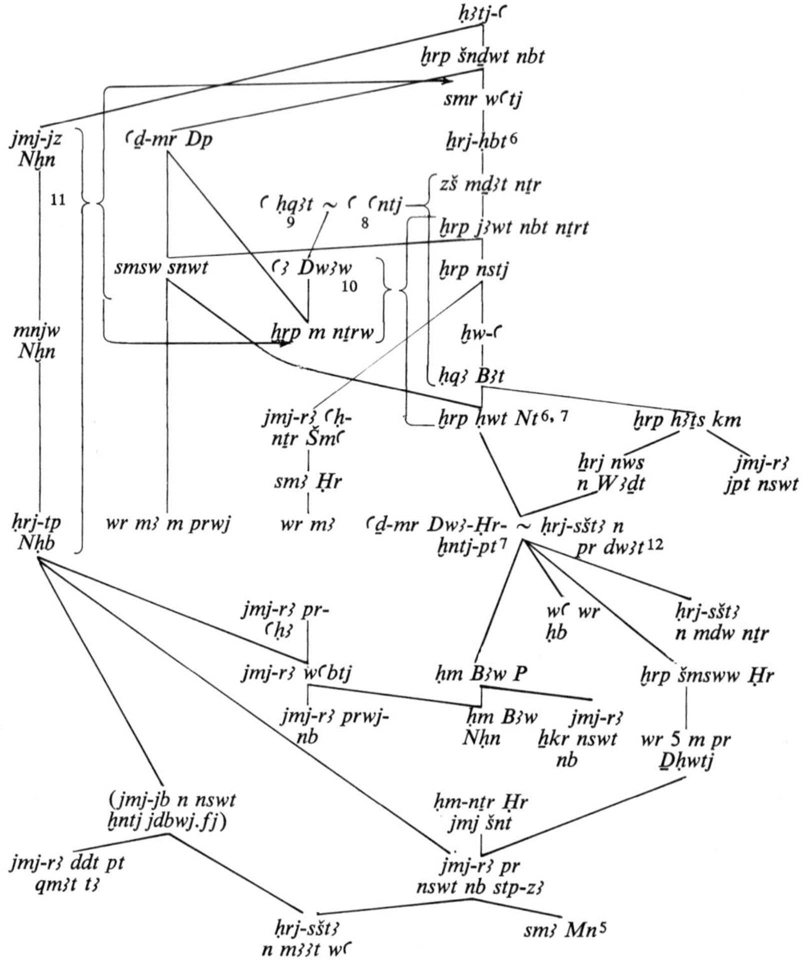

CHART I C

Titles of *MRRW-Kꜣ* [197] (Isolated Sequences)

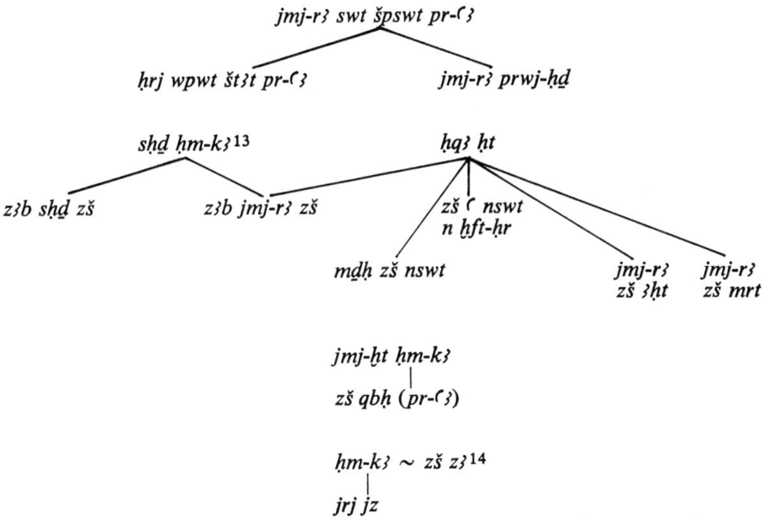

1 *R P nb* occurs twice in the vicinity of *smr wꜥtj* and, in the burial chamber, three times in the high-ranking position. Could the combination with *sḏtj nswt* be a different title?

2 *Jmꜣ-ꜥ* once precedes *ḫrj-ḥbt ḥrj-tp*. It probably is a mistake for *ḥꜣtj-ꜥ*, if the off-center position of the tree (cf. pl. 148) is taken seriously.

3 *Ḥts Jnpw* twice precedes *smr wꜥtj*. It occurs twenty-five times correctly.

4 *Wt Jnpw* precedes *ḥts Jnpw* thirteen times, follows fifteen times.

5 *Smꜣ Mn* occurs twice in the position of *Smꜣ Jnpw*.

6 *Ḫrj-ḥbt* occurs once (in the burial chamber) below *ḫrp ḥwt Nt*. The correct position is clearly attested four times.

7 *Ḫrp ḥwt Nt* once follows *ꜥḏ-mr Dwꜣ-Ḥr-ḫntj-pt*.

8 *ꜥ ḥqꜣt* precedes three times, follows five times.

9 These two titles occur twice at the lower end of their range, thirteen times at the upper end.

10 These two titles occur twice at the upper and twice at the lower end of their range of fluctuation.

11 This group of titles occurs twice at the upper end of its range and twice at the lower end.

12 *Ḥrj-sštꜣ n pr dwꜣt* precedes twice and follows once.

13 As the reader will notice, several passages in which this title occurs appear to have the hieroglyphs in a rather irregular order. The text has been emended in those cases. The sequences given here are, however, all attested in examples requiring no emendation.

14 *Ḥm-kꜣ* precedes in all except one case, the latter being, however, the only case where this group of titles occurs in a string written in large hieroglyphs and carefully carved. The passage has therefore been given equal weight with the others.

This is probably as good a place as any to mention one minor problem that is raised by two of the titles discussed in this study, *ḥqꜣ ḥt* and *zš zꜣ*. They both can refer to offices in the administration of the country, in which case they are of relatively high rank (*ḥqꜣ ḥt* regularly outranking *smr wꜥtj*) or to posts in the administration of private estates, in which case they are exceedingly unimportant. The matter is discussed more fully in chapter iv under 3/7 in the case of *ḥqꜣ ḥt*, for which the evidence is better. The situation seems to be similar for *zš zꜣ*, and we have avoided using it in the few cases that it occurs in a rankable context when held by *ḥm-kꜣ* or other offering bearers. It seemed safer to restrict our attention to those cases in which it was held by a tomb-owner or members of his family.

We continue our presentation with the titles in two more tombs of Sixth Dynasty date, that of *Jbj* of Deir el-Gebrawi and of *Ppjj-ꜥnḫ* the Middle at Meir.

[32] *Jbj* (the references are to the plates in Davies' publication):

3. jrj-pꜥt, ẖrj-ḥbt ḥrj-tp, stm, ḫrp šnḏwt nbt, [ḥrj]-tp [ꜥꜣ] Tꜣ-wr, jmj-rꜣ Šmꜥ, jmj-rꜣ šnwtj, jmj-rꜣ zšwwj, jmj-rꜣ prwj-ḥḏ.
   ḥꜣtj-ꜥ, ḥt-ꜥꜣt, jmꜣ-ꜥ, ḫrp nstj, ḫrp ḥꜣṯs km, jmj-jz, mnjw Nḫn, ḥrj-tp Nḫb, smsw snwt, ꜥꜣ Dwꜣw, ḫw-ꜥ, ḥqꜣ Bꜣt, ẖrj-ḥbt, zš mḏꜣt nṯr, ḫrp jꜣwt nbt nṯrt.
   mdw Ḥp, r P nb, ḫrp jbṯ Ḥr, ḫrp m nṯrw, ḫrp ḥwt Nt.
   jmj-rꜣ wpt ḥtp-ntr m prwj, ẖrj-tp nswt, ẖrj-ḥbt.
   *sḏꜣwtj bjtj, ḥqꜣ ḥt.
   *smr wꜥtj, ḥrj-tp ꜥꜣ Ḏw-f.
   *ḥqꜣ ḥt, smr wꜥtj, ẖrj-ḥbt.
   *ḥqꜣ ḥt, smr wꜥtj.
4. ḥꜣtj-ꜥ, ẖrj-ḥbt ḥrj-tp, stm, ḫrp šnḏwt nbt.
   ḥꜣtj-ꜥ, ḥqꜣ ḥt, smr wꜥtj.
5. ḥꜣtj-ꜥ, ḥqꜣ ḥt, smr wꜥtj.
   *sḏꜣwtj bjtj, ḥqꜣ ḥt, smr wꜥtj.
   *ḥqꜣ ḥt, smr wꜥtj.
6. ḥꜣtj-ꜥ, stm, q[. . .] wr ḫntt (?), ꜥḏ-mr Dwꜣ-Ḥr-ḫntj-pt.
   ḥrj-tp ꜥꜣ Tꜣ-wr, (wr m jꜣwt.f, smsw m sꜥḥ.f), ẖrj-ḥbt.
7. [sḥḏ] ḥm-[nṯr] Mn-ꜥnḫ-Nfrkꜣrꜥ, ẖrj-tp nswt. (First title very uncertain.)
   ḥqꜣ ḥt, smr wꜥtj mꜣꜥ, ḥrj-tp ꜥꜣ Tꜣ-wr.
   ḥꜣtj-ꜥ, ḥqꜣ ḥt, smr wꜥtj, ẖrj-tp nswt.
   ḥqꜣ ḥt Mn-ꜥnḫ-Nfrkꜣrꜥ, smr wꜥtj, ḥrj-tp ꜥꜣ [. . . , . . .] tp [. . .].
8. ḥꜣtj-ꜥ, ẖrj-ḥbt ḥrj-tp, stm, ḫrp šnḏwt nbt, jmꜣ-ꜥ, smr wꜥtj.
   smsw snwt, ꜥꜣ Dwꜣw, ḫw-ꜥ, ḥqꜣ [Bꜣt], ḫrp m nṯrw.
   ḫrp ḥwt Nt, ẖrj-ḥbt, zš mḏꜣt nṯr, <ḫrp> jꜣwt nbt nṯrt.
   ḥt-ꜥꜣt, ḥqꜣ ḥt mꜣꜥ.
   ḥꜣtj-ꜥ, sḏꜣwtj bjtj, ḥt-ꜥꜣt, ḥqꜣ ḥt, smr wꜥtj.
11. ḥꜣtj-ꜥ, ḥrj-tp ꜥꜣ Tꜣ-wr, ḥqꜣ ḥt, smr wꜥtj.
12. [. . .] sḏꜣwtj bjtj, smr wꜥtj.
13. jrj-pꜥt, ḥqꜣ ḥt, sḏꜣwtj bjtj, smr wꜥtj mꜣꜥ.
15. *sḏꜣwtj bjtj, ḥqꜣ ḥt.
   *smr wꜥtj, ẖrj-ḥbt. (two times).
17. ḥꜣtj-ꜥ, stm, ḫrp šnḏwt nbt, sḏꜣwtj bjtj, smr wꜥtj.
   ẖrj-ḥbt ḥrj-tp, jmꜣ-ꜥ, ḫrp nstj, ḫrp ḥꜣṯs km, jmj-rꜣ šnwtj.
   jmj-rꜣ Šmꜥ, ḥqꜣ ḥt, <jmj> jz, mnjw Nḫn, ḥrj-tp Nḫb.
   smsw snwt, ꜥꜣ Dwꜣw, ḫw-ꜥ, ḥqꜣ Bꜣt.
   ḥrj-tp ꜥꜣ Tꜣ-wr, ḥrj-tp ꜥꜣ Ḏw-f.
   ḥqꜣ ḥt, sḏꜣwtj bjtj, smr wꜥtj.
   ḥqꜣ ḥt, ḥt-ꜥꜣt, smr wꜥtj mꜣꜥ.

18. jmj-ẖt ḥm-nṯr, jmj-rꜣ wpt Mn-ꜥnẖ-Nfrkꜣrꜥ, ḥꜣtj-ꜥ, jmj-rꜣ Šmꜥ, jmj-rꜣ šnwtj, jmj-rꜣ zšwwj, jmj-rꜣ prwj-ḥḏ, ḥqꜣ ḥt, sḏꜣwtj bjtj, smr wꜥtj, ḥrj-tp ꜥꜣ Tꜣ-wr, ḥrj-tp ꜥꜣ Ḏw-f, ẖrj-ḥbt.
ḥꜣtj-ꜥ, ẖrj-ḥbt ḥrj-tp, stm, ẖrp snḏwt nbt, ḥrj-tp ꜥꜣ Tꜣ-wr.
jmj-rꜣ Šmꜥ, ḥqꜣ ḥt, sḏꜣwtj bjtj, smr wꜥtj.
*ḥqꜣ ḥt, smr wꜥtj.
ḥrj-tp ꜥꜣ Ḏw-f, ḥqꜣ ḥt.
stm, ẖrp šnḏwt nbt, sḏꜣwtj bjtj, smr wꜥtj, smsw snwt.
jmꜣ-ꜥ, ẖrp nstj, ẖrp hꜣṯs km, <jmj>-jz, mnjw Nẖn, ḥrj-tp Nẖb.
jmj-ẖt ḥm-nṯr Mn-ꜥnẖ-Nfrkꜣrꜥ, ḥrj-tp ꜥꜣ Tꜣ-wr.
ẖrp m nṯrw, ẖrp ḥwt Nt.

19. [jmj-rꜣ] Šmꜥ, sḏꜣwtj bjtj mꜣꜥ.
ḥqꜣ ḥt, [. . .], [jmj-jz, mnjw] Nẖn, ḥrj-tp Nẖb.
zš [mḏꜣt nṯr], ẖrp jꜣwt nbt nṯrt.
ḥqꜣ ḥt, sḏꜣwtj bjtj, smr wꜥtj.
*ḥqꜣ ḥt, smr wꜥtj.

23. sḏꜣwtj bjtj, ḥqꜣ ḥt, smr wꜥtj, ḥrj-tp ꜥꜣ Tꜣ-wr.
ḥꜣtj-ꜥ, smr wꜥtj, ḥrj-tp ꜥꜣ Ḏw-f.
(These are from his biography.)

The ranking is given on Chart II. The tomb of *Ppjj-ꜥnẖ* the Middle at Meir is probably somewhat later than that of *Jbj*. We now present his titles.

[133] *Ppjj-ꜥnẖ ḥrj-jb* (the references are to the plates in Blackman's publication):

4. smr wꜥtj, [ẖrj]-ḥbt, ḥrj-sštꜣ n pr dwꜣt.
ẖrj-tp nswt, mdw rẖjt, jwn Knmwt, ḥm-nṯr Mꜣꜥt.
ḥm-nṯr Jst Ḥtḥr, ḥm-nṯr Ḥr Stẖ, ḥm-nṯr Psḏt-ꜥꜣt.
ẖrj-tp nswt, jmj-rꜣ ḥm-nṯr.

4a. jrj-pꜥt, ḥꜣtj-ꜥ, jmj-jz, mnjw Nẖn, ḥrj-tp Nẖb, tꜣtj zꜣb ṯꜣtj, jmj-rꜣ zš ꜥ nswt, sḏꜣwtj bjtj, mdw Ḥp, r P nb, jmj-rꜣ šnwtj, jmj-rꜣ wꜥbtj, jmj-rꜣ šnꜥ, zꜣb ꜥd-mr, zš ꜥ nswt ẖft-ḥr, sḏꜣwtj nṯr, zš qd, jmj-rꜣ ḥm-nṯr n Ḥtḥr nbt Gsjw.
ẖrj-ḥbt ḥrj-tp, stm, smr wꜥtj, ẖrj-ḥbt, jmj-rꜣ Šmꜥ m spwt ḥrt-jb, ẖrj-tp nswt, mdw rẖjt, jwn Knmwt, ḥm-nṯr Mꜣꜥt, ḥrj-sštꜣ n wḏt-mdw nbt nt nswt.

6. ḥꜣtj-ꜥ, ḥrj-tp Nẖb, jmj-jz, mnjw Nẖn, sḏꜣwtj bjtj, smr wꜥtj, ẖrj-ḥbt, jmj-rꜣ [. . .] n bw mꜣꜥ.
smr wꜥtj, ẖrj-ḥbt, jmj-rꜣ ḥm-nṯr.
ḥꜣtj-ꜥ, jmj-jz, mnjw Nẖn, ḥrj-tp Nẖb, stm, ẖrp šnḏwt nbt, ẖw-ꜥ, ḥqꜣ Bꜣt, ẖrp hꜣṯs km.
smr wꜥtj, jrj nfr-ḥꜣt, jmj-rꜣ ḥm-nṯr n Ḥtḥr nbt Gsjw.
*sḥḏ ḥm-kꜣ, jmj-rꜣ pr.

CHART II

TITLES OF *JBJ* [32]

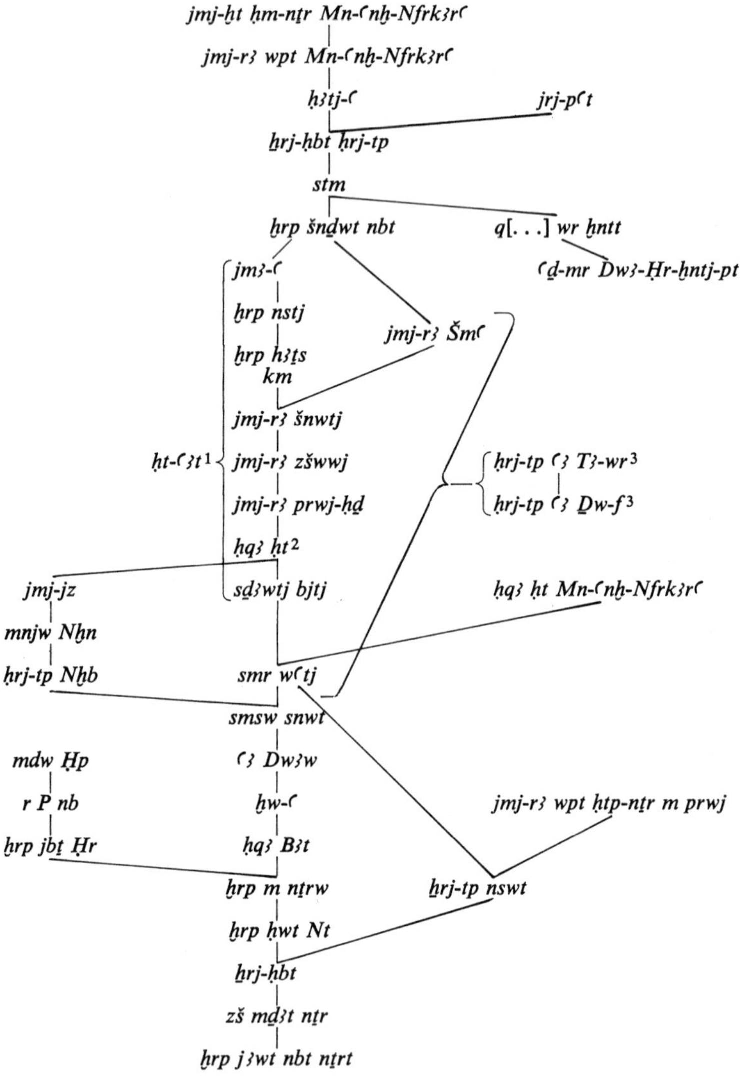

1 *Ḥt-ꜥꜣt* occurs twice at the higher and twice at the lower part of its range.
2 In the strings of the tomb-owner, *ḥqꜣ ḥt* occurs five times as listed and once below *sḏꜣwtj bjtj*. In the latter position it also occurs three times in the titles of dependents. We have preferred the position documented in the longer strings.
3 The nomarchies occur three times in the anomalous high position and four times in the more common low rank.

7. smr wꜥtj, ḥrj-sštꜣ n pr dwꜣt.
jmj-rꜣ gs-pr, ẖrj-tp nswt.
*špss nswt, sḥḏ ḥm-nṯr.
*špss nswt, jmj-rꜣ pr. (? A string of titles?)
8. ḥꜣtj-ꜥ, smr wꜥtj, ẖrj-ḥbt.
ẖrj-tp nswt, zš ꜥ nswt ẖft-ḥr.
*ẖrj-ḥbt, sḥḏ zš qdt.
9. ḥꜣtj-ꜥ, smr wꜥtj.
jmj-rꜣ gs-pr, ẖrj-tp nswt.
*špss nswt, jmj-rꜣ pr. (five times).
*špss nswt, smr pr.
11. jrj-pꜥt, smr wꜥtj, jmj-rꜣ ḥm-nṯr Ḥtḥr nbt Gsjw.
ḥꜣtj-ꜥ, smr wꜥtj, jmj-rꜣ ḥm-nṯr Ḥtḥr nbt Gsjw.
smr wꜥtj, ẖrj-ḥbt.
12. jrj-pꜥt, ḥꜣtj-ꜥ, [. . .].
jrj-pꜥt, ḥꜣtj-ꜥ.
jmj-rꜣ gs-pr, ẖrj-tp nswt.
smr wꜥtj, ẖrj-ḥbt.
*ẖrj-ḥbt, špss nswt.
*[sḥḏ] ḥm-nṯr, jmj-rꜣ pr.
14. ḥꜣtj-ꜥ, ẖrj-ḥbt ḥrj-tp.
ḥꜣtj-ꜥ, ẖrj-ḥbt ḥrj-tp, smr wꜥtj.
*ḥqꜣ ḥt, smr wꜥtj.
15. *zš ꜥ nswt, zꜣb jmj-rꜣ zš.
jrj-pꜥt, ḥꜣtj-ꜥ, jmj-jz, mnjw [Nḫn, . . .].
tꜣtj zꜣb ṯꜣtj, jmj-rꜣ zš ꜥ nswt, [. . .].
ẖrj-ḥbt ḥrj-tp, zš mḏꜣt nṯr, jmj-rꜣ Šmꜥ n bw [mꜣꜥ, . . .].
ẖrj-tp nswt, jmj-<rꜣ> ḥt-wrt, jmj-rꜣ ḥm-nṯr.
*ẖrj-tp nswt, jmj-rꜣ ḥm-nṯr n Ḥtḥr.
*ẖrj-tp nswt, zš ḥt-nṯr.
*ḥqꜣ ḥt, smr wꜥtj.
16. *špss nswt, sḥḏ ḥm-nṯr.
ḥꜣtj-ꜥ, smr wꜥtj.
*špss nswt, mtj n zꜣ.
17. smr wꜥtj, jmj-rꜣ ḥm-nṯr n Ḥtḥr.

These two tombs are typical samples of the average titulary of a high official of the later Sixth Dynasty. The ranking of *Ppjj-ꜥnḫ* is on Chart III; it is almost free of difficulties. In general, we find a much greater profusion of titles in the tombs of the Sixth Dynasty than in those of the Fifth. We shall now give three examples from the Fifth Dynasty, the titles of the vizier *Wꜣš-Ptḥ Jzj* from the time of Neferirkare, the vizier *Ptḥ-ḥtp* (the elder) from the time of Djedkare, and of his son the vizier *ꜣḫt-ḥtp*.

CHART III

TITLES OF *PPJJ-ꜥNḪ* THE MIDDLE [133]

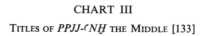

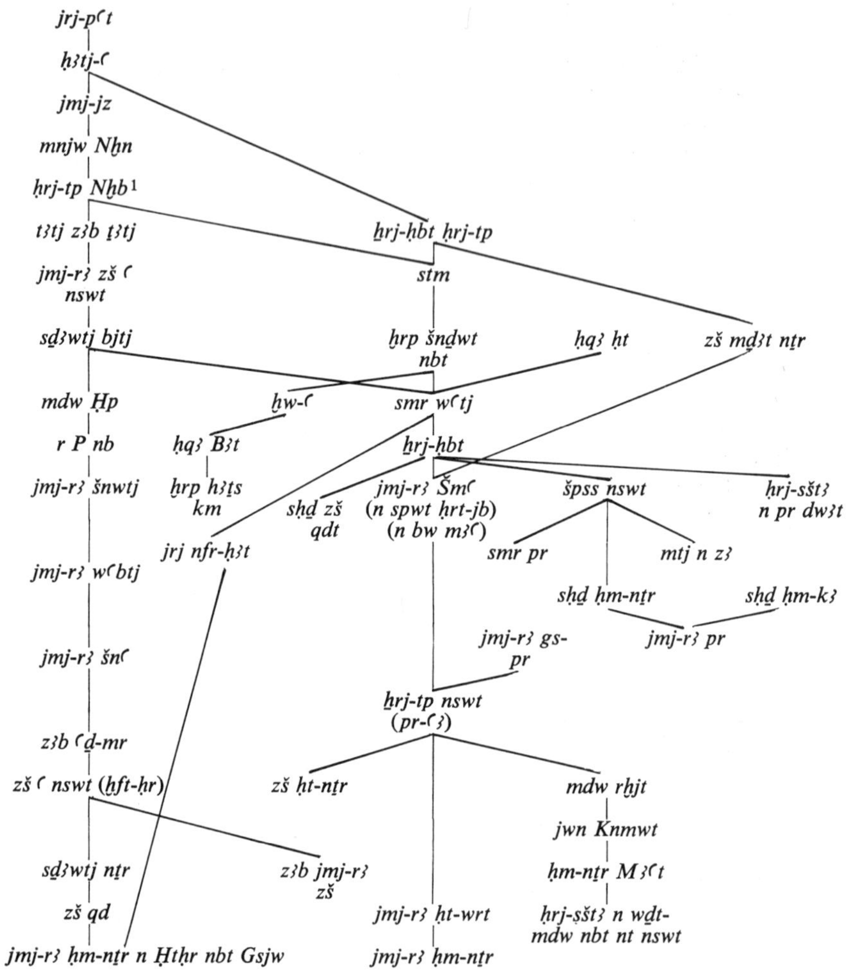

[1] *Ḥrj-tp Nḫb* once precedes *jmj-jz*, a mistake all the more blatant since the correct sequence is given on the opposite door thickness.

The following title sequence cannot be connected with the remainder:

ḥm-nṯr Jst Ḥtḥr
|
ḥm-nṯr Ḥr Stḫ
|
ḥm-nṯr Psḏt ꜥꜣt

[105] *Wꜣš-Ptḥ Jzj* (The tomb has been badly scattered. We give the texts in Mariette, *Mastabas*, D 38, first.):

ḥꜣtj-ꜥ, jmj-jz, mnjw Nḫn, tꜣtj zꜣb ṯꜣtj, ẖrj-ḥbt ḥrj-tp, zš mḏꜣt nṯr, smr wꜥtj.
ḥꜣtj-ꜥ, smr wꜥtj, jrj nfr-ḥꜣt, ẖrj-ḥbt.
ẖrj-ḥbt, ẖrj-tp nswt, mdw rḫjt, jwn Knmwt, ḫrp wsḫt, ḥm-nṯr Mꜣꜥt. (These three strings are on the upper lintel of the false door, now in the British Museum. Insofar as it is preserved, the remainder of the false door is in Copenhagen.)
ḥꜣtj-ꜥ, tꜣtj zꜣb ṯꜣtj, ẖrj-ḥbt ḥrj-tp, zš mḏꜣt nṯr, smr wꜥtj, jrj nfr-ḥꜣt, ḥrj-sštꜣ n pr dwꜣt, jmj-rꜣ kꜣt nbt nt nswt.
ḥꜣtj-ꜥ, tꜣtj zꜣb ṯꜣtj.
ẖrj-ḥbt ḥrj-tp, smr wꜥtj.
ẖrj-ḥbt ḥrj-tp, ḥrj-sštꜣ n mdw-nṯr.
smr wꜥtj, wr jdt.
smsw snwt, ꜥꜣ Dwꜣw.
**ẖrj-tp nswt, ẖrj-ḥbt.* (six times; in each case squeezed into a representation).
**ẖrj-tp nswt, jwn Knmwt, ẖrj-ḥbt.*
ḥꜣtj-ꜥ, tꜣtj zꜣb ṯꜣtj, smr wꜥtj.
tꜣtj zꜣb ṯꜣtj, jmj-rꜣ kꜣt nbt nt nswt, jmj-rꜣ zš ꜥ nswt.
ḥꜣtj-ꜥ, jmj-jz Nḫn, mnjw Nḫn, smr wꜥtj, jrj nfr-ḥꜣt, ḥrj-sštꜣ n pr dwꜣt.
ẖrj-ḥbt ḥrj-tp, zš mḏꜣt nṯr, ḥrj-sštꜣ n mdw nṯr, smsw snwt, ḫrp jꜣwt nbt nṯrt.
ḫt wr, ḫt *, ꜥꜣ Dwꜣw, jmj-rꜣ zš ꜥ nswt.*
smꜣ Ḥr, smꜣ Mn, ḥts Jnpw, ḫrp jꜣwt nbt nṯrt, ḥm jꜣqs.
smr wꜥtj, ḥrj-sštꜣ n pr dwꜣt, ḥm-nṯr Ḥr Jnpw ḫntj pr šmswt.
ẖrj-ḥbt ḥrj-tp, zš mḏꜣt nṯr, smsw snwt, sḏtj nswt, <ḥm> ḫtm (?).
ḥꜣtj-ꜥ, jmj-jz Nḫn, ḥrj-tp Nḫb, ḥm-nṯr Nḫbt, jmj-rꜣ zš ꜥ nswt.
tꜣtj zꜣb ṯꜣtj, jmj-rꜣ kꜣt nbt nt nswt.
ẖrj-ḥbt ḥrj-tp, zš mḏꜣt nṯr, smsw snwt, ꜥꜣ Dwꜣw, ḫt wr.
smr wꜥtj, jrj nfr-ḥꜣt, ḥrj-sštꜣ n pr dwꜣt.
ẖrj-ḥbt ḥrj-tp, zš mḏꜣt nṯr, ḥrj-sštꜣ n mdw nṯr, smsw snwt, ꜥꜣ Dwꜣw.
smr wꜥtj, ḥrj-sštꜣ n pr dwꜣt, ḥrj-tp Nḫb, ḥm-nṯr Ḥr Jnpw.
jmj-rꜣ zš ꜥ nswt, jmj-rꜣ kꜣt nbt nt nswt.

(The fragment published by Grdseloff has the following strings):

tꜣtj zꜣb ṯꜣtj, smr wꜥtj, jrj nfr-ḥꜣt.
ẖrj-ḥbt, jmj-rꜣ wꜥbt.

(In *Urkunden*, we find the following):

ẖrj-tp nswt, mdw rḫjt.
smr, ẖrj-ḥbt, wr zjnw. (In connected text in the biography and better discounted here.)

This is one of the earliest tombs to show a sufficiently consistent ranking of titles to be usable. Surprisingly enough, the only serious case of fluctuation encountered here is that of *ẖrj-ḥbt*, which precedes *ẖrj-tp nswt* in the one case where the combination occurs in a major string of titles belonging to the owner of the tomb, and follows in the titles added to the figures of members of his household. We have indicated both positions in Chart IV.

CHART IV

TITLES OF *WꜣŠ-PTḤ JZJ* [105]

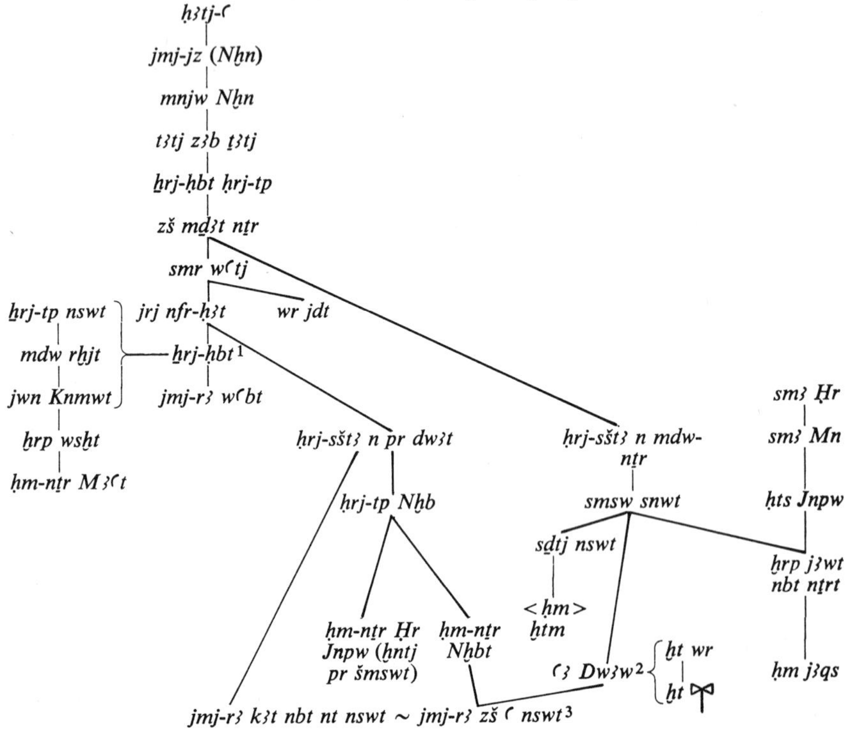

[1] *H̱rj-ḥbt* outranks *ẖrj-tp nswt* the only time the two titles occur together in a major string of titles belonging to the owner of the tomb. The reverse sequence occurs, in all, seven times, but in all cases in the short strings of titles written over the figures of members of the household. In such a case it seemed best simply to indicate a fluctuation.

[2] The title *ʿꜣ Dwꜣw* occurs once at each end of its range.

[3] Each title precedes once. The physicians' titles in the biography have not been included in this chart but can easily be inserted from the list of strings of titles.

[160] *Ptḥ-ḥtp* (the references are to the plates in Murray's publication):

8. *tꜣtj zꜣb ṯꜣtj, jmj-rꜣ kꜣt nbt nt nswt.*
   jmj-rꜣ zš ʿ nswt, ḥrj-sštꜣ n nswt.
   tꜣtj zꜣb ṯꜣtj, jmj-rꜣ kꜣt nbt nt nswt, jmj-rꜣ zš ʿ nswt, ḥrj-sštꜣ n wḏt-mdw nbt nt nswt, ẖrj-ḥbt, zš mḏꜣt nṯr.
   jrj-pʿt, tꜣtj zꜣb ṯꜣtj, sḏꜣwtj bjtj, r P nb, jmj-rꜣ kꜣt nbt nt nswt. (two times; the last title is immediately followed by *tꜣtj zꜣb ṯꜣtj* and then the name of the owner, one of the cases of repetition of a high title just before the name that was mentioned above.)

ḥꜣtj-ʿ, smr wʿtj n mrwt, jmj-rꜣ ẖt nbt nt nswt, jmj-rꜣ zš ʿ nswt, ḥrj-sštꜣ n nswt. (two times).
tꜣtj zꜣb ṯꜣtj, mdw rḫjt. (two times).
[. . .], *mdw rḫjt, ḫrp wsḫt, jwn Knmwt, jmj-rꜣ šnwtj, jmj-rꜣ prwj-ḥḏ, jmj-rꜣ jzwj ẖrj-ḫtm.* (two times).
[. . .] *wʿbt, jmj-rꜣ prwj-nb, ẖrj-ḥbt ḥrj-tp, zš mḏꜣt nṯr, ḥrj-sštꜣ n wḏt-mdw nbt nt nswt.* (two times).
9. *jrj-pʿt, ḥꜣtj-ʿ.*
tꜣtj zꜣb ṯꜣtj, jmj-rꜣ zš ʿ nswt, ḫrp wsḫt.
jmj-rꜣ kꜣt nbt nt nswt, jmj-rꜣ ḫkr nswt.
12. **ẖrj-tp nswt, mdw rḫjt.* (Restored from Mariette's copy.)
14. **ḥm-kꜣ, zš zꜣ.* (Inserted in scene.)
17. *jrj-pʿt, tꜣtj zꜣb ṯꜣtj, ḥꜣtj-ʿ, sḏꜣwtj bjtj, r P nb, jmj-rꜣ kꜣt nbt nt nswt, jmj-rꜣ zš ʿ nswt.*
jrj-pʿt, tꜣtj zꜣb ṯꜣtj, smr wʿtj. (two times).
jrj-pʿt, ḥꜣtj-ʿ, jmj-[. . .].

As was pointed out already, this tomb contains a good example of the Fifth Dynasty practice of repeating a high title at the end of the string just before the name of the owner of the tomb. The sequence *tꜣtj zꜣb ṯꜣtj, ḥꜣtj-ʿ* on the altar (pl. 17) is so unusual for a tomb of this period, that one is tempted to emend it, but it seemed safer to let it stand. Unfortunately there are no parallels against which to check it, or the copy of the text.

[13] *ꜣḫt-ḥtp* (the references are to the plates in Davies' publication):

6. *tꜣtj zꜣb ṯꜣtj, jmj-rꜣ wsḫt.*
ẖrj-tp nswt, mdw rḫjt, jwn Knmwt.
zꜣb ʿḏ-mr, ḥm-nṯr Mꜣʿt.
jmj-rꜣ njwt, sḥḏ ḥm-nṯr { *Nfr-Ḏdkꜣrʿ.* / *Nṯrj-swt-Mnkꜣwḥr.* / *Mn-swt-Nwsrrʿ.* }
**ẖrj-tp nswt, mdw rḫjt.*
9. **ẖrj-tp nswt, mdw rḫjt.*
**jmj-rꜣ njwt Nfr-*[. . .], *ẖrj-tp nswt.*
13. *tꜣtj zꜣb ṯꜣtj, ḫrp wsḫt.*
jmj-rꜣ [. . .], *jmj-rꜣ gs-pr.*
ẖrj-tp nswt, [*mdw rḫjt*], *jmj-rꜣ šnwtj.*
zꜣb ʿḏ-mr, nst ḫntt.
14. *tꜣtj zꜣb ṯꜣtj, ḫrp wsḫt.*
jmj-rꜣ Šmʿ, jmj-rꜣ šnwtj.
jmj-rꜣ gs-pr, ḫrp zš nb.
ẖrj-tp nswt, jmj-rꜣ prwj-ḥḏ.
zꜣb ʿḏ-mr, nst ḫntt.

CHART V

Titles of *PTḤ-ḤTP* [160]

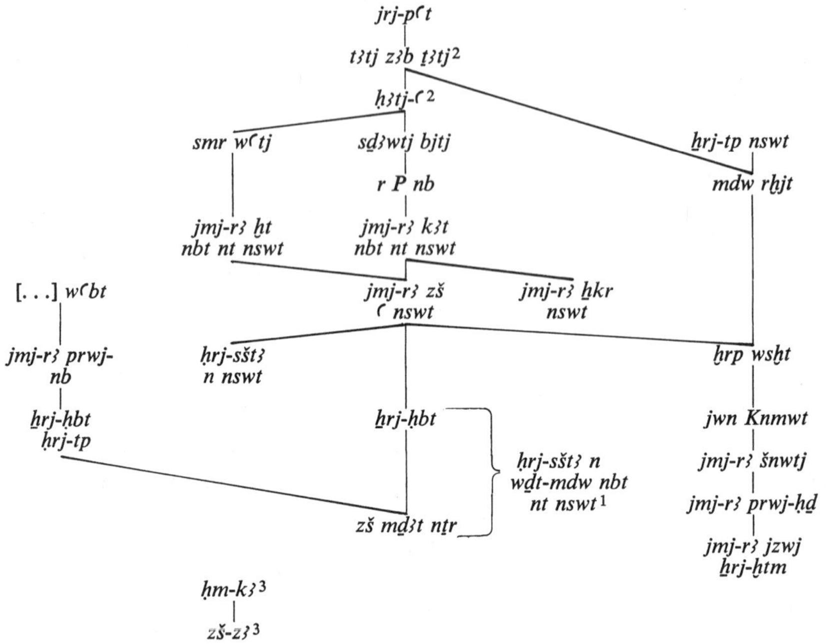

[1] This title occurs twice below *zš mḏꜣt nṯr* and once between *jmj-rꜣ zš ꜥ nswt* and *ẖrj-ḥbt*.
[2] This sequence is very unusual in a tomb of this period and is based on a single example on the altar or offering slab. It has seemed best not to emend the text, however, and it has been used as it stands in the discussion in chapter v.
[3] This is the *zš zꜣ* who is a domestic servant, as has already been discussed above.

18. *tꜣtj zꜣb ṯꜣtj, jmj-rꜣ zš ꜥ nswt.*
    jmj-rꜣ Šmꜥ, jmj-rꜣ gs-pr, mdw rḫjt.
    ẖrj-tp nswt, jmj-rꜣ prwj-ḥḏ, jmj-rꜣ šnwtj.
    zꜣb ꜥḏ-mr, ḫrp wsḫt.
19. **jmj-rꜣ sšr, ḥm-kꜣ.*
    **ḥm-kꜣ, sḏꜣwtj.*
20. *tꜣtj zꜣb ṯꜣtj, jmj-rꜣ zš ꜥ nswt.*
    jmj-rꜣ Šmꜥ, jmj-rꜣ gs-pr, mdw rḫjt.
    ẖrj-tp nswt, jmj-rꜣ prwj-ḥḏ, jmj-rꜣ šnwtj.
    zꜣb ꜥḏ-mr, ḫrp wsḫt, wr 10 Šmꜥ, ḫrp zš.
    **zꜣb jmj-rꜣ zš, jmj-rꜣ pr.*
23. **jmj-rꜣ sšr, ḥm-kꜣ.*
28. *mdw rḫjt, ḫrp wsḫt.*
    ẖrj-tp nswt, mdw rḫjt, ḥm-nṯr Mꜣꜥt. (partly on pl. 29).
    jmj-rꜣ njwt Nfr-Ḏdkꜣrꜥ, tꜣtj zꜣb ṯꜣtj, jmj-rꜣ zš ꜥ nswt, ḫrp wsḫt.
    [. . .], *ḥm-nṯr Mꜣꜥt, jmj-rꜣ wḏꜥ-mdw nb.*

29. *jmj-rꜣ njwt Nfr-Ḏdkꜣrꜥ, tꜣtj zꜣb ṯꜣtj, jmj-rꜣ zš ꜥ nswt, ḫrp wsḫt.*
   [. . .] *zš ꜥ nswt, ḫrj-tp nswt, mdw rḫjt, jwn Knmwt, ḥm-nṯr Mꜣꜥt, jmj-rꜣ wḏꜥ-mdw nb.*
   [. . .], *jmj-rꜣ prwj-ḥḏ, jmj-rꜣ šnwtj.*

CHART VI

TITLES OF *ꜣḪT-ḤTP* [13]

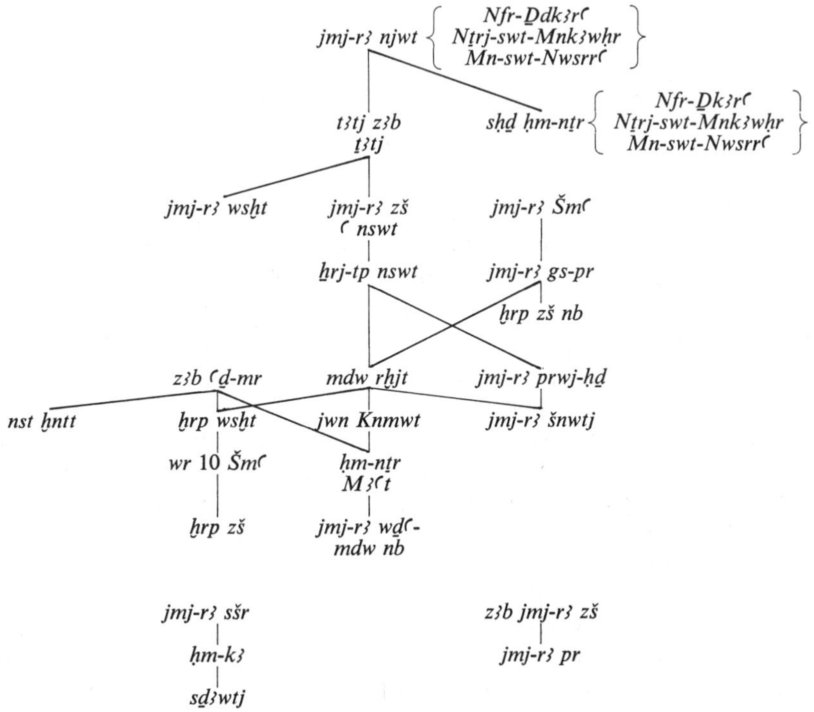

This is, I think, an adequate survey of the ranking of titles during the Fifth and Sixth Dynasties. The method followed should be evident upon comparison of the individual strings in a tomb with the ranking charts derived therefrom. It was stated earlier in the chapter that this system did not work during the Fourth Dynasty. We give two examples. The tomb of *Kꜣ-nfr* must date from about the middle of the Fourth Dynasty, since he was a son of Snefru.

[534] *Kꜣ-nfr:*
zꜣ nswt n ẖt.f mr.f, smr, ḫrp ꜥḥ, ḥrj-sštꜣ pr dwꜣt.
ḥꜣtj-ꜥ n jt.f, zꜣ Snfrw mr.f n jt.f hrw nb, ḫrp ꜥḥ, jmj-jz Nḫn, wr Npt.
ḥm-nṯr Ḥr-Nb-Mꜣꜥt, r P nb, mnjw Nḫn, sḏꜣwtj nṯr ḥꜥw, jmj-rꜣ wpwt, zꜣ nswt n ẖt.f.

zꜣ nswt n jt.f smsw, zꜣ Snfrw, ḥm-nṯr <Snfrw>, (nb jmꜣḫw ḫr jt.f), ḫrp wꜥbw. (Has the text been published correctly here?)
<ḥrj-tp> Nḫb, smr wꜥtj, ḫrp ꜥḥ, [ḥrj]-sštꜣ n pr dwꜣt, ḫt Ḥr (?).
ḥm Bꜣw Nḫn, ḥm-nṯr Ḥr mḥtj, ḥm-nṯr Sbk Šdjt, smꜣ Mn, jmj-rꜣ Ḫꜥ-Snfrw, smr n jt.f.
zꜣ nswt n ẖt.f mrjj.f mr.n.f jt.f, (nb jmꜣḫ [ḫr] jt.f), ḥm-nṯr Snfrw, ḫrp wꜥbw.
jrj-pꜥt, tꜣtj zꜣb ṯꜣtj, wr 5 pr Ḏḥwtj, ḥꜣtj-ꜥ, mnjw Nḫn, jmj-jz Nḫn, jmj-rꜣ wpwt.
sḏꜣwtj bjtj, wr mꜣ Jwnw, ḥm Bꜣw P, ẖrj-ḥbt, smsw jz, zꜣ nswt n [ẖ]t.f smsw, jmj-rꜣ Ḫꜥ-Snfrw.
ḥm-nṯr Wnwt Šmꜥ (??), *zꜣb ꜥḏ-mr, jwn Knmwt, wḏ-mdw n ḥrj-wḏbw, ḥts Jnpw. ḥm-nṯr Bꜣstt m swt nbt.*
ḥm-nṯr Ḥr-Nb-Mꜣꜥt, sḏꜣwtj nṯr ḥꜥw, ẖrj-tp nswt, mdw rḫjt, smꜣ Ḥr, nḫt <ḫrw?>, wꜥ wr ḥb, ḥm-nṯr Ḥr nb Mzn, ḫt Ḥr.

The quality of the publication is, unfortunately, not such as to inspire great feelings of confidence. The British Museum publication has been taken as a base, and, as a comparison with Plate 4 shows, I have taken it upon myself to make what amounts to a running emendation of the text. In any case, however questionable the details may be, the readings of the titles in general can hardly be open to question. Since this tomb contains more long strings of titles than any other tomb of so early a date, it is by far the best example of the confusion resulting from an attempt at conflating the strings. A comparison with the charts just given will show that the disorder here is of a completely different order of magnitude from the fluctuations found later; the latter, annoying as they are, are not enough to make the material unusable. Here the confusion is too great.

An offering slab found in the tomb of *Kꜣ-nfr* shows a feature that is very common in the tombs of Fourth and early Fifth Dynasty date: titles written in very short columns, sometimes separated by lines, sometimes not (as here), with most titles continuing from one column to the next. While it is tempting to treat such cases as a single string, experience has shown that this only adds to the confusion. The text is given here with slashes separating the short columns:

zꜣ nswt/ smsw/ n ẖt.f / mrjj.f /, smr wꜥtj/, ḫrp ḥm-nṯr Snfrw/, ḥrj/-sštꜣ/ Ḥr-Nb-Mꜣꜥt.

The titles of *Sšꜣt-ḥtp* offer a good example of the arrangement found in the Giza mastabas of the early Fifth Dynasty. The usual arrangement is in short columns, in this case separated by lines. By using only the relatively rare sequences of titles following each other within the same column, a consistent chart can be built up, but the rankings obtained are so odd as compared with the ones current somewhat later, particularly the low position of *zꜣ nswt*, as to lead one to suspect the validity of the ranking obtained. We present the title sequences, giving the short column series as for *Kꜣ-nfr* above.

CHART VII

TITLES OF *Kꜣ-NFR* [534]

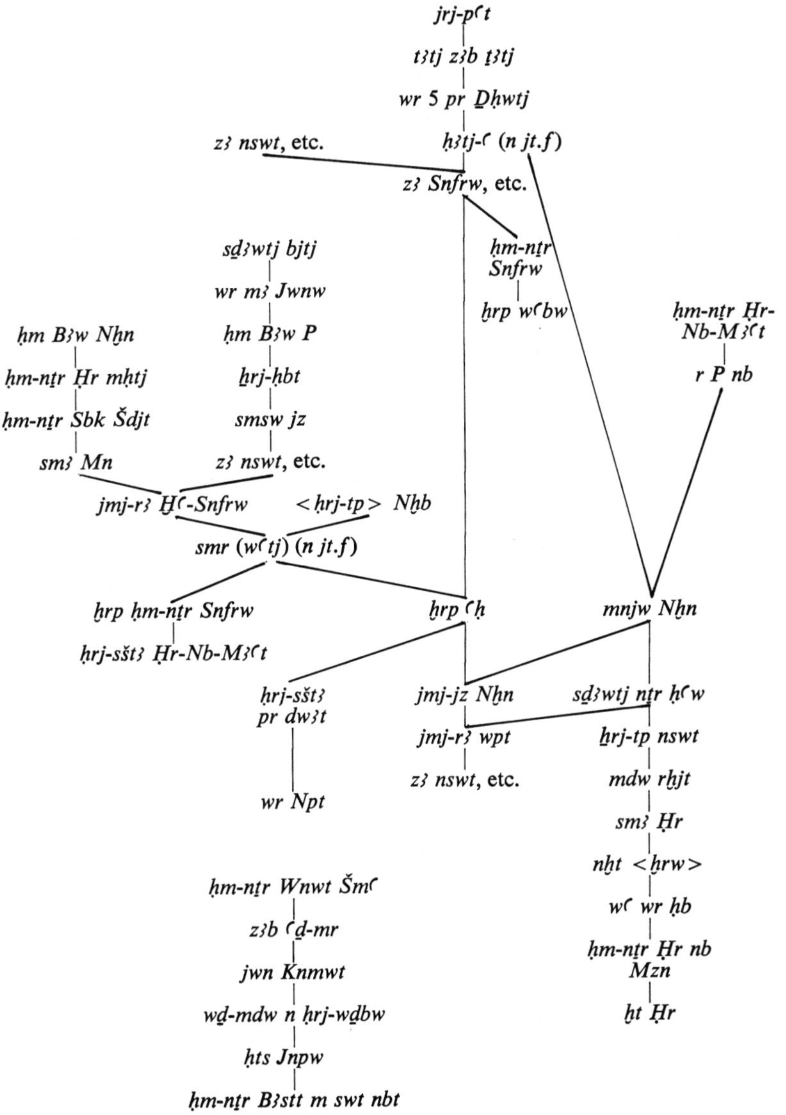

[473] *Sšꜣt-ḥtp Htj* (the references are to the figures in Junker's publication):

28. *zꜣ nswt/ n ẖt.f/, wt Jnpw/, wr* 10 *Šmꜥ, jrj-ḫt nswt/, ḥrj-sštꜣ/ kꜣt nbt nswt.*
smr, ḫrp ꜥḥ, zꜣ nswt n ẖt.f, ẖrj-ḥbt.
zꜣ nswt n ẖt.f, smr.
wt Jnpw, ẖrj-ḥbt. (two times).
wt Jnpw, ẖrj-ḥbt/, zꜣ nswt n ẖt.f.
smr, ḫrp ꜥḥ/, zꜣ nswt n ẖt.f/, wt Jnpw, ẖrj-ḥbt/, wr 10 *Šmꜥ, jrj-ḫt nswt/, ḥrj-sštꜣ/ kꜣt nbt nswt/, jmj-rꜣ kꜣt/ nbt nswt, smr.*
smr, zꜣ nswt n ẖt.f, wt Jnpw, ẖrj-ḥbt.
smr, zꜣ nswt.
smr, zꜣ nswt n ẖt.f.
33. *smr, ḫrp ꜥḥ, zꜣ nswt n ẖt.f.*
wt Jnpw, ẖrj-ḥbt, wr 10 *Šmꜥ, jrj-ḫt nswt.*

From this we obtain the following sequence of titles:

smr
|
ḫrp ꜥḥ
|
zꜣ nswt (n ẖt.f)
|
wt Jnpw
|
ẖrj-ḥbt
|
wr 10 *Šmꜥ*
|
jrj-ḫt nswt

Zꜣ nswt also occurs once before *smr*. If the short-column series are included, the result is somewhat more disordered than given here.

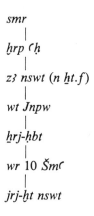

The system of ranking titles was still in full swing at the end of the Sixth Dynasty, as is shown, for instance by the strings of titles in the Koptos Decrees [602]. It did not survive into the Middle Kingdom, as far as can be concluded from an unsuccessful attempt to rank the titles in some of the tombs at Beni Hassan according to the methods used here. Since we made no attempt to collect tombs of obviously First Intermediate date, and included only those for which an Old Kingdom date seemed at least a possibility at the time, we are in no position to determine at what time the Egyptians ceased to write the titles in strict order of rank. Some of the tombs we collected titles from are, however, to be assigned to the First Intermediate Period, as became evident after study; as will be shown at the end of chapters iv and v, they still have internally consistent sequences of titles, but these sequences are often ones that could not occur during the Old Kingdom. Whether this is simply an intentional change or rather the first symptom of disintegration cannot be decided with the material at hand. I would suspect that an attempt was made to write the titles according to some system as long as the Heracleopolitans managed to preserve some of the traditions of the Old Kingdom. But this needs further study and is only presented as a guess.

A comparison of the ranking charts obtained for the six Fifth and Sixth Dynasty tombs presented here soon brings to light a bothersome fact. The strings of titles within each tomb show a considerable degree of consistency when conflated; and since this process has been carried out successfully for a very large number of tombs, it seems to the author that the validity of the ranking of titles within a tomb can be taken for granted in the remaining discussion. When the titles from different tombs, particularly tombs of different periods are compared, the sequences obtained definitely conflict. There is, to be sure, a large amount of general agreement, insofar as titles such as *jrj-pꜥt* and *ḥꜣtj-ꜥ* seem regularly to occur at, or near the top of a ranking chart, while others such as *smr wꜥtj* and *ẖrj-tp nswt* tend to occur around the middle and such titles as *ḥrj-sštꜣ* near the bottom. But the details differ sufficiently to make it quite impossible to conflate the titles from all the tombs into one large master chart. What is the explanation of this state of affairs?

Several possibilities come to mind. It is evident that the large mass of titles found in an Old Kingdom tomb can hardly represent titles held simultaneously; in all probability they are the accumulation of a lifetime. Varille compares a frequently recurring sequence of three titles to the Roman *cursus honorum*,* and this brings us to the first possibility that must be considered: that the sequence of titles in a tomb represents, in reverse, the order in which they were acquired. This can be disproved. To do so, we give the strings of titles from two tombs whose owners' detailed biographies permit one to compare the ranking and the order of acquisition of titles. They do not contain very many strings of titles and thus hardly strengthen the argument for the validity of the system of ranking titles; however, it still seemed useful to present the material in full. The tombs as a whole are not well preserved and contain a number of isolated titles which are not given here. The first is that of the nomarch *Jzj* at Edfu, who functioned in the time of Teti and possibly Pepi I.

* *La tombe de Ni-Ankh-Pepi à Zâouiyet el Mâyetîn*, p. 33.

[62] *Jzj*. (Titles of dependents have not been specially marked):
smr wꜥtj, ẖrj-tp nswt, zꜣb ꜥḏ-mr, mḏḥ zš nswt. (two times).
smr wꜥtj, ẖrj-tp nswt, ḥrj-tp ꜥꜣ n spt.
smr wꜥtj, ẖrj-tp nswt, mdw rẖjt, jwn Knmwt.
<tꜣtj> zꜣb ṯꜣtj, jmj-rꜣ zš [ꜥ] *nswt.*
smr wꜥtj, ẖrj-ḥbt. (two times).
ẖrj-tp nswt, jmj-rꜣ šnꜥ.
smr, sḥḏ ḥm-kꜣ.
ḥqꜣ ḥt, ẖrj-tp nswt pr-ꜥꜣ.
wꜥb, ḥm-kꜣ.
ḥqꜣ ḥt, wr 10 *Šmꜥ.*

From this we obtain ranking Chart VIII.

CHART VIII

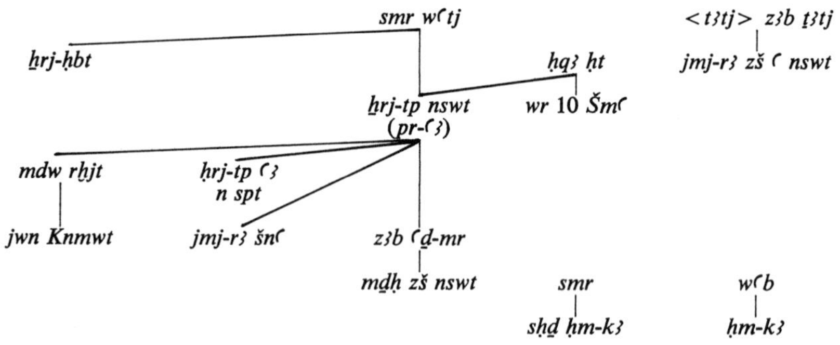

The details of his career are partially preserved. Under Djedkare he was *smsw hꜣjt nt* [. . .]; under Unis he was promoted to *ḥqꜣ ḥt*. Teti promoted him first to *mḏḥ zš nswt*, *zꜣb ꜥḏ-mr*, and *ẖrj-tp nswt*; later he became [*ḥꜣtj-ꜥ*, *smr wꜥtj*], *ḥrj-tp ꜥꜣ n spt*.* The remainder of his career, which presumably included promotion to *tꜣtj zꜣb ṯꜣtj*, is lost. Enough has been preserved, however, to show conclusively that the order of titles in the ranking system does not reflect the order in which the titles were acquired. The chances are that in any one promotion, the highest title granted (for it seems clear that titles were granted in groups—see also below), would tend to outrank any title held previous to the promotion; but there is an exception in the case just presented. The main point seems clear and is reinforced by the titles of the architect *Nẖbw*, who lived slightly later.

* The restoration seems reasonable but is far from certain, as Edel admits. However, it is hardly essential for our argument here.

[286] *Nḫbw:*

jmj-rꜣ kꜣt nbt nt nswt, smr wꜥtj. (two times).
ẖrj-ḥbt ḥrj-tp, smsw snwt.
smr wꜥtj, ẖrj-tp nswt.
jmj-rꜣ kꜣt nbt nt nswt, smr wꜥtj, mḏḥ qd nswt.
ẖrj-ḥbt ḥrj-tp, stm, ḫrp šnḏwt nbt, smr wꜥtj, smsw snwt, ꜥꜣ Dwꜣw.
smr wꜥtj, mḏḥ nswt. (two times).
smr wꜥtj, mḏḥ qd nswt m prwj.
ẖrj-tp nswt, mḏḥ qd nswt.
jmj-rꜣ qd, mtj n zꜣ.
sḥḏ n qd, mtj n zꜣ.

From this we obtain ranking Chart IX.

CHART IX

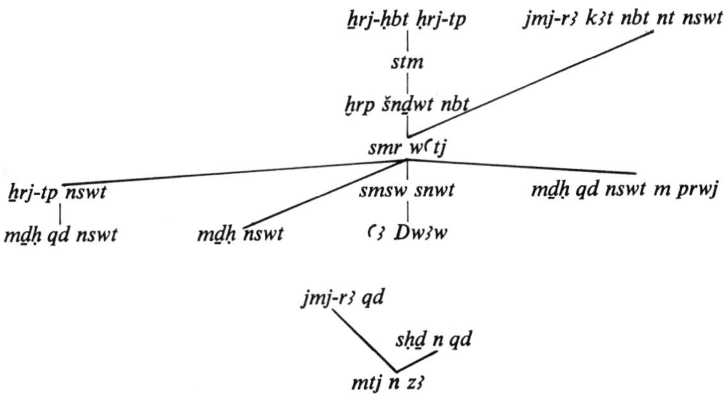

The stages in the career of *Nḫbw* and his brother are given in some detail. The careers are parallel, and are given below:

NḪBW	Brother of *NḪBW*
qd.	
sḥḏ n qd, mtj n zꜣ.	*sḥḏ n qd.*
jmj-rꜣ qd, mtj n zꜣ.	*jmj-rꜣ qd.*
mḏḥ qd nswt.	*mḏḥ qd nswt.*
ẖrj-tp nswt, mḏḥ qd nswt.	
smr wꜥtj, mḏḥ qd nswt m prwj.	*smr wꜥtj, mḏḥ qd nswt m prwj.*
	jmj-rꜣ kꜣt.

This list, while not as good evidence as the last example, does show that the mechanism of a promotion in ancient Egypt was not simple; it did not always consist of replacing a function by a new one but could, as here, involve simply the addition of a new title (honorific perhaps) while the title indicating the function remained unchanged.

The case of *Jbj* [32], whose titles have already been given (Chart II), hardly strengthens the argument, but is listed here for completeness' sake. Under Mernere he became *ḥ3tj-ʿ*, *smr wʿtj*, *ḥrj-tp ʿ3 Ḏw-f*; later under Pepi II he was promoted to *jmj-r3 Šmʿ*. In view of the fluctuation of the title of nomarch in this tomb, it can occur before that of the overseer of Upper Egypt, conflicting with the order in which the titles were acquired.

A second possibility that must be considered is that the different ranking sequences in the tombs are the result of individual preference, family or scribal tradition, or copying.

Individual preference seems inherently improbable as an explanation. In the first place, granted that the titles were written on the walls of the tomb according to some system, one would expect this system to have a somewhat greater significance than mere personal whim. Second, inspection of the charts presented here, and the much fuller material dealing with the common titles presented in chapters iv and v, shows that the variation from tomb to tomb stays within rather close limits. It is quite noticeable, but far from chaotic. Large numbers of tombs have title sequences that do not conflict with each other in any particular. Finally, it should be stressed that the system of ranked titles is found not only in private tombs but also in the pyramid temples of the kings of the Old Kingdom and in decrees and other documents issued from the royal chancellery; a comparison of the ranked titles from the pyramid of Pepi II with those of contemporary tombs shows great similarities in the ranking; on the other hand these titles [279] differ noticeably, for example, from the ranking patterns in the Dahshur Decree of Pepi I [153]. In the Koptos Decrees [602], document after document shows exactly the same ranking scheme. Personal whim hardly seems an adequate interpretation of these consistencies.

The question of family and scribal tradition can be answered more clearly by comparing the title sequences in tombs of known family groups with each other. A good case in point is the group of nomarchs of Meir, *N-ʿnḫ-Ppjj* [212] and his three sons named *Ppjj-ʿnḫ* [132–34]. A comparison of the titles given in the first part of chapter v will show a considerable degree of variation between these tombs. This case is particularly valuable, because it is in a provincial cemetery, for which a single scribal tradition could be assumed, if anywhere. Similarly, there are differences in the ranking patterns of the titles of *Mrrw-k3* [197] and his son *Mrjj-Ttj* [189], *Wjw* [106] and *Mrw Bbj* [192] at Sheikh Said, *Jzj* [62] and *Mrjjrʿ-nfr Q3r* [187] at Edfu, *Jj-mrjj* [21] and *Nfr-bꜣw-Ptḥ* [258] at Giza, to mention a few examples where family relationship seems reasonably certain.

The same evidence from the Upper Egyptian cemeteries also seems to exclude the possibility of scribal tradition. In the enormous Memphite Necropolis, tombs in small, clearly defined areas such as that around the pyramid of Pepi II or the Giza area show considerable variations in their title sequences.

Junker discusses at great length cases of the copying of scenes from one tomb into another, including cases where inscriptions were misunderstood and badly garbled in the process.* A cursory inspection of the material presented there shows, however, that the names and titles were the one element in the scenes that was not copied, and this is what one would expect. An Egyptian would hardly object to stereotyped representations of the good life on the walls of his tomb; his statues were in most cases mass-produced products not even attempting to reproduce his features. The essential point from the Egyptian standpoint seems to have been to have the tomb or statue "personalized" (to use a term from modern advertising lingo that seems quite appropriate here) by the addition of his names and titles; it had to be made clear to the visitor of the tomb chapel (and the soul returning to the statue) who the owner of the tomb was, and what his claims to power and distinction were.† Thus it seems unlikely that titles would be copied. Or take the case of the titles of *Mrrw-kꜣ* [197] and *Ḫntj-kꜣ Jḫḫj* [393]. Both tombs are in the Teti Cemetery, both are roughly contemporaneous, and as we shall show in the course of the discussion in chapter v, their title sequences are similar. Yet the individual strings written on the walls of their tombs differ widely. This then leads to our working hypothesis: at any given time there was a generally recognized system of ranking titles in use in Egypt. The titles held by an individual were arranged according to this scheme by the scribe planning the decoration of his tomb (or issuing a document) and then selections were made from this arrangement for each string of titles. This hypothesis is the only one that really satisfies the various points raised in the previous discussion: Similarities in the ranking of titles held by contemporaries, differences in the ranking of the titles of members of different generations of the same family, the fixed ranking of titles in documents issuing from the central government, and the fact that in two tombs of similar date the conflation of widely varying strings of titles may result in ranking charts that are very similar.

To the elucidation of this hypothesis we will devote the next three

* *Giza*, III, 63–77.

† See, for instance, Junker, *Giza*, XII, 87–94, for a recent discussion.

chapters. It is evident that, if it stands, it will provide a useful means of dating tombs on the basis of characteristic title sequences; at the same time this provides us with a method for testing the validity of the hypothesis. If we sort the tombs into groups on the basis of similar title sequences, do the groupings so obtained agree with the dates of these tombs as known from other sources? And do the title sequences in tombs known to be contemporary with others already assigned to such a group agree with the sequences characteristic for the group? The writer thinks that the evidence to be adduced in the following chapters allows one to answer both questions in the affirmative, and in chapter vi we shall attempt to study a few title sequences and their changes that are likely to shed some light on historical developments.

Here one objection still has to be answered: Granted that there was a generalized system of ranking titles in use at any given time and that the strings of titles found in the tombs are derived from such a system, what guarantee is there that the decoration of a tomb was not stretched out over so long a period of time that the recognized system of ranking titles was changed in the meantime, so that the strings actually represent two periods and give a false picture when conflated?

One can answer, of course, that more serious fluctuations in ranking would be expected in that case than are actually found; a better argument is the fact that there are almost no tombs showing any sign of a promotion of the owner during construction. The only cases known to me are the tomb of *Rʿ-špss* [315] and *Sšm-nfr* [478], both of whom were promoted to vizier after the greater part of their tombs had been completed. Otherwise, the titles are usually the same in all parts of the tomb, of course with variations due to differing availability of space and state of preservation.

The usual procedure seems to have been for a man to wait until relatively late in life before building his tomb. That a tomb could be built in a hurry is shown by the case of *Snḏm-jb Jntj* [455], whose tomb was built in only fifteen months and is one of the larger mastabas at Giza; there was thus no great pressure to begin building at an early stage in a man's career, when his station and finances would hardly enable him to erect a monument representative of the successful career he hoped for. One disadvantage of such a proceeding was, of course, that a man could wait too long and die before erecting his tomb. *Snḏm-jb* is a case in point; other examples are *Sḥtpw* [462], *Kꜣ-nfr* [534] *Ṯtj* [575], and *Ḏʿw* [592]. The list is not exhaustive and could be extended. A good many cases are mentioned in our list of sources in the next chapter. The building of a tomb by the father for the son is much rarer, an example being *Tp-m-ʿnḫ* [559], and it is always possible that in such cases the son died before the father.

In view of these remarks, it seems reasonably safe to treat the span of time consumed in decorating a tomb as negligible. In the mastaba of *Rʿ-špss*, the titles on the later, outer portions of the tomb excavated by Quibell only contain one short two-title sequence that is of little significance in any case. The titles of *Sšm-nfr* had to be divided into two groups.

The nature of the problem to be solved required the gathering of as complete a collection of ranked title sequences as possible. We begin with a survey of the sources.

III

LIST OF SOURCES USED

*

Accepting as a working hypothesis the likelihood that differences in ranking sequences are to be explained as the effect of changes brought about from time to time in a generally accepted system of ranking titles, our next step, and one that will occupy the bulk of this study, is to determine how well this hypothesis agrees with the facts. A complete proof is not possible with the material at our disposal. The procedure to be followed is roughly this. In this chapter, we will give a complete list of the approximately 675 sources from which we have drawn ranking charts or which contain other titles (such as priesthoods of kings or of kings' pyramids) which seemed worth collecting because their simple presence or absence could be used as a criterion for dating. The sources were numbered, and these numbers will be used to refer to them. Each entry is followed by bibliographical references and a brief paragraph summarizing whatever generally accepted evidence there seems to be for dating. In the next chapter, I will attempt to determine those ranking sequences of titles that continued unchanged throughout the period under consideration and thus can have no bearing on the problem. In chapter v, the variable sequences will be studied. We cannot work in a complete vacuum, considering nothing but the ranking charts—a method that would be ideal and greatly strengthen the proof of the hypothesis but that involves having at one's disposal a considerably greater body of material than is available. Until a reasonably well established group of title sequences characteristic for various parts of the later Old Kingdom has been established, we have to work from sources whose date is approximately known, grouping charts with similar titles that appear to be of the same date, checking whether their sequences agree or not, then finding other charts whose title sequences permit assignment to one or another of the groups so determined and then checking if this assignment agrees with the dating of the source on other grounds.

Before proceeding, then, we have to gather a certain amount of information about our sources other than the titles they contain, and this chapter will be devoted to a presentation of such data.

Each tomb or source is assigned a number. In general, the sequence of names is alphabetic, according to the order of the Egyptian alphabet, with unreadable names and sources that cannot be directly connected with the name of one individual at the end. For various reasons, the order was not always followed strictly at the time the reference numbers were assigned to the charts. Past experience has shown that the results of changing a system of reference numerals in the middle of a project can be disastrous. I hope that no names are so seriously out of place as to make them impossible to find. In this study, reference will always be by number in any case.

After the reference numbers were assigned, it was decided to include sources with few rankable titles but containing royal priesthoods. At the same time, a few other tombs that had been overlooked or unavailable previously were added to the collection. They were given numbers with a following letter and inserted into their proper alphabetic sequence.

A philological treatment of Old Kingdom personal names was not one of the author's aims. In view of the fact that even such an authority as Ranke changed his mind on numerous occasions as to the reading of these names, I have avoided the issue. The elements out of which the names are composed are read as simply as possible, without the addition of unwritten final weak consonants. In the arrangement of the elements, convenience rather than philological accuracy has been my main guide. Well known names such as *Ptḥ-ḥtp* (and of course all names similarly formed with a name of a god) are read in that order in spite of the fact that (at the moment) the reverse seems to me to be nearer the actual pronunciation. I hope that serious inconsistencies have been avoided and that no readings have been perpetrated that are unsupported in modern archeological literature. In view of the quite unsettled nature of the problems, it hardly seemed worthwhile to attempt to bring the names into conformity with the readings accepted by any one authority, such as Ranke or Junker. Names written in capitals are those of tomb owners. Second names, "beautiful names," and such are separated by a colon, while epithets follow directly.

Each entry contains two sections. The first contains the references to the works from which the ranking sequences given in the charts were derived. No attempt is made to replace Porter and Moss. The references are usually only to the more up-to-date and reliable publications, and only to those portions actually used. Some additional references are given in the discussion of the dating. Several works were regularly used without additional reference: the maps, plans and sections in Reisner, *Giza*, Vol. I, both those at the back of the book and those in the body of the text that are listed in the index of names of owners of mastabas on pages 529–32; the data in Smith, "Topography of the Old Kingdom Cemetery at Saqqarah," in Reisner, *The Development of the Egyptian Tomb*, pp. 390–411; archeological data and plans in publications referred to in the bibliographic section of each entry.

A certain number of sources to which I have had access are unpublished. Those at Giza I owe to the kindness of the authorities at the Boston Museum of Fine Arts, who allowed me to use the records of their Egyptian expedition. Unfortunately time did not permit me to utilize this material as fully as I should have wished. Most of the unpublished material from the Unis Causeway area at Saqqara I owe to notes kindly loaned me by Dr. Goedicke, then at Brown University. Material which I derived from the proofs of Dr. Selim Hassan's forthcoming volume on his excavations at Saqqara has been indicated as such. To Dr. Nims of the Oriental Institute I owe copies of texts in the mastaba of *Ptḥ-špss* [167] and *Mrjj-Ttj* [189]. The remaining unpublished materials are from my own copies.

The estimates given in the second entry for the date of the tomb are kept brief and are based only on criteria that appeared to be generally accepted. A thoroughgoing discussion of archeological details exceeds my competence, would in most cases require publications much more accurate and complete than are available at present, and would require a lengthy essay for almost every case. What is needed for our purposes here is simply enough information to permit an approximate check, and for this a rough, approximate dating seemed adequate.

The dates are given in terms of Dynasties (indicated by Roman numerals) with such appellations as early, middle, late, end, etc. being purposely kept rather vague. Where it seemed feasible to date in terms of reigns, however, they have been given. The criteria used to assign dates are of various kinds, of which the textual data are the easiest to handle; for a good many of the tombs discussed it is the only material available. In a few cases, biographies inscribed on the walls of tombs or plausible genealogies permit exact dating. Quarry marks on the blocks in a mastaba are also a reliable, if uncommon, means of dating. At Giza, however, one has to distinguish between the date of a mastaba core and the time at which the chapel was built and finished. If a person states in his tomb that he was *jmȝḫw ḫr* (revered before) a king, we take the statement to mean that he was a contemporary, as is generally held to be the case. However, in the case of [203B], Cooney changed the date of a statue that he would have assigned to the later

Sixth Dynasty on stylistic grounds to the end of the Fifth or early Sixth on the basis of a statement that the owner, *Mṯṯj*, was revered before Unis. I would not be surprised, then, if this criterion should turn out to be unreliable; for the time being, I have, however, continued to use it.

It is established by now beyond the slightest shadow of a doubt that titles such as *zꜣ nswt* and *zꜣ nswt n ẖt.f* cannot be interpreted to signify that the bearer was the direct offspring of a reigning monarch, and thus these titles become exceedingly difficult to use for chronological purposes.* The addition of the phrase *n jt.f* has been generally understood to indicate that the bearer was really the son of a king (cf. under [175]). We have accepted this interpretation for the Fourth Dynasty, in spite of the fact that Nims has shown conclusively (cf. under [303]) that this interpretation is quite unjustified at a later period.

All other occurrences of a king's name in a tomb, whether as an element in an estate name or personal name, or on a seal impression, or in a title—in short all occurrences that are not specifically written as dates—are, in agreement with Junker, who has, I think, adequately established his point, taken as indicating only *termini ante quem non* unless supported by other data.†

There is, however, one important point in which I disagree with Junker. In *Giza*, VI, 7–15 he gives one of the most complete discussions of the royal priesthoods to have appeared in recent years. This is not the place to go into a discussion of Junker's position on primeval monotheism and his resulting opinions about the divine status (or lack of it) of the king in the Old Kingdom. In his desire to demonstrate that the king of Egypt, at least while still alive, had a theological position different from, and lower than, the other gods, he states that the title of *ḥm-nṯr* of a king or of his pyramid temple only occurs after his death; in other words that he does not have a regular cult during his lifetime. This is demonstrably false.

Jbj [32] lived from the reign of Pepi I to the time of Pepi II as stated in his biography. He was *jmj-ḫt ḥm-nṯr* of the pyramid of Pepi II, whom he can hardly have outlived in view of his long reign.

Ḏꜥw Šmꜣj [592], the son of the last, is stated specifically in his tomb to have died during the reign of Pepi II and to have received posthumous favors from him. He was *sḥḏ ḥm-nṯr*, *jmj-ḫt ḥm-nṯr*, and *ḫntj-š* of his pyramid.

Wnj [110] mentions Mernere as the last king under whom he served. His tomb was thus presumably built in that reign. He was *sḥḏ ḥm-nṯr* and *mtj n zꜣ* of Mernere's pyramid.

Kꜣ-gm-nj [548] in his biography mentions Teti as the last king under whom

* Junker, *Giza*, II, 31–34.

† *Giza*, XII, 19–23 and references on p. 216.

he served, and since his tomb is probably the first major one erected to the north of the Teti Pyramid, it was in all probability built during the reign of Teti. *Kꜣ-gm-nj* was *jmj-rꜣ njwt* and *sḥḏ ḥm-nṯr* of the pyramid of Teti.

Ptḥ-ḥtp [157] describes himself as *jmꜣḫw ḫr* Userkaf on the same statue that lists among his titles *ḥm-nṯr Rʿ m Nḫn-Rʿ* and *ḥm-nṯr Wsrkꜣf m Wʿb-swt-Wsrkꜣf*.

Ptḥ-špss [164] probably built his tomb under Neuserre, at whose solar temple he was *ḥm-nṯr Rʿ*. This example and the last show that the cult at a royal solar temple also began before the death of its builder, though I do not think that this has ever been questioned.

Smnḫw-Ptḥ Jtwš [436] describes himself in his biography as *mjn ḫr Jzzj*, under whose reign the tomb was therefore probably built. He was *wʿb* at *Nfr-Jzzj*.

These are the clearest examples. In view of the general rarity of tombs with inscriptions permitting exact assignment of their construction to a definite reign, it is a considerable body of evidence against Junker's point. To it we might add tombs [84], [229A], [371], [409], [560], [587] of persons buried around the pyramid of Pepi II who held priesthoods at that establishment. It seems unlikely that so large a proportion of the owners of the major tombs in the area would have erected their tombs after the death of Pepi II and the fall of the Old Kingdom.

If I may digress briefly, I would like to add two points to Junker's discussion of the organization of the *ḥm-nṯr* of a king. First of all, the *ḥm-nṯr* of the pyramids of Khufu [9], Khafre [48], Menkaure [48], [319], and Sahure [486] are documented, though I do not maintain that these cases are even remotely contemporary with the reigns of these kings.

Second, in spite of Junker's assertion to the contrary, the title *jmj-rꜣ ḥm-nṯr* of the pyramid of Neferirkare is documented in the tomb of *Ṯjj* [564]. In view of the fact that the title *jmj-rꜣ ḥm-nṯr* of any god is uncommon (without the addition of the name of a god it is a common title among provincial magnates, but very probably indicates supervision of several cults at once), occurring in my collection only in the cases listed below, I suggest that there is really no evidence for supposing that the cult of the king differed in any particular, except greater elaboration possibly (cf. our list of the royal priesthoods in chapter vi), from that of any other god. The prevalence of the title *wʿb nswt* in connection with the king, which Junker stresses, can be explained by the fact that the divine king was, after all, also a living human being with demands considerably more extensive than any other god for personal service. The list of *jmj-rꜣ ḥm-nṯr* of other gods follows:

Onouris:	*Ggj* [556]
Antj:	*Ḥm-Rʿ Jzj* [333]
Mati:	*Ḥm-Rʿ Jzj* [333]
Hathor:	*Ppjj-ʿnḫ ḥrj-jb* and his father [133]
	Ppjj-ʿnḫ [132]
	N-kꜣ-ʿnḫ [237]
	Nbj-pw-Ppjj Nbj [247A]
Zokar:	*Sšm-nfr Mttj* (Cairo, *CG*, 1403)
Shezemtet:	*Sšm-nfr Mttj* (ibid.)

This is not a very impressive documentation.

Helck discusses the same titles rather briefly. He realizes that priesthoods at a king's pyramid can be contemporary with a king. His discussion largely stresses the social rank of the holders of these titles, a matter with which we are not directly concerned.* In a footnote, however, he does make a remark of chronological import. In discussing the tomb of *Sdꜣwg* [486], Helck disagrees with Junker's dating into the later Sixth Dynasty because he was a prophet of Re at the solar temple of Userkaf, "da Sonnenheiligtümer nach Aufgabe der Sitte, solche zu errichten, nicht mehr in Titulaturen genannt werden."† Junker's datings are usually based on sound archeological grounds and should not be rejected so cavalierly in any case, but Helck's statement is simply wrong.

Sꜣbw Jbbj [421] was a priest at the solar temples of Userkaf, Neferirkare, and Neuserre. His tomb must be dated at least to the reign of Teti, some three generations after the supposed cessation of the cult.

Kꜣ-pw-Ptḥ [517] was a priest at the solar temple of Neferirkare. Since he also was a priest of Djedkare, his tomb is certainly to be dated to a point after the construction of solar temples ceased.

Of the Abusir Papyri, the fragment published by Borchardt, "Ein Rechnungsbuch des königlichen Hofes aus dem Alten Reich," *Aegyptiaca*, pp. 8–15, shows that the solar temple of Neferirkare was still a functioning entity with prophets during the reign of Djedkare.

There is thus every indication that the cult of these temples continued into the Sixth Dynasty.

However that may be, the main point is clear: The occurrence of the name of a king in a title must be interpreted as a *terminus ante quem non*, as would be any other occurrence of such a name.

The architecture of a mastaba is our next criterion. In the case of most of the Giza Necropolis and portions of Saqqara, sufficiently detailed plans are available to permit a decision in the case of adjoining

* *Untersuchungen*, pp. 128–29.

† *Ibid.*, p. 128, n. 58.

tombs as to which one is the earlier. This is an invaluable source of reliable information as to relative dating.

Certain features of the plan, arrangement, and construction of the mastabas have also been used as criteria for dates. The discussion in Junker, *Giza*, IX, 23, is a useful summary of the dangers inherent in the process. One is dealing with large-scale features, thought out in advance, and subject to all the effects of whim, family or workshop tradition, conscious copying, and wild innovation. Certain plans or arrangements may be typical for a certain period, but they generally appeared at an earlier date in isolated cases and very commonly continued to be used after new plans had come into use, so that here too, we are faced largely with criteria offering a *terminus post quem*. Smith remarks that neighboring groups of tombs at Saqqara tend to show a "remarkable uniformity of chapel types" extending (as he does not state specifically but becomes clear upon examination of his list of tombs) over a considerable range in time at each place; to my mind a clear case of family or workshop tradition.*

Any dating on the basis of architectural criteria alone thus remains a somewhat impressionistic undertaking; and a comparison of the datings of Reisner and Junker for the Giza Necropolis shows that at present there is an inadequate body of reliably dated material to permit really secure datings even after consideration of fine points of style and workmanship, which are in any case impossible for a person working from publications only. The criteria given below must thus be used with some caution. They are largely based on those points where there appears to be a consensus of opinion between Reisner and Junker and which at the same time are likely to be of help when dealing with the extremely sketchy publications which are all that is available for much that remains from ancient Egypt.

Characteristic for the Fourth Dynasty are true cruciform chapels (largely at Saqqara),† large stone mastabas with no interior chapels and only a slab stela instead of a false door (Giza),‡ and survivals of the archaic corridor chapel types.§

With the Fifth Dynasty, interior chapels again were built at Giza,|| and various L-shaped,# short corridor,** and modified cruciform types were used. In general, the mastabas were largely solid with the interior chapels taking up only a relatively small proportion of the area.††

* Smith in Reisner, *Development of the Egyptian Tomb*, p. 392.
† Reisner, *Giza*, I, 183, 293; Junker, *Giza*, XII, 45.
‡ Reisner, *Giza*, I, 294; Junker, *Giza*, II, 2.
§ Reisner, *Giza*, I, 293; Junker, *Giza*, XII, 45.
|| Reisner, *Giza*, I, 296–97; Junker, *Giza*, II, 2–3; III, 21.
Reisner, *Giza*, I, 295–96; Junker, *Giza*, XII, 46.
** Reisner, *Giza*, I, 256, 302.
†† *Ibid.*, p. 302.

Around the middle of the Fifth Dynasty, chapels began to show more variation. The older types continued,* but new types developed. Corridor chapels, both exterior and interior with several offering places,† mastabas with multiple shafts,‡ east–west offering chambers,§ deep alcoves leading off a north–south corridor and practically forming a separate offering chamber,|| complex interior chapels with several rooms and pillared halls,# pillared porticoes,** and various odd arrangements such as entrances to interior chapels on the north or south,†† or L-shaped and other small chapel types at places other than the southeastern corner of the mastaba‡‡ appeared.

Toward the end of the Fifth Dynasty we find further features: decorated burial chambers,§§ sloping passages leading to the burial chamber, which had been the exception in the Fourth and Fifth Dynasties in built mastabas (but not in rock-cut tombs) now became common.|||| Mastabas are now found in which the interior is entirely filled with rooms.## Scenes became livelier,*** and a characteristic element of the decoration was lintels with a series of figures of the owner.†††

These features are the basis for much of the rough dating we will give in the list of sources. In addition, there are the various facts about the growth of the Giza Necropolis that have been noticed by Reisner and Junker, whose conclusions have been freely used, as are also opinions by Smith.

Location is also an element in dating, and for the large cemeteries at Giza and Saqqara it has seemed necessary to indicate the location of the tombs under discussion. At Giza, the terms established by Reisner and Junker are used, with the addition of the phrase "Khafre Cemetery" for the area excavated by Selim Hassan. All portions of this cemetery, with the exception of the fringes and other undesirable areas, came into use in the course of the Fourth Dynasty, and the problem is to distinguish the earlier tombs from the later ones at the same site.

* *Ibid.*, pp. 258, 304. † *Ibid.*, p. 302. ‡ Junker, *Giza*, IX, 10, 23.
§ Reisner, *Giza*, I, 261, 303; Junker, *Giza*, XII, 43–46.
|| Reisner, *Giza*, I, 257. # *Ibid.*, pp. 288, 301, 303–4, 361. ** *Ibid.*, p. 285.
†† *Ibid.*, pp. 258–60, 301–2. ‡‡ *Ibid.*, pp. 301–2. §§ Junker, *Giza*, IV, 43–46.
|||| Reisner, *Giza*, I, 101; Junker, *Giza*, VIII, 7–8.
Junker, *Giza*, VI, 95. *** *Ibid.*, p. 28.
††† Junker, *Giza*, IV, pp. 18–20. The archeological data, and particularly the discussion of the criteria used are very scattered in both of these publications, and these references do not approach exhausting all the passages in which pertinent data is discussed. The development of the Old Kingdom mastaba and rock-cut tomb is conveniently summarized, largely on the basis of Reisner's presentation, in Vandier, *Manuel d'archéologie égyptienne*, II, 251–312. Junker's frequently diverging views are largely ignored. Unfortunately, despite the index which appeared in Junker, *Giza*, XII, it is still quite difficult to find the places in which he has established his main criteria for dating.

At Saqqara, location is a more useful index. Following the order of Smith's description of the topography of the Saqqara Necropolis, the following terms have been used for the portions of the Saqqara Necropolis:

1. Northeast. Mariette's numbers 6 to 18, and Nord B on his map. This area is behind the archaic cemetery and seems to have been in use from the Fourth Dynasty onward.
2. Northwest knoll. Mariette's numbers 1 to 4 and Nord A. Fifth Dynasty onward.
3. Northwest. Mariette's numbers 19 to 33 and Nord C on his map (with a little of Nord D). The tomb of *Wꜣš-Ptḥ* belongs to this group [105] and is described in his biography (*Urkunden*, I, 44) as being in the cemetery of the pyramid of Sahure, the first king to build at Abusir. The chances are that all the tombs in the areas well to the north of the Step Pyramid and to the west of the archaic cemetery are to be dated to the reign of Sahure and onward into the Sixth Dynasty.
4. Mid-north. Mariette's numbers 34 to 56 and Nord D. Tombs apparently also from the early Fifth Dynasty onward.
5. Near-north. Mariette's numbers 57 to 71 and Nord E. Fifth Dynasty and later. The tomb of *Mṯn*, which Smith assigns to this group, lies at the very edge and perhaps was built as a portion of the northeastern group.
6. Near-north ridge. Mariette's numbers 72 to 77 and Nord F. The tomb of *N-ꜥnḫ-Sḫmt* [221] belongs to this group. It is dated to the reign of Sahure, and was indeed built with the express knowledge of the king. The cemetery that was established for the Abusir Pyramids probably extended this close to the Step Pyramid.
7. Teti area. The group of tombs to the north and northwest of the pyramid of Teti. With one or two possible exceptions, [527] and [528], all the tombs in this group seem to belong to the reign of Teti or later.
8. North of Step Pyramid. Mariette's numbers 78 to 88 and Nord G. This cemetery contains the tombs of contemporaries of King Djedkare (and later tombs of course), and appears to have been started under his reign as the main cemetery. His pyramid at the Haram el-Shauwaf appears to have been inconveniently far south for the inhabitants of Memphis. In any case, there is no trace of private tombs of his reign around his pyramid.
9. West of Step Pyramid. No tombs here are earlier than the Fifth Dynasty. The group around the mastaba of *Ptḥ-ḥtp* [160] seems to be a continuation of the Djedkare cemetery, but this indication of date has only been used for those tombs that are clearly part of this group.
10. East of Step Pyramid. Tombs south of the Teti Pyramid and the Pyramid of Userkaf and north of the southern limit of the Step Pyramid inclosure. This area appears to have come into use in the time of Userkaf.
11. Unis area. Tombs south and southeast of the Step Pyramid, around the Pyramid of Unis and the Unis Causeway. With the exception of one tomb

[25] that probably antedates the funerary complex of Unis, the rest certainly date from his reign or later.

12. South Saqqara. The tombs are located in reference to the pyramids they are closest to. All of them are from the Sixth Dynasty. Apparently the reasons that militated against moving the private cemetery from Djedisut to Mennefer in the Fifth Dynasty no longer held in the Sixth. It seems unlikely that any of the tombs here antedate the erection of the Sixth Dynasty pyramids near which they stand. The tombs in the group around the pyramids of Pepi I and Mernere are thus assigned at least to the reign of the former; those around the pyramid of Pepi II (and the Mastabet Faraun) are assigned to the reign of Pepi II or later.

In the case of the provincial cemeteries, the dating by location is easier. With the exception of the unusual rock-cut mastabas of Tihna and Hammamia, and numbers [114] and [457] at Sheikh Said, there seems to be very little reason for dating any of them earlier than the rise of the Sixth Dynasty, at least as far as the decorated rock-cut tombs are concerned, which are all that interest us here.*

That the criteria just given are far removed from the kind of archeological precision one would like is all too evident. The results should, however, be approximately correct, at least in a sufficiently large percentage of the cases to form a useful check and beginning point for our study of the titles. It is as far as we can go without undertaking extensive research in order to form an independent opinion on archeological indexes at present in dispute, and otherwise straying from the main subject of this study.

The remainder of this chapter will give the list of sources used; the author hopes it is a reasonably complete list of those tombs available to study that contain rankable sequences of titles longer than two or three items.

[1] *ꜣBBJ*	Mariette, *Mastabas*, Gc; Cairo, *CG*, 1341, 1406, 1459. Saqqara. Priest of Pepi I. Date: Pepi I or later.
[2] *ꜣBDW*	Abu-Bakr, *Giza*, I, 69–82; Chicago Art Institute No. 20.266 = Allen, *A Handbook of the Egyptian Collection*, p. 27. Giza, far northwest. Built after *Nfrj* [254] and *Nfr-jḥjj*, both of which have corridor chapels with several niches. This tomb has a complex interior chapel with a pillared chamber. Date: VI.

* Reisner, *Giza*, I, 220; Smith, *A History of Egyptian Sculpture and Painting*, pp. 214–17 and cf. our [397].

[3] *ꜣḪJ* — Junker, *Giza*, I, 234–42; Smith, "The Origin of Some Unidentified Old Kingdom Reliefs," *AJA*, XLVI, 528.
Giza 4750. A core mastaba with an added stone exterior chapel. Junker dates to Menkaure. Date: Menkaure.

[4] *ꜣḪJ* — Mariette, *Mastabas*, B 14; Cairo, *CG*, 44.
A true cruciform chapel from Saqqara. The statue is a family group with children, which Borchardt assigns to the Sixth Dynasty. The chapel type is usually earlier (Reisner, *Giza*, I, 302–4). Date: VI (?).

[5] *ꜣḪ-MRW-NSWT* — Boston Museum of Fine Arts No. 13.4352 = C. S. F(isher), "The Harvard University—Museum of Fine Arts Egyptian Expedition," *BMFA*, XI, 21–22. Also unpublished data.
Giza 2184. This mastaba is built against another which is itself built against a core mastaba. Date: end V or later.

[6] *ꜣḪT-ḤTP* — Mariette, *Mastabas*, A 1; Raymond Weill, *La II*^{e} *et la III*^{e} *Dynasties*, pp. 313–16.
Saqqara, northeast group No. 18 = FS 3076 in the archaic cemetery. A yellow brick mastaba with a cruciform chapel at the southern end of the row of early Old Kingdom mastabas. Date: IV.

[7] *ꜣḪT-ḤTP* — Smith, *HESP*, pp. 160–61, pls. 41, 42; also unpublished data.
Giza 7650. The stela of queen *Mrt-jt.s* (De Rougé, *Inscriptions hiéroglyphiques*, pl. 62) appears to come from this tomb, which Reisner, *Giza*, I, 212, also dates to the time of Khafre. Date: Khafre.

[8] *ꜣḪT-ḤTP* — Abu-Bakr, *Giza*, I, 1–9.
Giza, far northwest. Built against a mastaba which was itself built against a mastaba with a corridor chapel. Date: VI.

[9] *ꜣḪT-ḤTP* — Unpublished.
Giza 1204. Built between two core mastabas so as to block the passage. The chapel is composed of a north–south corridor with an east–west alcove. Date: mid-V or later.

[10] *ꜣḪT-ḤTP* — Unpublished.
Giza 1208. Location and type much like the last. Priesthood of Khufu. Date: mid-V or later.

[11] *ꜣḪT-ḤTP* Selim Hassan, *Giza*, I, 73–86.
Giza, Khafre cemetery. This mastaba is partly rock-cut. To judge from the published plans, it is built against a mastaba older than *Rꜥ-wr* [300] and precedes the mastabas in the so-called Street of Priests. Mention of Khafre. Date: early V—early VI.

[12] *ꜣḪT-ḤTP* *Encyclopédie photographique de l'art*, I, 17 ff.
Saqqara, southeast of the Step Pyramid. This mastaba has a modified cruciform chapel. *ꜣḫt-ḥtp* [14] is built against it. Date: V—early VI.

[13] *ꜣḪT-ḤTP* Davies, *The Mastaba of Ptahhetep and Akhethetep at Saqqareh*, Vol. II.
The son of *Ptḥ-ḥtp* [160]. The names of several kings ranging from Djedefre to Djedkare occur in this tomb. His father was a contemporary of Djedkare. This mastaba has a complex chapel with an east–west offering chamber. It is in Saqqara and one of the Ptahhotep group. A mastaba with the cartouche of Teti has been built against it. Date: Djedkare-Unis.

[14] *ꜣḪT-ḤTP* Mariette, *Mastabas*, E 17; Murray, *Seven Memphite Tomb Chapels*, pls. 3–8.
Saqqara, southeast of the Step Pyramid (in the Unis cemetery?). Later than [12] above. A modified cruciform chapel. Priesthood of Unis. Date: VI.

[14A] *ꜣḪT-ḤTP: ḤMJ* Unpublished.
The original owner of the mastaba of *Nb-kꜣw-ḥr*. Saqqara, Unis area some distance to east of the pyramid temple. A complex chapel with a court and pillared hall. Date: early VI.

[15] *JꜣRTJ* Maspero, "Trois années de fouilles," *MMAFC*, I, 200–201; Grdseloff, "Deux inscriptions juridiques de l'Ancien Empire," *ASAE*, XLII, 26–38.
South Saqqara, northwest of Mernere. A priest of Mernere. Date: Mernere or later.

[16] *JꜣZN* Reisner, "Report on the Egyptian Expedition during 1934–35," *BMFA*, XXXIII, 76; Smith, *HESP*, pls. 57b, 58c, 60. Also unpublished data.
Giza 2196. A fully decorated, rock-cut chapel approached by a long north–south corridor and with an east–west offering chamber. Reisner dates it to the Fifth Dynasty. Grdseloff, "Deux

inscriptions juridiques de l'Ancien Empire," *ASAE*, XLII, 40, n. 1, says it was built against *Pn-mrw* [140]. Date: VI.

[17] *JJJ* — Lepsius, *Denkmäler*, II, 100b; Mariette, *Mastabas*, C 26; Murray, *Seven Memphite Tomb Chapels*, pl. 2.
Saqqara, east of the Step Pyramid. Murray, in her plan *ibid.*, pl. 27, seems to have mixed up the location of this tomb (there listed under the name of the wife, *Nfrt*) with that of *Ḏfꜣw* [594]. This mastaba seems to have an east–west offering room reached by a north–south corridor. Date: V or later.

[18] *JJJ* — Unpublished.
Saqqara, Unis area. Priesthood of Pepi I. Date: Pepi I or later. Probably the father of *Rtj* [320].

[19] *JJJ* — Selim Hassan, *Giza*, I, 101–4.
Giza, Khafre cemetery. Built against the tomb of *Ffj* [488] in the Street of Priests, which itself was built against another tomb; also built against the tomb of *Wsr* [123]. Date: end V or later.

[20] *JJW* — Junker, *Giza*, IX, 226–31.
Giza, western end of western cemetery, in the confused mass of late tombs. This one is probably later than the one it joins. It has a row of niches in the eastern façade of the mastaba and several shafts in the mastaba. To the east is a sort of shapeless corridor chapel. Date: VI.

[21] *JJ-MRJJ* — Lepsius, *Denkmäler*, II, 49–54, *Erg.*, pp. 3–7; also in his son, *Nfr-bꜣw-Ptḥ* [258], Lepsius, *Denkmäler*, II, 55 ff.; Berlin Museum No. 1114 = Schäfer, *Aegyptische Inschriften*, I, 6–7.
Giza 6020. Son of *Špsskꜣf-ʿnḫ* [491]. A mastaba with a complex interior chapel. Priesthood of Neferirkare in son's tomb. Reisner, "A Family of Royal Estate Stewards of Dynasty V," *BMFA*, XXXVII, 29–35, dates to reign of Neuserre. Date: Neuserre or possibly a bit later.

[22] *JJ-MRJJ* — Junker, *Giza*, X, 143–47.
Giza, south of Khufu. A small later mastaba south of the original cores. Small squarish offering chamber, three shafts. Not built against any older structures; several later ones built

against it. Junker dates to Sixth Dynasty. Date: VI.

[23] *Jj-m-ḥtp* — Junker, *Giza*, VI, 239–40.
The son of *N-ʿnḫ-ʿntj* [207A] on his stela found reused among the later tombs of the western cemetery at Giza. Junker dates to Sixth Dynasty. Date: VI.

[24] *JJ-NFRT* — Wiedemann, Pörtner, *Aegyptische Grabreliefs aus der grossherzoglichen Altertümer-Sammlung zu Karlsruhe*, pp. 2–31, pls. 1–6.
A tomb chapel, presumably from Giza. Priesthood of Menkaure, but hardly likely to be from the core mastabas of the Fourth Dynasty. Date: V or later.

[25] *JJ-Kꜣ* — Zaki Saad, "A Preliminary Report on the Excavations at Saqqara," *ASAE*, XL, 676–80, pls. 73, 74.
Saqqara, Unis causeway. This mastaba is described as being under the causeway, and thus, presumably, earlier. Date: V.

[25A] *JJ-ṮMW* — Aberdeen No. 1046 = *Illustrated Catalogue of the Anthropological Museum, Marichal College, University of Aberdeen*, p. 155.
A miserable false door. The owner had a priesthood of Djedkare. Date: VI.

[26] *JJ-ḎFꜣ* — Lepsius, *Denkmäler*, II, 100a, 101a, *Erg.*, pl. 29b; Mariette, *Mastabas*, C 11.
Saqqara, east of Step Pyramid. The false door is in a niche in the east face of the mastaba. Date: early V (?) or later.

[27] *JWW* — Lepsius, *Denkmäler*, *Text*, II, 176; Mariette, *Catalogue général des monuments d'Abydos*, No. 540.
Abydos. Date: VI.

[28] *JWF* — Junker, *Giza*, IX, 67–68.
In the maze of late mastabas south of Giza 2000. Built against *Nfr-srs* [271] and another mastaba also built against *Nfr-srs*. All of them late with multiple shafts and corridor chapels. Date: VI and probably not too early.

[29] *JWNW* — Junker, *Giza*, I, 169–78.
Giza 4150. One of the very early cores. The inscriptions which concern us here were on the old slab stela which was later walled up when the mastaba was enlarged and provided with a stone chapel. Date: Khufu.

[30] *JWN-MN*
Lepsius, *Denkmäler*, II, 34g; Mariette, *Mastabas*, pp. 547 ff.; Selim Hassan, *Giza*, VII, 13–20.
Giza, Khafre cemetery; Lepsius No. 92. A partly rock-cut mastaba. The owner was a genuine prince, presumably a son of Khafre. Date: end IV.

[31] *JWN-Rʿ*
Selim Hassan, *Giza*, VI^{3}, 31–34.
Giza, Khafre cemetery. A partly rock-cut mastaba. The owner is stated to have been a son of Khafre. Date: end IV.

[32] *JBJ*
Davies, *The Rock Tombs of Deir el-Gebrawi*, Vol. I, pls. 3–15, 18.
Deir el-Gebrawi No. 8. *Jbj*'s career spans the reigns of Pepi I and Mernere. He presumably died in the first half of the reign of Pepi II. Date: Pepi II (early).

[33] *JB-JR*-[. . .]
Junker, *Giza*, IX, 102.
Giza. A small false door found in one of the late, small mastabas to the northwest (Junker's description, unfortunately, is not too clear) of Giza 4000. Date: VI.

[34] *JBW-NSWT*
Petrie, *Dendereh*, Vol. I, pl. 2.
Petrie dates this mastaba to the Fourth Dynasty, which is hardly likely for a decorated Upper Egyptian tomb. The mastaba has a rectangular brick retaining wall, two niches and an outside corridor; it is in a group with another that has a cruciform chapel and a corridor with several niches. Dating would require a detailed analysis far beyond the aims of this work. Date: ?

[35] *JPJ*
Lepsius, *Denkmäler*, II, 82f.
From Giza. Date: ?

[35A] *JPJ-ḤR-SSNB.F*
Firth, *Teti Pyramid Cemeteries*, pp. 190–91, 239.
Saqqara, Teti area. A shaft to the south of the mastaba of *Kꜣ-gm-nj* [548]. Priesthood of Teti. Coffin Texts in sarcophagus. Date: end VI or later.

[35B] *JFFJ*
Mariette, *Mastabas*, B 10; Cairo, *CG*, 1359.
Saqqara, northwest knoll No. 2. A stone mastaba with a modified cruciform chapel. Priesthoods of Userkaf. Date: V or later.

[36] *JMJ-ST-KꜣJ*
Junker, *Giza*, VI, 208–17.
Giza 4351. A small mastaba with a corridor chapel and an east–west alcove for the stela

built against a core mastaba. Junker dates it after the Sixth Dynasty. Date VI or later.

[37] *JMBJJ* — Selim Hassan, *Giza*, I, 91–95.
Giza, Khafre cemetery. A chapel with a corridor and an L-shaped chamber. Several shafts. From the published plan it looks like the last tomb on the south of the Street of Priests. Built against *Wsr* [123]. Date: end V or later.

[37A] *JMPJJ* — Hoelscher, *Chephren*, pp. 113–14.
Giza, Khafre cemetery. Apparently found in the rubble. Part of a false door with *wḏꜣt*-eyes on the lower lintel. Date: late VI to First Intermediate.

[38] *JNJ* — Reisner, *Giza*, I, 411–13, pl. 20b.
Giza 1235. A core mastaba with a slab stela. One of the original mastabas of the northwest cemetery. Date: Khufu.

[39] *JN-JT.F: MḪW* — Von Bissing, "Les tombeaux d'Assouan," *ASAE*, XV, 2–14.
Aswan. Reference to Pepi II in the inscription of his son, *Sꜣbnj*, in this tomb, who describes how he buried his father. Date: Pepi II.

[40] *JNPW-ḤTP* — Junker, *Giza*, IX, 154–69.
Giza. A small mastaba in the maze of late mastabas at the western end of the western cemetery. This one has a corridor chapel, several shafts, and in a string of adjoining mastabas was at least the fifth. Other mastabas built against it. Priesthood of Neuserre. Date: VI.

[41] *JN-Kꜣ.F* — Junker, *Giza*, IX, 170–78.
Giza, western end of western cemetery. A false door found in pieces in the midst of later Old Kingdom tombs. Date: VI.

[42] *JN-Kꜣ.F* — Selim Hassan, *Giza*, VI[3], 117–24.
Giza, Khafre cemetery. This mastaba is situated to the east of the mastaba of *Rwd-kꜣ* [316] and his son *Jn-kꜣ.f*, the sculptor, who *may* be the *Jn-kꜣ.f* who decorated the tombs of prince *Nb-m-ꜣḫt* [248] and *Mr-s-ꜥnḫ* III. It has a corridor chapel and appears to have been built against some other mastabas. Date: mid-V or later.

[43] *JN-Kꜣ.F* — Fakhry, "Stela of the Boat-Captain Inikaf," *ASAE*, XXXVIII, 35–45.
From Zawaydeh? Date: presumably VI (Fakhry).

[44] *JNTJ*

Petrie, *Deshasheh*, pp. 4–8, pls. 4–14.
A rock-cut tomb at Deshasha. Petrie dates to the middle of the Fifth Dynasty (*ibid.*, p. 4), largely on the basis of not very convincing philological arguments (the presence of the cartouche of Teti in the tomb of his son *Jttj* [73] and the existence in Deshasha of the tomb of a man called *Nn-ḫft-kꜣj Ṯjj*, which names he identifies with members of the families of the better known bearers of these names at Saqqara). The extreme liveliness and variety of the scenes on the walls of this tomb, for instance the siege (pl. 4), dancers (pl. 12), and butchers (pl. 12), would rather indicate a date in the Sixth Dynasty. Date: VI.

[45] *JR-JS*

Cairo, *CG*, 131.
Date: V (Borchardt).

[46] *JRW*

Selim Hassan, *Giza*, III, 57–71.
Giza, Khafre cemetery. A small free-standing mastaba with corridor chapel and three shafts near the inclosure wall of the pyramid city of *Ḫnt-kꜣw.s*. Date: end V or VI.

[47] *JRT-PTḤ: JRJJ*

University of Pennsylvania, *The University Museum Bulletin*, II, 58, pl. 9.
A false door from Saqqara. Dated by text to the Sixth Dynasty. Date: VI.

[48] *JR.N-ꜣḪT: JR.N-PTḤ: JRJ*

Selim Hassan, Giza, VI³, 9–17.
Giza, Khafre cemetery. Chapel with a corridor and an east–west alcove. Lintel with a series of figures of the owner. Built just in front of the tomb of queen *Rḫjt-Rʿ*. Date: VI.

[49] *JR.N-ꜣḪT: JRJJ*

"Archaeological News," *Archaeology*, VI, 185.
In the Minneapolis Institute of Arts. Provenience given in text as the western cemetery at Giza. The author dates it to the Fifth or Sixth Dynasties. Date: V or later.

[50] *JR.N-ꜣḪT: JRJ: N-ʿNḪ-PPJJ*

Junker, "Die Stele des Hofarztes 'Irj," *ZÄS*, LXIII, 53–70.
Giza, western cemetery. Found out of place in a shaft. Mention of Pepi (I?). Date: Pepi I or later.

[51] *JR.N-Rʿ*

Junker, *Giza*, III, 156–63.
Giza 4970 Ann. Great-grandson of *Kꜣ-nj-nswt* [531]. Built against *Nswt-nfr* [292]. Corridor chapel and multiple shafts. Date: early VI.

[52] *JR.N-SN*

Cairo, *CG*, 1391.

From Saqqara. A slab stela very much like those from the Fourth Dynasty mastabas at Giza. Date: IV ?

[53] *JR-SẖW* Selim Hassan, *Giza*, VII, 65–71.
Giza, Khafre cemetery. A rock-cut tomb at the southern end of the area excavated by Selim Hassan. Area only partially investigated. Date: ?

[54] *JRW-Kꜣ-PTḤ* Berlin Museum No. 1111–12, 1139–40, 1144–45, 1193–94, 1201–02 = Schäfer, *Aegyptische Inschriften*, I, 54–55; Lepsius, *Denkmäler*, *Text*, I, 12–14.
From Saqqara. Date: ?

[55] *JḤꜣ* Junker, *Giza*, VI, 74–77.
Giza, western cemetery. *Jḥꜣ* was a mortuary priest of *Nfr* [251] and occurs in his tomb. Date: early VI.

[56] *JḤJ* Lepsius, *Denkmäler*, II, 88; Berlin Museum No. 1146 = Schäfer, *Aegyptische Inschriften*, I, 67.
Giza 5330. A free-standing mastaba near the enclosure wall of the great pyramid. Chapel with north–south corridor and east–west offering chamber. Date: VI.

[57] *JḤJ* Macramallah, *Le mastaba d'Idout*.
The original owner of the mastaba of *Jdwt* in the Unis cemetery. A large mastaba with a complex interior chapel. It is hard to tell exactly from the photographs in the publication, but it seems to have been built against the mastaba of *Wnjs-ʿnḫ* [112] to the west, just as the mastaba of *Mḥw* [202] was built against this on the east. The name of Teti occurs in this mastaba. Date: Teti.

[58] *JḤJJ* Maspero, "Trois années de fouilles," *MMAFC*, I, 201–4.
Saqqara, near the pyramid of Mernere. Priesthood of Mernere. Date: Mernere or later.

[59] *JḤJJ* Newberry, "A Sixth Dynasty Tomb at Thebes," *ASAE*, IV, 97–100, pls. 1–3.
Date: VI.

[60] *JḤW* Cairo, *CG*, 1499.
Date: VI (Borchardt).

[61] *JẖJ* Jéquier, *La pyramide d'Oudjebten*, pp. 22–23, 26.
A funerary complex erected by his two sons in

the area of the pyramid of *Wḏbtn* in South Saqqara. These two sons, *Sʿnḫ.n-Ptḥ* and *Ḥm-ʿnḫ Ḥmj* as well as his grandson *Jqrj* are mentioned in a fragmentary decree of the year of the thirty-third numbering of Pepi II. Date: Pepi II.

[61A] *JZJ* — Louvre, stela No. 164. Unpublished.
Priest of Teti. Date: Teti or later.

[62] *JZJ* — Alliot, "Fouilles de Tell Edfou," *FIFAO*, X, 22–28; Edel, "Inschriften des Alten Reiches," *ZÄS*, LXXIX, 11–17.
Edfu. According to his biography, *Jzj* lived from the time of Djedkare to the time of Teti. Date: Teti.

[63] *JZJ-ʿNḪ* — British Museum No. 1383 = *Hieroglyphic Texts*, Vol. I, pl. 24.
Could this be the *Jzj-ʿnḫ* who occurs in several royal mortuary temples of the Fifth Dynasty, including that of Djedkare (unpublished)? In any case, the royal name with which his name is compounded dates the tomb to at earliest the middle of the Fifth Dynasty. Date: mid-V or later.

[64] *JZZJ-ʿNḪ* — Mariette, *Mastabas*, D 8.
Saqqara, north of Step Pyramid, No. 85 = QS 910. This tomb is much like the approximately contemporary one of *Kꜣ-m-ṯnnt* [530] with a multi-roomed interior chapel and pillared portico. A block intended for this tomb was delivered by mistake to that of *Pr-nb* [142] (cf. *The Tomb of Perneb*, p. 55), so both tombs were under construction approximately simultaneously. *Pr-nb* can be dated with some assurance to the reign of Djedkare. Date: Djedkare.

[64A] *JZZJ-Ḫʿ-*[. . .] — Mariette, *Mastabas*, H 10, p. 456; Cairo, *CG*, 1438.
Saqqara. Priesthood of Pepi I. Date: Pepi I or later.

[65] *JQRJ: N-ḤB.SN* — Mariette, *Mastabas*, Gd; Cairo, *CG*, 1340.
From Saqqara. Date: ?

[66] *JTJ* — Lepsius, *Denkmäler*, II, 59.
Giza 6030 = Lepsius No. 17. The brother-in-law of *Jj-mrjj* [21]. From the available plans (cf. also the references under [21]), both of these mastabas seem to have been provided with complex chapels with pillared courts at the same

time; the group seems to have been planned as a unit. *Jtj* had a north–south offering chamber. Date: mid-V

[67] *JTJJ* — Junker, *Giza*, VI, 229–31.
Giza. Built against *Jꜣbtjt* (Giza 4650). Multiple shafts. Corridor chapel using the back of a neighboring tomb. Date: VI.

[68] *JTJ* — Jéquier, *Tombeaux de particuliers*, p. 93.
South Saqqara around the pyramid of Pepi II. Date: Pepi II.

[69] *JTJ* — Lepsius, *Denkmäler*, II, 100e–g.
Zawiyet el-Maiyitin No. 5. Official of Pepi I. Date: Pepi I or later.

[70] *JTJ-SN* — Selim Hassan, *Giza*, V, 261–78.
Giza, Khafre cemetery. A rock-cut tomb, which looks as though it may have been cut in behind *Nfr-ḥr-n-Ptḥ* [267]. Date: mid-V or later.

[71] *JTTJ* — Lepsius, *Denkmäler*, II, 92b–c; Mariette, *Mastabas*, p. 541.
Giza. A rock-cut tomb in the scarp south of the Khufu causeway. Lepsius No. 68. East–west chapel. Date: V or later.

[72] *JTTJ: ꜤNḪ-JR.S* — Mariette, *Mastabas*, D 63; Murray, *Seven Memphite Tomb Chapels*, pls. 18, 19.
Saqqara, Ptahhotep group. Later than the mastaba of *Ptḥ-ḥtp* and *ꜣḫt-ḥtp* [13], part of which was broken away to make room for this tomb. Date: VI.

[73] *JTTJ: ŠDW* — Petrie, *Deshasheh*, pp. 9–11, pls. 15–25.
Deshasha. The rock-cut tomb of the son of *Jntj* [44]. The name of Teti occurs. Date: VI.

[73A] *JDJ* — Mariette, *Catalogue général des monuments d'Abydos*, No. 526; Cairo, *CG*, 1457, 1577; Weill, *Die Veziere des Pharaonenreiches*, p. 24; also occurs in the pyramid temple of Pepi II: Jéquier, *Le monument funéraire de Pepi II*, Vol. II, pls. 48, 61.
The identity of these various occurrences of the vizier *Jdj* has been maintained by Kees, "Beiträge zur Geschichte des Vezirats im Alten Reich," *Nachr. Gött.*, N.F. IV, Phil.-hist. Klasse, 39–54 and Helck, *Untersuchungen*, p. 141; this identity seems inherently probable. The names of his parents were *Ḫwj* and *Nbt*, as were those of *ḎꜤw* [591], who would thus be his brother, making him also the uncle of Pepi II. Kees, *op.*

cit., pp. 41–45 shows that the vizier *Jdj* in the pyramid temple of Pepi II cannot have lived much longer after the administration of *Ḏʿw*, which is attested for the year after the eleventh numbering of Pepi II. This would date him, and, incidentally, the completion of the decoration of the temple of Pepi II, to a point in about the second quarter of the ninety-four years that Pepi II reigned. The bulk of *Jdj*'s titles are available to me only in Weill's list, which does not permit ranking. For the question of the identity of *Ḫwj* and *Nbt* with the persons of the same name in Mariette, *op. cit.*, No. 525, which I tend to question, see under [366]. *Jdj* was probably the father of the vizier *N-ḥb-sd-Nfrkꜣrʿ* [229A]. Date: Pepi II, near the middle.

[74] *JDJ: TP-M-KꜣW* — Jéquier, *Tombeaux de particuliers*, pp. 12–21. South Saqqara, near the pyramid of Pepi II. Date: Pepi II.

[75] *JDJJ* — Cairo, *CG*, 1449. Provenience? Date: VI or later (Borchardt).

[76] *JDW* — Unpublished. Unis area. Date: VI.

[77] *JDW* — "Recent Discoveries at the Giza Pyramids," *BMFA*, XXIII, 13–14; Reisner, "Excavations in Egypt and Ethiopia 1922–25," *BMFA*, XXIII, 25–28; *Urkunden*, I, 203; Smith, *HESP*, Fig. 84b; unpublished data. Giza 7102. A rock-cut corridor chapel with an unusual false door. Priesthood of Pepi I. Date: Pepi I or later.

[78] *JDW: NFR* — Junker, *Giza*, VIII, 66–90. Giza, extreme east of western cemetery. A smallish, rectangular mastaba with an east–west offering alcove; sloping shaft to burial chamber. The owner was a vizier. The grave is very small for so high a rank. Date: VI.

[79] *JDW* — Junker, *Giza*, VIII, 90–107. Giza, far east of western cemetery. This tomb appears to have been dependent on the last. Models of daily life were found in it. Date: late VI.

[80] *JDW: TP-KꜣW* — Jéquier, *Le monument funéraire de Pepi II*, III, 55. South Saqqara, near pyramid of Pepi II. Date: Pepi II.

[81] *JDW* Petrie, *Dendereh*, Vol. I, pls. 5, 6; Vol. II, pl. 5a.
Dendera. Priesthood of Pepi II. Date: Pepi II or later.

[82] *JDW* Petrie, *Dendereh*, Vol. I, pls. 6, 7.
Dendera. According to Petrie, *ibid.*, p. 9, this tomb is somewhat later than the last. Date: end VI.

[83] *JDW: SNNJ* Montet, "Les tombeaux dits de Kasr el-Sayad," *Kemi*, VI, 110–25.
El-Qasr wa's-Saiyad. Priesthood of Pepi II. Date: Pepi II or later.

[84] *ꜥNW* Jéquier, "Tombes de particuliers," *ASAE*, XXXV, 147–55.
South Saqqara, near Pepi II. Priesthood of Pepi II. Date: Pepi II.

[85] *ꜥNḪ* Newberry, "The Inscribed Tombs of Ekhmîm," *LAAA*, IV, 114.
Akhmim No. 23. Date: VI or later.

[86] *ꜥNḪJ* Unpublished.
Saqqara, Unis area. A squarish chamber off the court in front of *Mḥw* [202]. Priesthood of Unis. Date: Pepi I or later.

[87] *ꜥNḪ-JR-PTḤ* Unpublished.
Giza 4811 + 4812. Built against Giza 4714, itself not one of the original mastabas on the site. In its final form, this mastaba is a complex involving at least two mastabas. Squarish offering chamber, pillared court and room. Date: VI.

[88] *ꜥNḪ-JR.S* Mariette, *Mastabas*, B 16.
Saqqara, northeast group No. 15. A mastaba with a true cruciform chapel. According to Reisner, *Giza*, I, 304, this type should not occur after the end of the Fourth Dynasty. Date: IV (?)

[88A] *ꜥNḪ-JR.S* Cairo, *CG*, 310.
Provenience? Priesthood at the solar temple of Neferirkare. Date: Neferirkare or later.

[89] *ꜥNḪ-WḎꜣ: JṮJ* Junker, *Giza*, 122–39.
Giza, at the extreme east of the western cemetery. A medium-sized, squarish mastaba with a chapel composed of a corridor with a deep east–west alcove at the south, apparently built against other mastabas. Date: VI.

[90] *ꜥNḪ-Mꜣꜥ* Mariette, *Mastabas*, D 27; Cairo, *CG*, 1464–65.
Saqqara, middle north No. 53. Stela described

as being "au fond d'une petite chambre." Date: ?

[91] *ʿNḪ-M-ʿ-Rʿ* — Selim Hassan, *Giza*, VI^{3}, 35–41.
Giza, Khafre cemetery. A rock-cut tomb. The owner was presumably a son of Khafre. Date: end IV.

[92] *ʿNḪ-M-ʿ-Rʿ* — Unpublished.
Giza 7837. An L-shaped rock-cut chapel, apparently later than Giza 7843, in the group of smallish tombs at the eastern end of the eastern cemetery. Reisner, *Giza*, I, 314 dates to Dynasties Five or Six. Date: V (I should guess not early) or later.

[93] *ʿNḪ-M-ʿ-Rʿ* — Mariette, *Mastabas*, D 40.
Saqqara. This mastaba has a complex interior chapel including three statue-niches and an east–west offering chamber. Priesthood of Menkauhor. Date: Menkauhor or later.

[94] *ʿNḪ-M-ʿ-ḤR: ZZJ* — Capart, *Une rue de tombeaux à Saqqarah*, pls. 18–73; Firth, *Teti Pyramid Cemeteries*, pp. 93 ff., pls. 6, 58.
Saqqara, Teti area. A large mastaba with a complex interior chapel built against that of *Nfr-sšm-Rʿ* [274]. Priesthood of Teti. Date: Pepi I.

[94A] *Jšfj* — Son of the last. Apparently a later addition to the tomb of his father. Date: about Pepi I—Mernere.

[95] *ʿNḪ-M-ʿ-KꜣJ* — Mariette, *Mastabas*, D 16; Cairo, *CG*, 1327, 1329, 1485.
Saqqara, near north No. 67. A stela in a niche or alcove in the east face of the mastaba. Priesthood of Neuserre. Date: Neuserre or later.

[96] *ʿNḪ-M-Zꜣ.F* — Selim Hassan, *Giza*, VI^{3}, 147–53.
Giza, Khafre cemetery. Built against the mastaba of *Kꜣ-dwꜣ* [550]. Date: end V or later.

[97] *ʿNḪ-NB.F* — Unpublished.
Giza, Mycerinus Quarry No. 3? A rock-cut tomb. Priesthood of Menkaure. Date: ?

[98] *ʿNḪ-NB.F* — Jéquier, "Tombes de particuliers," *ASAE*, XXXV, 134–36.
South Saqqara, near Pepi II. Date: Pepi II.

[99] *ʿNḪ-Ḥꜣ.F* — Unpublished. (The published relief fragments are useless for our purpose.)
Giza 7510. The first mastaba to be built east of

the nucleus of the eastern cemetery, and the largest mastaba in this area. Reisner, *Giza*, I, 28, dates the completion of this tomb to the first half of the reign of Khafre. Date: Khafre.

[100] *ʿNḪ-ḤꜢ.F: QꜢR* — Selim Hassan, *Giza*, III, 130–47.
Giza, Khafre cemetery. The father of *N-sʿnḫ-ꜣḫtj* [232]. A rock-cut tomb with a sloping passage to the burial chamber. Also other shafts. Date: VI.

[101] *ʿNḪ.T.F* — Selim Hassan, *Giza*, V, 225–35.
Giza, Khafre cemetery. This mastaba is built against an older tomb. The chapel has a corridor with an east–west alcove. Six shafts. Date: VI.

[102] *ʿNTJ-NFR* — Mariette, *Mastabas*, D 44; Cairo, *CG*, 123.
Saqqara, northeast group No. 13. A mastaba with a short corridor chapel with two niches. Date: V or later.

[102A] *ʿ[ṮM]ꜣ** — Cairo, *CG*, 99.
Saqqara. Priesthood of Sahure. Date: V 2 or later.

[103] *WꜢŠ-PTḤ* — Selim Hassan, *Giza*, III, 1–6.
Giza, Khafre cemetery. The southernmost mastaba in a row behind *Wp-m-nfrt* [109]. L-shaped chapel with one niche. Date: V (or later?).

[104] *WꜢŠ-PTḤ* — Selim Hassan, *Giza*, II, 5–14.
Giza, Khafre cemetery. A rock-cut tomb to the rear of that of queen *Ḫʿ-mrr-nbtj*, as whose servant he describes himself. Date: end IV—early V.

[105] *WꜢŠ-PTḤ: JZJ* — Mariette, *Mastabas*, D 38; Mogensen, *Inscriptions hiéroglyphiques du musée national de Copenhague*, No. 5129, pls. 10, 11; British Museum, *Hieroglyphic Texts*, Vol. I, pl. 10; Grdseloff, "Nouvelles données concernant la tente de purification," *ASAE*, LI, 141, pl. 1; *Urkunden*, I (2d ed.), 40–45.
Saqqara, northwest group No. 24 (described as being in the cemetery of Sahure). The biography dates the death of *Wꜣš-Ptḥ* and the erection of his tomb to the reign of Neferirkare. Date: Neferirkare.

* This name was read as *ʿ[šm]ꜣ* (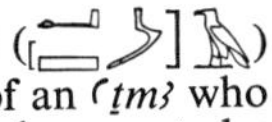) by Borchardt on the basis of an incorrect reading by Daressy of the name of an *ʿṯmꜣ* who occurs in the tomb of *Mrrw-kꜣ* [197], this name being apparently the only documented one that would fit the traces. The correct reading is given in *The Mastaba of Mereruka*, I, pl. 87, l. 38 (room A 10, east wall).

[105A]	*Wꜣš-Kꜣ*	British Museum No. 1156 = *Hieroglyphic Texts*, Vol. I, pls. 22, 23. From "Memphis," Priesthood of Userkaf. Date: Userkaf or later.
[106]	*WJW: JJJW*	Davies, *The Rock Tombs of Sheikh Saïd*, pls. 21–24. Shiekh Said No. 19. The father or the son of *Mrw Bbj* [192], who has the neighboring tomb, but nature of relationship not too certain. Pepi I mentioned. Date: Pepi I or later.
[107]	*Wꜥ*	Lepsius, *Denkmäler*, II, 93a. Giza. A rock-cut tomb in the scarp immediately to the south of the Khufu causeway. Lepsius No. 67. The tombs in this position are hardly likely to have been part of the original cemetery. Date: V or later.
[108]	*WP-M-NFRT*	Reisner, *Giza*, I, 385–89, pl. 17a. Giza 1201. One of the original cores in the northwest cemetery with a slab-stela. The mastaba was later converted into one with an interior chapel, but this does not affect the date of the inscriptions on the slab. Date: Khufu.
[109]	*WP-M-NFRT: WP*	Selim Hassan, *Giza*, II, 179–201. Giza, Khafre cemetery. A partly rock-cut mastaba in the same scarp as *Rꜥ-wr* [300] and some others. It is at the southern end, and thus likely to be later than those nearer the causeway of Khafre. The cartouche of Neferefre occurs here. *Wp-m-nfrt*'s son *Jbj* later carved himself an adjoining chapel on the corridor plan. Date: middle—late V.
[110]	*WNJ: JWN: ḪḎḎJ*	Cairo, *CG*, 1309–10, 1435, 1574, 1643, 1670; 175 (?); Mariette, *Catalogue général des monuments d'Abydos*, Nos. 529, 533; *Urkunden*, I, 98–110, 209. Abydos. According to his biography, his career continued into the reign of Mernere, at which time the tomb was presumably built. *Wnj* is mentioned in the Dahshur decree of Pepi I, dated to the year of the twenty-first numbering. Date: Mernere.
[111]	King *WNJS*	Unpublished. The titles of the officials depicted in the funerary temple of Unis. Date: Unis.
[112]	*WNJS-ꜥNḪ*	Unpublished. Partly in the Chicago Museum of Natural History.

The mastaba of *Jḥj* [57] appears to have been built against this one, which would make it one of the first to be built in this sequence of major mastabas in the Unis cemetery at Saqqara, behind the row of queens' tombs. Date: Unis—Teti.

[112A] *WNJS-ʿNḪ*
Davies, "The Work of the Robb de Peyster Tytus Memorial Fund at Thebes," *BMMA*, XIII, *Supplement*, 23, pl. 34.
Thebes. A small fragment of sunk relief found lying in the debris of the Theban necropolis with a figure of the owner and his son. Of his three titles, *ḫrj-tp nswt*, *jmj-rꜣ Šmʿ*, and *jmj-rꜣ šnwtj*, the first two are also found in [112], though in reversed order. One wonders if the fragment might be from some Upper Egyptian monument of the same person or a relative. The name is not very common. Date: VI?

[113] *WRJ*
Junker, *Giza*, VI, 195–98.
Giza, central portion of the western cemetery. A small mastaba built against another which was built against one of the original cores of the cemetery. Two shafts and a corridor chapel. Date: VI.

[113A] *WR-JR.N.J*
Mariette, *Mastabas*, D 20; Cairo, *CG*, 110, 114, 118–19, 211, 272.
Saqqara, near north No. 62. A large rectangular mastaba with an L-shaped interior chapel at the southern end. Next to the tomb of *Ṯjj* [564]. Priesthood at the solar temple of Neferirkare. Date: Neferirkare or later.

[114] *WR-JR.N.J*
Davies, *The Rock Tombs of Sheikh Saïd*, pls. 7–16.
Sheikh Said No. 25. The son of *Srf-kꜣ* [457]. Priesthood of Neuserre. Davies dates to the Fifth Dynasty; this tomb precedes those of the series of Sixth Dynasty nomarchs at this site. Date: Neuserre—end V.

[115] *WR-JR.N-PTḤ*
British Museum No. 718 = *Hieroglyphic Texts*, Vol. VI, pls. 1–12; Cairo, *CG*, 25.
Saqqara. Priesthood at the solar temple of Neferirkare. Date: Neferirkare or later.

[116] *WR-MRW*
Unpublished.
Giza 7851. A small rock-cut tomb in the cliff to the south of the Khufu causeway in the cluster of tombs at the eastern end of the eastern

cemetery. Priesthood of Khafre. Date: end V—VI.

[117] *WR-NWNW* — Zaki Saad, "Preliminary Report on the Excavations of the Department of Antiquities at Saqqara, 1942–43," *ASAE*, XLIII, 455, pls. 41, 42; Drioton, "Déscription sommaire des chapelles funéraires de la VIe Dynastie. . . . ," *ASAE*, XLIII, 496–501; Junker, "Zu den Titeln des 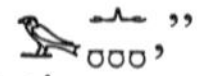," *ASAE*, XLIX, 207–15.
Saqqara, Teti area. A small mastaba with a corridor chapel (?) built against the tomb of *Mrrj* [195]. Priesthood of Teti. Date: mid-VI or later.

[118] *WR-ḪWW* — Lepsius, *Denkmäler*, II, 43–44; *Erg.*, pls. 38–39; *Urkunden*, I, 46–48; Selim Hassan, *Giza*, V, 237–56.
Giza, Khafre cemetery. A partly rock-cut tomb with an east–west alcove in the chapel. Serdab built against the tomb of *Ms-zꜣ* [203]. *Wr-ḫww* appears to occur in the Abusir Papyri (Borchardt, "Ein Rechnungsbuch des königlichen Hofes aus dem Alten Reiche," *Aegyptiaca*, p. 10) from the reign of Djedkare, where he is listed as a *ḥm-nṯr* of the solar temple of Neferirkare, a title he also has in his tomb. Date: end V.

[119] *WR-Kꜣ-PTḤ* — Mariette, *Mastabas*, B 15.
Saqqara, northwest group. A brick mastaba with an east–west offering chamber. Date: mid-V or later.

[120] (canceled)

[121] *WḤꜣ* — Selim Hassan, *Giza*, V, 255–56.
Giza, Khafre cemetery. A false door found out of place. Uses plural strokes. Hardly earlier than late Old Kingdom. Date: end VI or later.

[122] *WḤM-Kꜣ* — Lepsius, *Denkmäler*, II, 110h; *Text*, II, 61–62.
Zawiyet el-Maiyitin No. 6. Date: presumably VI.

[123] *WSR* — Selim Hassan, *Giza*, I, 95–97.
Giza, Khafre cemetery. A tomb in the Street of Priests. A chapel with a corridor and an east–west alcove. Built against the tomb of *Ffj* [488]. Date: mid-V or later.

[123A] *WSRKꜣF-ꜥNḪ* — Borchardt, *Das Grabdenkmal des Königs Neuser-reꜥ*, pp. 113–14.
Abusir. Appears to be the oldest mastaba in the group to the east of the temple of Neuserre,

possibly even older than the pyramid, if the odd skewed plan of the mortuary temple is the result of taking account of the presence of this mastaba. It has a short north–south corridor chapel with one niche to the south and several exterior chambers of brick. The owner probably occurs in the reliefs of the mortuary temple of Neuserre. Borchardt's publication of the statue of *Wsrkꜣf-ꜥnḫ* unfortunately does not indicate the line division of the text on his statue. The statue is now in the Liebighaus in Frankfurt/Main, Germany, and I owe to the kindness of Dr. Voss of the Staedel Museum of the same city information as to the line division. It is as follows (cf. with the printed text of Borchardt): (1) *jmj-rꜣ ḫt nbt nt pr-ꜥꜣ* to *ḥrj-sštꜣ n rꜣ-ꜥꜣ ḫꜣswt m gswj-pr*. (2) *ḥꜣtj-ꜥ* to *jmj-rꜣ kꜣt nbt nt nswt*. (3) *mdw Kꜣ-ḥḏ* to *jmj-rꜣ Ṯnw*. (4) *ẖrj-tp nswt* to *ḥm-nṯr Jnpw*. (5) *zꜣb ꜥḏ-mr* to *jmj-rꜣ spwt Tꜣ-mḥw m gswj-pr*. On the dorsal pillar, the titles are listed in the two long lines indicated by Borchardt. Date: Neuserre.

[124] *WTꜣ* *Urkunden*, I, 22; Cairo, *CG*, 1479, 1480, 1787; Junker, "Weta und das Lederkunsthandwerk im Alten Reich," *Sitzungsberichte der Österreichischen Akademie der Wissenschaften, Phil.-hist. Klasse*, Vol. CCXXXI, No. 1.
Giza. Junker proposes a date considerably later than the Fourth Dynasty, to which *Wtꜣ* had been assigned on the basis of his being a priest of Menkaure. Date: later Old Kingdom, say mid-V—VI.

[125] *WḎꜣW* De Morgan, *Fouilles à Dahchour*, II, 14–15.
Dahshur, No. 12. This mastaba has a chapel composed of a corridor with several niches and an east–west offering chamber. Date: mid-V or later.

[126] *Bꜣ-Kꜣ* Cairo, *CG*, 176; Chassinat, "À propos d'une tête en grès rouge du Roi Didoufrê," *Monuments Piot*, XXV, 67.
Abu Rawash. Apparently a son of Djedefre. Date: end IV.

[127] *BJW* Jéquier, *Tombeaux de particuliers*, pp. 98–100, 102–4, pl. 13.
South Saqqara, near Pepi II. Date: Pepi II.

[128] *BB-JB: SNḎM-JB* Mariette, *Mastabas*, B 13; Cairo, *CG*, 151.

Saqqara, northeast group No. 11. A yellow brick mastaba with a modified cruciform chapel. A man of this name occurs in the funerary temple of Neuserre; Borchardt assigns the statue to the Fifth Dynasty. Date: mid-V or later.

[129] *BḪN* Newberry, "The Inscribed Tombs of Ekhmîm," *LAAA*, IV, 108–9.
Akhmim No. 12. Date: VI or later.

[130] *PPJ* Jéquier, *Tombeaux de particuliers*, pp. 100–102, 104–5, pl. 14.
South Saqqara, near Pepi II. Date: Pepi II.

[130A] *Ppjj(Mrjj-Rʿ)-ʿnḫ* Unpublished.
Saqqara, Unis area. The son of *Mḥw* [202]. He had his own offering chamber within the mastaba of his father. It was probably built at the same time. Date: Pepi I.

[131] *PPJJ-ʿNḪ: ḪWJ* Smolenski, "Le tombeau d'un prince de la VIe Dynastie à Charouna," *ASAE*, VIII, 149–53; Broderick and Morton, "The tomb of Pepi Ankh (Khua) near Sharuna," *PSBA*, XXI, 26–33.
A tomb near Sharuna and Kom el-Ahmar Sawaris. Priesthood of Pepi I. Date: Pepi I or later.

[132] *PPJJ-ʿNḪ* M. Chaban, "Sur une nécropole de la VIe Dynastie à Koçeir el-Amarna," *ASAE*, III, 250–53.
Qoseir el-Amarna. The owner of this tomb may well have been the eldest son of *N-ʿnḫ-Ppjj* [212] at Meir across the Nile, as Blackman reconstructed the genealogy of the family (*The Rock Tombs of Meir*, I, 9–10). In this case the tomb would hardly have been excavated before the early years of Pepi II. Date: Pepi I or later, possibly Pepi II.

[133] *PPJJ-ʿNḪ ḤRJ-JB: NFR-Kꜣ: ḤNJ* Blackman, *The Rock Tombs of Meir*, Vol. IV.
Meir D 2. A son of *N-ʿnḫ-Ppjj* [212] and perhaps a (younger) brother of the last. Date: early Pepi II or later.

[134] *PPJJ-ʿNḪ: ḤNJ KM* Blackman, *The Rock Tombs of Meir*, V, 15–56, pls. 15–43.
Meir A 2. A son of *N-ʿnḫ-Ppjj* [212] and presumably a younger brother of the last. Date: early Pepi II or later.

[135] *PPJJ-NḪT* — Mariette, *Catalogue général des monuments d'Abydos*, No. 531; Cairo, *CG*, 1573.
Abydos. Date: Pepi I or later.

[136] *PPJJ-NḪT: ḤQ3-JB* — De Morgan, *Catalogue des monuments et inscriptions de l'Égypte antique*, I, 174–76; *Urkunden*, I, 131–35.
Aswan. Pepi II occurs in the titles and biography. Date: Pepi II.

[137] *PPJJ-SNB* — Mariette, *Catalogue général des monuments d'Abydos*, No. 530, 543.
Abydos. Date: Pepi I or later.

[138] *Ppjj-snb: Sn-jfd* — Newberry, "The Inscribed Tombs of Ekhmîm," *LAAA*, IV, 104.
Akhmim No. 5. The son of *Mmj*. Date: VI or later.

[139] *PNW* — Jéquier, *Tombeaux de particuliers*, pp. 41–47.
South Saqqara, near Pepi II. Date: Pepi II.

[140] *PN-MRW* — C. S. F(isher), "The Harvard University–Museum of Fine Arts Egyptian Expedition," *BMFA*, XI, 20–22; Grdseloff, "Deux inscriptions juridiques de l'Ancien Empire," *ASAE*, XLII, 39 ff.; Boston Museum of Fine Arts Nos. 12.1504, 12.1484; partly unpublished data.
Giza 2197. In his inscription, *Pn-mrw* describes the vizier *Sšm-nfr* [478] as his *jtjj* (patron). Thus they would be more or less contemporary. Date: end V.

[141] *PR-NB* — Selim Hassan, *Giza*, III, 157–59.
Giza, Khafre cemetery. A small rock-cut tomb in the quarry face around the tomb of *Ḫnt-k3w.s*. The tombs here are not likely to have been cut soon after the building of this so-called Fourth Pyramid. Date: V or later.

[142] *PR-NB* — Williams, *The Decoration of the Tomb of Perneb*; Lythgoe, *The Tomb of Perneb*.
Saqqara, north of Step Pyramid, QS 913. The son of *Rꜥ-špss* [315]. This mastaba was built against that of his father, but it appears in the published photographs as though a final casing were added to the tomb of *Rꜥ-špss* after the construction of the tomb of *Pr-nb*. This would make the construction of these tombs more or less contemporaneous. *Rꜥ-špss* was a vizier of Djedkare. Date: Djedkare.

[143] *PR-SN* — Lepsius, *Denkmäler*, II, 83; *Erg.*, pl. 8.
Giza, far northwest. A stone mastaba with an

L-shaped interior chapel that was planned from the beginning. Reisner, *Giza*, I, 311, dates to the first half of the Fifth Dynasty. Date: early V (or a bit later?)

[144] *PR-SN* — Mariette, *Mastabas*, D 45; Murray, *Seven Memphite Tomb Chapels*, pls. 9, 10; Berlin Museum No. 15004 = Schäfer, *Aegyptische Inschriften*, I, 20–22.
Saqqara, east of Step Pyramid. Chapel composed of a corridor and east–west alcove. Was made a grant of funerary income by Sahure. Date: Sahure.

[145] *PR-SNB* — Lepsius, *Denkmäler*, II, 34f, 94c; Mariette, *Mastabas*, p. 537.
Giza, Lepsius No. 78. A rock-cut tomb at the eastern end of the eastern cemetery. Date: mid-V or later.

[146] *PḤN-W-Kꜣ* — Lepsius, *Denkmäler*, II, 45–48; Berlin Museum No. 1131 = Schäfer, *Aegyptische Inschriften*, I, 13; Mariette, *Mastabas*, D 70.
Saqqara, near-north ridge. Large mastaba with a very complex plan. East–west offering rooms. The chambers take up a relatively small proportion of the area of the tomb. The plan is rather unusual and reminds one somewhat of the royal funerary temples of the early Fifth Dynasty. Neferirkare mentioned. Date: mid-V.

[147] *PḤ-R-NFR* — Zaki Saad, "Preliminary Report on the Excavations of the Department of Antiquities at Saqqara 1942–43," *ASAE*, XLIII, 453.
Saqqara, Teti area. To the west of *Mrrw-kꜣ* [197] and near *Kꜣ-m-ḥzt* [527]. Zaki Saad states that it was in the immediate vicinity of a brick tomb which he dates to the Fourth Dynasty. *Pḥ-r-nfr* was a priest at the solar temple of Userkaf. One would expect the mastabas in this area largely to date from the Sixth Dynasty, but it is impossible to tell without a plan of the site. Date: Userkaf or later, very possibly VI.

[148] *PTJW . . .* (?) — Unpublished.
Giza. A rock-cut tomb in the cliff to the east of the eastern cemetery, between Lepsius Nos. 67 and 68, immediately south of the Khufu causeway. Date: mid-V or later.

[149] *PTḤ-JW.F-N.J* — Junker, *Giza*, VII, 24–28.
Giza, western cemetery. This mastaba was

built against *Sšm-nfr* [476] and into the complex brick structure filling the space between it and the mastaba of *Wnšt* and Giza 4950. The owner was a priest of Pepi I and called himself revered (*jmꜣḫw*) before the famous sage *Ḏd.f-Ḥr*. Date: Pepi I or later.

[150] *PTḤ-ꜥNḪW* — Jéquier, *Tombeaux de particuliers*, pp. 65–66, pl. 7.
South Saqqara, near Pepi II. Date: Pepi II.

[151] *PTḤ-WSR* — Mariette, *Mastabas*, C 3.
Saqqara, northwest group No. 25. A yellow brick mastaba with a chapel composed of a corridor and an east–west alcove. Two niches in the east face. Date: mid-V or later.

[152] *PTḤ-Mꜣꜥ-ḪRW* — Berlin Museum No. 1159 = Schäfer, *Aegyptische Inschriften*, I, 54–58; Quibell, *Excavations at Saqqara*, III, 26.
Saqqara, north of Step Pyramid, QS 916. Priesthood at the solar temple of Neuserre. This part of the cemetery seems to have come into use during the reign of Djedkare. Date: Djedkare or later.

[153] *Ptḥ-mr-Mrjjrꜥ* — *Urkunden*, I, 209; Borchardt, "Ein Königserlass aus Dahschur," *ZÄS*, Vol. XLII, pl. 1; Helck, *Untersuchungen*, p. 140 (improved reading).
Addressee of the decree found at Dahshur dated to the twenty-first numbering of Pepi I. Date: Pepi I.

[153A] *PTḤ-MR-ZṮ.F* — Schäfer, *Priestergräber*, pp. 9–10; Borchardt, *Das Grabdenkmal des Königs Ne-user-reꜥ*, p. 137.
Abusir, Nos. VI, 10–11. Priesthood of Neferirkare, Khufu and Queen Khentkawes. Date: VI (Schäfer).

[154] *PTḤ-M-ḤꜣT* — Firth, *Teti Pyramid Cemeteries*, p. 245.
A pit in front of the tomb of *Mrrw-kꜣ* [197]. Coffin Texts in coffin. Date: end VI or later.

[155] *PTḤ-NB-NFRT* — Junker, *Giza*, VI, 226–28.
Giza, western cemetery. Built against the core Giza 4450. A dependent (*nj ḏt*) of the vizier *Mḥj*, presumably *Snḏm-jb Mḥj* [456]. Junker takes *Ptḥ-nb-nfrt* and *Mḥj* as being two names for the same person, interprets the *nj-ḏt* as a variant for the phrase, "also called" (*ḏd.tw n.f*), and then worries about the discrepancy in the titles affixed to the two names, which leads him

finally to assign a very late date to the tomb.* Actually he would be a (younger) contemporary of Unis. Date: early VI or later.

[156] *PTḤ-ḤTP* — Dennis, "New Officials of the IVth to Vth Dynasties," *PSBA*, XXVII, 34. No evidence given for a date.

[157] *PTḤ-ḤTP* — Mariette, *Mastabas*, D 51; Cairo, *CG*, 156. Saqqara, east of Step Pyramid. A mastaba with a slightly off-center modified cruciform chapel. *Ptḥ-ḥtp* was a contemporary of Userkaf and a priest at his temples. Date: Userkaf or slightly later.

[158] *PTḤ-ḤTP* and
[159] *PTḤ-ḤTP DŠR* — Mariette, *Mastabas*, C 6–7; Murray, *Saqqara Mastabas*, Vol. I, pls. 4–6. Saqqara, mid-north Nos. 41–42. Two tombs forming one complex whose architectural details and development are almost impossible to determine from the published plans. Both chapels are complex, with pillared porticoes and several chambers, including one with pillars. At the end of the open court separating the two was a false door of *Ptḥ-ḥtp*, who also had the northern chapel. Mariette believed that the tomb of *Ptḥ-ḥtp Dšr* was the older of the two, Petrie that the two chapels are later additions to the main mastaba. The complex is built against the mastaba of *Rʿ-nfr* [304] and another one to the west. The matter is discussed by Murray, *op. cit.*, pp. 5–6 and Smith in Reisner, *Development of the Egyptian Tomb*, p. 401. Date: mid-V or later.

[160] *PTḤ-ḤTP* — Mariette, *Mastabas*, D 62; Murray, *Saqqara Mastabas*, Vol. I, pls. 8–17. Saqqara, Ptahhotep group. A large mastaba with a complex chapel, pillared court and east–west offering chamber. The father of *ꜣḫt-ḥtp* [13] and the grandfather of *Ptḥ-ḥtp* [161] in the neighboring joint mastaba. Unlike the latter, the owner of this mastaba was vizier. The cartouche of Djedkare occurs in this tomb, and all evidence indicates that he was the famous sage who served that king as vizier. Selim Hassan found evidence (unpublished) for deification of this *Ptḥ-ḥtp* in the vicinity of this

* Already corrected by somebody as far as I can recall, but I am unable to find the reference.

tomb like that found for *Kȝ-gm-nj* [548] (Firth and Gunn, *Teti Pyramid Cemeteries*, p. 130) and *Ḏd.f-Ḥr* (Junker, *Giza*, VII, 26). Cf. also Goedicke, "Deification of a Private Person in the Old Kingdom," *JEA*, XLI, 31–33, though it does not bear on this specific case. Date: Djedkare.

[161] *PTḤ-ḤTP* Mariette, *Mastabas*, D 64; Pirie and Paget, *The Tomb of Ptah-hetep*; Davies, *The Mastaba of Ptahhetep and Akhethetep at Saqqareh*, Vol. I.
Grandson of the last. Complex mastaba with a north–south offering chamber. The chapel is part of the complex of *ȝḫt-ḥtp* [13], his father, and was probably built at the same time, but the plans are not clear on this point. Date: Djedkare–Unis.

[161A] *PTḤ-ḤTP: JJ-N-ʿNḪ* Unpublished.
Saqqara, Ptahhotep area. From Selim Hassan's excavations. He occurs also on an offering table found in or around the mastaba of the younger *Ptḥ-ḥtp* [161]. Priesthood of Sahure. Date: end V—early VI.

[162] *PTḤ-ḤTP* Lepsius, *Denkmäler*, II, 101b–104; *Erg.*, p. 43.
Saqqara, south of the Step Pyramid. A complex interior chapel with a pillared court and east–west offering chambers. Date: mid-V or later.

[163] *PTḤ-ḤTP* Junker, *Giza*, VII, 222–29.
Giza, western cemetery. The son of *Stj-kȝj* [485]. He enlarged the funerary complex begun by his father and built it against a mastaba which was built against that of *Kȝ-sḏȝ* [546]. Date: VI.

[164] *PTḤ-ŠPSS* Mariette, *Mastabas*, C 1, H 14, pp. 112–13, 451–53 (an absolutely identical lintel with the same name and titles as on the lintel of C 1, also in C 9); British Museum No. 682 = *Hieroglyphic Texts*, I, 10–13; Cairo, *CG*, 93, 368; *Urkunden*, I, 51–53.
Saqqara, mid-north No. 48 (C 9 is No. 50). Both mastabas have modified cruciform chapels. C 1 has two subsidiary niches in the eastern face, C 9 has one. In view of the text on the lintels, which is the same sign for sign in the two tombs, one would suppose them to have been built at approximately the same time. However, for the purposes of the book we can disregard C 9. C 1 is dated to the reign of

Neuserre by the biography of the owner. Date: Neuserre.

[165] *PTḤ-ŠPSS* Mariette, *Mastabas*, C 10; Cairo, *CG*, 28, 54, 77, 81, 83, 207, 214.

Saqqara, mid-north No. 49. A large, free-standing mastaba with a modified cruciform chapel and one subsidiary niche. Much like the last two, and very close to them. One would suppose it to belong to a member of the same family, and at approximately the same date; say, the middle of the Fifth Dynasty. Date: V.

[166] *PTḤ-ŠPSS* Mariette, *Mastabas*, D 54.

Saqqara, east of Step Pyramid. A mastaba with a modified cruciform chapel and a corridor. A subsidiary niche in the corridor. Priesthood at the solar temple of Neferirkare. Date: mid-V or later.

[167] *PTḤ-ŠPSS* De Morgan, "Découverte du Mastaba de Ptah-Chepsés dans la Nécropole d'Abou-sir," *Revue Archéologique*, Ser. 3, XXIV, 18–33, pls. 1, 2; Dittmann, "Zum Titel ," *ZÄS*, LXXVII, 7; also unpublished data.

Abusir. A large mastaba with an interior chapel of complex plan, with pillared court, statue shrines, and many other chambers. *Ptḥ-špss* was a son-in-law of Neuserre, or perhaps it would be safer to say that he was married to a woman with the title of princess (cf. references above, also those in Helck, *Untersuchungen*, p. 136, nn. 24, 25). The genealogical conclusion is not quite as self-evident as there assumed. The name is, furthermore, much too common to permit secure identification with officials called *Ptḥ-špss*, but with differing titles, that occur in the pyramid temples of Sahure and Neferirkare (see references under Helck). Date: V, probably later than Neuserre.

[167A] *PTḤ-ŠPSS* Badawi, "Denkmäler aus Saḳḳarah II," *ASAE*, XL, 573–77.

Saqqara, Ptahhotep group. A lintel found out of place. The owner was a *ka*-priest of *Ptḥ-ḥtp* and a priest of Djedkare. Date: VI.

[168] *PTḤ-ŠPSS* Mariette, *Mastabas*, E 1–2; Murray, *Saqqara Mastabas*, Vol I, pls. 28–31.

Saqqara, mid-north No. 38. Shares mastaba

with *Sȝbw Jbbj* [421]. The owner had a priesthood of Unis and Teti. He appears, from location and name to have been a later member of the family of [164] and [165]. *Sȝbw Jbbj* was high priest of Ptah under Unis and Teti according to his biography. *Ptḥ-špss* is likely to have held office slightly later, probably still within the reign of Teti. Date: Teti—Pepi I.

[168A] *PTḤ-ŠPSS* Quibell, *Teti Pyramid, North Side*, pp. 20–23. Saqqara, Teti area. Situated to the north of the tomb of *Kȝ-gm-n.j* [548] and at a higher level. Date: mid-VI or later.

[169] *FTK-Tȝ* Lepsius, *Denkmäler*, II, 96; *Erg.*, pl. 40; *Text*, I, 141.
Saqqara, far northwestern knoll, Lepsius No. 1. A mastaba with a complex chapel including a pillared chamber. Date: mid-V or later.

[170] *Mȝ-NFR* Lepsius, *Denkmäler*, II, 65–70; Mariette, *Mastabas*, H 2; Berlin Museum No. 1108 = Schäfer, *Aegyptische Inschriften*, I, 101–18.
Saqqara, east of Step Pyramid, Lepsius No. 17. A complex chapel with east–west offering chambers. Priesthood of Djedkare. Date: Djedkare or later.

[171] *Mȝ-NFR* Mariette, *Mastabas*, D 37.
Saqqara, northwest No. 26. A small brick mastaba built against an older tomb. Date: VI ?

[172] *MJNWW* Junker, *Giza*, VI, 232–36.
Giza, western cemetery. A small mastaba with a corridor chapel and several shafts built against Giza 4860. Date: VI.

[173] *MN-ʿNḪ* Dennis, "New Officials of the IVth to Vth Dynasties," *PSBA*, XXVII, 33–34.
Giza 1047. A small mastaba in the maze of late tombs to the west of Giza 2000 with a chapel composed of a corridor and an east–west offering chamber. A sloping passage to the burial chamber. Priesthood of Menkauhor. Date: VI.

[174] *MN-ḪʿF* Lepsius, *Denkmäler*, II, 82d; also unpublished data.
Giza 7430 + 7440. One of the nucleus mastabas in the eastern cemetery. *Mn-ḫʿ.f* was presumably a son of Khufu. According to Reisner (*Giza*, I, 209, 211), the mastaba would have

been finished about the time of Khafre or Menkaure. Date: Khafre–Menkaure.

[175] *MN-ḎD.F* Lepsius, *Denkmäler*, II, 33; also unpublished data.
Giza 7760. Reisner, *Giza*, I, 209 guesses that he might be a son of *Kꜣ-wꜥb* [513]; and his mastaba is certainly later than the nucleus cemetery. However, he did have a damaged title ending with [. . .] *n jt.f*, and this class of titles, unlike the title *zꜣ nswt n ẖt.f*, appears to be a good criterion for its bearer's being an actual son of a king (Junker, *Giza*, II, 33–34). Since the filiation assumed by Reisner does not appear to be specifically stated anywhere, it is probably safer for the time being to assume that he was a son, perhaps, of Khufu. The tomb would be later, of course. Date: Menkaure or so.

[176] *MMJ* Selim Hassan, *Giza*, VII, 45–48.
Giza, Khafre cemetery. The first in a street of rock-cut tombs to the south of the cemetery. Date: hardly Fourth Dynasty; V or later.

[177] *MNJW* Blackman, *The Rock Tombs of Meir*, Vol. V, pls. 47, 48.
Meir, E 1. Date: VI.

[177A] *MN-ꜥNḪ-PPJJ: MNJ* Petrie, *Dendereh*, Vol. I, pls. 1–4; Vol. II, pl. 2a; *Urkunden*, I, 268-70.
Dendera. Priesthood of Mernere. According to Petrie, *op. cit.*, p. 14, the tomb of *Mn-ꜥnḫ-Ppjj* precedes that of *Jdw* [81]. Date: Mernere or later.

[178] *MN-ḤBW* Junker, *Giza*, VIII, 159–65.
Giza, extreme east of western cemetery. A chapel with pillars. The plan of the mastaba takes account of previous structures on the site. Date: VI, probably not too early.

[179] *MN-SWT-JT-NSWT* Junker, *Giza*, V, 190.
Giza, far west of western cemetery. A small mastaba built against *Jṯw* and another one built against that of *Dmg* [585]. Date: late VI.

[179A] *MR* (?) Cairo, *CG*, 1441.
Provenience? This piece is published without a picture and a date based solely on the presence of a priesthood of Menkaure. Hard to date, though one would expect such a small, miserable piece to be relatively late. Date: ?

[180] *MRJJ* Smith, "The Origin of Some Unidentified Old

Kingdom Reliefs," *AJA*, XLVI, 510–15 = Louvre No. B 49 a–c; Chicago Museum of Natural History No. 31300 bis; Cairo *CG*, 1388. Saqqara, probably the early Old Kingdom cemetery in the north. Smith dates to the middle of the Fourth Dynasty. Date: IV.

[181] *MRJJ: JDW* British Museum No. 1191 = *Hieroglyphic Texts*, Vol. I, pl. 33.
Provenience? Date: ?

[182] *MR-JB* Lepsius, *Denkmäler*, II, 18–22; Berlin Museum No. 1107 = Schäfer, *Aegyptische Inschriften*, I, 88–100; Junker, *Giza*, II, 121–35.
Giza 2100 Ann. I. An annex or expansion of the original core mastaba Giza 2100, which presumably belonged to *Mr-jb*'s father. Junker dates it to the early Fifth Dynasty. Date: early V.

[183] *MR-JB* and Junker, *Giza*, VIII, 140–51.
[183A] *JR-N-ȝḪTJ* Junker, *Giza*, VIII, 151–53.
Giza, extreme east of western cemetery. These two tombs, whose owners had the same titles, are situated near the tomb of *Jṯj*. The superstructures of both are destroyed. Junker dates both to the very end of the Old Kingdom or the First Intermediate Period. Date: end VI or later.

[183B] *MRJJ-JZZJ* Smith in Reisner, *The Development of the Egyptian Tomb*, p. 411.
Saqqara, Unis area. An unpublished mastaba excavated by Firth. The owner was a priest of Unis. Date: VI.

[184] *MRJJRꜤ-JȝM* Jéquier, *Le monument funéraire de Pepi II*, III, 50–56, pls. 52, 53.
South Saqqara, near Pepi II. The dating of this tomb is discussed by Kees, "Beiträge zur Geschichte des Vezirats im Alten Reich," *Nachr. Gött.*, N.F., IV, phil.-hist. Klasse, 44–45. He identifies the owner of this tomb with a *Ppjj-jȝm* with much lower titles who occurs in the mortuary temple of Pepi II. Since he himself admits the existence of another *Ppjj-jȝm* in the late Menkaure-temple decree of Pepi II, the identification hardly is compelling, particularly considering the difference in titles. The conclusion drawn by Kees, that this tomb must be later than the completion of the temple of Pepi

II, loses much of its force—the official in the reliefs could just as well be the *Ppjj-jꜣm* of the late decree at an early stage of his career. Likewise, the conclusion that he must have been born under Pepi I, on the basis of his name, is hardly tenable any more (cf. Junker, *Giza*, II, 30, which is quite conclusive). The tomb under consideration must, however, be rather older than that of *N-ḥb-sd-Nfrkꜣrꜥ*, which was secondarily inserted into it. This would place it at some point before the middle of the reign of Pepi II. Date: Pepi II, first half.

[185] *MRJJRꜥ-ꜥNḪ: N-SW-JḤJJ* — Mariette, *Mastabas*, E 13; Cairo, *CG*, 1483.
Saqqara, east of Step Pyramid? Mention of Pepi I. Date: Pepi I, or later.

[186] *MRJJRꜥ-ꜥNḪ: ḤQꜣ-JB* — Firth, *Teti Pyramid Cemeteries*, pp. 167–68, pl. 64.
Saqqara, Teti area. A stela found thrown in a shaft. Date: mid-VI or later.

[187] *MRJJRꜥ(PPJJ)-NFR: QꜣR* — Daressy, "Inscription du mastaba de Pepi-Nefer à Edfou," *ASAE*, XVII, 130–40 = *Urkunden*, I, 251 ff. = Cairo, *CG*, 43371.
Edfu. A son of *Jzj* [62]. His biography dates the tomb to Mernere. Date: Mernere.

[188] *MRJJRꜥ-Ḥꜣ-JŠT.F* — Petrie, *Sedment*, Vol. I, pls. 7–12.
Sedment. Wooden statues, servant figurines, coffin with offering list. Date: late VI.

[189] *MRJJ-TTJ* — Daressy, "Le mastaba de Mera," *Mémoires de l'Institut Égyptien*, III, 521–74; Wreszinski, *Atlas zur altägyptischen Kulturgeschichte*, III, 90.
Saqqara, Teti area. The son of *Mrrw-kꜣ* [197]. and a later addition to his father's tomb. Priesthood of Pepi I. The alterations in the texts in this tomb and *Mrjj-Ttj*'s relationship to *Mrrw-kꜣ* have been discussed at length by Nims, "Some Notes on the Family of Mereruka," *JAOS*, LVIII, 638–47. In the course of the work on this study, I was largely dependent on Daressy's text, which is not completely reliable and does not always indicate the line divisions; it was not much use as a guide for distinguishing the original texts from the recuttings and later additions. A certain element of uncertainty thus enters into the ranking chart obtained from this tomb. At the last minute,

Nims's misplaced copies of the texts in this mastaba were found, which indicate the alterations in the texts. The title sequences used in this study are the original ones. The later additions involved only a small number of high-ranking titles, which were, however, fitted into erasures and at the ends of lines in such a fashion that the result, if read as a continuous string, would produce wildly fluctuating sequences. They must be treated as separate strings. Date: Pepi I or somewhat later.

[190] *MR-ʿNḪ.F* Selim Hassan, *Giza*, III, 14–22.
Giza, Khafre cemetery. A rock-cut mastaba apparently cut in the rock face left when the big anonymous rock-cut mastaba of Selim Hassan, *Giza*, I, 89 was cut free in the rear. Therefore later. This tomb is quite irregular and miserable. Date: VI.

[190A] *MRW* Drioton, "Description sommaire des chapelles funéraires de la VIe Dynastie," *ASAE*, XLIII, 506–9.
Saqqara, Teti area. A small stone-lined short corridor chapel with an antechamber to the south. Immediately north of *Mrrw-kꜣ* [197]. Mention of Pepi I. Date: Pepi I or later.

[191] *MRW* Daressy, "La nécropole des grands prêtres d'Héliopolis sous l'Ancien Empire," *ASAE*, XVI, 195–98.
Heliopolis. Decorated burial chamber. The tombs appear to have been similar in many respects to the late Sixth Dynasty ones found in the vicinity of the pyramid of Pepi II. Daressy dates them to the Sixth Dynasty. Date: VI.

[192] *MRW: BBJ* Davies, *The Rock Tombs of Sheikh Saïd*, pls. 17–21.
Sheikh Said No. 20. Next to the tomb of *Wjw* [106]. A relative? Pepi I is mentioned in this tomb. Date: Pepi I or later.

[193] *MRW-Kꜣ* Junker, *Giza*, IX, 70–83.
Giza, western cemetery in group of late tombs immediately to the south of Giza 2000. This mastaba was built against that of *Nfr-srs* [271] and another one. It has a corridor chapel and a pillared portico. Date: VI.

[194] *MRW-Kꜣ* Selim Hassan, *Giza*, I, 62–63.

Giza, Khafre cemetery. Built against *Rʿ-wr* [300]. Date: mid-V or later.

[195] *MRRJ*

Zaki Saad, "Preliminary Report on the Excavations of the Department of Antiquities at Saqqara 1942–43," *ASAE*, Vol. XLIII, pl. 39; Drioton, "Description sommaire des chapelles funéraires de la VIe Dynastie," *ASAE*, XLIII, 488–96.

Saqqara, Teti area. This mastaba was built to the north of *Mrrw-kꜣ* [197] and is evidently later, but other tombs were afterward built against it. Date: mid-VI.

[196] *MRRJ*

Lepsius, *Denkmäler*, II, 111.

Zawiyet el-Maiyitin No. 17. Priesthood of Pepi I. Date: Pepi I or later.

[197] *MRRW-Kꜣ: MRJ*

Duell *et al.*, *The Mastaba of Mereruka*, Vols. I and II.

Saqqara, Teti area. A large mastaba with a complex interior chapel built against *Kꜣ-gm-n.j* [584] in the front row of major mastabas. Zaki Saad states ("Preliminary Report on the Excavations of the Department of Antiquities at Saqqara 1942–43," *ASAE*, XLIII, 451) that the bonding of the joint between the two mastabas shows that they were built simultaneously; the photograph, *ibid.*, pl. 36, looks to me as though the mastaba of *Mrrw-kꜣ* were the later of the two. In any case, the two are likely to be nearly contemporary. Date: Teti.

[198] *MR*(?)-*ḤTP*

Mariette, *Mastabas*, D 15.

Saqqara, near north No. 69. A smallish stone mastaba with an L-shaped interior chapel. Date: V or later.

[199] *MR-ḪWFW*

Fakhry, *Sept tombeaux à l'est de la Grande Pyramide de Guizeh*, pp. 19–25.

Giza, in the cliff north of the Khufu causeway. A rock-cut tomb. Hard to date, but one would hardly imagine the cluster of small rock-cut tombs to date from the earlier years of the cemetery. Date: V or later.

[200] *MR-SW-ʿNḪ*

Selim Hassan, *Giza*, I, 104–17.

Giza, Khafre cemetery. A dependent of the estate (*ḏtj*) of *Rʿ-wr* [300]. The mastaba is built against that of *Rʿ-wr* and has a corridor chapel. A lintel bears a row of figures of the owner, which would not indicate an early date for the tomb. Date: *ca.* end V.

[201] *MḤJ* — Jéquier, *Tombeaux de particuliers*, pp. 70–75, pls. 9, 10.
South Saqqara, near Pepi II. Date: Pepi II.

[202] *MḤW* — Zaki Saad, "A Preliminary Report on the Excavations at Saqqara 1939–1940," *ASAE*, XL, 687–90, pls. 80, 81; also unpublished data.
Saqqara, Unis area. Abdel Salam Ḥussein, "The Reparation of the Mastaba of Meḥu at Saqqara," *ASAE*, XLII, 417–45 gives plans and architectural details, which show that this mastaba was built against that of *Jḥj* [57]. Complex interior chapel with east–west offering chambers and pillared court. Priesthood of Pepi I. Date: Pepi I, perhaps slightly later.

[203] *MS-Zꜣ* — Selim Hassan, *Giza*, V, 289–92.
Giza, Khafre cemetery. A rock-cut tomb which looks on the published plans as though it might be earlier than that of *Wr-ḫww* [118]. Date: mid-V.

[203A] *MŠT* — Junker, *Giza*, IX, 234.
A small mastaba with a corridor chapel and several shafts built against Giza 1351 and another mastaba built against it. Date: VI.

[203B] *MṮṮJ* — Cooney, "The Wooden Statues Made for an Official of King Unas." *Brooklyn Museum Bulletin*, XV, No. 1, 1–25.
Saqqara, probably Unis area. *Mṯṯj* was *jmꜣḫw* before Unis, thus probably a contemporary. Date: Teti.

[204] *MDW-NFR* — Reisner, *Giza*, I, 491–95; Cairo, *CG*, 57189.
Giza 4630. A core mastaba expanded so as to block the street. Complex chapel with a north–south corridor with subsidiary niches, a square chamber with a column; several shafts in the later masonry. A sealing with the name of Userkaf was found here (Reisner and Smith, *Giza*, II, 51–52). Date: end V or later.

[205] *MDW-NFR* — Selim Hassan, *Giza*, III, 115–18.
Giza, Khafre cemetery. A rock-cut tomb near the mausoleum of queen *Ḫnt-kꜣw.s*. It seems possible that the tomb of *Sšmw* [474] was built in the courtyard of this tomb. Date: V or later.

[206] *N-*[. . .]*-Rꜥ* — Selim Hassan, *Giza*, VII, 73-79.
Giza, Khafre cemetery. A mastaba with an

L-shaped interior chapel at the north end. A sloping passage opens in the floor of the offering chamber and leads to the burial chamber. This type is usually considered characteristic for the later Fifth and Sixth Dynasties (Reisner, *Giza*, I, 150–55; Junker, *Giza*, VIII, 4–8). The chances are that this tomb is then to be dated at least to the middle of the Fifth Dynasty, despite the title *zꜣ nswt* borne by the owner. Date: mid-V or later.

[207] *NJ-MZTJ** — Unpublished.
Giza 2366. I cannot find this mastaba on any plan of the Giza necropolis, but to judge from its number, it probably was one of the small, later mastabas to the immediate west of the *Snḏm-jb* family. Date: VI ?

[207A] *N-ʿNH̱-ʿNTJ: NJJ* — Junker, *Giza*, VI, 239–40.
Giza, western cemetery. The father of *Jj-m-ḥtp* [23], listed separately, on a stela found reused. None of the titles are recorded in a rankable sequence, and he is only included here because of a priesthood of Khufu. Date: VI.

[208] *N-ʿNH̱-Bꜣ(H̱NMW)* — Selim Hassan, "Excavations at Saqqara (1937–1938)," *ASAE*, XXXVIII, 506–8.
Saqqara, Unis area. A large mastaba with an interior court, pillared hall, stairway to roof, and a decorated burial chamber. Date: VI.

[209] *N-ʿNH̱-PPJJ: ḤPJ* — Unpublished.
Unis area. Date: Pepi I or later.

[210] *N-ʿNH̱-PPJJ* — Selim Hassan, "Excavations at Saqqara (1937–1938)," *ASAE*, XXXVIII, 508–12; also unpublished data.
Saqqara, Unis area. A partly rock-cut tomb. Date: Pepi I or later.

[211] *N-ʿNH̱-PPJJ: H̱NMW-ḤTP: ḤPJ* — Varille, *La Tombe de Ni-Ankh-Pepi à Zâouyet el Mayetîn.*
Zawiyet el-Maiyitin. Date: Pepi I or later.

[212] *N-ʿNH̱-PPJJ: SBK-ḤTP: ḤPJ KM* — Blackman, *The Rock Tombs of Meir*, V, 1–15, pls. 4–14.
Meir A 1. The father of the three *Ppjj-ʿnḫ*'s [132–34]. Date: Pepi I or later.

* This name is written . In my notes I find a transliteration *Sḏb-ztnj*, which I can no longer trace to a source, and probably found in the records of the Harvard–Boston excavation. The name is actually a formation like *Nj-Ptḥ* with a (male) god 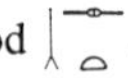. He occurs in the unpublished reliefs from the temples of Djedkare and Unis. For reading cf. *Wörterbuch*, II, 136.

[213] *N-ʿNḪ-PPJJ KM* — Cairo, *CG*, 60, 236.
From Meir. Probably the same as the last. Date: Pepi I or later.

[214] (canceled)

[215] *N-ʿNḪ-Rʿ* — Selim Hassan, *Giza*, IV, 151–56.
Giza, Khafre cemetery. A rock-cut tomb in the rock face immediately to the east of the pyramid of Khafre. The sloping passage to the burial chamber is not diagnostic for date in the case of rock-cut tombs. *N-ʿnḫ-Rʿ* bore the title *zȝ nswt*, but that hardly permits any conclusions as to his parentage. The brick wall of his court seems to have been built so as to block the entrance to another rock-cut tomb. Date: V (?).

[215A] *N-ʿNḪ-Rʿ* — Cairo, *CG*, 55.
From Saqqara. Priesthoods of Neferirkare. Date: Neferirkare or later.

[216] *N-ʿNḪ-Rʿ* — Mariette, *Mastabas*, F 1; British Museum Nos. 1429, 658 = *Hieroglyphic Texts*, Vol. I, pl. 25; Cairo, *CG*, 62.
Saqqara. Pieces not found *in situ.* Borchardt dates the statue of the family group to the Fifth Dynasty. Date: V (?)

[217] *N-ʿNḪ-Rʿ* — Lepsius, *Denkmäler*, II, 91a; Junker, *Giza*, XI, 86.
Giza, south of the Great Pyramid. A tomb which seems to have had a corridor chapel. The complex of the family of *Sšm-nfr* [479] was built against it. Date: later V—early VI.

[218] *N-ʿNḪ-ẖNMW* — Selim Hassan, *Giza*, VI³, 133–42.
Giza, Khafre cemetery. A mastaba with a corridor chapel built against the tomb of *Rwd-kȝ* [316]. Several shafts. Date: VI.

[219] *N-ʿNḪ-ẖNMW NMḤW* — Grdseloff, "Notes sur deux monuments inédites de l'Ancien Empire," *ASAE*, XLII, 121–125.
Provenience? Office at the solar temple of Userkaf, to whose reign Grdseloff dates *N-ʿnḫ-ẖnmw*. Date: V.

[220] *N-ʿNḪ-SNFRW: FFJ* — De Morgan, *Fouilles à Dahchour*, II, 11–13.
Dahshur No. 8. A brick mastaba with a north–south corridor with a niche and an east–west offering chamber. Other rooms added on the outside of the mastaba. An earlier mastaba was partly demolished to make room for this one. Date: VI.

[221] *N-ʿNḪ-SḪMT* — Mariette, *Mastabas*, D 12; Cairo, *CG*, 1482.
Saqqara, near north ridge No. 74. A mastaba with a stela in a niche in the east face. The erection of the tomb is dated by the biography to the reign of Sahure. Date: Sahure.

[222] *N-WSR-Rʿ* — Selim Hassan, *Giza*, IV, 185–88.
Giza, Khafre cemetery. A rock-cut tomb belonging to a prince, presumably a son of Khafre. Date: end IV.

[223] King *N-WSR-Rʿ* — Borchardt, *Das Grabdenkmal des Königs Ne-user-Reʿ*, pp. 71–74 and *passim*.
The titles of the officials depicted in the funerary temple of Neuserre. Date: Neuserre.

[224] *NJWTJ* — Lepsius, *Denkmäler*, II, 89a; *Erg*., pp. 10c, 30–31.
Giza 4611, Lepsius No. 50. A mastaba built so as to block the road between two core mastabas. Corridor chapel and several shafts. Date: end V or later.

[225] *NJ-PPJJ* — Mariette, *Abydos*, Vol. II, pl. 43b.
Abydos. Priesthood of Mernere. Date: Mernere or later.

[226] *N-MꜣʿT-PTḤ* — Mariette, *Mastabas*, D 24.
Saqqara, mid-north No. 56. A small stone mastaba with a modified cruciform chapel. Priesthood of Neferirkare. Date: Neferirkare or later.

[227] *N-MꜣʿT-Rʿ* — Selim Hassan, *Giza*, II, 202–25.
Giza, Khafre cemetery. A small tomb, partly rock-cut, to the east of *Wp-m-nfrt* [109] and apparently backing on to the court. Later than [109] ? Priesthood of Neuserre. Date: Neuserre or later.

[228] *N-MꜣʿT-Rʿ* — Mariette, *Mastabas*, D 17; Cairo, *CG*, 51.
Saqqara, near north No. 65. A large mastaba with an exterior corridor chapel that has serdabs in its east wall. A sloping passage leads to the burial chamber. Date: mid-V or later.

N-MꜣʿT-SD see *SD-N-MꜣʿT*

[229] *N-ḤB-SD-PPJJ* — Wreszinski, *Aegyptische Inschriften aus dem K. K. Hofmuseum in Wien*, pp. 6–7.
From El-Kab. Date: Pepi I (end) or later.

[229A] *N-ḤB-SD-NFRKꜣRʿ* — Jéquier, *Le monument funéraire de Pepi II*, III, 56–60.
South Saqqara, near Pepi II. This vizier's tomb

was inserted into that of *Mrjjrʿ-jꜣm* [184] and thus is evidently later. It seems possible that he is the *N-ḥb-sd-Ppjj* who is listed as the eldest son of the vizier *Jdj* [73A] on his monument at Abydos. His administration would then come after the middle of the reign of Pepi II. Cf. Kees, "Beiträge zur Geschichte des Vezirats im Alten Reich," *Nachr. Gött.*, N.F. IV, Phil.-hist. Klasse, 46–47. Date: Pepi II, second half.

[230] *N-ḤTP-ẖNMW* Abu-Bakr, *Giza*, I, 11–25.
Giza, far northwest. The first mastaba in the group. Corridor chapel with several stelae. Date: mid-V or later.

[231] *N-ḪWT* Jéquier, *Tombeaux de particuliers*, p. 54.
South Saqqara, near Pepi II. Date: Pepi II.

[231A] *N-ḪNZW* Quibell, *Excavations at Saqqara*, Vol. III, pl. 61, Fig. 1.
Saqqara, north of Step Pyramid, QS 906. Priesthood of Teti. Date: Teti or later.

[232] *N-SʿNḪ-ꜣḪTJ: JṮJ* Selim Hassan, *Giza*, III, 119–29.
Giza, Khafre cemetery. The son of *ʿnḫ-ḥꜣ.f Qꜣr* [100]. A rock-cut tomb. Among the reliefs a lintel with a series of figures of the owner. Date: VI.

[233] *N-SW-MNꜣ* Lepsius, *Denkmäler*, II, 92d–e; *Erg.*, pl. 33.
Giza, Lepsius No. 64. A rock-cut tomb just south of the Khufu causeway. A squarish chamber with several stelae, situated in the cluster of small tombs at the extreme east of the eastern cemetery. Date: mid-V or later.

[234] *N-SW-ḤNW* Junker, *Giza*, X, 181–83.
Giza, south of the Great Pyramid. Added to *N-sw-sʿnḫ* [235]. Date: VI.

[235] *N-SW-SʿNḪ* Junker, *Giza*, X, 175–81.
Giza, south of the Great Pyramid. One of the mass of small, late mastabas around the Fourth Dynasty cores. Corridor chapel and seven shafts. Date: VI.

N-SW-QD see *QD-N-S*

[236] *N-Kꜣ-ʿNḪ* Mariette, *Mastabas*, D 48; British Museum No. 1275 = *Hieroglyphic Texts*, Vol. I, pl. 28; Murray, *Seven Memphite Tomb Chapels*, pl. 3.
Saqqara, east of Step Pyramid. A mastaba with two niches in the east face. A corridor with windows was later added along the entire east side of the mastaba. A mastaba adjoins to the

east, but the relationship between the two cannot be determined from the published data. *N-kȝ-ʿnḫ* was a priest of the solar temple of Neferirkare. Date: Neferirkare or later.

[237] *N-Kȝ-ʿNḪ*

Fraser, "The Early Tombs at Tehneh," *ASAE*, III, 122–30; Moret and Lefebvre, "Un nouvel acte de fondation à Tehneh," *Revue Égyptologique*, N.S., I, 30–38; *Urkunden*, I, 24–32, 161–62.

Tihna No. 13. *N-kȝ-ʿnḫ* became priest of Hathor, lady of Ra-one, under Userkaf. Date: early V.

[238] *N-Kȝ-ʿNḪ*

Cairo, *CG*, 136.

Provenience? Borchardt dates the statue to the Fifth Dynasty. Date: V (?).

[239] *N-KȝW-PTḤ*

Murray, "Some Fresh Inscriptions," *Ancient Egypt*, IV, 62–64.

From Saqqara or Abusir. Priesthood of Sahure. Date: Sahure or later.

[240] *N-KȝW-NSWT*

Cairo, *CG*, 1307.

Provenience? A circular offering plate which Borchardt doubtfully dates to the Fifth Dynasty. Date: (?).

[240A] *N-Kȝ-Rʿ*

Cooney, "Three Egyptian Families of the Old Kingdom," *Brooklyn Museum Bulletin*, XIII, No. 3, 1–9.

From Saqqara. A tomb which, to judge from the remarks in Cooney's article, must once have been of considerable size. The pieces from it are widely scattered and apparently mostly unpublished. Among his many titles was a priesthood at the solar temple of Neuserre. Date: Neuserre or later.

[241] *N-KȝW-Rʿ*

Lepsius, *Denkmäler*, II, 15; *Erg.*, pl. 35; Mariette, *Mastabas*, p. 549.

Giza, Khafre cemetery. Lepsius No. 87. A rock-cut tomb belonging to a prince, presumably a son of Khafre. Date: end IV.

[242] *N-KȝW-Rʿ*

Mariette, *Mastabas*, D 50.

Saqqara, east of Step Pyramid. Priesthood of Neferefre. Corridor chapel? Date: Neferefre or later.

[243] *N-KȝW-Rʿ*

Cairo, *CG*, 1414, 1416.

Saqqara. Priesthood at the solar temple of Neferirkare. Date: Neferirkare or later.

[243A] *N-KȝW-Rʿ*

De Rougé, *Inscriptions hiéroglyphiques*, pl. 91.

South Saqqara? Priesthood of Djedkare. Date: Djedkare or later.

[243B] *N-K3W-ḤR* — Fakhry, *Sept tombeaux à l'est de la Grande Pyramide de Guizeh*, p. 7.
Giza. A small rock-cut tomb in the cliff to the north of the Khufu causeway. Hardly likely to date from the earliest period of the cemetery. Priest of Shepseskaf, the only such in this collection. Date: V or later.

[244] *N-K3W-ḤR* — Lepsius, *Denkmäler*, II, 94d; Selim Hassan, *Giza*, IV, 189–95.
Giza, Khafre cemetery. A mastaba built against the rock face near *Dbḥn* [583]. Has an east–west offering chapel and a sloping passage to the burial chamber. Junker, *Giza*, VIII, 7, dates it to the Sixth Dynasty. Date: mid-V or later.

[245] *N-K3W-ḤR* — Quibell, *Excavations at Saqqara*, III, 25, pls. 62-66.
Saqqara, north of Step Pyramid, QS 915. A mastaba with a short corridor chapel ("oblong"), apparently T-shaped with two false doors. The exact location is uncertain. Priesthood of Userkaf. Date: Djedkare or later?

[246] *NB*-[. . .] — Berlin Museum No. 1124 = Schäfer, *Aegyptische Inschriften*, I, 26–27.
Saqqara. Priesthood of Teti. Date: Teti or later.

[247] *NBJ* — Maspero, "Trois années de fouilles," *MMAFC*, I, 199–200; Cairo, *CG*, 1525, 1687.
Saqqara, west of Mernere. Date: VI.

[247A] *NBJ-PW-PPJJ: NBJ* — Jéquier, *Tombeaux de particuliers*, p. 105.
South Saqqara, near Pepi II. Priesthood of Pepi I. Date: Pepi II.

[248] *NB-M-3ḪT* — Lepsius, *Denkmäler*, II, 12–14; *Erg.*, pl. 34; Selim Hassan, *Giza*, IV, 125–50.
Giza, Khafre cemetery. A rock-cut tomb belonging to a son of Khafre. Date: end IV.

[249] *NB-K3W-ḤR* — Selim Hassan, "Excavations at Saqqara (1937–1938)," *ASAE*, XXXVIII, 512–14; also notes taken from the proof sheets of Selim Hassan's final publication of the tomb, which has, however, not yet appeared.
Saqqara, Unis area. The tomb was usurped from *3ḫt-ḥtp Ḥmj* [14A]. Date: VI.

[250] *NFR* — Reisner, *Giza*, I, 422–25, pls. 29–33, 34a–f.
Giza 2110. An original core mastaba later provided with a new casing and a stone

exterior chapel with one niche. Reisner dates to the later Fourth Dynasty. Date: end IV—early V.

[251] *NFR* — Junker, *Giza*, VI, 26–74.
Giza 4761. Built against a core mastaba so as to almost block the passage. Corridor chapel. Some scenes are copied from the mastaba of *Kꜣ-n-nswt* the younger [532]. Date: end V or somewhat later.

[252] *NFR* — Lepsius, *Denkmäler*, II, 95f; Selim Hassan, *Giza*, III, 200–218.
Giza, Khafre cemetery, Lepsius No. 99. A rock-cut tomb with a sloping passage to the burial chamber. According to Junker, *Giza*, VIII, 6, it is later than the tomb of *Mdw-nfr* [205]. Date: mid-V or later.

[253] *NFR* — Fisher, *The Minor Cemetery at Giza*, p. 147.
Giza 3015. A small stone mastaba built against others at several removes. It has a corridor chapel using two older tombs as walls. Date: VI.

[253A] *NFR* — Cairo, *CG*, 1462; Berlin Museum No. 11665 = Schäfer, *Aegyptische Inschriften*, I, 62.
Provenience? Priesthood at the solar temple of Userkaf. Date: V or later.

[254] *NFRJ* — Abu-Bakr, *Giza*, I, 39–67.
Giza, far northwest. A mastaba built in several stages with a corridor chapel with a deep alcove for a main false door and several more niches along the corridor. The first tomb in its group. Date: mid-V or later.

[255] *NFR-JRT-PTḤ* — Mariette, *Mastabas*, D 53.
Saqqara, east of Step Pyramid. The chapel has an east–west offering chamber, and a north–south corridor with a niche. Priesthood of Menkauhor. Date: Menkauhor or later.

[256] *NFR-JRT-N.F* — Mariette, *Mastabas*, D 55; Cairo, *CG*, 21, 157; Speleers, *Recueil des inscriptions égyptiennes des Musées Royaux du Cinquantenaire à Bruxelles*, pp. 8–12.
Saqqara, east of Step Pyramid. A mastaba with a modified cruciform chapel. Priesthood at the solar temple of Neferirkare. Date: Neferirkare or later.

[257] *NFR-JḤJ* — Unpublished.
Giza 4513. A mastaba with a corridor and

pillared chamber built against another tomb itself built against a core mastaba. Date: VI.

[258] *NFR-BȝW-PTḤ* Lepsius, *Denkmäler*, II, 55–58; Berlin Museum No. 1114 = Schäfer, *Aegyptische Inschriften*, I, 6–7.

Giza 6010 = Lepsius No. 15. Son of *Jj-mrjj* [21]. Complex chapel. Priesthood of Neuserre. Date: mid-V—end V.

[259] *NFRFRʿ-ʿNḪ* Mariette, *Mastabas*, D 58; Cairo, *CG*, 87.

Saqqara, east of Step Pyramid. A mastaba with a modified cruciform chapel and a corridor. Date: Neferefre or later.

[260] *NFR-MȝʿT* Petrie, *Medum*, pls. 16–28.

Meydum. One of the large mastabas of the early Fourth Dynasty. *Nfr-mȝʿt* was probably the father of *Ḥm-Jwnw* [331]; cf. Junker, *Giza*, I, 151–52. Date: early IV.

[261] *NFR-MȝʿT* Barsanti, "Rapport sur la fouille de Dahchour," *ASAE*, III, 203–4.

Dahshur. Priesthood of Khafre. See under [264]. Date: mid-V.

[262] *NFR-MȝʿT* Lepsius, *Denkmäler*, II, 17a–c; Reisner, "Nefertkauw, the Eldest Daughter of Sneferuw," *ZÄS*, LXIV, 98-99.

Giza 7060 = Lepsius No. 57. According to Reisner, *Giza*, I, 309, this mastaba was built between the middle of the reign of Khafre and the middle of the reign of Menkaure. *Nfr-mȝʿt* was a grandson of Snefru. Date: Khafre–Menkaure.

[263] *NFRT-NSWT* Unpublished.

Giza 1457. A free-standing mastaba with an L-shaped interior chapel with a single niche. Reisner, *Giza*, I, 210, dates to the later Fourth Dynasty on the basis of a sealing of Menkaure found in the shaft (cf. Reisner and Smith, *Giza*, II, 50). According to Junker, *Giza*, V, 3, the sealing would hardly permit an exact dating. He places the tomb rather later. In orientation, alignment, and size it does not really seem to belong to the Fourth Dynasty core cemetery 1200. Date: V (?).

[264] *Nfrt-nswt* Barsanti, "Rapports sur la fouille de Dahchour," *ASAE*, III, 204.

Dahshur. Priesthood of Khafre. Fischer writes me that he is now convinced that [261] and

[264] actually come from one tomb, belonging to [261], who now can definitely be shown to have been the son of *Nswt-nfr* [292]. At the time the manuscript was prepared for press (July, 1959) his article on this point had not yet appeared. *Nfrt-nswt* can well be a variant for *Nswt-nfr* (assuming thot the final *t* is not simply an error of Barsanti's); and the titles listed here would be those of [292] as recorded later in the tomb of his son. The reading *Nswt-nfr* was taken from Junker, and the transposition is, of course, no problem. Date: mid-V.

[265] *NFR-RNPT* — Selim Hassan, *Giza*, III, 160–65.
Giza, Khafre cemetery. A rock-cut tomb next to that of *Pr-nb* [141] with several shafts. *Nfr-rnpt* was a prophet of the mother of the king, presumably *Ḫnt-kꜣw.s*, beside whose tomb he had his cut. Date: V or later.

[266] *NFR-ḤR-N-PTḤ* — Abu-Bakr, *Giza*, I, 121–23.
Giza, far northwest. A rock-cut tomb. Considering location at extreme edge of the cemetery, one would hardly date it to the earliest years of its existence. Date: V or later?

[267] *NFR-ḤR-N-PTḤ: FFJ* — Selim Hassan, *Giza*, V, 279–87.
Giza, Khafre cemetery. A rock-cut tomb with a corridor chapel and several shafts. Earlier than that of *Jtj-sn* [70]? Priesthood of Menkaure. Date: V or later?

[268] *NFR-ḤR-N-PTḤ* — Mariette, *Mastabas*, D 21; Cairo, *CG*, 76.
Saqqara, near north No. 61. A mastaba near the tomb of *Ṯjj* [564] with a short corridor chapel. Date: V or later.

[268A] *NFR-ḤR-N-PTḤ* — Ny Carlsberg Glyptothek No. 1446 = Koefoed-Petersen, *Recueil des inscriptions hiéroglyphiqes de la Glyptothèque Ny Carlsberg*, p. 32.
Provenience: Priesthood of Khufu. Date: ?

[268B] *NFR-ḤTP* — Selim Hassan, *Giza*, VII, 55–56.
Giza, Khafre cemetery. A mastaba built against the rock face. It has an east–west offering chamber. Priest of Menkaure. Date: mid-V or later.

[269] *NFR-ḤTP* — Cairo, *CG*, 206.
From Saqqara. Borchardt dates to the Fifth Dynasty. Date: V (?).

[269A] *NFR-ḪWW* — Selim Hassan, *Giza*, VI[3], 158–62.

Giza, Khafre cemetery. A large rectangular mastaba with an L-shaped chapel with one niche. Several shafts. Built against Selim Hassan's mastaba 17. The chapel of *Kꜣ-ꜥpr* [511] appears to have been added later in the northeast corner of the block. Date V or later.

[270] *NFR-SFẖ-PTḤ* Lepsius, *Denkmäler*, II, 94e; also unpublished data.
Giza. A rock-cut tomb in the eastern cliff, Lepsius No. 79. The location does not indicate an early date. Date: V or later.

[271] *NFR-SRS* Junker, *Giza*, IX, 60–63.
Giza. A mastaba with a corridor chapel and east–west alcove in the maze of small mastabas to the south of Giza 2000. This one was the first to be built in its group. Date: VI, probably not too late.

[272] *NFR-SŠM-PPJJ: SNNJ* Petrie, *Dendereh*, Vol. I, pl. 7; Vol. II, pl. 7a.
Dendera. Mention of Pepi I. Date: Pepi I or later.

[273] *NFR-SŠM-PTH: WḎꜣ-Ḥꜣ-TTJ: ŠŠJ* Capart, *Une rue de tombeaux à Saqqarah*, pls. 76–102.
Saqqara, Teti area. The third major tomb in the Street of Tombs, built against that of *ꜥnḫ-m-ꜥ-Ḥr* [94]. Is the owner of this tomb the *Ššj* who occurs as a son in the tomb *Nfr-sšm-Rꜥ* [274], the first in the Street of Tombs? Mention of Teti. Date: Pepi I.

[273A] *NFR-SŠM-PTḤ: SꜥNḪ-PTḤ-MRJJRꜥ: ŠŠJ* Cairo, *CG*, 1404.
Abydos, Kom el-Sultan. The identification of the owner of this false door with the preceding entry was made by Capart, *op. cit.*, pp. 74–76. In view of the difference not only in the name but also in the titles, this identification should be viewed with caution. Date: Pepi I or later.

[274] *NFR-SŠM-Rꜥ: ŠŠJ* Capart, *Une rue de tombeaux à Saqqarah*, pls. 8–17; Firth and Gunn, *Teti Pyramid Cemeteries*, pp. 103–4, pl. 58, Figs. 5, 6.
Saqqara, Teti area. The first tomb in the Street of Tombs, and the third from the west in the line of great viziers' tombs to the north of the Pyramid of Teti. Complex plan with pillared court and east–west chapel. Priesthood of Teti. Date: Teti—Pepi I.

[275] *NFR-SŠꜣT: ḪNW* Mariette, *Mastabas*, E 11; Cairo, *CG*, 1490–92.
Saqqara, a tomb situated southeast of the Step

Pyramid about where the Unis area ends and the Userkaf cemetery east of the Step Pyramid starts. A brick mastaba with two rooms lined with stone, including an east–west chapel. The names of both Userkaf and Unis occur in the inscriptions. Date: VI.

[275A] *NFR-SŠM-SŠꜣT: SꜤNḪ-PTḤ-PPJJ: ŠŠJ* Daressy, "La nécropole des grands prêtres d'Héliopolis sous l'Ancien Empire," *ASAE*, XVI, 211–12.
Heliopolis. A pair of obelisks found out of place. Date: Pepi I or later.

[276] *Nfr-sšm-kꜣ* Reisner, *Giza*, I, 502.
Giza 4420. *Nfr-sšm-kꜣ* was the son of *Ttw*. The mastaba is one of the original cores, but it was evidently not used for a long time. Despite the archaic looking titles, the crudely scratched offering table scene (in a later form, with husband and wife seated side by side) on the uncased core and, as Reisner points out, *op. cit.*, p. 518, "the type and small size of the burial chamber and . . . the cheap finishing of the old core" all point to a relatively late date. Reisner also shows that *Ttw* is mentioned as a *ka*-priest in the tomb of *Sḫm-kꜣ* [466] immediately to the south. The reuse of the old core by *Ttw* would be even later. Date: VI.

[277] *NFR-QD* Dennis, "New Officials of the IVth to Vth Dynasties," *PSBA*, XXVII, 34.
Giza, western cemetery, No. 1151. A mastaba with a corridor and east–west alcove built against Giza 1101 = D 91, which, though freestanding, does not belong to the original layout of the northwestern portion of the cemetery. Priesthood at the solar temple of Neuserre. Date: end V or later.

[278] *NFR-KꜣW* Legrain, "Notes archéologiques prises à Gebel Abou Fodah," *ASAE*, I, 13.
Sheikh Atiya. Date: VI (?).

[279] King *NFR-Kꜣ-RꜤ: PPJJ* II Jéquier, *Le monument funéraire de Pepi II*, Vols. II–III, *passim*.
The titles of the officials depicted in the funerary temple of Pepi II. The decoration of this temple was apparently completed about the middle of the ninety-four years that Pepi II reigned (cf. discussion under [73A]). Date: Pepi II, middle.

[280] *NFRKꜣRꜥ-NḪT: ḪTWJ* — Jéquier, "Tombes de particuliers," *ASAE,* XXXV, 136–40.
South Saqqara, near Pepi II. Date: Pepi II.

[281] *NNJ* — Petrie, *Sedment*, Vol. I, pl. 1.
Sedment. Dated to the Sixth Dynasty by Petrie, *ibid.*, 4. Date: VI.

[282] *NN-ḪFT-KꜣJ* — Mariette, *Mastabas*, D 47; Cairo, *CG*, 30–31, 69, 94, 103, 170, 174, 178, 266, 285–86, 321–23; 1484.
Saqqara, east of Step Pyramid. The mastaba originally had only a modified cruciform chapel. Later additions were built on the east including a room with a pillar. A person bearing this not very common name occurs in the temple of Sahure (Borchardt, *Das Grabdenkmal des Königs S'aꜣḥu-reꜥ*, II, 91, 120, 124) with the titles *smr*, *ḫrp ꜥḥ* also found in the tomb. The owner of the tomb was a priest of Sahure. The alteration of the tomb so as to obtain a complex chapel would indicate a date somewhat before the middle of the Fifth Dynasty for the erection of the original structure, which agrees well with the mention in the temple of Sahure. Date: Neuserre or a bit earlier.

[283] *NN-KJ: NNJ-PPJJ* — *Urkunden*, I, 260; Maspero, "Trois années de fouilles," *MMAFC*, I, 196–99, pls. 6, 7.
South Saqqara, near Pepi II. Date: Pepi II.

[284] *NN-GM* — Unpublished.
Saqqara, Unis area. Priesthood of Unis and Teti. Date: VI.

[285] *NḤRJ* — Jéquier, *Le monument funéraire de Pepi II*, III, 61.
South Saqqara, near Pepi II. Inserted into the tomb of *Mrjjrꜥ-jꜣm* [184]. Date: Pepi II, second half.

[286] *NḪBW: PTḤ-MR-ꜥNḪ-MRJJRꜥ* — *Urkunden*, I, 215–21; Dunham, "The Biographical Inscriptions of Nekhebu in Boston and Cairo," *JEA*, XXIV, 1–8; Reisner, "New Acquisitions of the Egyptian Department," *BMFA*, XI, 53–66; Boston Museum of Fine Arts Nos. 13.3161, 13.4339, 13.4348; some unpublished data.
Giza 2381–2382. A tomb with a sloping passage to the burial chamber. *Nḫbw* was probably a grandson of *Sndm-jb Jntj* [455] and lived,

according to his biography, in the time of Pepi I. Date: Pepi I.

[286A] *Ptḥ-mr-ʿnḫ-Ppjj: Ptḥ-špss:Jmpj* — Unpublished. Cf. Reisner, *Giza*, I, 153; Reisner and Smith, *Giza*, II, 54.

[286B] *Sꜣbw-Ptḥ: Jbbj* — Giza 2381–2382. Two of the sons of *Nḫbw*. The father was buried in 2382A; in 2381A, also a burial chamber reached by a sloping shaft, was found a coffin bearing the names and titles of *both* the sons of *Nḫbw*. Since we are only concerned with the titles here, we need not discuss the problem raised by this, nor try to determine who was actually buried where; in any case, we have no access to the pertinent archeological records. A sealing of Pepi II was found here, which is what one would expect considering the known date of the father. Date: Pepi II, early.

[287] *NḪTJ: ʿNḪ-JRTJ-TTJ* — Quibell, *Excavations at Saqqara*, I, 20, pl. 11.
Saqqara, east of Teti area. A stela probably of the Tenth Dynasty, since it was found in a line with others mentioning King Merikare. Included as a warning that some other pieces listed here that appeared to be of the late Old Kingdom might also, like this one, be completely outside the range of time considered here. Date: X.

[288] *NḪT-Zꜣ.S* — Mariette, *Mastabas*, D 67; Cairo, *CG*, 1440.
South Saqqara. No plan available. Priesthood of Neuserre. Date: Neuserre or later.

[289] *NḪT-Zꜣ.S* — Cooney, "Three Egyptian Families of the Old Kingdom," *Brooklyn Museum Bulletin*, XIII, No. 3, 13–18; Elmar Edel, "Ein 'Vorsteher der Farafra-Oase' im Alten Reich?" *ZÄS*, LXXXI, 67–68.
Provenience? A statue of the Fifth or Sixth Dynasty. Date: V–VI.

[290] *NḪT-Kꜣ* — Selim Hassan, *Giza*, VII, 21–33.
Giza, Khafre cemetery. A mastaba with a north–south corridor and a pillared chamber. Priesthood of Sahure. Date: mid-V or later.

[291] *NS* (or [. . .]-*NS*?) — Selim Hassan, *Giza*, V, 276.
Giza, Khafre cemetery. A block found loose. Reproduced in type only, and with misprints. Turned up apparently in the vicinity of the tomb of *Jtj-sn* [70]. Date: ?

[292] *NSWT-NFR* — Junker, *Giza*, III, 75, 163–87.

Giza 4970. One of the cores in the westernmost row of the cemetery *en échelon*, later converted to a mastaba with an interior L-shaped chapel with two false doors. A scene in this tomb was copied from the mastaba of *Sšꜣt-ḥtp* [473], a particularly clear case since a portion of the original was misunderstood and badly garbled in the copying. Date: early—mid-V.

[293] *NṮR-ꜤPR.F* Fakhry, "The Excavation of Snefru's Monuments at Dahshur. Second Preliminary Report," *ASAE*, LII, 591, pl. 21.

Dahshur. This large, monumental, round-topped stela was found in the central court of the Valley Temple of Snefru. *Nṯr-ꜤPr.f* was a *zꜣ nswt*, which at the presumed early date of this stela might still indicate that he was a son of the king. The stela is dated by Fakhry to the Fourth Dynasty. Date: IV.

[294] *NṮR-WSR* Mariette, *Mastabas*, D 1; Murray, *Saqqara Mastabas*, pls. 20–25.

Saqqara, north of Step Pyramid No. 78. A mastaba with a complex interior chapel and an east–west offering room. It is situated near the eastern end of the row of mastabas along the north of the Step Pyramid. A son of his was called *RꜤ-šps*, and may well have been the vizier of that name who erected his tomb nearby [315]. Since, however, the latter also had a son named *Nṯr-wsr*, the relationship is far from certain. The two tombs are likely to have been roughly contemporary. Date: Neuserre–Djedkare.

[295] *NḎM-JB* Cairo, *CG*, 1443.

Provenience? Userkaf is mentioned, but the stela could, of course, be much later. Date: V–VI.

[296] *NḎM-JB* Cairo, *CG*, 219.

Abydos. Borchardt suggests a Sixth Dynasty date. Date: VI (?).

[297] *RꜤ-WR* Junker, *Giza*, III, 121, 217–23.

Giza 5270. A large mastaba immediately to the east of the cemetery *en échelon*. It was designed from the beginning for an interior L-shaped chapel with two false doors and a northern niche on the eastern face. A serdab was built against the back of the mastaba of *Ḏꜣtjj* [589];

the serdab chamber of *Sšm-nfr* [478] was later built against the back of the mastaba of *Rʿ-wr*. He was presumably a son of the eldest *Sšm-nfr* in the western cemetery at Giza [476]. Date: mid-V.

[298] *Rʿ-WR*

Lepsius, *Denkmäler*, II, 84; *Erg.*, pp. 25–26; Junker, *Giza*, III, 223–35.

Giza 5470 = Lepsius No. 32. A mastaba somewhat smaller than the last with an L-shaped chapel with one false door and a northern niche. A mastaba was later built against this on the south, and then a serdab and court were added to the east of the main mastaba of *Rʿ-wr* and were built against this later mastaba; one presumes that a considerable interval elapsed between the erection of the main mastaba and the completion of the complex. *Rʿ-wr* was probably a son of *Sšm-nfr* [477] and thus a generation later than his namesake above [297]. A sealing of Djedkare was found in the shaft. Date: end V.

[299] *Rʿ-WR*

Lepsius, *Denkmäler*, II, 95e; Selim Hassan, *Giza*, V, 293–97.

Giza, Khafre cemetery. A mastaba with a pillared room and serdab built against the east face. A sloping passage leads to the burial chamber. Reisner, *Giza*, I, 152, dates to "late Dyn. IV or Dyn. V." The burial chamber was decorated, and its shape, with the north–south orientation and the shaft entering it by the east wall, all would indicate a much later date. Cf. Junker, *Giza*, VIII, 7. Date: VI.

[300] *Rʿ-WR*

Selim Hassan, *Giza*, I, 1–61, pls. 1–41; Cairo, *CG*, 197–200, 216–17, 280, 287, 318, 350, 365–367, 815; 1675; also some statues in the Brooklyn Museum.

Giza, Khafre cemetery. A vast, meandering chapel complex, with numerous passages, chambers, courts, and serdabs, ending in a rock-cut, cruciform offering chamber. It has evidently been fitted into the space left between several earlier mastabas. The biographical inscription refers to an event which took place under the reign of Neferirkare. It does not, of course, follow that the tomb was erected under his reign. The complex plan might indicate a slightly later date. Date: Neferirkare—mid-V.

[301] (canceled)

[302] *Rʿ-PTḤ-MR* — Mariette, *Mastabas*, C 22.
Saqqara, mid-north No. 51. A mastaba with an L-shaped (or modified cruciform?) chapel, a corridor along its east face, and a serdab at the southern end of the corridor. In the serdab was found a statue pair of a man and his wife, not the owner of the mastaba. Date: V or later.

[303] *Rʿ-M-KȝJ* — Mariette, *Mastabas*, D 3; Metropolitan Museum of Art No. 08.201.1 = Hayes, *The Scepter of Egypt*, I, 94–102.
Saqqara, north of Step Pyramid No. 80. A mastaba with a short corridor chapel. *Rʿ-m-kȝj* bore the title of *zȝ nswt smsw n ẖt.f* and *ḥrj-tp Nḫb n jt.f*. According to generally accepted ideas (see above under [175]) this would definitely prove that he was an actual king's son. However, Nims ("Some Notes on the Family of Mereruka," *JAOS*, LVIII, 638–47) shows that *Mrjj-Ttj* [189], who bore the titles *zȝ nswt n ẖt.f* and *ẖrj-ḥbt n jt.f* was definitely the son of *Mrrw-kȝ* [197] and not of a king. If this rule is then of dubious validity in the Sixth Dynasty, we have to consider the possibility of its also being inoperative in the late Fifth. Since the tomb stands in the cemetery of Djedkare, *Rʿ-m-kȝj* may, but need not, have been a son of his. The name *Jzzj*, without a cartouche, occurs in one of the estate names: it could be the second name of Djedkare. Date: end V.

[304] *Rʿ-NFR* — Mariette, *Mastabas*, C 5; Cairo, *CG*, 18–19.
Saqqara, mid-north No. 40. A mastaba with a brick outside chapel and a brick casing. The mastaba of *Ptḥ-ḥtp* and *Ptḥ-ḥtp Dšr*, [158], [159], was built against it on the south. The well known statues of *Rʿ-nfr* in the Cairo Museum came from this tomb. Date: early V.

[305] *Rʿ-ḤR-Kȝ: JPJ* — Jéquier, *Tombeaux de particuliers*, pp. 121–25, pl. 17.
South Saqqara, near Pepi II. Date: Pepi II.

[306] *Rʿ-ḤR-TP: JTJ* — Firth and Gunn, *Teti Pyramid Cemeteries*, p. 212, pl. 77.
Saqqara, Teti area. *Rʿ-ḥr-tp* describes himself as revered before the vizier *Kȝ-gm-nj* [548], which would date his monument to a later time. The archeological circumstances of the finding of

this tomb are rather confused. Date: mid-VI or later.

[307] *Rʿ-ḤTP* Petrie, *Medum*, pls. 9–15; Cairo, *CG*, 3. Meydum. One of the large brick mastabas of the Fourth Dynasty cemetery. Date: early IV.

[308] *Rʿ-ḤTP* Mariette, *Mastabas*, C 12. Saqqara. A mastaba with the chapel composed of a large square room and corridors. Date: mid-V or later?

[309] *Rʿ-ḤTP* Unpublished. Giza 4241. A small, squarish mastaba built against that of *Snfrw-snb* [451]. It has several shafts, a short corridor chapel on the east with a niche; to the north of this an interior, L-shaped chapel with one niche was later cut (? if I interpret the plan correctly). Date: end V or later.

[310] *Rʿ-ḤTP* Selim Hassan, *Giza*, V, 206. Giza, Khafre cemetery. Found out of place. Date: ?

[311] *Rʿ-ḤTP* Selim Hassan, *Giza*, VII, 81–84. Giza, Khafre cemetery. A mastaba with an L-shaped interior chapel with a single false door, more or less in the middle of the east face of the mastaba, and a single northern niche. An elaborate outside chapel with a pillared room was added. A sloping passage leads from the inside chapel to a burial chamber. *Rʿ-ḥtp* was a *zꜣ nswt*, but in view of the archeological data, I would hesitate to assign this mastaba to the Fourth Dynasty. Date: mid-V or probably later.

[312] *Rʿ-ḤTP* Mariette, *Mastabas*, C 24; Cairo, *CG*, 127, 130, 163, 172, 182–85, 187–88, 192, 194, 205, 303, 312. Saqqara, near north No. 66. A mastaba with an east–west offering chamber or alcove reached by a corridor from the north. Borchardt ascribes the statues to the Fifth Dynasty. Date: V (or later?).

[313] *Rʿ-ḪW.F* Selim Hassan, *Giza*, VII, 95–99. Giza, Khafre cemetery. A small mastaba largely filled by a modified cruciform chapel with two false doors. A masonry block behind it, which is entered on the plan as a separate unit but contains the only shafts in the area which could correspond to the shafts described as belonging

to this tomb, is built against another mastaba. Date: V or later.

[314] *Rʿ-Ḫ̮W.F*
Selim Hassan, "Excavations at Saqqara (1937–1938)," *ASAE*, XXXVIII, 506.
Saqqara, Unis area. A brick mastaba south of that of *Ḥtp* [352]. Date: VI.

[315] *Rʿ-ŠPSS*
Lepsius, *Denkmäler*, II, 60–64 *bis*; *Erg.*, pls. 39a–c, 41–42; Quibell, *Excavations at Saqqara*, III, 23–24, 79–82, pl. 61.2; *Urkunden*, I, 179–80.
Saqqara, north of Step Pyramid, Lepsius No. 16 = QS 902. This tomb was apparently only partly seen by Lepsius, who published the only plan available to me. The mastaba had a complex chapel with a pillared hall and statue shrines. In the portion published by Lepsius, his highest title is *jmj-rꜣ Šmʿ*; in the portion uncovered by Quibell was found the copy of the letter sent to him by Djedkare, in which he is addressed as vizier. This is one of the rare cases in which a man's position changed during the construction of his tomb; cf. *Sšm-nfr* [478]. *Rʿ-špss* was the father of *Pr-nb* [142] and either the father or the son of *Nṯr-wsr* [294]. He was evidently a contemporary of Djedkare, and the tomb was erected during his reign. Date: Djedkare.

[316] *RWD-Kꜣ*
Selim Hassan, *Giza*, VI^3, 125–32.
Giza, Khafre cemetery. A large mastaba with two niches in the eastern face. There was no interior chapel, and the remains of an exterior one have disappeared. The mastaba of *Jn-kꜣ.f* [42] was erected very close to the eastern face of *Rwd-kꜣ*'s mastaba. At first sight it might appear that [42] was built first and the mastaba of *Rwd-kꜣ* backed against it so as to provide a corridor chapel. However, there seems to be no trace of there ever having been any walls to close off the corridor; and the structure at the north which now forms an entrance to the "corridor chapel" of *Rwd-kꜣ* is evidently, if Selim Hassan's plans are correct, later than both mastabas. It seems that the mastaba of *Rwd-kꜣ* is older, and that the mastaba of *Jn-kꜣ.f* was built later, either displacing a former exterior chapel on the east of the mastaba of *Rwd-kꜣ* or possibly built close because there had

never been any. *Rwd-kꜣ* had a son, also named *Jn-kꜣ.f*, who was a sculptor and may have been the sculptor of that name who decorated the tombs of *Nb-m-ꜣḫt* [248] and queen *Mr-s-ʿnḫ* III in the late Fourth Dynasty. The mastaba is drawn with several shafts, but since the area was used as a cemetery at a later period, some of them may have nothing to do with the original structure. Date: early V.

[317] *RWḎ* — Fisher, *The Minor Cemetery at Giza*, pp. 34–35, 141–43.
Giza 2086. A mastaba with a corridor, an alcove with a pillar and one other room. It was built against Giza 2085 which was itself built against earlier tombs. Date: VI.

[318] *RWḎ-Kꜣ* — British Museum No. 1268–69 = *Hieroglyphic Texts*, Vol. I, pl. 20.
Giza. Priesthood of Khafre. Date: ?

[319] *RMNW-Kꜣ: JMJ* — Selim Hassan, *Giza*, II, 169–78.
Giza, Khafre cemetery. A small mastaba with an alcove for the false door. It was built against the same mastaba as that of *Ḫnw* [388] in a cluster of small, later tombs. Date: VI.

[320] *RTJ* — Zaki Saad, "A Preliminary Report on the Excavations at Saqqara 1939–1940," *ASAE*, XL, 682; also unpublished data.
Saqqara, Unis area. A small, squarish chapel on the north of the court in front of *Mḥw* [202]. Probably identical with the *Rtj*, who is the eldest son of *Jjj* [18] in his nearby tomb. Date: mid-VI or later.

[321] *RDJ.N-PTḤ* — Petrie, *Gizeh and Rifeh*, pl. 7a.
South Giza. A lintel from a rock-cut tomb. Date: ?

[322] *RDJ-N.S* — Unpublished.
Giza 2156. Note that in the numbering system used in Reisner, *Giza*, Vol. I, the number 2156 is used both for the tomb of the younger *Kꜣ-n-nswt* [532], an annex to a tomb which in that book still bears the number 2155 but later (Junker, *Giza*, Vol. XII, map 4) was changed to 4870, and this tomb, a miserable, small mastaba with an alcove for the false door, which was built against Giza 2220. Date: VI.

[323] *HNQW: ḪTTJ* — Davies, *The Rock Tombs of Deir el-Gebrawi*, Vol. II, pl. 28.

Deir el-Gebrawi No. 39. It is clear from Davies' remarks, p. 31, that this is not one of the first tombs in the hillside, since it broke into an older gallery. Davies himself feels uncertain as to the relative dating of this and the other decorated tombs at this site as compared with *Jbj* [32] and his son *Ḏʿw* [592], who are both securely dated to the reign of Pepi II. Since his arguments for the earlier dating (pp. 38–41) are based on the names only, whereas those for a later date are archeological, I feel there can be little doubt that this tomb and the others in the northern group were later. Date: end VI or later.

[324] *HNQW: JJ-[. . .]F* — Davies, *The Rock Tombs of Deir el-Gebrawi*, Vol. II, pls. 23–36.
Deir el-Gebrawi No. 67. This tomb belongs to the same group as the last, and according to Davies, p. 38, it should be a bit earlier. Date: end VI or later.

[325] *Ḥꜣ M-Kꜣ J* — Junker, *Giza*, VII, 253.
Giza, western cemetery. An architrave found out of place. Junker dates it to the Sixth Dynasty. Date: VI.

[326] *ḤꜣSJ* — *Urkunden*, I, 151–52 = Cairo, *CG*, 1649.
Provenience? The use of plural strokes indicates a relatively late date in the Old Kingdom. Date: VI or later.

[327] *ḤꜣGJ* — Unpublished.
Giza 2352. A smallish, free-standing mastaba between the cemetery *en échelon* and the *Snḏm-jb* family group. Djedkare is mentioned. Date: end V or later.

[328] *ḤWTJ* — Mariette, *Mastabas*, B 9; Cairo, *CG*, 64; 1392.
Saqqara, north of Step Pyramid (?) No. 88. A brick mastaba with possibly a modified cruciform chapel. Its location is rather uncertain. Date: ?

[329] *ḤBJ* — Junker, *Giza*, IX, 119–21.
Giza, western cemetery. A mastaba with a corridor chapel. It was built against mastaba D 100 and is the third member in another chain. Date: VI.

[330] (canceled)

[331] *ḤM-JWNW* — Junker, *Giza*, I, 122–62; Smith, "The Origin of

Some Unidentified Old Kingdom Reliefs," *AJA*, XLVI, 520–30.
Giza 4000. This great mastaba was the starting point for laying out the 4000 cemetery and is certainly of the time of Khufu. Quarry marks on the masonry indicate that the construction took place during the eighth to the tenth numbering. *Ḥm-Jwnw* was probably the son of *Nfr-mꜣꜥt* [260]. Date: Khufu.

[332] *ḤMW* Selim Hassan, *Giza*, VI³, 81–91.
Giza, Khafre cemetery. A mastaba with a corridor and alcove, also several shafts. A man of the same name occurs as son in the neighboring tomb of *Kꜣ-dwꜣ* [550]. Both of these mastabas were built against the same older tomb. *Kꜣ-dwꜣ* had an interior L-shaped chapel with two false doors and a northern niche. When the tomb of *Ḥmw* was added on the east, the resulting corridor in front of the mastaba of *Kꜣ-dwꜣ* was provided with a door on the south. *Ḥmw* was a priest of Menkauhor. Date: end V or later.

[333] *ḤM-Rꜥ: JZJ* Davies, *The Rock Tombs of Deir el-Gebrawi*, Vol. II, pls. 17–21.
Deir el-Gebrawi No. 72. For the date see the remarks under [323]. Davies, pp. 38–40, gives good reasons for supposing this to be one of the earliest tombs in the northern group. A biographical inscription in the tomb of *Hnqw* [324] (Davies, pl. 25, l. 22) indicates that he became ruler (*ḥqꜣ*) of the nome at the same time as his brother *Ḥm-Rꜥ*. The two tombs are close to each other; the identification seems reasonably certain. Date: end VI or later.

[334] *ḤNW* Cairo, *CG*, 1411.
Provenience? A false door with cavetto cornice and molding surrounded by an outside frame. Borchardt dates to the Sixth Dynasty or later. Date: VI or later.

[335] *ḤNNJ* Junker, *Giza*, XI, 70.
Giza, south of Great Pyramid. A small mastaba with an east–west offering chamber built against another tomb itself built against the outer court of *Sḫm-kꜣ* [467]. Date: VI.

[336] *ḤNNJ* Maspero, "Trois années de fouilles," *MMAFC*, I, 208.

Saqqara, west of Pepi I. *Ḥnnj* held office at a pyramid the last written element of which was *nfr*. Unfortunately this can be reconstructed to fit the names of either of the pyramids of Djedkare, Pepi I, or Mernere, all three of which were in the immediate vicinity. Date: VI.

[337] *ḤNNJ* — Jéquier, *Tombeaux de particuliers*, pp. 27–30. South Saqqara, near Pepi II. Date: VI 4.

[338] *ḤNNJ* — Ahmed Kamal, "Fouilles à Dara et à Qoçéîr el-Amarna," *ASAE*, XII, 133.
Dara. Fragments of a wooden coffin with an offering list inscribed on it found in the necropolis surrounding the brick tomb of an obscure local king, Khui, who must date at the very earliest from the last years of the Sixth Dynasty. Date: end VI or later.

[338A] *ḤN-Kꜣ* — Berlin Museum No. 7334 = Schäfer, *Aegyptische Inschriften*, I, 70; Von Bergmann, "Inschriftliche Denkmäler der Sammlung ägyptischer Alterthümer des Österr. Kaiserhauses," *Recueil de travaux*, VII, 179.
Meidum. The publications give no indications for a date except the fact that *Ḥn-kꜣ* was an official at the two pyramids of Snefru, which still leaves the bulk of the Old Kingdom as a possible range of time. Date: ?

[339] *ḤNTJ* — Spiegelberg and Pörtner, *Aegyptische Grabsteine und Denksteine aus süddeutschen Sammlungen*, Vol. I, pl. 1.
Provenience? Now in Karlsruhe. Spiegelberg dates to the Sixth Dynasty. Date: VI or later.

[340] *ḤRWJ* — Newberry, "The Inscribed Tombs of Ekhmîm," *LAAA*, IV, 105.
Akhmim No. 7. Date: VI or later.

[341] *ḤRWJ* — Newberry, "The Inscribed Tombs of Ekhmîm," *LAAA*, IV, 109–10.
Akhmim No. 13. Date: VI or later.

[342] *ḤRWJ* — Newberry, "The Inscribed Tombs of Ekhmîm," *LAAA*, IV, 112.
Akhmim No. 19. It is highly unlikely that these three high officials of the nome of Akhmim, two of whom bore the title of vizier ([340] and [342]) were contemporary, but there is no way of determining their sequence from the published data. Date: VI or later.

[343] *ḤR-MRW: MRRJ* Unpublished.
Saqqara, Unis area. A mastaba with a corridor chapel with several false doors. Offering chamber? It was situated immediately to the north of the mastaba of *ꜣḫt-ḥtp Ḥmj* [14A], but I am unable to tell from the notes available to me whether it was built against it or not. Date: VI.

[344] *ḤR-NḪT* Jean Sainte Fare Garnot, "Les mastabas," *Fouilles Franco-Polonaises*, I, 48–51.
Edfu, No. VI. This mastaba appears to be later than mastaba No. II (*ibid.*, pp. 36, 50, n. 3), which Garnot dates to the reign of Pepi I or Mernere. That would place this tomb at least in the reign of Pepi II. Date: Pepi II or later.

[345] *ḤR-ḪW.F* *Urkunden*, I, 120–31; De Morgan, *Catalogue des monuments et inscriptions de l'Égypte antique*, I, 162–74.
Aswan. *Ḥr-ḫw.f* served Mernere and Pepi II. The well known letter sent him by the latter king in the year of the second numbering addresses him by titles considerably below the highest ones he has in the tomb itself. It would seem probable then that the tomb was built some time later. Date: Pepi II, first half.

[346] *ḤRJ-Š.F-ŠMꜣ* Jéquier, "Tombes de particuliers," *ASAE*, XXXV, 133–34.
South Saqqara, near Pepi II. Date: Pepi II.

[347] *ḤZJ* Selim Hassan, *Giza*, III, 245–56.
Giza, Khafre cemetery. A mastaba with a corridor chapel and five shafts, situated to the east of the Street of Priests and built against a tomb built against the easternmost mastaba in that street. Date: VI.

[348] *ḤZJ* Junker, *Giza*, VI, 164–68.
Giza, western cemetery. A small mastaba with an exterior corridor or court and an east–west alcove. It is at least the fourth in a string of mastabas built against each other in the group of small, later mastabas between the central and northern sections of the western cemetery. Date: VI.

[349] *ḤZZJ* Maspero, *Le Musée Égyptien*, I, 19–21, pl. 22.
Saqqara, apparently from one of the areas north of the Step Pyramid. Now in the Cairo Museum (Journal d'Entrée No. 34568). An elongated false door with cornice and molding which

Maspero dates to the Fifth Dynasty. The cornice is hardly likely to appear much before the middle of that dynasty (cf. Reisner, *Giza*, I, 378). Date: mid-V or later.

[349A] *Ḥ̣ZZJ* — Cairo, *CG*, 1407.
Provenience? A rather crude false door. Priesthood of Pepi I. Date: Pepi I or later.

[350] *ḤKNJ-H̱NMW* — Selim Hassan, *Giza*, VII, 49–52.
Giza, Khafre cemetery. A mastaba with a north–south corridor and east–west alcove built against a rock face. The only inscriptions found were the long strings of titles on the limestone sarcophagus. Date: mid-V or later.

[351] *ḤTP* — Mariette, *Mastabas*, C 2.
Saqqara, northeast group No. 8. This mastaba was built of stone and had three niches for false doors on the east. Date: mid-V or later?

[352] *ḤTP* — Selim Hassan, "Excavations at Saqqara 1937–1938," *ASAE*, XXXVIII, 503–5.
Saqqara, southeast of the entrance to the Step Pyramid, possibly already within the Unis area. This mastaba had a complex interior chapel including a court. A sloping passage leads from the south to the burial chamber. The sarcophagus was carved and provided with inscriptions. Date: end V or later.

[353] *ḤTPJ* — Selim Hassan, *Giza*, VII, 101–5.
Giza, Khafre cemetery. A large mastaba only partly excavated. No traces remain of a chapel, only two niches in the eastern face of the mastaba. The sarcophagus found in the burial chamber was extensively decorated and had lengthy inscriptions, including an offering list. Date: end V or later.

[354] *ḤTP-JB* — Lutz, *Statues*, p. 24; Lutz, *Steles*, pls. 6-8.
Giza 1032. A small tomb subsidiary to a minor mastaba in the maze of small tombs west of Giza 2000. Date: VI.

[355] *ḤTP.N-PTḤ* — Unpublished.
Giza 2350. A medium-sized, free-standing mastaba more or less on a line with that of *Rʿ-wr* [297] and *Pḥ.n-Ptḥ* between the cemetery *en échelon* and the *Snḏm-jb* group. The tomb of *Ḥ3gj* is immediately to the east [327]. Date: mid-V or later.

[356] *ḤTP.N-PTḤ* — Lepsius, *Denkmäler*, II, 71–72; *Erg.*, pls. 9, 10a–b.
Giza, northeastern end of western cemetery. A mastaba with a corridor chapel and pillared room erected to the north of the *Snḏm-jb* group. A considerable mass of tombs was built against it later. King Djedkare is mentioned. Date: early VI.

[357] *ḤTP-ḤR-ꜣḪTJ* — Mariette, *Mastabas*, D 60; Mohr, *The Mastaba of Hetep-her-akhti*; Boeser, *Beschreibung der aegyptischen Sammlung des Niederländischen Reichsmuseums der Altertümer in Leiden*, pls. 5–21.
Saqqara, west of Step Pyramid. A mastaba with a long east–west chapel with its entrance on the east. Priesthood at the solar temple of Neuserre. Date: Neuserre or later.

[358] *ḤTP-ḤR-N-PTḤ* — *Urkunden*, I, 231; Helck, *Untersuchungen*, p. 112, n. 5.
Provenience? A doorjamb, now in the Cairo Museum with a most astonishing collection of inexpertly archaized titles. In addition to old titles of the Third Dynasty we find spellings of more current titles attempting to arouse the impression of antiquity. Some of the titles appear to be complete inventions on the part of *Ḥtp-ḥr-n-Ptḥ*. As Helck indicates, an archaizing text of this type is not likely to be earlier than the end of the Fifth Dynasty. It remains to be seen whether the ranking of titles in a text as wilful as this is of any value to our problem. Date: end V or later.

[358A] *ḤTP-Kꜣ* — Koefoed-Petersen, *Recueil des inscriptions hiéroglyphiques de la Glyptothèque Ny Carlsberg*, p. 76 = Ny Carlsberg Glyptothek No. 25.
Provenience? A priesthood of Userkaf. Date: V–VI.

[358B] *Ḥtp-kꜣ* — Unpublished.
Saqqara, Unis area. The inscriptions of the grandson of *Mḥw* [202] which were later added on the eastern wall of the court of the tomb of his grandfather. He was a priest of Pepi I and Pepi II. Date: Pepi II.

[359] *ḤTP-Kꜣ-ḪWFW* — Mariette, *Mastabas*, Gi; Cairo, *CG*, 1324.
Saqqara. Borchardt wonders if this piece could be of the Fifth Dynasty. Date: ?

[360] *Ḫꜥ-BꜣW-PTḤ* — Mariette, *Mastabas*, D 42; Oriental Institute Nos. 10810, 10815 (unpublished).
Saqqara, northwest No. 19. A mastaba with a series of interior chambers and a pillared portico. Priesthood of Neuserre. Date: Neuserre or later.

[361] *Ḫꜥ-BꜣW-ḪNMW: BJW* — Jéquier, *Le monument funéraire de Pepi II*, III, 62–67, pls. 52, 55.
South Saqqara, near Pepi II. A man with a great many titles, the bulk of which are listed in a fashion that does not permit ranking. His name was entered secondarily in the reliefs of the temple of Pepi II, and with relatively low titles. He eventually became vizier. Kees, "Beiträge zur Geschichte des Vezirats im Alten Reich," *Nachr. Gött.*, N.F. IV, phil.-hist. Klasse, 48, believes that archeological evidence also indicates that this tomb was erected later than the complex around *Mrjjrꜥ-jꜣm* [184]. Date: Pepi II, second half.

[362] *ḪꜥFRꜥ-ꜥNḪ* — Lepsius, *Denkmäler*, II, 8–11; *Erg.*, pls. 28a–c.
Giza 7948 = Lepsius No. 75. A rock-cut tomb at the eastern end of the eastern cemetery. Reisner, *Giza*, I, 314, dates it to the Fifth or Sixth Dynasties. Date: V or later.

[363] *Ḫꜥ-MRR-PTḤ* — Mariette, *Mastabas*, C 4.
Saqqara, near north No. 68. A mastaba with the false door in an alcove in the east face. Date: V or later.

[364] *ḪWJ* — Quibell, *Excavations at Saqqara*, I, 22, pl. 14.
Saqqara, east of the pyramid of Teti. One of the row of Tenth Dynasty tombs uncovered by Quibell. *Ḫwj* was a priest of Teti and a physician with several interesting titles. Date: X.

[365] *ḪWJ* — Zaki Saad, "Preliminary Report on the Excavations of the Department of Antiquities at Saqqara 1942–1943," *ASAE*, Vol. XLIII, pl. 44; Drioton, "Description sommaire des chapelles funéraires de la VIe dynastie," *ASAE*, XLIII, 502–4.
Saqqara, Teti area. A mastaba situated to the north of that of *Wr-nwnw* [117]. It had a lintel with a series of figures of the owner. Priesthoods of Teti and Pepi I. Date: mid-VI or later.

[366] *ḪWJ* — Mariette, *Catalogue général des monuments d'Abydos*, No. 525.

Abydos. The general date of this monument is hardly in doubt since *Ḫwj* had a son whose name was compounded with that of Pepi II. His name is an exceedingly common one; his wife was called *Nbt*, also a common name. However, these are the names of the parents of the viziers *Jdj* [73A] and *Ḏʿw* [591] and the parents-in-law of Pepi I. Despite the frequency of the names, it was only natural to suggest the identity of the owner of the monument being discussed here with the latter *Ḫwj*; see Kees, "Beiträge zur Geschichte des Vezirats im Alten Reich," *Nachr. Gött.*, N.F. IV, phil.-hist. Klasse, 40. However, there are certain arguments which should induce us to treat this identification with caution, quite aside from the common occurrence of both names. They were already raised by Mariette in his publication. First of all, the completely different titles of both husband and wife on this monument and on the monuments of *Jdj* and *Ḏʿw* should lead one to hesitate. Second, Mariette No. 525 lists four children of *Ḫwj*. It would be surprising that of the highly distinguished children of the *Ḫwj* of No. 523 (*Ḏʿw* and *ʿnḫ-n.s-Mrjjrʿ*) and 526 (*Jdj*) only the exceedingly common name *Jdj* should recur on the monument of the supposed father. Mariette concludes, "Il est donc probable que nous avons affaire ici à un *Khua* et à une *Nebet* qui, . . . se sont appelés plus tard comme le beau-père et la belle-mère d'Apappus. Il ne serait pas difficile de réunir d'autres exemples de cet usage." Date: Pepi II.

[367] *ḪWJ* De Morgan, *Catalogue des monuments et inscriptions de l'Égypte antique*, I, 157; Newberry, "Three Old Kingdom Travellers to Byblos and Pwenet," *JEA*, XXIV, 182; Griffith, "Notes on a Tour in Upper Egypt," *PSBA*, XI, 228–34, pl. 1. Aswan. An inscription in this tomb indicates that *Ḫwj* was a contemporary of *Ṯṯj* [575]. This *Ṯṯj* (cf. Newberry, *op. cit.*, p. 183) almost certainly left an undated graffito in the Wadi Hammamat and may possibly also be referred to in another one dated to the eighteenth numbering of Pepi I, though the title differs. Date: VI, perhaps Mernere—early Pepi II.

[368] *ḪWW* British Museum No. 199 = *Hieroglyphic Texts*, Vol. I, pl. 21.
From "Memphis." Date: ?

[369] *ḪWWJ* Jean Sainte Fare Garnot, "Les Mastabas," *Fouilles Franco-Polonaises*, I, 38–41.
Edfu, No. IV. A slab with a very crudely incised text comes from this mastaba. Could well be from the First Intermediate. Date: VI or later.

[370] *ḪW-BꜣWJ* Jéquier, *La pyramide d'Oudjebten*, p. 27.
South Saqqara, near Pepi II. A *stèle-maison* found near the entrance to the annex to the temple of Queen *Wḏbtn*. Date: Pepi II.

[371] *ḪW-BꜣWJ* Maspero, "Trois années de fouilles," *MMAFC*, I, 199, pls. 1–4.; Fischer, *JAOS* LXXIV, 31–32.
South Saqqara, near Pepi II. Priesthood of Pepi II. The owner of this tomb is almost certainly the same person as the owner of the memorial stela in the previous entry, particularly if the hopelessly garbled title reproduced in type by Maspero () is emended to read *ḥrj-tp ꜥꜣ Tꜣ-wr*, one of the titles of [370]. Date: Pepi II.

[372] *ḪWFW-ꜥNḪ* Reisner, *Giza*, I, 503–8, pls. 65a–b, 66a–f, 67a–e.
Giza 4520. A core mastaba later converted by breaking an L-shaped chapel into the center of the eastern face and adding an outside stone chapel. The mastaba was left uncased. The position of the interior chapel is not what would be expected for the earlier Fifth Dynasty. The tomb has been dated to the time of Userkaf by the excavators on the basis of a sealing of his found in the burial chamber (Reisner and Smith, *Giza*, II, 52). However, as we have already stated several times, this only gives us a *terminus a quo*. Smith, *HESP*, pp. 71–72, discusses the statue of *Ḫwfw-ꜥnḫ* and his wife and decides that it belongs to the second half of the Fifth Dynasty. Since he accepts the dating of the tomb itself to the time of Userkaf, he supposes that it was placed in the chapel at a much later date. All things considered, it seems probable that the date of the tomb is approximately that of the statue. Date: later V.

[373] *ḪWFW-ʿNḪ* Maspero, *Le Musée Égyptien*, I, 18–19, pl. 21. Giza. A granite sarcophagus decorated with elaborate false doors and the name and titles of the owner. It was excavated by Mariette and its exact provenience is apparently unknown. The lid has a curved top and heavy bosses at each end. According to Junker, *Giza*, II, 23, this would certainly indicate a later date than the Fourth Dynasty. Date: V–VI.

[373A] *ḪWFW-ʿNḪ* Labib Habachi, "A Group of Unpublished Old and Middle Kingdom Graffiti on Elephantine," *WZKM*, LIV, 55–71.
A graffito on Elephantine. Labib Habachi dates it to the Fourth or Fifth Dynasties basing his judgment on the quality of the carving. Date: ?

[374] *ḪWFW-ḤTP* Lepsius, *Denkmäler*, *II*, 34c; Mariette, *Mastabas*, p. 539; also unpublished data.
Giza, Lepsius No. 76. A rock-cut tomb situated in the cliff to the east of the eastern cemetery. It had a long east–west corridor leading to a north–south offering chamber. Considering the location, it is hardly likely to belong to the earliest period of the cemetery. Date: V or later.

[375] *ḪWFW-Ḫʿ.F* Daressy, "Le mastaba de Khâ-f-Khoufou à Gizeh," *ASAE*, XVI, 257–67; Reisner, "The Servants of the *Ka*," *BMFA*, XXXII, 1–9; Capart, *L'art Égyptien*, Vol. I, pl. 26; Reisner and Smith, *Giza*, II, 10, Fig. 11.
Giza 7130 + 7140. One of the mastabas of the nucleus cemetery east of the pyramid of Khufu. The owner was presumably a son of Khufu. The core was converted to admit an interior chapel (Reisner, *Giza*, I, 206). Capart insists (*op. cit.*, p. 7) that the inscription he photographed in his pl. 26 comes from this tomb, and expresses his astonishment that Daressy should not have noticed it. The titles, however, are not otherwise recorded for this *Ḫwfw-ḫʿ.f* elsewhere in his tomb but do occur in the mastaba of *Ḫwfw-ḫʿ.f* [376] who owned the neighboring mastaba Giza 7150. Capart's photograph does not show enough of the surroundings to permit one to check with certainty, but I am convinced he confused the two. Date: mid—end IV.

[376] *H̱WFW-H̱ʿ.F* — Capart, *L'art Égyptien*, Vol. I, pl. 26; mostly unpublished data.
Giza 7150. A smallish mastaba built just to the south of the last. It had an L-shaped interior chapel at the northern end of the eastern face, a relatively uncommon position. The owner lived from the time of Menkaure to that of Neuserre. As stated above, the photograph which Capart ascribed to [375] probably represents a corner of this mastaba. Date: Neuserre.

[377] *H̱WFW-SNB* — Junker, *Giza*, VII, 117–26.
Giza, western cemetery. A smallish mastaba to the east of the cemetery *en échelon*. It was originally free-standing, having several shafts and a chapel composed of a north–south corridor and a square room with a pillar. Date: end V or later.

[378] *H̱WFW-SNB* — Junker, *Giza*, VII, 126–33.
Giza, western cemetery. A small mastaba with the main axis east–west. It has several shafts and a short corridor chapel opening from the south. It was built just to the east of [377] and probably belongs to his son. Junker dates both this mastaba and that of his father to the end of the Sixth Dynasty, but since a considerable number of later mastabas were built against the two, while they themselves were built on an independent site, an earlier date might be possible. Date: VI.

[379] *H̱W.N-PTḤ* — Selim Hassan, *Giza*, VII, 35–41.
Giza, Khafre cemetery. A mastaba with multiple shafts and a corridor chapel opening from the south. It was built against the rock face in front of the window of an uninscribed rock-cut tomb. The drawings and plans published do not permit one to decide which of the two took account of which in its construction. Date: end V or later.

[380] *H̱W.N-PTḤ* — Mariette, *Mastabas*, B 8; Cairo, *CG*, 1295, 1297, 1513.
Saqqara. A mastaba with a corridor chapel and several false doors. Date: mid-V or later.

[381] *H̱W.N-ḤR: H̱WJ* — Daressy, "La nécropole des grands prêtres d'Héliopolis sous l'Ancien Empire," *ASAE*, XVI, 209–11.

Heliopolis. A tomb with a decorated burial chamber, apparently much like that of *Mrw* [191]. Date: VI.

[381A] *Ḫ̮W-NḪRJ* Daressy, "La nécropole des grands prêtres d'Héliopolis sous l'Ancien Empire," *ASAE*, XVI, 212.
Heliopolis. An obelisk found out of place, possibly mentioning a priesthood of Pepi I, among other titles. Date: Pepi I or later.

[382] *Ḫ̮W.N-H̱NMW* De Morgan, *Catalogue des monuments et inscriptions de l'Égypte antique*, I, 197–99.
Aswan. A tomb with priesthoods of Pepi II. Date: Pepi II.

[383] *Ḫ̮W-NS* Lepsius, *Denkmäler*, II, 105–9.
Zawiyet el-Maiyitin No. 2. The tomb was dated by Lepsius to the Sixth Dynasty (why?). The scenes show considerable parallelism, both in subject matter and in arrangement of the scenes on the walls, with the nearby tomb of *N-ʿnḫ-Ppjj* [211], which is clearly to be dated to the Sixth Dynasty, and with the scenes in the tombs of *Wr-jr.n.j* [114] and *Srf-kꜣ* [457] at Sheikh Said (about forty-one kilometers to the south), which are generally dated to the Fifth. It would appear that the decoration of these tombs was definitely influenced by each other, either due to direct copying, or more probably due to their being designed by the same group of artists. The dating of the Sheikh Said tombs is largely based on the royal priesthoods mentioned therein, and is thus open to question; they could perhaps also date from the Sixth Dynasty. Smith, *HESP*, pp. 215–17, remarks on the similarities, but decides to date *Ḫ̮w-ns* to a period later than that of the above-mentioned tombs at Sheikh Said on the basis of the wider range of the repertory of scenes in the former. He says, "Although all of these subjects (except spear-making), can be traced back to Dyn. V originals, they are a regular part of the scenic equipment of the late Dyn. VI provincial tombs." I would be inclined to be very much on the cautious side here, and leave considerable leeway in the dating of these tombs. Date: mid-V—first half VI.

[384] *Ḫ W-NS* — De Morgan, *Catalogue des monuments et inscriptions de l'Égypte antique*, I, 158–62.
Aswan. Date: VI.

[384A] *Ḫ W-Tꜣ* — Selim Hassan, *Giza*, III, 4.
Giza, Khafre cemetery. A small rock-cut mastaba with a corridor chapel. The relationship to the neighboring tombs seems unclear. Date: mid-V or later.

[385] *Ḫ PṮT* — Junker, *Giza*, VI, 231.
Giza, western cemetery. Inscribed fragments found out of place but probably belonging to one of the small, later mastabas in the area. The pieces were found near the core mastaba Giza 4860. Date: VI.

[386] *Ḫ MT.NW* — Lepsius, *Denkmäler*, II, 26; Mariette, *Mastabas*, pp. 517 ff.
Giza 5210 = Lepsius No. 43. A medium-sized mastaba with an exterior stone chapel, built to the east of (and apparently later than) the mastaba of Prince *Dwꜣ-n-Rꜥ* (Giza 5110), which appears to be later than the original middle cemetery and precedes the cemetery *en échelon*. *Ḫmt.nw* states that he served Prince *Kꜣ-wꜥb*, his wife *Ḥtp-ḥr.s*, and their daughter, queen *Mr-s-ꜥnḫ* III, in whose tomb (Giza 7530) he also occurs. Date: end IV—beginning V.

[387] *Ḫ MT.NW* — Mariette, *Mastabas*, Gn.
Saqqara. Date: ?

[388] *Ḫ NW* — Selim Hassan, *Giza*, II, 159–68.
Giza, Khafre cemetery. A somewhat irregular, small mastaba with several shafts built against a tomb itself built against another in the mass of smallish, late tombs to the west of that of *Kꜣ-m-nfrt* [522]. Date: VI.

[389] *Ḫ NW* — Mariette, *Mastabas*, D 6; Cairo, *CG*, 102, 171; *Urkunden*, I, 34.
Saqqara, north of Step Pyramid No. 83 = QS 907. A mastaba with a modified cruciform chapel. According to its location, it could hardly be earlier than the time of Djedkare. Date: Djedkare or later.

[389A] *Ḫnw* — Firth and Gunn, *Teti Pyramid Cemeteries*, pp. 27, 42, pl. 17D.
Saqqara, Teti area. A son of *Mrrw-kꜣ*, who had his figure and name and titles inserted at a later date into the reliefs of the tomb of his father,

according to Firth. Duell, *et al.*, *The Mastaba of Mereruka*, I, 3 (cf. also pls. 6, 7), is rather doubtful about this assertion. Firth suggests that this *Ḫnw* may be identical with the *Ḫnw* called *Kꜣ-nbw.f*, who was buried just inside the temenos wall of *Mrrw-kꜣ* [533]. In view of the difference in their titles and the fact that another *Ḫnw* (*Ṯmj*) was buried just outside the temenos wall beside *Kꜣ-nbw.f Ḫnw* [533], and considering how common the name is, I would suggest treating this identification with caution. Date: Pepi I or later.

[390] *ḪNW* — Zaki Saad, "A Preliminary Report on the Excavations at Saqqara 1939–1940," *ASAE*, XL, 681; also unpublished data; Schott, "Zur Krönungstitulatur der Pyramidenzeit," *Nachr. Gött.*, Phil.-hist. Klasse, 1956, No. 4, pl. 3.
Saqqara, Unis area. A mastaba with a pillared chamber in a street of smallish tombs to the north of the Unis Causeway. Date: VI.

[391] *ḪNW* — British Museum No. 1272 = *Hieroglyphic Texts*, Vol. I, pl. 8.
From "Memphis." Priesthood of Menkaure. Date: ?

[392] *ḪNT* — Selim Hassan, *Giza*, VI^3, 197–200.
Giza, Khafre cemetery. A small, free-standing, square mastaba with several shafts and presumably an open-air chapel, situated just to the north of the wall of the Pyramid City of *Ḫnt-kꜣw.s*. Date: end V or later.

[393] *ḪNTJ-Kꜣ: JḪḪJ* — James, *The Mastaba of Khentika Called Ikhekhi*.
Saqqara, Teti area. A large mastaba with a complex interior chapel filling it almost completely, much like the mastaba of *Mrrw-kꜣ* [197]. It is the easternmost of the series of great mastabas built next to the inclosure wall of the Teti Pyramid and is probably the latest, particularly considering that some of the scenes seem to have been directly influenced by the decoration of the mastaba of *Mrrw-kꜣ* (owner painting a picture of the seasons, for instance). *Ḫntj-kꜣ* had a priesthood of Pepi I. Date: Pepi I.

[394] *ḪNT-KꜣW-ḤR* — Unpublished.
Saqqara, Unis area. Date: VI.

[395] *ḪZW* — Berlin Museum No. 7764 = Schäfer, *Aegyptische Inschriften*, I, 41–42.

Provenience? Priesthood of Mernere. Date: Mernere or later.

[396] *H̱N-ꜥNH̱: H̱NJ* — Newberry, "The Inscribed Tombs of Ekhmîm," *LAAA*, IV, 118–19.
Akhmim No. 27. Date: VI or later.

[397] *H̱NW-Kꜣ* — Fraser, "The Early Tombs at Tehneh," *ASAE*, III, 72, 74–75.
Tihna No. 14. Just possibly he is to be identified with the *H̱nw-kꜣ* part of whose burial was found in a shaft of the tomb of *Kꜣ-ḥp* (No. 10). Fraser identifies the owner of this tomb with the *H̱nw-kꜣ* who is listed in the tomb of *N-kꜣ-ꜥnẖ* [237] as his father or ancestor. In that case, this tomb would have to be dated to the Fourth Dynasty, which would be a most unexpected date for an Upper Egyptian rock-cut tomb, particularly considering that this is a regular rock-cut tomb, whereas the others at Tihna are rock-cut mastabas. The plan, with a long entrance corridor and a symmetrical, cruciform layout, is rather unusual for Upper Egypt. Reisner, *Giza*, I, 220, finds a Fourth Dynasty date improbable. One would rather expect this tomb, which is also situated higher up the hillside than the rock-cut mastabas, to be somewhat later. Date: mid-V or later?

[398] *H̱NMW* — Unpublished.
Giza 2191. A mastaba with a corridor chapel built against a core mastaba. Date: mid-V or later.

[399] *H̱NMW-Bꜣ.F* (better *Bꜣ-Bꜣ.F*) — Junker, *Giza*, VII, 151–58; unpublished data.
Giza 5230 = Lepsius No. 40. A large, extremely well preserved mastaba with an exterior chapel formed by the mastaba itself and the symmetrically disposed serdab-houses in front of it. The serdab-houses each contained four serdabs and a T-shaped interior offering chamber. It was built subsequent to the easternmost row of the cemetery *en échelon* and the mastaba of Prince *Dwꜣ-n-Rꜥ* (Giza 5110) who may have been his father (Reisner, *Giza*, I, 248). All indications point to a date early in the Fifth Dynasty. Date: early V.

[400] *H̱NMW-Bꜣ.F* (better *Bꜣ-Bꜣ.F*) — Selim Hassan, *Giza*, VII, 7–11.
Giza, Khafre cemetery. A good-sized, rectangular mastaba with no interior chapel. In

addition to a vertical shaft this mastaba also had a sloping passage leading to the burial chamber from the north. The owner probably was a son of Khafre. Date: end IV—early V.

[401] *H̱NMW-NFR* Junker, *Giza*, X, 111.
Giza, south of the Great Pyramid. A small, square mastaba with a chapel composed of a corridor and an east–west alcove, situated to the south of the row of Fourth Dynasty cores. Its plan takes account of the presence of an earlier sloping passage leading to the burial chamber of another tomb. Date: VI.

[402] *H̱NM-NTJ* Unpublished.
Giza 2374. A tomb squeezed in between Giza 2370 (*Snḏm-jb Jntj* [455]) and 2375 (*Mḥw-ꜣḫtj*). He is almost certainly to be identified with the son of *Snḏm-jb Jntj*, and according to Reisner, "Preliminary Report on the Work of the Harvard–Boston Expedition in 1911–1913," *ASAE*, XIII, 249, and Reisner, "New Acquisitions of the Egyptian Department," *BMFA*, XI, 62, he may be the father of *Nḫbw* [286]. The names of Unis and Teti occur in this mastaba. In the mastaba of *Mḥw-ꜣḫtj* was found a sealing with a damaged Horus-name ending in [. . .]-*ḫꜥw*, preceded by a tall, narrow sign to the left. (Reisner and Smith, *Giza*, II, 53, Fig. 57.) This could be restored as the Horus-names of Neferirkare, Neferefre, Djedkare, Mernere, or Pepi II. Smith decides for the latter two on the basis of the argument that in the Fifth Dynasty cases the first hieroglyph would ordinarily be written above rather than beside the other two, but cf., e.g., Gauthier, *Le livre des rois*, I, 134; Schott, "Zur Krönungstitulatur der Pyramidenzeit," *Nachr. Gött.*, Phil.-hist. Klasse, 1956, No. 4, Abb. 12. The restoration of a Fifth Dynasty title thus is possible, as Reisner originally suggested, and there is no compelling need to date the tomb of *H̱nm-ntj* to the later Sixth Dynasty, which would be very awkward in view of his almost certain genealogy. Date: Teti.

[403] *H̱NMW-ḤTP* Lepsius, *Denkmäler*, II, 88c; Junker, *Giza*, VIII, 60–65.
Giza, western cemetery. Lepsius No. 38, but not

Giza 5550 as indicated on Reisner's map, which is rather *Jdw* [78]. A small mastaba, free-standing, with an L-shaped chapel. The mastaba is deeper than long and is situated near to the eastern end of the cemetery. The titles are from a broken architrave found by Junker in the general area. Date: VI.

[404] *H̱NMW-ḤTP* — Junker, *Giza*, IX, 199–208.
Giza, western end of the western cemetery. A small mastaba with an L-shaped chapel and several shafts, the first mastaba in a cluster of connected tombs in the general mass of late tombs in this portion of the cemetery. Date: VI.

[405] *H̱NMW-ḤTP* — Mariette, *Mastabas*, B 11, Gb; Cairo, *CG*, 96; 1306.
Saqqara, northwest knoll No. 4. A mastaba with a modified cruciform chapel. Borchardt suggests Fifth and Fourth Dynasty, respectively, as a date for the two pieces in Cairo. Date: ?

[406] *H̱NMW-ḤTP* — Mariette, *Mastabas*, D 49; Murray, *Seven Memphite Tomb Chapels*, pls. 15–17.
Saqqara, east of Step Pyramid. A mastaba with a modified cruciform chapel. Priesthoods of Userkaf. Date: V (or later?).

[407] *H̱NMW-ḤTP* — Jéquier, *Le monument funéraire de Pepi II*, III, 38.
South Saqqara, near Pepi II. Date: Pepi II.

[408] *H̱NMW-ḤTP* — Jéquier, *Le monument funéraire de Pepi II*, III, 61.
South Saqqara, near Pepi II. Date. Pepi II.

[409] *H̱RD-NJ* — Jéquier, *Tombeaux de particuliers*, pp. 111–12, pl. 15.
South Saqqara, near Pepi II. Priesthood of Pepi II. Date: Pepi II.

[410] *Zꜣ-N-JT.F* — Berlin Museum No. 7722 = Schäfer, *Aegyptische Inschriften*, I, 59.
Provenience? Date: ?

[411] *ZWF* — Selim Hassan, *Giza*, V, 257–60.
Giza, Khafre cemetery. A rock-cut tomb with a modified cruciform (T-shaped) chapel. Since the surroundings are largely unexcavated, it is difficult to tell, but it seems, by size and workmanship and layout to be earlier than the usual small, constricted mastaba of the later type. Date: V or later.

[412] *Zp-n* — Abu-Bakr, *Giza*, I, 31-37.

Giza, far northwest. The owner of one of the false doors in the corridor chapel with several niches in the mastaba of *Nfr-Jḥjj*, which was built against the similar mastaba of *Nfrj* [254]. Date: end V or later.

[413] *Z-NFR* Junker, *Giza*, IX, 127–34.
Giza, western part of western cemetery. A small mastaba with a corridor chapel and three niches built against another small mastaba in the vicinity of Giza D 100. Date: VI.

[414] *ZZJ* Mariette, *Mastabas*, E 16.
South Saqqara, near Mastabet Farʿun and Pepi II. Priesthoods of Pepi I. Date: Pepi II?

[415] *Zzj* *Urkunden*, I, 94.
Graffito in Wadi Hammamat. A member of an expedition led by *Ptḥ-mr-ʿnḫ-Mrjrʿ* (i.e., *Nḫbw* [286]). The year was the year after the . . . numbering, with the number destroyed, but may well have been the year after the eighteenth, from which a graffito of his has been preserved giving much the same staff. Date: Pepi I.

[416] *ZṮW* Lepsius, *Denkmäler*, II, 38.
Giza, Mycerinus quarry. A rock-cut tomb to the east of the pyramid of Menkaure. Date: V–VI.

[417] *ZṮW* Mariette, *Mastabas*, B 7; Cairo, *CG*, 1298, 1301, 1377–78, 1494.
Saqqara. A mastaba with a T-shaped chapel and a long north–south corridor to the east along the eastern face of the mastaba with an entrance in the middle. Borchardt hesitatingly dates to the Fourth Dynasty. The relief is very crude, the main figures lumpy, the subsidiary ones excessively elongated and incised. Inscription incompetent (e.g., use of the *ḫ*-sign for the city-sign), the titles odd (*tꜣtj* as a separate title before *zꜣb jmj-rꜣ zš*). The possibility of a late attempt at archaism should not be overlooked. Date: ?

[417A] *ZṮW* Cairo, *CG*, 190; 1300.
Provenience? Borchardt suggests Mariette, *Mastabas*, B 6, but the titles are different. Date according to Borchardt is Fifth Dynasty. Date: V (?).

[418] *ZṮW* Lepsius, *Denkmäler*, II, 86b–87; *Erg.*, pl. 27b; Reisner, *Giza*, I, 521–23, pls. 74b–d, 75.
Giza 4710 = Lepsius No. 49. A core mastaba

later converted to an interior L-shaped chapel with one niche and a northern niche in the eastern face. Also several outside additions. Date: V.

[419] *ZṮW* — Mariette, *Mastabas*, D 46.
Saqqara, east of Step Pyramid. A mastaba with a short corridor (L-shaped) chapel. Date: V (or later).

[420] *SꜣBW KM* — Mariette, *Mastabas*, C 23.
Saqqara, mid-north No. 44. A stone mastaba with an L-shaped interior chapel. Date: V.

[421] *SꜣBW: JBBJ* — Mariette, *Mastabas*, E 1–2; Cairo, *CG*, 1418–19, 1565; *Urkunden*, I, 82–84.
Saqqara, mid-north Nos. 37–38. *Sꜣbw* shares a mastaba complex with *Ptḥ-špss* [168], and also had a priesthood of Unis and Teti in addition to being high priest of Ptah, as were so many of the *Ptḥ-špss* and *Sꜣbw* buried in this area. Date: Teti (biography).

[422] *SꜣBW: ṮTJ* — Mariette, *Mastabas*, E 3; Cairo, *CG*, 1709, 1756; *Urkunden*, I, 84–85.
Saqqara, mid-north No. 47. A mastaba with a modified cruciform chapel. From the plan it is clearly later than the last. Date: Pepi I or later.

[423] *SꜣB.N.F: JBJ* — Cairo, *CG*, 1497.
Provenience? Borchardt suggests a dating to the Sixth Dynasty. Date: VI (?).

[424] *SꜣBW-SW* — Montet, *Abou-Roach*, pp. 216–17.
Abu-Rawash. A tomb with a stone sarcophagus inscribed in ink. Could *Sꜣbw-sw* be the same as the man with the same name who occurs as a *ka*-priest in the tomb of the father of *Sḥtpw* [460]? Priesthood of Djedefre. Date: end V or later.

[425] *SʿNḪW* — Selim Hassan, *Giza*, III, 219–22.
Giza, Khafre cemetery. A small rock-cut tomb cut in the scarp to the north of the tomb of *Ḫnt-kꜣw.s*. Date: mid-V or later.

[426] *SʿNḪW-PTḤ* — Cairo, *CG*, 37, 196, 201.
Saqqara. Three statues. According to Smith, *HESP*, p. 79, they are to be dated to the Fifth Dynasty. Date: V.

[427] *SʿNḪ.N-PTḤ* — Maspero, "Trois années de fouilles," *MMAFC*, I, 205–6.
South Saqqara. A mastaba situated to the north of the Haram el-Shauwaf with the typical

painted burial chamber of the later Old Kingdom. Date: VI.

[428] *SWḎꜣ-Kꜣ* — Selim Hassan, *Giza*, VI³, 187–95.
Giza, Khafre cemetery. A rock-cut tomb opening off the passageway leading to the tomb of *Jwn-Rꜥ* [31]. Date: V or later.

[429] *SBKJJ* — Daressy, "La nécropole des grands prêtres d'Héliopolis sous l'Ancien Empire," *ASAE*, XVI, 198–204.
Heliopolis. A tomb with a decorated burial chamber much like the others at this site, e.g., [191], [381]. Date: VI.

[430] *SBKJJ: BJJ* — Daressy, "La nécropole des grands prêtres d'Héliopolis sous l'Ancien Empire," *ASAE*, XVI, 204–9.
Heliopolis. A tomb much like the last. Date: VI.

[430A] *SBKJ* — Firth and Gunn, *Teti Pyramid Cemeteries*, pp. 213–14.
Saqqara, Teti area. A loose block bearing some titles, including an office at the pyramid of Pepi I. Date: Pepi I or later.

[431] *SBK-M-ḪNT: SBKJJ* — Leclant, "Compte-rendu des fouilles et travaux menés en Égypte durant les campagnes 1948–1950," *Orientalia*, N.S. XIX, 492, pl. 57.
Saqqara, southeast of Step Pyramid. A large false door with cornice and molding. Office of Pepi I. Date: Pepi I or later.

[432] *SBK-ḤTP* — Jéquier, "Tombes de particuliers," *ASAE*, XXXV, 155–59.
South Saqqara, near Pepi II. Date: Pepi II.

[433] *SBK-ḤTP* — De Morgan, *Catalogue des monuments et inscriptions de l'Égypte antique*, I, 195–97.
Aswan. Date: VI.

[434] *SBK-Qꜣ.F: SBKJJ: SBKW* — Oriental Institute No. 11049.
Saqqara. A small false door with cornice and molding, according to label "late Old Kingdom." Date: VI.

[435] *SMꜣ-ꜥNḪ* — Selim Hassan, *Giza*, VI³, 163–71.
Giza, Khafre cemetery. A small mastaba with several shafts, an L-shaped chapel and an open passage on the east built against the mastaba of *Jr.n-ꜣḫt* [48]. Date: VI.

[436] *SMNḪW-PTḤ: JTWŠ* — Mariette, *Mastabas*, D 43; *Urkunden*, I, 191–93; Capart, "Pour reconstituer la biographie de Itoush," *Chronique d'Égypte*, XIV, 339–40.
Saqqara, northeastern group No. 14. A mastaba

with a complex interior chapel dated by the biography to the reign of Djedkare. Date: Djedkare.

[436A] *SMR-Kꜣ* — Fisher, *The Minor Cemetery at Giza*, pp. 96–101, 146–47.
Giza 3020 (probably). A mastaba with a corridor chapel and several shafts built at several removes against a free-standing mastaba in this group of small, later tombs. Date: VI.

[437] *SMDNTJ* () — Zaki Saad, "Preliminary Report on the Excavations of the Department of Antiquities at Saqqara 1942–43," *ASAE*, XLIII, 456–57, pl. 46; Drioton, "Description sommaire des chapelles funéraires de la VIe Dynastie," *ASAE*, XLIII, 509–11.
Saqqara, Teti area. A mastaba with four rooms including an east–west offering chamber situated to the north of *Mrrw-kꜣ* [197]. Date: Pepi I or later.

[438] *SNJ* — Jéquier, *Tombeaux de particuliers*, pp. 35–40, pl. 3.
South Saqqara, near Pepi II. Date: Pepi II.

[439] *SNW* — Lutz, *Statues*, pl. 3, No. 4; Lutz, *Steles*, pl. 24; *Urkunden*, I, 230.
Giza 1206. A mastaba with six shafts and originally no internal offering chamber (one appears to have been broken out later, a short north–south corridor chapel) built against a core mastaba of the northwest cemetery. Date: mid-V or later.

[440] *SN-WḤM* — Boston Museum of Fine Arts No. 27.444 (unpublished).
Giza 2132. A wretched little mastaba with several shafts and probably an open-air chapel built against a core mastaba. Date: VI.

[441] *SNB* — Junker, *Giza*, V, 3–124.
Giza, western cemetery. A smallish, rectangular mastaba with a complex exterior chapel including a chamber roofed with a true dome, situated at the western end of the central strip. It was built against the mastabas of *Jṯw* and *ʿnḫw*, of which the former has a corridor chapel with several stelae and several shafts. The latest king mentioned is Djedefre, and this combined with the deep false door apparently led some to date it quite early, but Junker points

out that the scenes of daily life (rather than offering bearers only) on the jambs and the thicknesses as well as the projecting flanges and eyes on the lower lintel indicate a late date. Date: mid-VI or later.

[442] *SNB* — Lepsius, *Denkmäler*, II, 94a.
Giza? An architrave or lintel found reused in a house in Kafr el-Batran (the modern Nazlet el-Simman?). Date: ?

[443] *SNB.F* — Cairo, *CG*, 1334.
Provenience? Borchardt suggests Sixth Dynasty or later. Date: ?

[444] *SNBW-Kȝ* — Selim Hassan, *Giza*, VI^3, 67–71.
Giza, Khafre cemetery. A rock-cut tomb leading off from the entrance passageway to the tomb of princess *Ḥmt-Rʿ*, a daughter of Khafre, in whose tomb he is also mentioned. Date: early V.

[445] *SNFRW-JN-JŠT.F* — De Morgan, *Fouilles à Dahchour*, II, 6; Balcz, "Zur Datierung der Mastaba des *Snofru-ỉni-ỉštef* in Dahšûr," *ZÄS*, LXVII, 9–15.
Dahshur. A brick mastaba with a north–south corridor and an east–west offering chamber at the end, also several niches in the corridor and four shafts. It was built against another mastaba much like it. Balcz summarizes the arguments for a dating to the Sixth Dynasty. Date: VI.

[446] *SNFRW-NFR* — Junker, *Giza*, VII, 32–44.
Giza, western cemetery. A mastaba with a corridor chapel built so as to block the north–south passage between two mastabas of the cemetery *en échelon*. Later tombs were built against it. Junker suggests a date early in the Sixth Dynasty and suggests that the owner may have been related to the next two, who were also musicians. Date: end V or later.

[447] *SNFRW-NFR* — Mariette, *Mastabas*, E 6.
Saqqara, near north No. 58. A mastaba with an east–west chapel built against the mastaba of *Kȝ-m-nfrt* [523]. Priesthood of Djedkare. Date: Djedkare or later.

[447A] *SNFRW-NFR* — Mariette, *Mastabas*, E 7; Cairo, *CG*, 1328, 1420–21, 1436, 1461.
Saqqara, near north No. 59. A mastaba situated near the last and probably belonging to a close relative, perhaps the son of this name occurring

in [447]. Priesthood of Djedkare. Date: end V or later.

[448] *SNFRW-ḤTP* Fisher, *The Minor Cemetery at Giza*, pp. 157–66, pls. 53–55.
Giza 3008. A mastaba with a corridor chapel and several shafts built against a similar mastaba. Date: VI.

[449] *SNFRW-ḤTP* Unpublished.
Saqqara, Unis area. A false door cut into the rock-scarp somewhat to the east of the tomb of *Mḥw* [202]. Date: VI.

[450] *SNFRW-Ḫʿ.F* Lepsius, *Denkmäler*, II, 16; Reisner, "Nefertkauw, the Eldest Daughter of Sneferuw," *ZÄS*, LXIV, 98–99; also unpublished data.
Giza 7070. A medium-sized mastaba with an L-shaped interior chapel belonging to the son of *Nfr-mꜣʿt* [262]. *Snfrw-ḫʿ.f* was thus a great-grandson of Snefru and belonged to the generation of Menkaure. The chapel contained only one false door. Date: end IV—early V.

[451] *SNFRW-SNB* Reisner, *Giza*, I, 465–71, pl. 57b.
Giza 4240. One of the core mastabas of the western cemetery, later finished by the addition of a casing and outside chapel (with one false door) of limestone and brick dependencies that effectively block the passage between this tomb and the next. Reisner, *Giza*, I, 307, dates the chapel to the Fourth Dynasty. Date: mid-IV—early V.

[451A] *SNNW* Smith, *HESP*, p. 70 = Boston Museum of Fine Arts No. 06.1877.
Giza 2032. A small mastaba with a corridor chapel in the mass of small, late tombs to the east of Giza 2000. Priesthood at the solar temple of Neuserre. Date: end V or later.

[451B] *SNNW* British Museum No. 1136 = *Hieroglyphic Texts*, Vol. I, pl. 27.
Provenience? A false door whose owner held office at the solar temple of Neuserre. Could this be the same person as the owner of the statue in [451A]? The titles are *wʿb* and *sḥḏ šnʿ* of *Šzp-jb-Rʿ*, respectively. Date: mid-V or later.

[452] *SNNW-ʿNḪ* Mariette, *Mastabas*, D 52.
Saqqara, east of Step Pyramid. A mastaba with a modified cruciform chapel and a corridor

(and other rooms?) to the east. Priesthoods of Userkaf and Sahure. Date: Sahure or later.

[452A] *SNNW-Kȝ: KKJ* — Reisner, *Giza*, I, 217, 311; Smith, *HESP*, pl. 45; Junker, *Giza*, VI, 20; Reisner, "Preliminary Report on the Work of the Harvard–Boston Expedition in 1911–13," *ASAE*, XIII, 248; Boston Museum of Fine Arts No. 07.1000.
Giza 2041. A smallish, free-standing mastaba with an L-shaped chapel built behind the tomb of *Nfr* [250], in whose tomb he is mentioned as a scribe. This mastaba stands at the edge of the mass of small, later mastabas to the east of Giza 2000, but is much larger and to judge by the plan evidently precedes them in time. Date: early—middle V.

[453] [*S*]*ND*[*M*]*-JB* — Selim Hassan, *Giza*, V, 276.
Giza, Khafre cemetery. A reused block whose text is reproduced in type only. Date: ?

[454] *SNḎM-JB* — Mariette, *Mastabas*, D 28.
Saqqara, mid-north No. 46. A mastaba with a corridor chapel and a long north–south corridor connecting it to a transverse entrance chamber and an entrance on the north side of the mastaba. Priesthood of Neuserre. Date: Neuserre or later.

[455] *SNḎM-JB: JNTJ* — Lepsius, *Denkmäler*, II, 76–78a–b; *Erg.*, pls. 17–21, 22b, 23c; *Urkunden*, I, 59–67.
Giza 2370 = Lepsius No. 27. A large mastaba with a complex interior chapel including a pillared hall, at the northeastern corner of the western cemetery. It is dated by the biography to the reign of Djedkare, presumably later than the sixteenth numbering which dates one of the letters he received from that king. The tomb was erected after his death by his son, while the father's body was being embalmed. The construction took fifteen months, an unexpectedly short time for a mastaba measuring about 23 × 16 meters. According to Reisner and Smith, *Giza*, II, 57, an offering list was inscribed on the walls of the burial chamber. This would make the tomb of *Snḏm-jb* one of the earliest securely dated examples of the practice of decorating the walls of the burial chamber. Date: Djedkare, second half.

[456] *SNḎM-JB: MḪJ* — Lepsius, *Denkmäler*, II, 73–75; *Erg.*, pls. 11–16;

Mariette, *Mastabas*, pp. 500–504; *Urkunden*, I, 68.
Giza 2378 = Lepsius No. 26. A mastaba, rather smaller than the last, with a complex interior chapel, built near [455] and belonging to the son of *Snḏm-jb Jntj.* According to his inscriptions, he served Djedkare and Unis. Date: Unis.

[456A] *SNḎM-JB* — Chicago Museum of Natural History No. 31705 (unpublished).
Provenience? A block containing portions of a few lines of titles or text, including what may be the remnant of a priesthood of Djedkare, which is the reason for including it here. The text is covered by a sheet of glass, reflections from which effectively thwart any attempts to make out the text with the help of a flashlight, but I thought I saw the remains of the title *jmj-rꜣ kꜣt nbt nt nswt*, which makes it probable that it comes from one of the two last tombs, which are known to have been plundered around the turn of the century, when the majority of the Old Kingdom reliefs in this collection were acquired. Date: end V.

[457] *SRF-Kꜣ* — Davies, *The Rock Tombs of Sheikh Saïd*, pls. 4–6, 17.
Sheikh Said No. 24. The tomb of the father of *Wr-jr.n.j* [114]. Priesthoods of Userkaf and Khufu, on the basis of which Davies dated the tomb to the earlier Fifth Dynasty, but cf. the remarks under [383]. Date: early V (or later?).

[458] *SR-NFR* — Dennis, "New Officials of the IVth to Vth Dynasties," *PSBA*, XXVII, 32.
Giza, Priesthood of Sahure. Date: Sahure or later.

[459] *SRḤW* — Unpublished.
Giza, Mycerinus Quarry No. 2. Priesthood of Menkaure. Date: ?

[460] *Sḥtpw* — Montet, *Abou-Roach*, pp. 218–20.
Abu Rawash. The son of a man whose name has been destroyed. The false door of the mastaba had a broad inner niche decorated with scenes. It could be relatively early in the Old Kingdom. Priesthood of Khafre. This tomb was later re-excavated by Bisson de la Roque, *Rapport sur les fouilles d'Abou-Roasch (1922–*

1923), *FIFAO*, I[3], 55–56, pls. 25, 26, who gives a brief description of the tomb and a plan. It had a stone retaining wall on three sides and two square brick chapels, in one of which was found the false door. The tombs at this site (M) are much smaller than those of the main cemetery (F). Despite the effect of the false door, the tomb does not seem to have been early. Date: mid-V or later?

[461] *SḤTPW* — Junker, *Giza*, XI, 55.
Giza, south of the Great Pyramid. A mastaba with a small, squarish offering chamber built against the tomb of *Sḫm-kȝ* [467]. Date: VI.

[462] *SḤTPW* — Firth and Gunn, *Teti Pyramid Cemeteries*, p. 165, pl. 63.
Saqqara, Teti area. The chapel of *Sḥtpw* is in a multiple-chapel mastaba erected by his son *Kȝ-m-snw* [528], who also provided the false door and decoration of his father's chapel together with *Wȝš-Ptḥ*, another son of *Sḥtpw*. The father was a priest of Neferirkare, the son also of Neuserre. The excavator dated this mastaba to a period earlier than the erection of the pyramid of Teti; Kees (cf. under [527], [528]) prefers a dating to the Sixth Dynasty. Date: mid-V or later.

[463] *SḪM-ʿNḪ-PTḤ* — Unpublished.
Giza 7152. A mastaba, with an interior short corridor chapel (L-shaped, but to the north rather than to the south of the entrance as usual at Giza) situated approximately in the middle. The tomb is at the southwestern edge of the eastern cemetery, southeast of the pyramids of Khufu's queens. It is evidently not part of the original Fourth Dynasty layout of the cemetery, and according to Reisner, *Giza*, I, 312, is later. The owner bore the title of vizier, with which the relatively small size of the mastaba ill accords. Date: V–VI.

[464] *SḪM-ʿNḪ-PTḤ: SḪM-PTḤ* — Selim Hassan, *Giza*, II, 32–45.
Giza, Khafre cemetery. A very small mastaba largely filled by a squarish offering chamber with three false doors. It was built against the tomb of *Dȝg* [577] in a group of later tombs to the east of *Rʿ-wr* [300]. Date: VI.

[465] *SḪM-ʿNḪ-PTḤ* — Mariette, *Mastabas*, D 41; L. E[arle] R[owe],

"Two Mastaba Chambers," *BMFA*, VIII, 19–20; Dunham, "Some Old Kingdom Tomb Reliefs," *BMFA*, XXVII, 35–36; Boston Museum of Fine Arts No. 04.1761; also unpublished data.
Saqqara, northwest No. 20. A mastaba with an east–west offering chamber approached through a corridor entered through a door in the northern face of the mastaba. Date: mid-V or later.

[466] *SḪM-Kꜣ* Lepsius, *Denkmäler*, II, 89b–c; Reisner, *Giza*, I, 516–18; Berlin Museum No. 1186 = Schäfer, *Aegyptische Inschriften*, I, 8–9.
Giza 4411 = Lepsius No. 51. A mastaba with a two-room chapel, a north–south offering room and a north–south antechamber. It was inserted into the east–west passage between Giza 4410, a mastaba inserted at a later date into the space of one of the core mastabas, and possibly built of reused materials, and Giza 4420, at that time an unfinished and uncased core mastaba of the original series. This latter was later used by *Ttw*, the father of *Nfr-ssm-kꜣ* [276], who also occurs as a *ka*-priest in the tomb of *Sḫm-kꜣ*. Reisner thinks that Giza 4410 and 4411 were built simultaneously as one complex, possibly for husband and wife. Giza 4410, which is now uninscribed, is badly aligned with the remainder of the mastabas of the original cemetery. It was provided with an exterior chapel with an L-shaped offering chamber and a serdab so designed as to block the north–south road between the core mastabas. In the shaft of 4410 a sealing of Userkaf was found. Such a complex involving the destruction of an older core, the blocking of several roads and multiroomed interior chapels is not likely to be earlier than the later part of the Fifth Dynasty. Date: mid-V or later.

[467] *SḪM-Kꜣ* Junker, *Giza*, XI, 1–48.
Giza, south of the Great Pyramid. A Fourth Dynasty core later converted into a mastaba with a complex chapel by breaking out space for a cruciform offering chamber in the core, building a complex series of rooms before it and adding other structures, including a court to the

		south. In addition to the original shafts, a sloping passage was excavated to lead to the burial chamber from the east. A jar with an ink inscription including the name of Djedkare was found here and may come from the burial. Junker, *Giza*, X, 2, dates this to the Sixth Dynasty. Date: end V or later.
[468]	*SḪM-Kꜣ*	Mariette, *Mastabas*, C 19. Saqqara, mid-north No. 54. A yellow brick mastaba with a short corridor chapel. Date: mid-V or later.
[469]	*SḪM-Kꜣ*	Murray, *Saqqara Mastabas*, I, 7–10, pl. 7. Saqqara, west of Step Pyramid. A mastaba with a short corridor (L-shaped) chapel with a single false door in the middle of the west wall and the entrance at the southern end of the east. Priesthood of Neuserre. Date: Neuserre or later.
[470]	*SḪM-Kꜣ*	Unpublished. Giza. An architrave found loose in the vicinity of Giza 2364 and 2365. This extreme north-eastern corner of the eastern cemetery does not seem to have been used before the latter part of the Fifth Dynasty (the *Snḏm-jb* family). Date: end V or later.
[471]	*SḪM-Kꜣ-Rꜥ*	Lepsius, *Denkmäler*, II, 41–42; *Erg.*, pls. 36, 37; Selim Hassan, *Giza*, IV, 103–23. Giza, Khafre cemetery. A rock-cut tomb in the scarp nearest the Second Pyramid, belonging to a prince, presumably a son of Khafre. According to his inscriptions, he was born under Khafre and lived until the time of Sahure.* Date: Sahure.
[472]	*SḪNTJW-Kꜣ: DŠRJ*	Mariette, *Mastabas*, Gh; Cairo, *CG*, 1316, 1353. Probably from Abydos. Date: VI (?).
[473]	*SŠꜣT-ḤTP: HTJ*	Lepsius, *Denkmäler*, II, 23–25; Junker, *Giza*, II, 172–95. Giza 5150 = Lepsius No. 36. A core in the easternmost row of the cemetery *en échelon*. It was converted to a mastaba with an interior L-shaped chapel with two false doors by expanding the mastaba to the east. In front of that were built extensive structures of brick that were almost completely destroyed by later

* This should serve as a warning not to trust genealogical information to give an exact date. This man is of the generation of Menkaure, yet died fifteen to twenty years later.

activity on the site. Enough remains to show that these were built against the mastaba of *Ṯntj* (Giza 5250??—it has no number on Reisner's map, but this is the one it should have by interpolation into his system). This latter lies to the east of the cemetery *en échelon* and has proportions totally different from those of the original planned core mastabas of the cemetery, and thus is hardly likely to be earlier than the beginning of the Fifth Dynasty. The mastaba of *Sšꜣt-ḥtp* would then have been completed correspondingly later. Date: early V. A scene from here was copied by *Nswt-nfr* [292].

[473A] . . . (name lost) Junker, *Giza*, II, 189–92.
Giza 5150. A statue of husband and wife found in one of the serdabs of *Sšꜣt-ḥtp* [473]. The titles on it are completely different from those given in the chapel of *Sšꜣt-ḥtp*, and Junker finally decides that in all probability it represented his parents. Date: early V.

[474] *SŠMW* Selim Hassan, *Giza*, III, 78–92.
Giza, Khafre cemetery. A small mastaba with a corridor chapel and five shafts situated in the mass of small mastabas to the north of the tomb of *Ḫnt-kꜣw.s*. Date: VI.

[475] *SŠMW* Lepsius, *Denkmäler*, II, 97a; Berlin Museum No. 1110 = Schäfer, *Aegyptische Inschriften*, I, 25.
Saqqara, mid-north, Lepsius No. 5. A mastaba with a north–south corridor and east–west alcove. Priesthood at the solar temple of Neferirkare. Date: mid-V or later.

[476] *SŠM-NFR* Lepsius, *Denkmäler*, II, 27–29; Junker, *Giza*, III, 9.
Giza 4940 = Lepsius No. 45. A converted core in the westernmost row of the cemetery *en échelon* with an L-shaped interior chapel with two false doors. The last king mentioned is Djedefre. This *Sšm-nfr* was in all probability the father of [477] and the grandfather of [478], of whom the latter can be dated on independent evidence to the earlier years of Djedkare. This leaves little leeway in dating this *Sšm-nfr* to the early Fifth. Date: Sahure–Neferirkare.

[477] *SŠM-NFR* Junker, *Giza*, III, 9, 187–92; also unpublished data.

Giza 5080 = 2200. A mastaba in the second row of the cemetery *en échelon* later converted to a mastaba with an interior L-shaped chapel and one of the peculiar halls surrounded by serdabs that seems to have been favored by this family. The serdab-structure was inserted into the space between Giza 5080, 5070, and 5170. A sealing of Shepseskaf was found in this tomb (see Reisner and Smith, *Giza*, II, 51). According to Junker, *Giza*, III, 71, a scene in this mastaba was copied from the mastaba of *Jj-mrjj* [21], and that there was some relationship between the two seems to be indicated by the occurrence of an estate named *Grgt-Jj-mrjj* in the tomb of the former. *Sšm-nfr* was apparently the son of [476] and the father of [478]. All this leaves very little leeway for the dating of the tomb, which must have been completed about the time of Neuserre. Date: Neuserre.

[478] *SŠM-NFR* Junker, *Giza*, III, 73, 192–215, pls. 1–4. Giza 5170. A mastaba in the easternmost row of the cemetery *en échelon*, later converted into an establishment much like [477], but more elaborate, since it contains a pillared hall connecting the L-shaped chapel and the serdab hall. These latter structures were built against the mastaba of *Rʿ-wr* [297], who was according to Junker an uncle of the owner of this tomb. Unlike the last three, [297] erected his own mastaba instead of converting an older core, so that the joint between the two indicates that [478] was completed later. This mastaba is one of the rare ones which reveal a promotion in the course of construction. *Sšm-nfr* had been an *jmj-rꜣ zš ʿ nswt*, as were other members of the family, and apparently was suddenly promoted to *tꜣtj zꜣb ṯꜣtj* and even *zꜣ nswt n ẖt.f*. These titles are only found on the south wall of the offering chamber. The latest king's name found here is that of Neferirkare. A scene in this tomb was copied from [477], which belonged to his father. Grdseloff, "Deux inscriptions juridiques de l'Ancien Empire," *ASAE*, XLII, 58–61, shows that he must have held the office of vizier for a short period near the beginning of the reign of Djedkare. Date: early Djedkare.

[479] *SŠM-NFR* — Lepsius, *Denkmäler*, II, 79–81; *Erg.*, pl. 23b; Junker, *Giza*, XI, 92–241.
Giza, south of the Great Pyramid. A large family-complex built to the south of the row of Fourth Dynasty cores and built against the mastaba of *N-ꜥnḫ-Rꜥ* [217]. The mastaba of *Sšm-nfr* had a complex interior chapel with an offering chamber in an inverted T-shape (a short north–south corridor with an east–west alcove and false door in the center), a design also found in such mastabas as that of *ꜣḫt-ḥtp* [13]. A sloping passage leads to a decorated burial chamber. Junker thinks that the owner of this tomb is related to the family of the last three. The name is, however, quite common, and the tomb itself built at a considerable distance from the others, so that the genealogy seems highly uncertain to me. The name of Djedkare occurs. Date: very end V or later.

[480] *SŠM-NFR* — Selim Hassan, *Giza*, VI[3], 201–6.
Giza, Khafre cemetery. An irregular mastaba with its interior largely filled by a complex chapel. One of the offering chambers is an L-shaped short corridor with two false doors, the other one has the false door in an east–west alcove. This family-complex was built against one of the mastabas against which the tomb of *Jn-kꜣ.f* [43] was also built. Date: mid-V or later.

[481] *SŠM-NFR: JWFJ* — Selim Hassan, *Giza*, VII, 57–63.
Giza, Khafre cemetery. The chapel of this tomb consists of a rock-cut east–west alcove at the end of which was carved the false door. From beside it, a sloping passage leads to the decorated burial chamber. Date: VI.

[482] *SŠM-NFR: ḤBꜣ* — Mariette, *Mastabas*, E 8.
Saqqara, west of Step Pyramid. No plan of this tomb has been published. Mariette assigns it to the Sixth Dynasty. Priesthood of Menkauhor and Djedkare. Date: Djedkare or later.

[483] *SŠM-NFR* — Barsanti, "Fouilles autour de la pyramide d'Ounas," *ASAE*, I, 150–60; Zaki Saad, "Preliminary Report on the Royal Excavations at Saqqara, 1942–1943," *Supplément aux ASAE*, Cahier No. 3 (1947), pp. 56–62, pls. 18–23.
Saqqara, Unis area. A tomb situated to the

west of the pyramid of Unis. It has a small north–south chapel and an antechamber to the north. Date: VI.

[484] *ST-Kꜣ* — Chassinat, "A propos d'une tête en grès rouge du foi Didoufrē," *Monuments Piot*, XXV, 66.
Abu Rawash. A statue found in a court of the temple of Djedefre belonging to a prince, apparently a son of Djedefre. Date: middle—end IV.

[485] *STJ-KꜣJ* — Junker, *Giza*, VII, 193–222.
Giza, western cemetery. No number on Reisner's map, but in the location for 5360. A smallish mastaba with a short corridor interior chapel situated to the east of the cemetery *en échelon*. It was later expanded by his son *Ptḥ-ḥtp* [163] into a tomb with a complex chapel built against Giza 5460 and 5350, which latter had been built against the mastaba of *Kꜣ-sḏꜣ* [546], all three of which are large mastabas erected subsequent to the cemetery *en échelon*. Date: mid-V or later.

[486] *SDꜣWG* — Junker, *Giza*, IX, 107–18.
Giza, western cemetery. A mastaba with a corridor chapel and several shafts in the mass of small, late tombs to the southwest of Giza 2000. Junker dates to the later Sixth Dynasty. Date: VI.

[487] *SD-N-MꜣꜤT* (read *N-MꜣꜤT-SD*) — Mariette, *Mastabas*, D 56; Cairo, *CG*, 58, 88, 113, 133.
Saqqara, east of the Step Pyramid. No plan available. Priesthood of Neuserre. Date: Neuserre or later.

[487A] *SḎFꜣW* — Petrie, *Meydum and Memphis* (*III*), pl. 31.
Meydum. A libation trough found in a mastaba in the northern group. Date: ?

[488] *SḎFꜣ-PTḤ: FFJ* — Selim Hassan, *Giza*, I, 97–101.
Giza, Khafre cemetery. A mastaba in the Street of Priests, on the south side. It had a roofed corridor chapel and was built against a tomb to the east. The mastabas of *Jjj* [19] and *Wsr* [123] were built against it to the west. In the burial chamber was a sarcophagus decorated with elaborate false-door paneling and inscribed with the name and titles of the owner. Date: mid-V or later.

[489] *ŠPSJ* — Mariette, *Mastabas*, D 13; Cairo, *CG*, 1379.

Saqqara, north ridge No. 73. A mastaba with a modified cruciform chapel and a corridor, apparently added later, on the eastern face. Date: V or later.

[490] *ŠPSS-ꜣḪTJ* Selim Hassan, *Giza*, III, 93–97.
Giza, Khafre cemetery. A small, irregular tomb with an east–west offering chamber in the group of later, small tombs to the north of the tomb of *Ḫnt-kꜣw.s*. Date: VI (?).

[490A] *ŠPSJ-KꜣW* Lepsius, *Denkmäler*, II, 110 l–n; *Text*, II, 63.
Zawiyet el-Maiyitin No. 9. Priesthood of Pepi I. Date: Pepi I or later.

[491] *ŠPSSKꜣF-ʿNḪ* Unpublished.
Giza 6040. The tomb of the father of *Jj-mrjj* [21] and the grandfather of *Nfr-bꜣw-Ptḥ* [258]. He appears to have held much the same titles as his son, and is represented in the tomb of his son and of his grandson, where also most of his known titles are given. His own tomb is now virtually uninscribed. The titles found in the other tombs are, of course, included in the later ranking-sequences, but he is listed separately for the sake of the royal priesthoods he held. In the tomb of his grandson he is recorded as holding priesthoods of Khufu, Sahure, and Neferirkare. His own mastaba originally had an interior L-shaped chapel. Later this was walled up as a serdab and a large pillared court was added on the east. Reisner, *Giza*, I, 217, suggests the reign of Neferirkare for the construction of the original mastaba, which is very probable but leaves the date of the later expansion undetermined. It might coincide with the construction of the tombs of his son and other members of his family on adjoining sites, but is of little importance to us as it is completely blank. Date: Neferirkare.

[492] *ŠPSSKꜣF-ʿNḪ* Selim Hassan, *Giza*, II, 15–31.
Giza, Khafre cemetery. A mastaba with a corridor chapel and several shafts, situated to the east of the mastaba of *Rʿ-wr* [300]. Several mastabas were later built against it. Date: end V—mid-VI.

[493] *Špsskꜣf-ʿnḫ* Selim Hassan, *Giza*, VI[3], 88–91.
Giza, Khafre cemetery. The owner of the southernmost of the two false doors in the

corridor of the mastaba of *Ḥmw* [332]. Date: end V or later.

[493A] *ŠNʿJJ** — British Museum No. 212 = *Hieroglyphic Texts*, Vol. I, pl. 45.
Provenience? A false door with a priesthood of Pepi II. Date: Pepi II.

[493B] *ŠNʿJJ* — Jéquier, *Tombeaux de particuliers*, pp. 108–9.
Saqqara, near Pepi II. *Šnʿjj* had his name and title added in the temple of Pepi II at a date subsequent to its completion (Jéquier, *Le monument funéraire de Pepi II*, Vol. II, pl. 73. Date: Pepi II, second half.

[494] *ŠTWJ* — Junker, *Giza*, IX, 184–90.
Giza, western cemetery. An isolated, squarish, small mastaba near the western end of the cemetery. It had an L-shaped chapel and an exterior court. Date: end V or later?

[494A] *QꜣJJ* — Lepsius, *Denkmäler*, II, 34a–b; *Text*, I, 89–90.
Giza, Lepsius No. 69. A rock-cut tomb immediately to the south of the causeway of Khufu. Considering its location, it would hardly belong to the earliest years of the cemetery's history. Date: V–VI.

[495] *QꜣR: MRJJRʿ-NFR* — Reisner, "Excavations in Egypt and Ethiopia 1922–1925," *BMFA*, XXIII, 25–28; Smith, *HESP*, Fig. 84a; Boston Museum of Fine Arts No. 27.1134; also unpublished data.
Giza 7101. A mastaba partly built and partly rock-cut, situated beside the tomb of *Jdw* [77], to whom he was probably related. The chapel was composed of a sunk court approached by a staircase with decorated walls leading down from ground level. Beyond the court were two rock-cut chambers. *Qꜣr* held priesthoods of Khufu, Khafre, Menkaure, and Pepi I. Reisner considers *Qꜣr* to have been the son of *Jdw* and dates his tomb a generation later (*Giza*, I, 317), but according to the evidence offered by the tombs, the genealogy could just as well be reconstructed the other way. I do not know if there is any archeological data permitting one to assign a relative date to the tombs. According

* This name was read *Prjj* by the editors of both [493A] and [493B]. It is written  in [493A] and  in [493B]. But we certainly have here the name *Šnʿjj* recorded in Ranke, *Die ägyptischen Personennamen*, I, 328, 23; II, 390.

to Reisner's map, they are beside each other but not in contact. Date: Pepi I or later.

[496] *QꜣR* — Selim Hassan, *Giza*, VI³, 207–11.
Giza, Khafre cemetery. A small mastaba block with four shafts and a corridor chapel using the back of an older mastaba to the east. Date: end V or later.

[497] *QꜣR: MRJJRꜥ-NFR* — British Museum No. 1319, 1341–42 = *Hieroglyphic Texts*, Vol. I, pls. 34–36.
From "Memphis." Date: Pepi I or later.

[498] *QꜣR* — Newberry, "The Inscribed Tombs of Ekhmîm," *LAAA*, IV, 101–2.
Akhmim No. 1. Date: VI or later.

[499] *QDFJJ* and — Junker, *Giza*, VI, 80–92.
[499A] *WSR* — Junker, *Giza*, VI, 186–88.
Giza, western cemetery. These two tomb-owners have exactly the same titles and are therefore treated together.
Qdfjj erected himself a mastaba with a portico chapel built against Giza 4770, a core mastaba. It stands at right angles to the mastaba of *Nfr* [251]. The plans and drawings indicate a sort of low screen-wall connecting the two, but I can find no indications as to the relative dating either in the plans or in the text. Junker suggests a dating to the later Fifth Dynasty. Date: end V or later.
Wsr erected his mastaba about thirty meters away from the last as one of a mass of small, later tombs in the space between the old central and northern sections of the western cemetery. It had a corridor chapel, several shafts and was built against several older tombs in the area. Date: VI.

[500] *QD-NS* — Mariette, *Mastabas*, E 5.
Saqqara, northwestern group No. 23. A brick mastaba with several chambers including an east–west offering chamber. Date: mid-V or later.

[500A] *QD-NS* — Mariette, *Mastabas*, E 10, pp. 402–4.
Saqqara. A rock-cut tomb with statues in niches cut in the rock. Priesthood of Menkauhor. Date: end V or later.

[501] *QD-NS* — Junker, *Giza*, VI, 244–48.
Giza, western cemetery. A small, now rather shapeless mastaba with an L-shaped chapel

built against the mastaba of *Mjnww* [192]. Date: VI.

[502] *QD-NS* Junker, *Giza*, VII, 133–38.
Giza, western cemetery. A small mastaba with a corridor chapel inserted into the space between *Ḫwfw-snb* [377] and Giza 5160. Date: VI.

[502A] *QD-ŠPSS* De Morgan, *Fouilles à Dahchour*, II, 22; Cairo, *CG*, 1390.
Dahshur. A mastaba built against that of *Kꜣ-nfr* [534]. Its interior is largely filled by two chambers. Priesthood of Snefru. Date: mid-V or later.

[503] *KꜣJ* Selim Hassan, *Giza*, III, 29–40.
Giza, Khafre cemetery. A mastaba, partly rock-cut and partly built, with a chapel composed of a modified cruciform offering chamber, an antechamber and three symmetrically disposed rooms before that. It is the largest and rather obviously the first in that part of the necropolis. The eastern façade is paneled. Reisner suggested that *Kꜣj* might have been a son or descendant of Queen *Ḫꜥ-mrr-nbtj* II, on the basis of some model bowls of alabaster bearing that name with one of his titles, *zꜣ nswt*, that were found deposited in the floor of her pyramid temple (Reisner, *Mycerinus*, p. 55). The name of the mother of the owner of this tomb was *Ḫnwt*, so he cannot have been the son of the queen. The deposit in the queen's temple seems to have been later than the erection of the temple, so that, even accepting the not improbable identification of the two *Kꜣj*'s, we have here no secure criterion for dating the tomb. But a dating to the earlier Fifth Dynasty seems likely from size and position of the tomb. Date: early—mid-V.

[504] *KꜣJ* Mariette, *Mastabas*, C 21.
Saqqara, mid-north No. 45. A "très ancien mastaba sans forme, de briques jaunâtres." Date: V or VI.

[505] *KꜣJ* Mariette, *Mastabas*, D 19; Cairo, *CG*, 1299, 1302–3.
Saqqara, near north No. 63. An elongated mastaba with two chapels opening from a corridor on the east side. One is a short cor-

ridor chapel, the other a complex one with a pillared hall. The plan looks as though the tomb might have been built against another one on the east. Date: mid-V or later.

[506] *KꜣJ* — Mariette, *Mastabas*, Gj; Berlin Museum No. 7723 = Schäfer, *Aegyptische Inschriften*, I, 61. Saqqara. Date: ?

[507] *KꜣJ: SNJ* — Zaki Saad, "A Preliminary Report on the Excavations at Saqqara 1939–1940," *ASAE*, XL, 685–86; also unpublished data.
Saqqara, Unis area. Zaki Saad states that this tomb was built over an earlier one on the site. It contains a frieze of figures of the owner. Date: VI.

[508] *Kꜣ-jrj.s* — Selim Hassan, *Giza*, III, 171.
Giza, Khafre cemetery. A person in Mastaba "H," a tomb with an irregular rock-cut chapel cut just to the east of the tomb of Queen *Bw-nfr*, and apparently later. The chapel is more or less vaguely a north–south corridor with an additional chamber to the north and an alcove on the east. The irregularity is largely caused by the collapse of a rock wall on the west that was cut too thin. Date: mid-V or later?

[509] *Kꜣ-JRW-ẖWFW* — Lepsius, *Denkmäler*, II, 17d.
Giza, Lepsius No. 21. The owner of the false door in the northern niche of the mastaba of *Pr-sn* [143]. Date: early V?

[510] *Kꜣ-ʿPR* — Selim Hassan, *Giza*, II, 155–58.
Giza, Khafre cemetery. A rock-cut mastaba with a rather irregular chapel, probably unfinished. It is situated in the group of tombs to the west of *Kꜣ-m-nfrt* [522], but differs from the majority of them, which are built and have a large number of shafts. Date: later V?

[511] *Kꜣ-ʿPR* — Selim Hassan, *Giza*, VI[3], 155–62.
Giza, Khafre cemetery. This tomb has been built against, or rather added to, the mastaba of *Nfr-ḫww* [269A], and thus is not likely to have belonged to the *Kꜣ-ʿpr* who was the father of the former. Date: VI.

[511A] *Kꜣ-ʿḤꜣ.F* — De Morgan, *Fouilles à Dahchour*, I, 12; Cairo, *CG*, 1381–83.
Dahshur. This mastaba is one of a group of brick tombs built against each other. It appears that it may have had a cruciform chapel. The

other tombs that formed part of this complex have corridor chapels. The total gives the appearance of a compound mastaba with four chapels, something like the tomb of *K3-m-snw* [526]. This could hardly be early, despite the priesthood of Snefru and the title *z3 nswt n ẖt.f*. Date: mid-V or later.

[512] *K3W* — Bisson de la Roque, *Rapport sur les fouilles d'Abou-Roasch (1922–1923)*, *FIFAO*, I³, 29.
Abu Rawash, F 15. A small, brick mastaba with two chapels, one a corridor, the other L-shaped with an antechamber. It was built behind F 11, a mastaba with a complex interior chapel and portico entrance, itself built against an older mastaba. The titles *z3 nswt* and *smr wˁtj n jt.f* were found here, but in view of the archeological data it seems highly improbable that the owner of this mastaba was a son of Djedefre, whom one would expect to have been buried in one of the original mastabas of the cemetery. Date: end V or later.

[513] *K3-WˁB* — Reisner, "The Tomb of Meresankh, a Great-Granddaughter of Queen Hetep-Heres I and Sneferuw," *BMFA*, XXV, 69–70, 75; Reisner, "Report on the Egyptian Expedition during 1934–35," *BMFA*, XXXIII, 75.
A. Giza 7120, one of the great double mastabas of the eastern nucleus cemetery. The chapel was virtually completely destroyed, and titles are only available to me from a statue. *K3-wˁb* was a son of Khufu. Date: mid-IV.
B. Giza 7530, the rock-cut chapel of his daughter *Mr-s-ˁnḫ* III, where he is depicted with the greater part of the titles preserved. The chapel was cut underneath a mastaba definitely later than the original nucleus cemetery. Reisner dates to the reign of Menkaure (*Giza*, I, 310). Date: later IV.

[514] *K3-WḎ3* — Cairo, *CG*, 1398.
Provenience? Borchardt suggests Fifth Dynasty. Date: V (?).

[515] *K3-PW-JNPW* — Mariette, *Mastabas*, D 57; Murray, *Seven Memphite Tomb Chapels*, pls. 11–13.
Saqqara, east of Step Pyramid. A mastaba with two modified cruciform chapels and a niche between them. To the east was a corridor,

apparently widening into a hall or court opposite the entrance to the southern chapel. Date: mid-V or later.

[516] *Kꜣ-PW-JNPW* — Mariette, *Mastabas*, E 12.
Saqqara, east of Step Pyramid. A mastaba with a plan much like that of *Nfr-sšm-Sšꜣt* [275]. Date: VI.

[517] *Kꜣ-PW-PTḤ* — Cairo, *CG*, 1563 (still unpublished); Helck, *Untersuchungen*, p. 82.
From Saqqara? A false door with titles including priesthoods of Neferirkare, Neuserre, and Djedkare. Date: Djedkare or later.

[518] *Kꜣ-PW-NSWT: Kꜣj* — Junker, *Giza*, III, 123–45.
Giza 4651. A mastaba with an L-shaped interior chapel inserted into the space between the core mastaba of *Jꜣbtjt* (Giza 4650) and Giza 4660. It blocks the passage between the two. *Kꜣ-pw-nswt* was a *ka*-servant of *Jꜣbtjt* and rebuilt her tomb, apparently after finishing his own (cf. also Junker, *Giza*, I, 216–26). His name, of course, also occurs in her chapel. Junker dates the entire complex to the middle of the Fifth Dynasty, since these various alterations block the passages between mastabas. Date: early—middle V.

[519] *Kꜣ-PW-Rʿ* — Mariette, *Mastabas*, D 39; Dam, "The Tomb Chapel of Ra-ka-pou," *University of Pennsylvania Museum Journal*, XVIII, 188–200; also unpublished data.
Saqqara, northwest group No. 22. A mastaba with a corridor chapel and apparently other rooms. Priesthood of Djedkare. Date: Djedkare or later.

[520] *Kꜣ-M-ʿNḪ* — Junker, *Giza*, IV.
Giza 4561. A mastaba built between two core mastabas so as to block the north–south passage. The chapel consists of a north–south corridor and an east–west alcove with the false door. The burial chamber was fully decorated with scenes. Date: VI.

[521] *Kꜣ-M-ʿḤ* — Reisner, *Giza*, I, 398–403, pl. 19a.
Giza 1223. One of the original core mastabas of the northwest cemetery. The inscriptions come from the slab stela that was set into the core. The mastaba was later enlarged and provided with an interior L-shaped chapel, the slab-stela

being covered by the masonry. The conversion may have occurred as late as the Fifth Dynasty. The original core dates from the time of Khufu. Date: Khufu.

[522] *Kꜣ-M-NFRT* — Selim Hassan, *Giza*, II, 104–38.
Giza, Khafre cemetery. A large, irregular mastaba, partly built and partly rock-cut situated immediately to the northwest of *Rꜥ-wr* [300], and like that mastaba squeezed in an irregular fashion into the available space. It also provided an unusually large amount of serdab space, like *Rꜥ-wr*. The chapel is complex and contains both north–south and east–west offering chambers. According to the plans, this mastaba is definitely later than *Rꜥ-wr*, and probably is to be dated to the second half of the Fifth Dynasty. Date: mid-V or later.

[523] *Kꜣ-M-NFRT* — Mariette, *Mastabas*, D 23; Dunham, "A 'Palimpsest' on an Egyptian Mastaba Wall," *AJA*, XXXIX, 300–309; Boston Museum of Fine Arts No. 04.1761 (still largely unpublished).
Saqqara, near north No. 57. A mastaba with a modified cruciform offering chamber approached by a north–south corridor and an antechamber. Priesthoods of Khafre, Userkaf, Sahure, Nefirkare, and Neuserre. Date: Neuserre or later.

[524] *Kꜣ-M-NFRT* — Petrie, *Athribis*, pls. 1–5.
Hagarsa. Petrie assigns this rock-cut tomb to the Fourth Dynasty, but the date seems highly improbable (Reisner, *Giza*, I, 220). Smith, *HESP*, p. 217, compares this with the rock-cut mastabas of Hemamiya and assigns it to the Fifth. Date: V (?).

[525] *Kꜣ-M-RḤW* — Mariette, *Mastabas*, C 25; Cairo, *CG*, 1370; *Urkunden*, I, 33–34.
Saqqara. A rock-cut tomb with a built façade. The chapel is composed of a corridor and an alcove. Date: mid-V or later?

[526] *Kꜣ-M-RḤW* — Mariette, *Mastabas*, D 2; Cairo, *CG*, 1534; Mogensen, *Le mastaba égyptien de la Glyptothèque Ny Carlsberg.*
Saqqara, north of Step Pyramid No. 79. A mastaba with a short corridor chapel. Priesthood of Neuserre. Date: Neuserre (probably Djedkare) or later.

[527] *K3-M-ḤZT*

Quibell and Hayter, *Teti Pyramid North Side*, pp. 16–20, pls. 27–29; *Urkunden*, I, 206–7 = Capart, *Monuments pour servir à l'étude de l'art égyptien*, I, pl. 13; Kees, "Eine Familie königlicher Maurermeister aus dem Anfang der 6. Dynastie," *WZKM*, LIV, 91–100; Abd el-Hamid Zayed, "Réflexions sur une statue de  menuisier et constructeur de la fin de l'Ancien Empire," *Trois études d'égyptologie*, pp. 1–11.

Saqqara, Teti area. A brick mastaba situated to the west of the mastaba of *Mrrw-k3* [197] and behind that of *K3-m-snw* [528]. The mastaba is largely filled by three chapels forming a suite of rooms. The chapel of *K3-m-ḥzt* at the south has a short corridor offering chamber and an antechamber with three pillars. The northern chapel (owner?) was much like it. A corridor joining the two served as offering chamber for *K3-pw-nswt*, the brother of *K3-m-ḥzt*. The tomb appears to have been built at one time, so conflation of the titles seemed justifiable. In the mastaba was found a wooden seal of Pepi I, but according to the excavator was later than the building. Firth considered the mastaba to be the oldest on the site and to antedate the building of the pyramid of Teti. Kees is of the opposite opinion. He thinks it is to be dated later than [528] as it is situated behind it. Some of the scenes are quite unusual (the siege), a factor which would rather indicate the Sixth Dynasty. It is to be noted that both this tomb and the next were buried under a mass of debris which, according to the excavators, partly came from the construction of the late Sixth Dynasty cemetery to the north. Date: early VI.

[528] *K3-M-SNW*

Firth and Gunn, *Teti Pyramid Cemeteries*, p. 157, pls. 62, 63.

Saqqara, Teti area. A brick mastaba with four modified cruciform (T-shaped chapels), some of which appear to have had a corridor or other antechamber, situated to the southeast of the mastaba of *Mrrw-k3* [197], just around the corner of the Teti Pyramid inclosure, and to the east of [527]. The two northernmost chapels were finished in stone. One was occupied by

Kꜣ-m-snw and *Wr-ḏdd-Ptḥ* (relationship?), the other by *Sḫtpw* [462]. Since the latter was finished posthumously by two of his sons, the chances are that all three were built at the same time. The titles can be conflated easily, and indeed largely overlap. *Sḫtpw* has, however, also been listed separately, since he did have a separate chapel. Kees (see above) dates this mastaba into the Sixth Dynasty; the excavators suggested a date possibly preceding the erection of the mastabas of *Mrrw-kꜣ* [197] and *Kꜣ-gm-nj* [548]. *Sḫtpw* was a priest of Sahure and Neferirkare; his son added a priesthood of Neuserre. The false door has the elongated form found commonly in the Fifth Dynasty. The debris under which this tomb was buried seems to exclude a date in the later Sixth Dynasty. Date: Neuserre—early VI.

[529] *Kꜣ-M-QD*

Lepsius, *Denkmäler*, II, 100c.

Saqqara, Lepsius No. 14. A mastaba with a north–south corridor chapel situated in the northern group on the Abusir track. Priesthood at the solar temple of Neferirkare. Date: mid-V or later.

[529A] *Kꜣ-M-QD*

Barsanti, "Rapport sur la fouille de Dahchour," *ASAE*, III, 202–3.

Dahshur. A tomb belonging to a prince, presumably a son of Snefru. His mother had the title *zꜣt nswt*. The tomb appears to have been a small one. There is a possible reference to "The foremost of the westerners" (in the plural ), but this, if not miscopied, need by no means be interpreted as an occurrence of Osiris in an invocation offering (the context rather looks like an epithet or a title). Date: IV (?).

[530] *Kꜣ-M-ṮNNT*

Mariette, *Mastabas*, D 7; *Urkunden*, I, 180–86; Cairo, *CG*, 1371, 1456.

Saqqara, north of Step Pyramid No. 84 = QS 919. A mastaba with a multiroomed chapel approached by a pillared portico, a plan much like that of the tomb of *Jzzj-ʿnḫ* [64]. The much damaged biographical inscription mentions service under the vizier *Rʿ-špss* [315], which dates the tomb to the reign of Djedkare. Date: Djedkare.

[531] *K3-N-NSWT* — Junker, *Giza*, II, 135–72.
Giza 4870 = 2155. A core mastaba of the northern group in the western cemetery, later expanded to contain an interior, two-niched, L-shaped chapel. Junker dates to the earlier Fifth Dynasty, basing his argument for the lower limit on an independent dating for the adjoining mastaba of *K3-n-nswt*'s son [532]. Date: early V.

[532] *K3-N-NSWT* — Junker, *Giza*, III, 145–56.
Giza 2156. This is the same number as that assigned to the totally different mastaba of *Rdj-n.s* [322]. Probably the number was changed at the same time as that of the mastaba of his father [531], but to what? The mastaba is a small annex with an L-shaped, two-niched chapel built against the eastern side of the mastaba of his father, *K3-n-nswt* [531]. The tomb was still unfinished at the time of his death and was completed by his son, also called *K3-n-nswt* (III). In the burial chamber were found four pottery canopic jars, which, according to Junker, *Giza*, III, 15, is a characteristic of the period after the middle of the Fifth Dynasty. Date: middle V.

[533] *K3-NBW.F: ḪNW* — Firth and Gunn, *Teti Pyramid Cemeteries*, pp. 27, 38, 42, 186, 209, 270, pls. 17, 74, 76.
Saqqara, Teti area. A small tomb erected within the temenos wall of *Mrrw-k3* (197). For the rather dubious identification with a son of *Mrrw-k3*, see [389A]. Date: Pepi I or later.

[534] *K3-NFR* — De Morgan, *Fouilles à Dahchour*, II, 23; British Museum Nos. 1324, 1345 = *Hieroglyphic Texts*, Vol. I, pls. 4, 5.
Dahshur. A mastaba with a large brick retaining wall and two exterior chapels (one for his wife?). The aim appears to have been a double mastaba something like the great mastabas of the nucleus eastern cemetery at Giza. *K3-nfr* is stated to have been a son of Snefru. The tomb was erected after his death by his son, approximately in the reign of Khafre. Date: Djedkare–Khafre.

[535] *K3-NFR* — Reisner, *Giza*, I, 389–92, pl. 17b.
Giza 1203. One of the original cores of the northwestern section of the western cemetery. It

had an exterior brick chapel around a slab stela and apparently never was converted. Date: middle IV.

[536] *Kꜣ-NFR* Reisner, *Giza*, I, 437–46, pls. 38c–e, 39b, 40a–b, 43a–c.

Giza 2150. A core mastaba of the northern section of the western cemetery, converted later to a mastaba with an L-shaped interior chapel with two false doors and a northern niche on the outside. Junker, *Giza*, VII, 162, wonders if he could be a son or grandson of [535]; Reisner, *Giza*, I, 422, thinks that he was probably the son of *Nfr* [250], whose mastaba was nearby, and with its one-niched exterior chapel belongs to a somewhat earlier type. *Nfr*'s wife was called *Mr-s-ʿnḫ*, and a woman of the same name occurs in the tomb of *Kꜣ-nfr* in a position that could well be that of a mother (much like in *Ḫwfw-ḫʿ.f* [375]; *Kꜣ-nfr* was married to *Špst-kꜣw*). His son was called *Kꜣ-sḏꜣ* and may well be our [546]. Date: early V.

[537] *KꜣW-NSWT* Selim Hassan, *Giza*, II, 75–86.

Giza, Khafre cemetery. A large rock-cut tomb with built additions on top situated beside the "Galarza Tomb" of Queen *Ḫʿ-mrr-Nbtj* at the eastern end of the Khafre cemetery. A son of his was named after Shepseskaf. Date: early V or later.

[538] *Kꜣ-RS* Barsanti, "Rapport sur la fouille de Dahchour," *ASAE*, III, 201–2.

Dahshur. Priesthood of Snefru. Date: ?

[539] *Kꜣ-ḤJ.F* Junker, *Giza*, VI, 94–152.

Giza 2136. A smallish mastaba built against a core. It had several shafts and a square offering chamber with a pillar and two false doors. The lively nature of some of the scenes and the beginning elongation of the figures point to a relatively late date, according to Junker the middle of the Sixth Dynasty. Date: mid-VI.

[540] *Kꜣ-ḤJ.F* Bisson de la Roque, *Rapport sur les fouilles d'Abou-Roasch (1924)*, *FIFAO*, II[1], 53 ff., pls. 14–17, 33.

Abu Rawash F 21. A mastaba with a retaining wall and rubble filling, an east–west offering chamber approached by an antechamber, and two burial chambers approached from the east by sloping passages. Its other structures appear to have been built against the back of a much larger mastaba with L-shaped, two-niched chapels much like those of the Fifth Dynasty at Giza; the types of mastabas found there seem to occur also at Abu Rawash, but the cemetery there has been little studied as yet. A man with the same name and one of the titles of this *Kꜣ-ḥj.f* occurs in the badly damaged mastaba F 19, the one against which F 21 has been built, as a son (Bisson de la Roque, *Rapport sur les fouilles d'Abou-Roasch* (*1922–1923*), *FIFAO*, I^3, 39). Date: end V or later.

[540A] *Kꜣ-ḤJ.F* Cairo, *CG*, 268.
Saqqara. Priesthood of Neuserre. Date: Neuserre or later.

[540B] *KꜣJ-ḤP* Berlin Museum Nos. 11467, 11469 = Schäfer, *Aegyptische Inschriften*, I, 44–45.
Provenience? Priesthood of Userkaf. Date: V or later.

[541] *Kꜣ-ḤP: ṮTJ JQR* Newberry, "The Inscribed Tombs of Ekhmîm," *LAAA*, IV, 116–18.
Akhmim, No. 26. Date: VI or later.

[542] *Kꜣ-ḤR-ST.F* Selim Hassan, *Giza*, VI^3, 73–79.
Giza, Khafre cemetery. A mastaba with a rock-cut chapel and a built superstructure. The chapel is approached from the west by a staircase that leads to a partly built antechamber with four statues carved out of the rock. To the south is the square offering chamber with two false doors in the west wall. This tomb appears to antedate the mass of later mastabas with corridor chapels and multiple shafts that were built immediately to the south, in part against the tomb of *Kꜣ-ḥr-st.f*. Date: V—early VI?

[543] *Kꜣ-ẖNT* Petrie and Mackay, *Bahrein and Hemamieh*, pls. 9–19.
Hemamia. A rock-cut mastaba, or rather a transitional form between the rock-cut mastaba of Tihna and a rock-cut tomb. The chapel is formed by a long, narrow north–south corridor, with a main entrance leading to it at right angles from the south and a secondary passage leading out again at the north. The entrance is unroofed and the wall on the side of the tomb is battered to give the effect of a mastaba. An

attempt has evidently been made to imitate the mastaba with the long corridor of the later Fifth Dynasty. This tomb and the next are close to each other and evidently belong to members of the same family. Both had sons named *Kꜣ-ḫnt*, but the following factors indicate that the owner of [543] was the son of [543A]: [543] is situated higher on the spur of the cliff on which the tombs were built, an inherently more unfavorable situation. [543] was married to a *Ḫnt-kꜣw.s* and had a daughter named *Jwfj*, while [543A] was married to an *Jwfj*. It seems more likely that a man would name one of his daughters after his mother than that his son should marry a woman with the same name as his sister (agreeing with Černý, "Consanguineous Marriages in Pharaonic Egypt," *JEA*, XL, 23–29, that a brother–sister marriage would be extremely unlikely). Date: end V—early VI.

[543A] *Kꜣ-ḪNT*

Petrie and Mackay, *Bahrein and Hemamieh*, pls. 20–28.

Hemamia. A rock-cut mastaba much like the last and situated below it, presumably belonging to the father of [543]. Date: mid—end V.

[544] *Kꜣ-ḪR-PTḤ: FTK-Tꜣ*

Lepsius, *Denkmäler*, II, 78; *Text*, I, 62; Junker, *Giza*, VIII, 108–22.

Giza 5560 = Lepsius No. 35. A medium-sized mastaba situated immediately to the west of the enclosure wall of the Great Pyramid. Its interior is largely filled with rooms, including an east–west offering chamber. The burial chamber is decorated and reached through a sloping passage from the east. The owner held office at the pyramid of Djedkare. Date: VI.

[545] *Kꜣ-ḪR-NSWT*

Selim Hassan, *Giza*, II, 65–71.

Giza, Khafre cemetery. A mastaba with a corridor chapel entered from the west, with several stelae. The mastaba had several shafts and was built against that of *Dꜣg* [577]. The owner was a dependent (*nj ḏt*) of (the estate of) *Rꜥ-wr* [300]. Date: VI.

[546] *Kꜣ-SḎꜣ*

Lepsius, *Denkmäler*, II, 85; *Erg.*, pls. 27a–28d; Junker, *Giza*, VII, 158–84.

Giza 5340 = Lepsius No. 37. A large mastaba with an interior L-shaped chapel with two false doors and a northern niche. It is situated two rows to the east of the cemetery *en échelon* and was planned with an interior chapel from the beginning. An extension for a serdab was added on the south and a mastaba much like it on the north, against which were later built innumerable small, multishafted later tombs. This second mastaba, Giza 5350, probably was built for the son of *Kꜣ-sḏꜣ*, and against it was built the small mastaba of a *Kꜣ-nfr*, perhaps a grandson. Junker shows that *Kꜣ-sḏꜣ* was almost certainly a descendant, probably the son of *Kꜣ-nfr* [536], who has a son with the name *Kꜣ-sḏꜣ* depicted in his tomb and who bore titles very similar to those in [546]. Date: mid-V.

[546A] *Kꜣ-SḎꜣ* Berlin Museum No. 7969 = Schäfer, *Aegyptische Inschriften*, I, 35.
Provenience? Priesthood of Menkaure. Date: ?

[547] *KꜣKꜣJ-ꜤNḪ* Selim Hassan, *Giza*, VI³, 24–25.
Giza, Khafre cemetery. The owner of the northern chapel in the compound tomb of which *Jr-n-ꜣḫt* [48] held the entrance and the southern chapel, while a *Kꜣ-m-nfrt* used the long connecting corridor as his. This latter had himself depicted making offerings to Queen *Rḫjt-Rꜥ*, in front of whose tomb this was built, and the *ka*-servants of whose estate (*ḏt*) he supervised. It does not follow that the tombs must have been approximately contemporary. Date: VI.

[548] *Kꜣ-GM-NJ* Von Bissing, *Die Mastaba des Gemnikai*, Vols. I–II; Firth and Gunn, *Teti Pyramid Cemeteries*, pp. 108–26, pls. 5, 52–53, 59–60; Edel, "Inschriften des Alten Reiches, II," *MIOF*, I, 210–26.
Saqqara, Teti area. A large, complex mastaba against which that of *Mrrw-kꜣ* [197] was built. It may very well have been the first in the row of great mastabas immediately to the north of the enclosure wall of the pyramid of Teti. According to his biography, his career extended from the reign of Djedkare to that of Teti. A son of *Kꜣ-gm-nj* was named *Mr-Ppjj* and has been used as evidence for dating the tomb into the reign of Pepi I. He occurs, however, only on

a slab found in the debris west of *Mrrw-kꜣ* (Firth and Gunn, *op. cit.*, p. 167), and cannot be used as evidence for the date of the tomb or even to date the death of *Kꜣ-gm-nj*, since such court names apparently were assumed later in life on occasion (cf. [153], who was a vizier, named after Pepi I, and who served in about the twenty-first year of that king's reign, and thus could hardly have been born after the accession of Pepi I). Date: Teti.

[549] *Kꜣ-TP* British Museum Nos. 1181, 1173–74, 1288 = *Hieroglyphic Texts*, Vol. I, pl. 9; Vol. VI, pl. 19; Chicago Museum of Natural History No. 31709–10 (unpublished).
Saqqara? Fragments of a tomb of which the reliefs have been badly scattered. *Kꜣ-tp* was a priest of Khufu, and the high relief used on the Chicago fragments might indicate a relatively early date. Date: ?

[550] *Kꜣ-DWꜣ* Selim Hassan, *Giza*, VI^3, 93–110.
Giza, Khafre cemetery. The tomb of the father of *Ḥmw* [332], which see for description and relationship between the two mastabas. The tomb of *Kꜣ-dwꜣ* was built against the façade of the rock-cut tomb of Princess *Ḥmt-Rʿ*. A stela of *Ḥmw* was also found in this tomb [550]; he is listed as a priest of Neuserre. Date: Neuserre or later.

[551] *Kꜣ-DBḤ.N* Selim Hassan, *Giza*, V, 213–23.
Giza, Khafre cemetery. A mastaba with a north–south corridor and an east–west alcove. It had nine shafts and was built against the mastaba of *Ḫʿfrʿ-ʿnḫ*, a large mastaba with a complex chapel, including an L-shaped offering chamber and a large pillared hall. Date: VI.

[552] *GM.N.J* Firth and Gunn, *Teti Pyramid Cemeteries*, pp. 197–98.
Saqqara, Teti area. A shaft to the east of the mastaba of *Kꜣ-gm-nj* [548], containing a coffin with coffin texts. *Gm.n.j* held office at the pyramid of Pepi I. Date: mid-VI—First Intermediate.

[553] *GM.N.J-M-ḤꜣT: GM.N.J* Firth and Gunn, *Teti Pyramid Cemeteries*, pp. 187–88, pl. 27b.
Saqqara, Teti area. Priesthood of Teti and Merikare. Another example, like *Ḫwj* [364], of the

survival of Old Kingdom cults into the First Intermediate Period. Date: X.

[554] *GḤJJ* — Newberry, "The Inscribed Tombs of Ekhmîm," *LAAA*, IV, 111.
Akhmim, No. 17. Date: VI or later.

[555] *GḤSꜣ: NBJJ* — Newberry, "The Inscribed Tombs of Ekhmîm," *LAAA*, IV, 102–3.
Akhmim, No. 2. Date: VI or later.

[556] *GGJ* — Cairo, *CG*, 70–75, 213, 369; 1455.
Saqqara. Priesthood of Mernere. Date: Mernere or later.

[557] *TP-M-ʿNḪ* — Lepsius, *Denkmäler*, II, 152b.
Giza, western cemetery. Apparently from a tomb situated in the group of smaller mastabas to the north of the group Giza 6000 and to the west of Giza 4000. Date: VI (?).

[558] *TP-M-ʿNḪ* — Mariette, *Mastabas*, D 10, H 11; Cairo, *CG*, 154, 162; 1509, 1510.
Saqqara, north ridge No. 75. A mastaba with a modified cruciform chapel and a northern subsidiary niche. Priesthood of Unis. Date: Unis–VI.

[559] *TP-M-ʿNḪ* — Mariette, *Mastabas*, D 11; Cairo, *CG*, 1415, 1417, 1541, 1556, 1564; Smith, "The Origin of Some Unidentified Old Kingdom Reliefs," *AJA*, XLVI, 515–18.
Saqqara, north ridge No. 76. A mastaba with a corridor chapel with two false doors and an east–west offering alcove for the owner. The entrance was from the north. The latest king mentioned is Sahure. Smith assigns the mastaba to the first half of the Fifth Dynasty; the reasons are not expressly stated, but seem to be in part the occurrence of Sahure as the last king mentioned. He was the brother-in-law of a *Sꜣbw* who was a *ḥm-nṯr* of Ptah and almost certainly belonged to the family of *Sꜣbw*'s and *Ptḥ-špss*'s that appears to have held that office during the greater part of the Fifth and at least the earlier Sixth Dynasties. Date: mid-V.

[559A] *TP-M-ʿNḪ* — Borchardt, *Das Grabdenkmal des Königs Ne-user-Reʿ*, pp. 117–26.
Abusir. The northernmost mastaba in the first row to the east of the pyramid temple of Neuserre. It was built before the mastaba that joins it to that of *Wsrkꜣf-ʿnḫ* [123A] but after

the mastaba of the princesses (a chapel with a long north–south corridor and several false doors). It has a complex interior chapel with three rooms, including two east–west chapels. Date: Neuserre—end V (at the latest).

[560] *TTJ*

Jéquier, *Le monument funéraire de Pepi II*, III, 67–75.

South Saqqara, near Pepi II. Priesthoods of Pepi I and Pepi II. Kees, "Beiträge zur Geschichte des Vezirats im Alten Reich," *Nachr. Gött.*, N.F. IV, Phil.-hist. Klasse, 48, gives grounds for thinking that he was vizier after *N-ḥb-sd-Nfrkꜣrꜥ* [229A]. Date: Pepi II, second half.

[561] *TTJ-ꜥNḪ: JJ-M-ḤTP*

Davies, *The Rock Tombs of Sheikh Saïd*, pls. 27–30.

Sheikh Said No. 15. Pepi I is mentioned. Date: Pepi I or later.

[562] *ṮꜣWTJ*

Montet, "Les tombeaux dits de Kasr el-Sayad," *Kemi*, VI, 84–109.

El-Qasr wa's-Saiyad. Priesthood of Pepi II. Date: Pepi II (or later?).

[563] *ṮꜣWTJ: RSJ*

Petrie, *Dendereh*, Vol. I, pl. 7.

Dendera. According to Petrie, Sixth Dynasty. Date: VI or later.

[564] *ṮJJ*

Épron and Wild, *Le tombeau de Ti*; Steindorff, *Das Grab des Ti*; Mariette, *Mastabas*, D 22.

Saqqara, near north No. 60. A large mastaba with a complex chapel, still largely designed so as to be outside the main mastaba block on the east. It includes a pillared portico, a pillared court, corridors and two east–west offering chambers, one of which also has two pillars. The burial chamber is approached by a sloping passage from the northeast. Priesthoods of several kings, of which the latest is Neuserre. Date: Neuserre—end V.

[565] *ṮJJ*

Mariette, *Mastabas*, C 15; Cairo, *CG*, 95; 1380.

Saqqara, northeastern group No. 6. A mastaba with a modified cruciform chapel. Priesthood at the solar temple of Sahure. Date: Sahure or later.

[566] *ṮJJ*

Cairo, *CG*, 1522.

Provenience? Priesthood of Pepi I. Date: Pepi I or later.

[567] *ṮNTJ*

Lepsius, *Denkmäler*, II, 30–31; *Erg.*, pl. 26b.

Giza 4920 = Lepsius No. 47. A core of the first row of the cemetery *en échelon*. It was later converted into a mastaba with a two-niched, L-shaped interior chapel and a small northern niche. Reisner, *Giza*, I, 214, dates it to the early Fifth Dynasty. Date: early V or later.

[568] *ṮNTJ* Lepsius, *Denkmäler*, II, 34d–e; Mariette, *Mastabas*, p. 538; also unpublished data.
Giza. A rock-cut tomb in the cliff in the east of the eastern cemetery. It is hardly likely, because of its position, to belong to the earlier years of the cemetery. Date: V or later.

[569] *ṮNTJ* Mariette, *Mastabas*, B 1.
Saqqara, near north No. 71. A mastaba with a true cruciform chapel, dated by Smith in Reisner, *The Development of the Egyptian Tomb*, p. 392, to the Fourth Dynasty. The mastaba was situated near that of *Mṯn*. *Ṯntj* was a priest of Khufu. Date: mid-IV or later.

[569A] *ṮNTJ* Maspero, "Trois années de fouilles," *MMAFC*, I, 191.
Dahshur. Priesthood of Snefru. Date: ?

[570] *ṮNTJ* Moret, "Une nouvelle disposition testamentaire de l'Ancien Empire égyptien," *CRAIBL* (no volume number), 1914, pp. 539–46; Cairo, *CG*, 57139; *Urkunden*, I, 163–65.
Giza. One wonders whether this *Ṯntj*, of whose tomb only the legal text seems to be known, could have been related in any way to our [567]. The names of the wives are different, and thus preclude identity, but of the five *ka*-priests mentioned in the contract (*Jwfj*, *Pr-sn*, *Nfr-ḥr*, *Snb*, *Kꜣ-m-nfrt*) all except *Pr-sn* (or at least individuals of the same name) occur also in [567], the last two with the same title. Date: ?

[570A] *ṮNTJ* Ahmed Kamal, "Notes prises aux cours des inspections," *ASAE*, IX, 86–87.
South Giza. Two small, miserable false doors, one of which had a series of figures of members of *Ṯntj*'s family on the lower lintel. On the jambs were also pictures of members of the family and offering-bearers. According to Junker, *Giza*, VI, 241, this might indicate a late date in the Old Kingdom. Date: ?

[571] *ṮNTJ* Mariette, *Mastabas*, C 18.
Saqqara, northern ridge No. 72. A mastaba

with a complex interior chapel with corridor-type offering chambers. The entrance is to the south. Date: mid-V or later.

[572] *ṮNTJ*
Berlin Museum No. 7721 = Schäfer, *Aegyptische Inschriften*, I, 62.
Provenience? Date: ?

[573] *ṮRW*
Selim Hassan, *Giza*, III, 23–25.
Giza, Khafre cemetery. A small, squarish mastaba with an open-air chapel built against one of the small tombs to the southwest of *RꜤwr*. [300]. Date: VI.

[574] *ṮṮJ*
British Museum No. 157a–c = *Hieroglyphic Texts*, Vol. I, pls. 5–7; Lepsius, *Auswahl der wichtigsten Urkunden des aegyptischen Alterthums*, pl. 8.
Giza. A chapel with two false doors. Date: ?

[575] *ṮṮJ*
De Morgan, *Catalogue des monuments et inscriptions de l'Égypte antique*, I, 199–200; Newberry, "Three Old Kingdom Travellers to Byblos and Pwenet," *JEA*, XXIV, 183.
Aswan. For discussion of date, see his contemporary, *Ḫwj* [367]. Date: VI, perhaps Mernere—early Pepi II.

[576] *ṮṮW*
Firth and Gunn, *Teti Pyramid Cemeteries*, pp. 151–56; pl. 61.
Saqqara, Teti area. A tomb built into the angle formed by the mastabas of *Mrrw-kꜣ* [197] and *Kꜣ-gm-nj* [548] on the south. Priesthood of Pepi I. Date: Pepi I or later.

[577] *DꜣG*
Selim Hassan, *Giza*, II, 46–64.
Giza, Khafre cemetery. A mastaba with a corridor chapel with several false doors and a pillared hall. It had numerous shafts. It was built against the tomb of *Wꜣš-Ptḥ* [104], and is one of the earliest of a cluster of late tombs in that area, some of which were built against it. Date: VI.

[578] *DWꜣ.N-RꜤ*
Mariette, *Mastabas*, D 61, H 15; Cairo, *CG*, 1511.
Saqqara, west of Step Pyramid, very close to the Ptah-hotep group, but not necessarily a part of it. The chapel was composed of a square room with pillars. Priesthood at the solar temple of Neferirkare. Date: mid-V or later.

[579] *DWꜣ.N-ḤR*
Lepsius, *Denkmäler*, II, 82a–b.
Giza 7550 = Lepsius No. 58. According to

Reisner, *Giza*, I, 208, the son of *Kꜣ-wꜥb* [513]. However, he had the titles *zꜣ-nswt n ẖt.f, smr n jt.f*. See under *Mjn-ḏd.f* [175], whose mastaba was also very similar to this. Both apparently had an L-shaped chapel with one niche as an originally planned interior chapel. Date: end IV or somewhat later.

[580] *DWꜣ-Rꜥ: JTJJ* — Mariette, *Mastabas*, E 15.
Saqqara, west of Step Pyramid. A mastaba with a multiroomed chapel including an east–west offering chamber. Priesthood of Menkauhor. Date: Menkauhor or later.

[581] *DWꜣ-Rꜥ* — Maspero, "Trois années de fouilles," *MMAFC*, I, 190–91; Cairo, *CG*, 1325, 1375, 1389, 1552.
Dahshur. A mastaba with a corridor chapel with two stelae. At the southern end was an undecorated east–west room. Priesthood of Userkaf. Date: mid-V or later.

[582] *DWꜣ-ḤP* — Mariette, *Mastabas*, D 59.
Saqqara, west of Step Pyramid. A mastaba with a long east–west chapel with entrance on the east, much like *Ḥtp-ḥr-ꜣḫtj* [357]. Priesthood of Neuserre. Date: Neuserre or later.

[583] *DBḤ-N* — Lepsius, *Denkmäler*, II, 35–37; *Text*, I, 111–12; *Erg.*, pl. 34b; Selim Hassan, *Giza*, IV, 159–84.
Giza, Khafre cemetery, Lepsius No. 90. A rock-cut tomb with a burial chamber reached through a sloping shaft from the east (which thus is *not* a good criterion for a late date in rock-cut tombs; cf. Junker, *Giza*, VIII, 5). It was built, according to an inscription, in the reign of Menkaure. Date: Menkaure.

[583A] *DBḤ-N* — Oriental Institute No. 10734 (unpublished).
Provenience? A small false door of a man who was a priest of Sahure, Neferirkare, and Neuserre. Date: Neuserre or later.

[584] *DMWT* — Junker, *Giza*, IX, 37–38.
Giza, western cemetery. A drum found loose among the later, small mastabas in the section between the central and northern core cemeteries. Date: VI (?).

[585] *DMG* — Junker, *Giza*, V, 186–87.
Giza, western cemetery. A mastaba with a corridor chapel built against that of *Zꜣ-Nḫn* at the extreme western end of the western cemetery. Date: VI.

[586] *DNDNW* — Lepsius, *Denkmäler*, II, 93d–e.
Giza, eastern cemetery, Lepsius No. 73. A rock-cut tomb in the cliff at the eastern limit of the cemetery. One would hardly expect tombs in this location to date from the earliest years of the cemetery. Date: V–VI.

[587] *DR-SNḎ: NFRKꜣRꜥ-ꜥNḪ* — Jéquier, *Tombeaux de particuliers*, pp. 110–12.
South Saqqara, near Pepi II. Priesthood of Pepi II. Date: Pepi II.

[588] *DGM: PPJJ-MR* — Jéquier, *Tombeaux de particuliers*, pp. 117–20, pl. 16.
South Saqqara, near Pepi II. Date: Pepi II.

[589] *ḎꜣTJJ* — Lepsius, *Denkmäler*, II, 86a; Junker, *Giza*, VII, 231–40.
Giza 5370 = Lepsius No. 31. A mastaba of considerable size with an L-shaped chapel with two false doors, situated two rows to the east of the cemetery *en échelon* in the area occupied by the *Sšm-nfr* family. The mastaba was designed with an interior chapel from the beginning. It appears to be the oldest mastaba in that particular part of the cemetery; *Rꜥ-wr* [297] built his serdab against it. Sealings of Neferirkare were found here. Date: Neferirkare—mid-V.

[590] *ḎꜣTJ* — Boston Museum of Fine Arts No. 27.446 (unpublished); also unpublished data from excavation.
Giza 2337X. No archeological data available. The mastaba of a dependent of the estate (*nj ḏt*) of the vizier *Snḏm-jb* (i.e., either [455] or [456], both of which are nearby). The relationship is similar to that of *Ptḥ-nb-nfrt* [155] and [456], *Mr-sw-ꜥnḫ* [200] and *Rꜥ-wr* [300], *Kꜣkꜣj-ꜥnḫ* [547], and Queen *Rḫjt-Rꜥ*. The last two examples show that one cannot conclude from such a relationship that the lives of the persons concerned must have coincided. Date: end V or later.

[590A] *ḎꜣTJ* — Berlin Museum No. 7765 = Schäfer, *Aegyptische Inschriften*, I, 52.
Provenience? Priesthood of Mernere. Date: Mernere or later.

[591] *ḎꜥW* — Mariette, *Catalogue général des monuments d'Abydos*, No. 523; Mariette, *Abydos*, Vol. I, pl. 2; Cairo, *CG*, 1431.
Abydos. The brother of *Jdj* [73A], brother-in-

law of Pepi I and uncle of Pepi II. According to his biography he served under Pepi I, Mernere, and Pepi II. He was a vizier in the earlier years of Pepi II (decree of the year after the eleventh numbering, *Urkunden*, I, 280) and was probably listed among the courtiers in the temple of Pepi II. (Jéquier, *Le monument funéraire de Pepi II*, Vol. III, pl. 42; see Helck, *Untersuchungen*, p. 141.) His family relationships are discussed under [73A]. Date: Pepi II, early.

[592] *Ḏ*ʿ*W: ŠM*ꜣ*J* — Davies, *The Rock Tombs of Deir el-Gebrawi*, Vol. II, pls. 3–15.
Deir el-Gebrawi No. 12. The owner of this tomb was a son of *Jbj* [32]. The tomb was built after *Ḏ*ʿ*w Šm*ꜣ*j*'s death by his son *Ḏ*ʿ*w*, both for his father and himself, and he says, "Moreover, I caused myself to be buried in one tomb with this *Ḏ*ʿ*w* in order that I might be with him in one place and not because there were not the means for building two tombs." The mortuary equipment was given by King Pepi II, including, as a special honor, a posthumous promotion to the title of *ḥ*ꜣ*tj-*ʿ. Date: Pepi II, middle or somewhat later.

[593] *ḎFJ* — Seattle Art Museum No. Eg. 11.1 = *Handbook, Seattle Art Museum*, 1951, p. 9.
El-Kab. A rectangular slab with the elongated figures of the owner of the tomb and his wife preceded by his titles. Date: end VI—First Intermediate.

[594] *ḎF*ꜣ*W* — Mariette, *Mastabas*, D 25; Murray, *Seven Memphite Tomb Chapels*, pl. 14.
Saqqara, mid-north No. 55. Note that Miss Murray seems to have confused the location of this tomb with that of *Jjj* [17]. A mastaba with a small, squarish, east–west chapel entered from the east. *Ḏf*ꜣ*w* may have been a priest of Neuserre (the cartouche is damaged and restoration not absolutely certain). Date: mid-V or later.

[595] *ḎD-W*ʿ*J* — Lutz, *Steles*, pls. 3, 4.
Giza 1452 + 1453. A mastaba at the western end of the western cemetery with two L-shaped chapels and a niche. It was built against Giza 1451 which appears to have had four niches in

the eastern face (and an open-air chapel?). These are smallish tombs definitely not part of the original plan for the cemetery. Date: mid-V or later.

[596] *ḎD.F-ḪNMW* Gauthier, "Deux nouveaux princes de l'Ancien Empire à Guizeh," *ASAE*, XXII, 27; also unpublished data.
Giza 7711a. A rock-cut tomb at the northeast of the eastern cemetery. The owner had the title *zꜣ nswt*, but considering the small size of the tomb and its location is hardly likely to have been a prince of the Fourth Dynasty. Gauthier suggests a date in the Fifth Dynasty. Date: V–VI.

[597] . . . Petrie, *Medum*, pl. 16.
Meydum No. 7. A small mastaba to the east of that of *Rꜥ-ḥtp* [307]. It apparently had a passage or corridor along the east side, bulging out to form a court in the middle. There were two false doors, the southern one in a niche of some sort (the plan is too small and indistinct to reveal any details). The titles come from a fragmentary lintel of the southern false door. The mastaba seems to be composed of a retaining wall with rubble filling. Date: certainly later than the great tombs at this site, otherwise uncertain.

[598] . . . Junker, *Giza*, I, 242–48.
Giza 4860. A core mastaba in the easternmost row of the central section. It had a (now destroyed) exterior chapel around a slab stela and had never been converted to a more modern type. Junker dates the core to the reign of Menkaure. Date: mid-IV—late IV.

[599] . . . Selim Hassan, *Giza*, II, 134.
Giza, Khafre cemetery. Two pieces of a broken lintel found lying in the courtyard of the eastern section of the tomb of *Kꜣ-m-nfrt* [522] and probably belonging to a member of his family. Date: mid-V or later.

[600] . . . Unpublished.
Giza 1012. A small, free-standing mastaba in the group of small mastabas to the west of Giza 2000. On Reisner's map it looks as though it was later expanded by the addition of a

corridor on the east. Priesthood of Sahure. Date: end V or later?

[601] . . . Unpublished.
Giza 1673. A loose lintel (No. 32-4-12) apparently from this mastaba. It had a corridor chapel with at least three niches, eleven shafts, and was built between two of the core mastabas of the northwest cemetery so as to block the passage. Date: end V or later.

[601A] . . . Unpublished.
Saqqara, Unis area. A chapel to the east of that of *Ḫnw* [390]. Priesthood of Unis. Date: VI.

[601B] . . . Mariette, *Mastabas*, H 6, p. 445.
Saqqara. A fragment of an inscription. Priesthood of Userkaf. Date: V or later.

[601C] -*ḎR* Cairo, *CG*, 1349.
Provenience? Priesthood at the solar temple of Neferirkare. Date: Neferirkare or later.

[601D] Decree of Pepi II from the Valley Temple of Menkaure.
Urkunden, I, 277.
According to Smith, "Inscriptional Evidence for the History of the Fourth Dynasty," *JNES*, XI, 113, this is dated to the thirty-fifth numbering. Date: Pepi II, middle—late.

[602] Decrees of Neferkauhor from Koptos.
Urkunden, I, 295–305; Hayes, "Royal Decrees from the Temple of Min at Coptus," *JEA*, XXXII, 3–23.
A series of decrees addressed to the vizier and overseer of Upper Egypt, *Šmꜣj*, and his son, *Jdj*, in the first year of Neferkauhor. Hayes shows that the latter must have been one of the ephemeral kings of the Eighth Dynasty at the end of the Old Kingdom. Date: VIII.

[603] Expedition sent by the nomarch *Ṯꜣwtj Jqr* to Wadi Hammamat.
Urkunden, I, 258–59.
The graffiti left by this expedition giving the titles of both the nomarch and his subordinates probably date from the First Intermediate Period. There is no reference to a king in the dating. Plural strokes are used, and the title *jmj-rꜣ jḥw* is once written . Date: end VI or First Intermediate.

IV

STANDARD TITLE SEQUENCES

*

In the foregoing chapter we have listed the sources on the basis of which we intend to discuss the various datable phenomena connected with titles and their ranking sequences. The purpose of this and the following chapter is to determine what sequences of titles are characteristic for the different periods of the Old Kingdom. Later, we shall analyze some datable features of titles not directly connected with the ranking patterns; for this reason some of the sources in the preceding section have been included despite the fact that they contain relatively few rankable titles.

A collection of the titles in use in the Old Kingdom (Dynasties Four through Six) was made relatively early in the research for this investigation. I have not made an accurate count, but it seems clear that the total number of titles in use at that period was at least 1,600, most of which occur in the sources listed in chapter iii. Two problems have to be dealt with before the changes in title sequences are discussed. First of all, the vast array of titles, many of which are rare or documented only once, must be reduced somehow to more manageable proportions. Then those title sequences which remained unchanged throughout the period under consideration, the standard sequences which can serve as a useful framework for analyzing the changes in the rank of other titles but are of no help for purposes of dating themselves, have to be determined.

Most of the 1,600 or more titles fall into clearly marked groups characterized by a similar beginning. Thus there are between 400 and 500 titles beginning with *jmj-r3* (a very good illustration of the complexity of the government of Egypt at the time) and about 70 beginning with *ḥrj-sšt3*. Many of the latter seemed to be variants of each other and appeared to occur frequently in ranking charts bracketed by the same titles. It was tempting to test the possibility of simplifying the enormous mass of titles by lumping together those that showed such similarities. The results were not encouraging.

The following list indicates the sources in which more than one kind of *ḥrj-sštȝ* title occurs. An "S" after the number indicates that the titles are found in the same sequence in the ranking chart (not necessarily the same string on the wall); an "I" indicates that other titles are inserted between those beginning with *ḥrj-sštȝ*.

1
14
24
31—SI
36
41
48
49
63—SI
78—S
93
94
94A
95—SI
105
109—SI
117
123A
133
142
152
163—S (? restoration!) I
164
166—SI
167
168
170
178
189
195
197—S (twice) I (once)
215—S
215A
256
276
288
294
300
315—S
345
356
360
365
376
389
393
399
402
419
421
437—SI
475
477
478—S
479
482
487
495
523
527—SI
528
532—SI
534
548—SI
558
564—S (twice) I (twice)
574—SI
576

The majority have the titles in question in separate sequences, regularly in environments which do not indicate positively that the titles formed with *ḥrj-sštȝ* could not be of approximately the same rank. But the evidence from the 17 cases where they do occur in the same sequence is conclusive: In 13 of them other, unrelated titles intervene. In 6 of the cases one of the titles concerned is *ḥrj-sštꜣ n pr-dwꜣt*, but that is what one would expect in view of the frequent occurrence of that title.

After obtaining such negative results with the relatively small and simple group of titles beginning with *ḥrj-sštꜣ*, a glance at a chart such as that of *Ḫntj-kꜣ* [393] suffices to show that a lumping such as proposed above is certainly impossible for the enormous group of titles beginning with *jmj-rꜣ*. They occur in at least three positions: between *ḥꜣtj-ꜥ* and *tꜣtj zꜣb ṯꜣtj*, between *smr wꜥtj* and *ẖrj-tp nswt*, and below *ẖrj-tp nswt*.

Undoubtedly some of the titles in such groups did have similar rank, but the details of such groupings cannot be established until we know the ranking of all such titles throughout the course of the Old Kingdom —which still is to be established. The lumping of titles was attempted as a means for simplifying the solution to that problem; evidently it is of little use to us for that purpose.

The only remaining means for simplifying the work is to restrict the number of titles under consideration. At first an attempt was made to work with a list of 335 titles, all of which were documented at least four times in our charts. Even this restriction soon turned out to be inadequate. The ranking schemes soon became unmanageably complex and eventually a little calculation showed that a documentation of conclusions would require over a thousand pages of manuscript for this chapter alone. Finally, therefore, the 50 commonest titles in the collection, each one of which is documented at least thirty-five times, were chosen.

This restriction actually imposes itself for another reason. A preliminary survey showed that we have to reckon with about ten periods showing different characteristic title sequences in the course of the Fifth and Sixth Dynasties. In these circumstances, title sequences based on titles occurring less frequently than those in the list are not likely to carry much conviction; nor will one be able to deduce from them more than a highly fragmentary picture of the changes in rank that such titles underwent.

We will first of all give a list of the 50 (or rather 51, since it seemed wise to treat *smr* and *smr wꜥtj* as separate titles) titles whose ranking will be studied in detail. Before giving the list (which is in transliteration and follows the usual order of the Egyptian alphabet), a few remarks are in order. For the reading of the main elements of which the titles are composed, the index in Junker, *Giza*, XII, 166–76, has been followed, unless the contrary has been indicated. Nonessential matters such as capitalization and hyphenization have not been followed, nor has Junker's practice of separating nominal endings from the stem by a dot. Final weak consonants have not been indicated in those cases where the Egyptian writing does not usually indicate them. The hieroglyphic writing of titles during the Old Kingdom was usually quite abbreviated, not indicating plurals and generally omitting prepositions and connective particles. We have in general followed the Egyptian practice, thus writing *jmj-rꜣ ḫntj-š pr-ꜥꜣ* even though rare variants show that the reading was in all probability *jmj-rꜣ ḫntjw-š pr-ꜥꜣ* in all cases.

Certain variations in the titles have been ignored, and to that extent titles have been lumped: First of all, all variations caused by writing of singular and plural, or the presence and absence of the genitive particle and prepositions. A dual, however, seems not to be a permissible variant for a spelling with a singular. Then certain additions at the end of titles do not appear in our collection to produce the slightest change in the rank of the titles to which they are added. Such are:

pr-ꜥꜣ after titles ordinarily ending in *nswt* (but not otherwise)
mꜣꜥ
mꜣꜥ n jꜣwt.f
mrjj.f
m swt.f nbt
n jt.f
n bw mꜣꜥ
n mrwt
n ẖt.f
n st-jb.f
n st-jb nb.f
n swt (j)ptn
smsw

These additions can occur quite freely after a great number of titles. There are undoubtedly restrictions of usage, but since our purpose here is not a philological analysis of the titles themselves, we have not gone into the matter. It is of interest, however, that the additions such as *mꜣꜥ*, which have quite commonly been taken as indications of the declining value of the titles to which they are appended,* do not by themselves produce any change in the rank of these titles.

Besides these common additions, which will not be listed separately for each title, certain titles show other variations that do not appear to affect the ranking. These are indicated by placing the words concerned in parentheses.

* For instance, Erman and Ranke, *Ägypten und ägyptisches Leben im Alterṭum*, p. 109. But cf. *Wörterbuch*, II, 13.

The titles that will be discussed in this chapter and the next are the following:

jwn Knmwt	*ḫntj-š pr-ʿȝ*
jmj-rȝ wpt	*ḫrp ʿḥ*
jmj-rȝ pr	*ḫrp zḥ*
jmj-rȝ prwj-ḥḏ	*ḫrp šnḏwt (nbt)*
jmj-rȝ ḥm-kȝ	*ḫrj-ḥbt*
jmj-rȝ ḫntj-š pr-ʿȝ	*ḫrj-ḥbt ḥrj-tp*
jmj-rȝ zš ʿ nswt	*ḫrj-tp nswt*
jmj-rȝ sšr	*zȝ nswt*
jmj-rȝ Šmʿ	*zȝb jmj-rȝ zš*
jmj-rȝ šnwtj	*zȝb ʿḏ-mr*
jmj-rȝ kȝt nbt nt nswt	*zȝb zš*
*jrj-pʿt**	*zȝb sḥḏ zš*
jrj nfr-ḥȝt	*zš*
wʿb nswt	*zš ʿ nswt (ḫft-ḥr)§*
wr 10 *Šmʿ*	*zš mḏȝt nṯr*
mdw rḫjt	*zš n zȝ*
nst ḫntt†	*smr*
rḫ nswt‡	*smr wʿtj‖*
ḥȝtj-ʿ	*smr pr*
ḥm-nṯr Mȝʿt	*sḥḏ ḥm-kȝ*
ḥm-nṯr Ḫwfw	*sḥḏ ḫntj-š pr-ʿȝ*
ḥm-kȝ	*stm#*
ḥrj-sštȝ	*sḏȝwtj bjtj*
ḥrj-sštȝ pr dwȝt	*špss nswt***
ḥrj-tp Nḫb	*tȝtj zȝb ṯȝtj*
ḥqȝ ḥt	

* This title is discussed at length by Gardiner, *Onomastica*, I, 14°–19,° whose reading I follow.

† The reading follows *Wörterbuch*, II, 323. It cannot be correct as it stands, but there is no evidence for prefixing a *nj*, as is done by Junker.

‡ Helck, *Untersuchungen*, pp. 26–28, shows that *jrj-ḫt nswt* is the proper reading for this title and that the interpretation as "royal acquaintance" is secondary, though ancient. The older reading has been retained purely for reasons of convenience.

§ *Rʿ-wr* [297] has both *zš ʿ nswt* and *zš ʿ nswt ḫft-ḥr* in the same string, separated by other titles also beginning with *zš*, which are, however, rare and not discussed here. It occurs only once, and is the only example in the whole collection indicating a different ranking for the two; and since it disappears on the elimination of the rare titles, it has been ignored for the present.

‖ The study will show that there is no reason for supposing that *smr* and *smr wʿtj* were ranked differently during the period for which the organized system of ranking lasted. But the data on the two are listed separately.

The reading of this title is discussed in Gardiner, *Onomastica*, I, 39°–41°.

** Edel writes me that the reading *špss nswt* actually is unproved, and that he expects to publish soon an article demonstrating that *špsj nswt* is actually the correct reading. Since there is, however, no risk of confusion, we shall retain Junker's reading here.

The next step is to determine what are the *standard sequences* of these titles that remain unchanged throughout the period under consideration. First of all, a considerable number of sources (generally containing a very small number of titles in rankable sequence anyway) can be eliminated as containing no rankable sequence of these common titles. They are:

2, 4, 14A, 17, 20, 23, 28, 29, 33, 34, 35, 35A, 35B, 37, 37A, 38, 41, 42, 43, 46, 50, 51, 52, 53, 54, 58, 61A, 65A, 69, 72, 76, 87, 88A, 93, 96, 97, 99, 102, 102A, 105A, 107, 108, 113A, 116, 119, 122, 130A, 141, 144, 148, 151, 153A, 157, 161A, 165, 167A, 168A, 169, 173, 176, 179, 179A, 180, 183B, 190A, 194, 200, 203A, 203B, 205, 207A, 208, 216, 217, 219, 221, 226, 230, 231A, 234, 237, 239, 240A, 243A, 243B, 247A, 253, 253A, 255, 261, 264, 265, 266, 268B, 269, 269A, 270, 271, 276, 278, 283, 284, 289, 291, 295, 302, 304, 308, 310, 312, 314, 316, 319, 321, 326, 327, 328, 339, 343, 344, 347, 348, 353, 354, 358A, 358B, 362, 369, 373A, 374, 377, 379, 380, 381A, 384A, 385, 387, 389A, 403, 405, 410, 413, 417A, 420, 423, 427, 430A, 436, 436A, 442, 443, 446, 451A, 451B, 452A, 453, 454, 456A, 459, 460, 461, 462, 468, 469, 472, 487, 487A, 490, 491, 494A, 496, 500A, 503, 506, 508, 511A, 519, 521, 524, 527, 529, 529A, 535, 537, 538, 540A, 540B, 546A, 547, 551, 554, 557, 559, 565, 569A, 570A, 574, 580, 583A, 584, 585, 589, 594, 597, 599, 601, 601B, 601C.

Many of these contain titles and title sequences that will concern us later. Some of them are unpublished or only partly published, and it is possible that, if they were more completely available, they would also exhibit rankable sequences of the common titles.

The amount of data left even after elimination of all but the commonest titles is still quite enormous, and it soon became obvious that it was hopeless to attempt to obtain results by direct examination of the charts. The following procedure was therefore followed. First of all, all existing relative rankings of all possible combinations of two titles were recorded. The results were then entered on a large sheet of squared paper, with the lines indicating the first title and the columns the second title of each such combination. From this chart it was relatively easy to establish which sequences occurred only one way, and thus presumably could be considered as valid for the whole period under consideration, and which occurred both ways and thus fluctuated and would, if our working hypothesis is validated, be evidence for dating. In principle, the ranking chart of standard sequences given at the end of the chapter could then be directly drawn up. In practice certain difficulties are encountered.

In the first place, it was already obvious at the time that the material was gathered, that the system of ranking titles that was established on the basis of tombs of the Fifth and Sixth Dynasties was not likely to work at an earlier date. Most of the tombs of the Fourth Dynasty, at least as preserved, contain relatively few titles and tend to arrange them in very short lines giving only one title, or even only part of a title. It thus becomes quite difficult to obtain reliable ranking sequences from them, and those that one does obtain from the few lines of text containing more than one title appear odd. One factor that is quite obvious even before any of the charts are studied in detail is the fact that the title *zꜣ nswt*, which one would expect to rank very highly, and which during the Fifth and Sixth Dynasties is only outranked by *jrj-pꜥt*, can occur in the tombs of the Fourth and early Fifth Dynasties in positions where it is outranked by most titles. The complete data will be given at the end of the chapter, where we will discuss the tombs that violate the standard sequence of titles. Here we can point out such cases as that of *Ḥm-Jwnw* [331], where *zꜣ nswt* is outranked by *tꜣtj zꜣb ṯꜣtj*, *sḏꜣwtj bjtj*, and *jmj-rꜣ kꜣt nbt nt nswt*, among the common titles, or *Kꜣ-nfr* [534], where the position of *zꜣ nswt* is quite irregular, occurring at odd places in the strings, usually at the beginning or end, but not always. All relative sequences of two titles that occurred in tombs which appeared to belong to the early period from the data given in the list in the last chapter, were therefore marked, and if a sequence only occurred in such tombs, it was ignored for purposes of establishing the standard sequence of titles.

Likewise, an attempt at applying our ranking procedures to the titles in the tomb of Amenemhat at Beni Hassan (No. 2) very rapidly showed that the procedure followed for ranking titles in the Old Kingdom did not work for the Middle Kingdom. It was to be assumed that some of the later tombs in our collection might already be from the period when the system had begun to break down. Any odd sequence from such a tomb was therefore marked and generally ignored if it conflicted with a very well documented and otherwise uncontradicted sequence from earlier tombs.

Even in tombs from the period in which the ranking system was certainly operative, a certain amount of error has to be expected. If the relative ranking of two titles fluctuated, it was entered both ways into the chart, unless there was very good reason to suspect a mistake (sequence occurring many times one way, only once the other—indicated by a question mark). A few other cases where error might be suspected, generally only contradictions of exceedingly well documented sequences, and then only if the contradiction was virtually unparalleled, were also marked with question marks. This was done with relatively little hesitation in such cases as in [361] and [560], which have one string each in which *ẖrj-ḥbt* occurs where one would expect *ẖrj-ḥbt ḥrj-tp*. In any case, all places where there is reason to suspect an error are marked.

Another difficulty that has to be faced is that of poor documentation. When a sequence such as *smr wʿtj, ẖrj-ḥbt* occurs ninety-nine times without being contradicted, there can be little question that this is a standard sequence, but what if such a sequence is documented only once? The accidents of preservation of what is obviously an uncommon grouping may simply have left us without any documentation for the reverse. In actual practice the risk has turned out to be a possibility for uncontradicted sequences documented fewer than ten times and acute for those documented fewer than four times. In some cases we must face the situation helplessly. In other cases better documented sequences serve as a check. To give a simplified example, let us assume that the following diagram represents the true standard sequence of a group of titles:

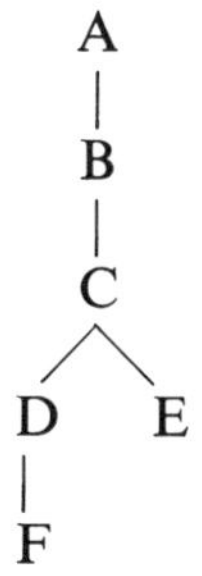

It is quite conceivable that the relationship of E to D and F is not well documented and that only the sequence FE is found. One would be tempted to insert E into the chart below F. Before doing so, it is absolutely necessary to check the relationship of E to the titles which have already been established, we assume, as outranking F. If the sequence ED is found, it is evident that FE cannot be part of the permanent sequence. Of course, neither can ED. On the other hand, if AB, BC, and CD are all well documented sequences, it is evident that AD is also valid, even if it is documented only once.

The procedure followed in setting up the chart of standard sequences was therefore to begin with the best documented uncontradicted sequences and then to work back to the rarer combinations. In the event two not directly contradicted sequences could not both be worked into the standard sequence chart because of indirectly implied contradictions, the better documented one was given preference.

As was already remarked earlier, one of the less pleasant aspects of the problem being studied in this book is that the bulk of material involved makes the full presentation of the material contained in the ranking charts, not to mention the individual strings of titles on which they are based, quite impractical, and there is unfortunately not enough space available to give even the simplified charts that are left after removal of all except the commonest titles. The reader will have to be content with the samples given in chapter ii, the long list of references in chapter iii (from whose not inconsiderable length one can obtain some idea of the bulk that a full documentation would occupy), and the selected sequences in chapters v and vi. However, the reader has a right to expect a minimum of documentation. I have therefore copied in the following pages the list giving all the documented sequences of two titles in the group of 51 that are found in the charts. If the diagram on the preceding page represents the ranking chart for a tomb, the reference number for this tomb would be entered under AB, AC, AD, AF, AE, BC, BD, BF, BE, CD, CF, CE, and DF. Clumsy as it looks, this procedure is an absolute necessity in any case for establishing the standard sequences of as large a body of material as is being considered here. By collecting all the sequences of two titles listed for a given source, it would also be possible to reconstruct the ranking sequence of the common titles documented for that tomb, though admittedly it would be a rather wearisome process. But in any case, the material both for the standard sequences and for the variable ones is given.

Before proceeding to give the data, some of the symbols employed should be explained. The numbers, of course, refer to the sources listed in chapter iii. A Roman (IV) in parentheses after a number indicates that the tomb probably dates from the Fourth or early Fifth Dynasties. Sequences that seem to be the result of an error or to be odd sequences from late tombs are marked by a question mark and some comment in parentheses. A sequence of titles that is part of the chart of *standard* sequences is marked by an [S] in brackets. A sequence that *violates* the standard sequence chart (evidently only supported by early or otherwise dubious examples) is marked by a [V]. A sequence not directly contradicted but which cannot be admitted to the standard sequence chart because of an implied *contradiction* is marked by a [C] followed by a brief indication of the reasons for its inadmissibility. Sequences whose reverse also occurs in charts presumably dating from the Fifth or Sixth Dynasties are left unmarked, as are also sequences agreeing with the chart of standard sequences that happen to be documented only in early or otherwise uncertain examples.

The sequences are numbered by two Arabic numerals separated by a diagonal stroke (e.g., 12/35) and referred to by those numbers. It will be easier to follow the remarks made about the various sequences by referring to the charts of standard sequences at the end of the chapter.

1. Sequences beginning with *JWN KNMWT:*

1/1. *jmj-rꜣ prwj-ḥd:* 160, 274. [C]. (Cf. 4/9, 4/11.)
1/2. *jmj-rꜣ šnwtj:* 57, 160, 274, 315. [C] (Cf. 10/8, 10/13, 10/15.)
1/3. *wr* 10 *Šmꜥ:* 90, 95, 294, 315, 333, 482, 523.
1/4. *mdw rḫjt:* 26 (? Documented only once.) 95 (? Only once on an offering slab which also contradicts the usual sequence in this tomb on other occasions), 215 (IV), 467 (? Again documented only once. In view of the exceedingly common occurrence of the reverse sequence 16/1, the chances are that this is a mistake.) [V].
1/5. *nst ḫntt:* 161, 294, 315 (? Restored and very doubtful as it disagrees with the regular position of this title in this tomb), 333, 363, 482, 500.
1/6. *rḫ nswt:* 523.
1/7. *ḥm-nṯr Mꜣꜥt:* 13, 14, 77, 94, 95, 105, 133, 161, 181, 294, 315, 381, 467, 480, 482, 505, 523.
1/8. *ḥm-kꜣ:* 6 (IV).
1/9. *ḥrj-sštꜣ:* 14, 470, 482, 523. [C]. (Cf. 23/3.)
1/10. *ẖrj-ḥbt:* 105, 394.
1/11. *zꜣb ꜥḏ-mr:* 161, 333, 363, 500.
1/12. *zš ꜥ nswt:* 77, 381. [S].

2. Sequences beginning with *JMJ-Rꜣ WPT:*

2/1. *jmj-rꜣ ḫntj-š pr-ꜥꜣ:* 131.
2/2. *wꜥb nswt:* 543. [S].
2/3. *mdw rḫjt:* 536 (IV).
2/4. *nst ḫntt:* 48.
2/5. *rḫ nswt:* 536 (IV), 543A, 570.
2/6. *ḥqꜣ ḥt:* 131. [C]. (Cf. 26/27.)
2/7. *ḫrp ꜥḥ:* 536 (IV).
2/8. *ẖrj-ḥbt:* 131.
2/9. *ẖrj-tp nswt:* 48, 131.
2/10. *zꜣ nswt:* 534 (IV). [V].
2/11. *zꜣb ꜥḏ-mr:* 48, 558.
2/12. *zꜣb zš:* 558. [S].
2/13. *zꜣb sḥḏ zš:* 558. [S].
2/14. *zš ꜥ nswt:* 131. [S].
2/15. *smr:* 131, 536 (IV). [C]. (Cf. 43/10 and 31/2.)
2/16. *smr wꜥtj:* 131, 536 (IV).
2/17. *smr pr:* 210. [S].
2/18. *špss nswt:* 210. [S].

3. Sequences beginning with *JMJ-Rꜣ PR:*

3/1. *jmj-rꜣ ḥm-kꜣ:* 123, 251, 329, 404, 444 (IV), 518. [S].
3/2. *jmj-rꜣ sšr:* 207. [S].
3/3. *jmj-rꜣ šnwtj:* 553. [C]. (Cf. 10/8, 10/11, 10/13, 10/15.)
3/4. *wꜥb nswt:* 518.
3/5. *rḫ nswt:* 553.
3/6. *ḥm-kꜣ:* 145, 590. [S].
3/7. *ḥqꜣ ḥt:* 167 (? This is the title of a servant. Assuming that this is not a mistake, it would still be most astonishing to have a title that is well documented in a high-ranking position [26/24] suddenly outranked by a title close to the bottom of the standard ranking chart. According to Junker, *Giza*, III, 90–96, one must distinguish two uses of this title. When held by household officials, it indicates a man, barely ranking above the menials, engaged in managing a portion of his lord's domain. When held by an official engaged in the administration of the public domains, it indicates a rather exalted office. Evidently we have here an example of the former usage—something which would occur only rarely since the titles of household officials rarely are given in any rankable sequence. They generally do not have enough.) [V].
3/8. *ḫrp zḥ:* 483. [S].
3/9. *zš n zꜣ:* 155, 590.
3/10. *sḥḏ ḥm-kꜣ:* 479.

4. Sequences beginning with *JMJ-Rꜣ PRWJ-ḤḎ:*

4/1. *jmj-rꜣ šnwtj:* 361, 393.
4/2. *ḥrj-tp Nḫb:* 32.
4/3. *ḥqꜣ ḥt:* 32. [C]. (Cf. 26/4, 44/10.)
4/4. *ḫrp šnḏwt nbt:* 361 (? Dubious since one link in the sequence is 31/29), 560.
4/5. *ḫrj-ḥbt:* 32, 361, 560. [C]. (Cf. 31/5, 31/7.)
4/6. *ḫrj-ḥbt ḥrj-tp:* 560.
4/7. *ḫrj-tp nswt:* 32.
4/8. *zš mḏꜣt nṯr:* 32, 361, 560. [C]. (Cf. 41/2, 41/3, 41/4.)
4/9. *smr wꜥtj:* 32, 560.
4/10. *stm:* 361 (? cf. 4/4), 560.
4/11. *sḏꜣwtj bjtj:* 32.

5. Sequences beginning with *JMJ-Rꜣ ḤM-Kꜣ:*

5/1. *wꜥb nswt:* 518.
5/2. *rḫ nswt:* 435.
5/3. *sḥḏ ḥm-kꜣ:* 492. [C]. (Cf. 46/1.)

6. Sequences beginning with *JMJ-Rꜣ ḪNTJ-Š PR-ꜥꜣ:*

6/1. *jmj-rꜣ wpt:* 556.

6/2. *jmj-rꜣ prwj-ḥḏ:* 393. [C]. (Cf. 4/9, 4/10, 4/11.)
6/3. *jmj-rꜣ šnwtj:* 393. [C]. (Cf. 10/4, 10/5, 10/13, 10/14, 10/15.)
6/4. *ḥrj-sštꜣ:* 356. [S].
6/5. *ḫrp ꜥḥ:* 356. [C]. (Cf. 28/11.)
6/6. *ẖrj-ḥbt:* 15, 131, 247, 280, 305, 562.
6/7. *ẖrj-tp nswt:* 86, 185.
6/8. *zꜣb ꜥḏ-mr:* 36. [S].
6/9. *zš mḏꜣt nṯr:* 562. [C]. (Cf. 41/14.)
6/10. *zš n zꜣ:* 556. [S].
6/11. *smr pr:* 356, 437. [S].
6/12. *špss nswt:* 15, 437, 556. [S].
6/13. *ḥrj-sštꜣ pr dwꜣt:* 562. [C]. (Cf. 24/5.)

7. Sequences beginning with *JMJ-Rꜣ ZŠ ꜥ NSWT:*

7/1. *jwn Knmwt:* 13, 57, 133, 160, 171, 274, 275, 294, 315. [S].
7/2. *jmj-rꜣ pr:* 133. [S].
7/3. *jmj-rꜣ prwj-ḥḏ:* 57, 158, 160, 202, 229A, 274, 402, 548, 560. [S].
7/4. *jmj-rꜣ Šmꜥ:* 133, 602.
7/5. *jmj-rꜣ šnwtj:* 13, 57, 133, 158, 160, 197, 202, 274, 315, 465, 548, 560. [S].
7/6. *jmj-rꜣ kꜣt nbt nt nswt:* 57, 105, 158, 159, 189, 274, 315, 455, 548.
7/7. *jrj nfr-ḥꜣt:* 133.
7/8. *wr 10 Šmꜥ:* 13, 294, 315.
7/9. *mdw rḫjt:* 13, 57, 133, 274, 275.
7/10. *nst ḫntt:* 294, 315 (? cf. 1/5).
7/11. *ḥꜣtj-ꜥ:* 229A, 602.
7/12. *ḥm-nṯr Mꜣꜥt:* 13, 133, 294, 315.
7/13. *ḥrj-sštꜣ:* 477. [S].
7/14. *ḥrj-sštꜣ pr dwꜣt:* 133, 197, 419.
7/15. *ḥrj-tp Nḫb:* 197, 602.
7/16. *ḫrp šnḏwt nbt:* 135, 189, 197, 229A, 560, 591. [C]. (Cf. 41/13, 13/2, 28/3.)
7/17. *ẖrj-ḥbt:* 133, 160, 189, 197, 455, 560, 602. [S].
7/18. *ẖrj-ḥbt ḥrj-tp:* 135, 189, 197, 560, 591.
7/19. *ẖrj-tp nswt:* 13, 57, 133, 274, 275, 602.
7/20. *zꜣb jmj-rꜣ zš:* 133. [S].
7/21. *zꜣb ꜥḏ-mr:* 133.
7/22. *zš:* 133. [S].
7/23. *zš ꜥ nswt:* 133. [S].
7/24. *zš mḏꜣt nṯr:* 160, 189, 197, 560.
7/25. *smr wꜥtj:* 133, 135, 189, 197, 229A, 419, 560, 602.
7/26. *smr pr:* 133. [S].
7/27. *stm:* 135, 189, 197, 229A, 560, 591. [C]. (Cf. under 7/16.)
7/28. *sḏꜣwtj bjtj:* 133, 135, 197, 229A, 591, 602.
7/29. *špss nswt:* 133. [S].

8. Sequence beginning with *JMJ-Rꜣ SŠR:*

8/1. *ḥm-kꜣ:* 13, 161.

9. Sequences beginning with *JMJ-Rꜣ ŠMꜤ:*

9/1. *jwn Knmwt:* 13, 133, 315, 505. [S].
9/2. *jmj-rꜣ pr:* 134. [S].
9/3. *jmj-rꜣ prwj-ḥḏ:* 32, 212, 274, 393, 505, 592. [S].
9/4. *jmj-rꜣ ḫntj-š pr-Ꜥꜣ:* 110, 131, 134, 187, 393, 562. [S].
9/5. *jmj-rꜣ zš Ꜥ nswt:* 315, 505.
9/6. *jmj-rꜣ šnwtj:* 13, 32, 112A, 134, 212, 274, 315, 393, 533. [S].
9/7. *jmj-rꜣ kꜣt nbt nt nswt:* 135, 315. [S].
9/8. *wr* 10 *ŠmꜤ:* 13, 315, 505. [S].
9/9. *mdw rḫjt:* 13, 133, 192, 315, 505. [S].
9/10. *nst ḫntt:* 315, 505. [S].
9/11. *ḥm-nṯr MꜣꜤt:* 13, 112, 133, 315, 505. [S].
9/12. *ḥrj-sštꜣ:* 187, 323. [S].
9/13. *ḥrj-sštꜣ pr dwꜣt:* 187, 562. [S].
9/14. *ḥrj-tp Nḫb:* 32, 110, 212, 602.
9/15. *ḥqꜣ ḥt:* 32, 81, 106, 110, 131, 562, 592.
9/16. *ḫrp šnḏwt nbt:* 110, 131, 134, 212, 592.
9/17. *ẖrj-ḥbt:* 32, 39, 81, 106, 131, 134, 187, 212, 323, 345, 395, 562, 592, 602.
9/18. *ẖrj-ḥbt ḥrj-tp:* 110, 131, 134, 137, 212.
9/19. *ẖrj-tp nswt:* 32, 106, 112, 131, 133, 192, 212, 315, 393, 505, 602.
9/20. *zꜣb jmj-rꜣ zš:* 133. [S].
9/21. *zꜣb Ꜥḏ-mr:* 315, 505. [S].
9/22. *zš Ꜥ nswt:* 131, 133. [S].
9/23. *zš mḏꜣt nṯr:* 32, 110, 323, 562, 592.
9/24. *smr:* 110, 131. [C]. (Cf. 43/10 and 31/5.)
9/25. *smr wꜤtj:* 32, 39, 81, 106, 110, 131, 134, 135, 137, 187, 212, 213, 323, 345, 395, 562, 592, 602.
9/26. *stm:* 131, 134, 212, 592.
9/27. *sḏꜣwtj bjtj:* 32, 81, 106, 212, 213, 345, 562.

10. Sequences beginning with *JMJ-Rꜣ ŠNWTJ:*

10/1. *jmj-rꜣ prwj-ḥḏ:* 32, 146, 158, 160, 162, 202, 274, 349, 548, 560, 592.
10/2. *ḥrj-sštꜣ:* 376, 475. [S].
10/3. *ḥrj-tp Nḫb:* 32.
10/4. *ḥqꜣ ḥt:* 32.
10/5. *ḫrp šnḏwt nbt:* 361 (? cf. 4/4), 560.
10/6. *ẖrj-ḥbt:* 32, 361, 560.
10/7. *ẖrj-ḥbt ḥrj-tp:* 560.
10/8. *ẖrj-tp nswt:* 32.
10/9. *zꜣb jmj-rꜣ zš:* 133. [S].
10/10. *zꜣb Ꜥḏ-mr:* 133.
10/11. *zš Ꜥ nswt:* 133. [C]. (Cf. 40/2 and 3/3.)
10/12. *zš mḏꜣt nṯr:* 32, 361, 560. [C]. (Cf. 41/2, 41/3, 41/4.)
10/13. *smr wꜤtj:* 32, 560.

10/14. *stm:* 361 (? cf. 4/4), 560.
10/15. *sḏꜣwtj bjtj:* 32.

11. Sequences beginning with *JMJ-RꜢ KꜢT NBT NT NSWT:*

11/1. *jwn Knmwt:* 57, 160, 215 (IV), 274, 275, 294, 505. [S].
11/2. *jmj-rꜣ prwj-ḥḏ:* 57, 158, 160, 274, 505. [S].
11/3. *jmj-rꜣ ḫntj-š pr-ꜥꜣ:* 185. [C]. (Cf. 6/8 and 36/6, also 17/5.)
11/4. *jmj-rꜣ zš ꜥ nswt:* 105, 146, 160, 197, 274, 363, 455, 505, 564, 590.
11/5. *jmj-rꜣ šnwtj:* 57, 158, 160, 197, 274, 315, 402. [S].
11/6. *wr* 10 *Šmꜥ:* 294, 473 (IV), 505.
11/7. *mdw rḫjt:* 57, 94, 215 (IV), 274, 275, 505.
11/8. *nst ḫntt:* 294, 505.
11/9. *rḫ nswt:* 473 (IV).
11/10. *ḥm-nṯr Mꜣꜥt:* 294, 505. [S].
11/11. *ḥrj-sštꜣ:* 236, 463, 475. [S].
11/12. *ḥrj-sštꜣ pr dwꜣt:* 197.
11/13. *ḥrj-tp Nḫb:* 197.
11/14. *ḥqꜣ ḥt:* 185. [C]. (Cf. 26/4.)
11/15. *ḫrp ꜥḥ:* 473 (IV).
11/16. *ḫrp šnḏwt nbt:* 197.
11/17. *ẖrj-ḥbt:* 160, 182 (IV), 185, 197, 455, 473 (IV).
11/18. *ẖrj-ḥbt ḥrj-tp:* 197.
11/19. *ẖrj-tp nswt:* 57, 94, 185, 215 (IV), 274, 275, 286, 505.
11/20. *zꜣ nswt:* 331 (IV), 473 (IV). [V].
11/21. *zꜣb ꜥḏ-mr:* 505.
11/22. *zš mḏꜣt nṯr:* 160, 197.
11/23. *smr:* 182 (IV), 473 (IV).
11/24. *smr wꜥtj:* 182 (IV), 185, 197, 286, 286A–B.
11/25. *stm:* 197.
11/26. *sḏꜣwtj bjtj:* 197.

12. Sequences beginning with *JRJ-PꜤT:*

12/1. *jwn Knmwt:* 57, 133, 160, 274, 333. [S].
12/2. *jmj-rꜣ wpt:* 279, 342, 534 (IV). [S].
12/3. *jmj-rꜣ pr:* 133. [S].
12/4. *jmj-rꜣ prwj-ḥḏ:* 32, 57, 158, 160, 202, 229A, 274, 279, 361, 393, 408, 548, 560, 576, 592. [S].
12/5. *jmj-rꜣ ḫntj-š pr-ꜥꜣ:* 279, 393, 562. [S].
12/6. *jmj-rꜣ zš ꜥ nswt:* 57, 94, 133, 135, 158, 159, 160, 189, 197, 202, 229A, 274, 324, 340, 393, 455, 456, 548, 560, 591, 602. [S].
12/7. *jmj-rꜣ sšr:* 393. [S].
12/8. *jmj-rꜣ Šmꜥ:* 32, 133, 135, 202, 279, 395, 493B, 562, 592, 602, 603. [S].
12/9. *jmj-rꜣ šnwtj:* 32, 57, 133, 158, 160, 197, 202, 274, 279, 361, 393, 408, 548, 560, 576. [S].
12/10. *jmj-rꜣ kꜣt nbt nt nswt:* 57, 94, 135, 158, 159, 160, 189, 197, 260 (IV), 274, 331 (IV), 393, 399 (IV), 455, 456, 548. [S].

12/11. *jrj nfr-ḥꜣt:* 133, 202, 279, 285, 361, 408, 548. [S].
12/12. *wr* 10 *Šmʿ:* 333, 473A (IV). [S].
12/13. *mdw rḫjt:* 57, 94, 133, 160, 274, 333, 534 (IV). [S].
12/14. *nst ḫntt:* 333. [S].
12/15. *ḥꜣtj-ʿ:* 31 (IV), 57, 94, 132, 133, 135, 153, 158, 159, 160, 174 (IV), 184, 189, 197, 202, 229A, 249, 260 (IV), 272, 274, 279, 285, 324, 331 (IV), 333, 338, 340, 342, 361, 366, 393, 395, 399 (IV), 402, 408, 409, 438, 450 (IV), 455, 456, 493B, 534 (IV), 548, 560, 562, 571, 576, 591, 592, 602, 603. [S].
12/16. *ḥm-nṯr Mꜣʿt:* 133, 576. [S].
12/17. *ḥrj-sštꜣ:* 399 (IV).
12/18. *ḥrj-sštꜣ pr dwꜣt:* 133, 197, 202, 249, 471 (IV), 484 (IV), 534 (IV), 562, 576. [S].
12/19. *ḥrj-tp Nḫb:* 32, 133, 189, 197, 303, 399 (IV), 548, 576, 602. [S].
12/20. *ḥqꜣ ḥt:* 32, 562, 592. [S].
12/21. *ḫrp ʿḥ:* 30 (IV), 399 (IV), 471 (IV), 484 (IV), 534 (IV).
12/22. *ḫrp šndwt nbt:* 32, 133, 135, 189, 197, 229A, 279, 324, 333, 361, 393, 560, 571, 576, 591, 592. [S].
12/23. *ẖrj-ḥbt:* 30 (IV), 32, 132, 133, 160, 189, 197, 202, 241 (IV), 272, 279, 285, 311, 324, 333, 338, 342, 361, 393, 395, 399 (IV), 438, 455, 484 (IV), 560, 562, 576, 592, 602, 603. [S].
12/24. *ẖrj-ḥbt ḥrj-tp:* 30 (IV), 32, 91 (IV), 132, 133, 135, 189, 197, 241 (IV), 248 (IV), 249, 279, 303, 324, 333, 361, 393, 399 (IV), 471 (IV), 548, 560, 571, 576, 591. [S].
12/25. *ẖrj-tp nswt:* 32, 57, 94, 133, 202, 274, 279, 311, 333, 342, 393, 534 (IV), 602. [S].
12/26. *zꜣ nswt:* 30 (IV), 80, 91 (IV), 174 (IV), 223, 241 (IV), 248 (IV), 260 (IV), 262 (IV), 303, 311, 331 (IV), 386 (IV), 399 (IV), 400 (IV), 450 (IV). 471 (IV), 484 (IV), 502A, 534 (IV), 560, 601D. [S].
12/27. *zꜣb jmj-rꜣ zš:* 133. [S].
12/28. *zꜣb ʿḏ-mr:* 133, 333. [S].
12/29. *zš:* 133. [S].
12/30. *zš ʿ nswt:* 133, 576. [S].
12/31. *zš mḏꜣt nṯr:* 30 (IV), 32, 133, 160, 189, 197, 248 (IV), 249, 303, 361, 393, 548, 560, 562, 571, 576, 592. [S].
12/32. *smr:* 174, 399 (IV). [S].
12/33. *smr wʿtj:* 30 (IV), 32, 57, 73A, 132, 133, 135, 160, 174 (IV), 189, 197, 202, 229A, 249, 272, 274, 279, 285, 303, 324, 333, 338, 342, 361, 393, 395, 399 (IV), 408, 409, 438, 450 (IV), 456, 471 (IV), 484 (IV), 548, 560, 562, 571, 576, 592, 602, 603. [S].
12/34. *smr pr:* 133. [S].
12/35. *stm:* 32, 133, 135, 189, 197, 229A, 279, 324, 333, 361, 393, 560, 571, 576, 591, 592. [S].
12/36. *sḏꜣwtj bjtj:* 30 (IV), 32, 132, 133, 135, 160, 175 (IV), 189, 197, 229A, 249, 260 (IV), 262 (IV), 279, 285, 331 (IV), 361, 395, 408, 409, 450 (IV), 548, 562, 576, 591, 592, 602. [S].

12/37. *špss nswt:* 133. [S].
12/38. *ṯ3tj ṯ3b ṯ3tj:* 30 (IV), 57, 73A, 94, 133, 135, 153, 158, 159, 160, 174 (IV), 184, 189, 197, 202, 229A, 241 (IV), 248 (IV), 249, 260 (IV), 274, 279, 324, 331 (IV), 340, 375, 393, 399 (IV), 402, 455, 456, 471 (IV), 473A (IV), 534 (IV), 548, 560, 571, 591, 602. [S].

13. Sequences beginning with *JRJ NFR-Ḥ3T:*

13/1. *jmj-r3 prwj-ḥḏ:* 361. [C]. (Cf. 4/4, 4/6, 4/10.)
13/2. *jmj-r3 zš ʿ nswt:* 105.
13/3. *jmj-r3 šnwtj:* 361. [C]. (Cf. 10/5, 10/7, 10/14.)
13/4. *jmj-r3 k3t nbt nt nswt:* 105. [C]. (Cf. 11/16, 11/18, 11/25, 11/26.)
13/5. *wʿb nswt:* 360. [S].
13/6. *rḫ nswt:* 360. [C]. (Cf. 18/18.)
13/7. *ḥrj-sšt3:* 288, 360, 401, 564. [S].
13/8. *ḥrj-sšt3 pr dw3t:* 105, 411, 559A, 564. [C]. (Cf. 24/8.)
13/9. *ḥrj-tp Nḫb:* 105, 142, 223, 246, 564.
13/10. *ḫrp ʿḥ:* 154, 559A, 564, 583 (IV).
13/11. *ḫrp šnḏwt nbt:* 361 (? Mistake, cf. 4/4.) [V].
13/12. *ḫrj-ḥbt:* 105, 361, 564.
13/13. *zš mḏ3t nṯr:* 361, 564.
13/14. *smr wʿtj:* 170, 411.
13/15. *smr pr:* 170.
13/16. *stm:* 361 (? Mistake, cf. 4/4.) [V].

14. Sequences beginning with *WʿB NSWT:*

14/1. *jmj-r3 pr:* 190, 207, 251, 258, 386 (IV), 550.
14/2. *jmj-r3 ḥm-k3:* 140, 251, 492, 550, 577.
14/3. *jmj-r3 sšr:* 207. [S].
14/4. *wr* 10 *Šmʿ:* 517.
14/5. *rḫ nswt:* 16, 22, 25, 115 (?), 124, 199, 243, 251, 258, 332, 360, 428, 458, 486, 528, 550, 600.
14/6. *ḥm-nṯr Ḫwfw:* 16, 21, 36, 172, 190, 193, 235, 251, 355, 378, 386 (IV), 398, 501, 502, 539.
14/7. *ḥm-k3:* 440. [S].
14/8. *ḥrj-sšt3:* 16, 36, 75, 115, 172, 235, 245, 277, 322, 332, 520.
14/9. *ḫntj-š pr-ʿ3:* 172, 322.
14/10. *ḫrp zḥ:* 464. [S].
14/11. *z3b jmj-r3 zš:* 452.
14/12. *z3b zš:* 452.
14/13. *zš:* 514. [S].
14/14. *sḥḏ ḥm-k3:* 242, 492. [C]. (Cf. 46/6.)
14/15. *sḥḏ ḫntj-š pr-ʿ3:* 378, 398, 539.

15. Sequences beginning with *WR* 10 *ŠMʿ:*

15/1. *jwn Knmwt:* 171, 338A, 350, 465, 505, 515, 523.
15/2. *jmj-r3 wpt:* 543, 570. [C]. (Cf. 2/14 and 41/5, etc.)

15/3. *jmj-r3 zš ˁ nswt:* 171.
15/4. *jmj-r3 k3t nbt nt nswt:* 143 (IV?), 376.
15/5. *wˁb nswt:* 511, 543.
15/6. *mdw rḫjt:* 123A, 171, 350, 515.
15/7. *nst ḫntt:* 8, 9, 70, 187, 257, 294, 315 (? Restored, cf. 1/5), 338A, 376, 465, 532, 544, 578.
15/8. *rḫ nswt:* 128, 182 (IV), 187, 250, 313, 351, 448, 473 (IV), 476 (IV), 489, 523, 532, 543, 543A, 570, 581, 596.
15/9. *ḥm-nṯr M3ˁt:* 45, 70, 123A, 171, 294, 465, 482, 505, 523, 544.
15/10. *ḥrj-sšt3:* 88 (IV), 257, 376, 482, 523, 581.
15/11. *ḥq3 ḥt:* 307 (IV).
15/12. *ḫrj-tp nswt:* 171, 187, 350, 489.
15/13. *z3b jmj-r3 zš:* 70, 198, 489.
15/14. *z3b ˁḏ-mr:* 187, 350.
15/15. *zš:* 448. [S].
15/16. *zš ˁ nswt:* 143 (IV?).
15/17. *zš mḏ3t nṯr:* 293 (IV).
15/18. *smr:* 182 (IV), 358 (? This is the tomb with the odd assemblage of archaizing titles; and it is rather doubtful that the rankings given here are of any value.) [C]. (Cf. 43/12 and 33/10.) (If, as is maintained in this study, *smr* is only a variant for *smr wˁtj*, [V].)
15/19. *ḫrp ˁḥ:* 182 (IV).
15/20. *smr wˁtj:* 182 (IV). [V].
15/21. *ḫrj-ḥbt:* 182 (IV).

16. Sequences beginning with *MDW RḪJT:*

16/1. *jwn Knmwt:* 13, 14, 56, 57, 59, 62, 77, 78, 105, 133, 160, 161, 171, 181, 273, 274, 275, 281, 294, 315, 333, 350, 363, 381, 394, 396, 402, 465, 470, 480, 481, 482, 495, 500, 505, 515, 516, 523, 559A, 560. [S].
16/2. *jmj-r3 prwj-ḥḏ:* 160, 274. [C]. (Cf. 4/7, 4/9, 4/11.)
16/3. *jmj-r3 zš ˁ nswt:* 146, 171, 294, 315, 505.
16/4. *jmj-r3 šnwtj:* 13, 57, 160, 274, 315. [C]. (Cf. 10/8, 10/13, 10/15.)
16/5. *jmj-r3 k3t nbt nt nswt:* 146, 294, 315.
16/6. *wr* 10 *Šmˁ:* 13, 294, 315, 333, 482, 505, 523.
16/7. *nst ḫntt:* 161, 294, 315 (? Restored, cf. 1/5), 333, 363, 482, 500.
16/8. *rḫ nswt:* 523, 536 (IV).
16/9. *ḥm-nṯr M3ˁt:* 13, 14, 77, 105, 123A, 133, 161, 181, 294, 315, 381, 467, 480, 482, 505, 523.
16/10. *ḥrj-sšt3:* 14, 470, 482, 523.
16/11. *ḫrj-ḥbt:* 105, 394.
16/12. *z3b ˁḏ-mr:* 161, 294, 333, 363, 500.
16/13. *zš ˁ nswt:* 77, 381. [S].
16/14. *smr:* 536 (IV). [V].

17. Sequences beginning with *NST ḪNTT:*

17/1. *jwn Knmwt:* 14, 90, 95, 171, 294, 315, 338A, 465, 515, 523.

17/2. *jmj-rꜣ wpt:* 540.
17/3. *jmj-rꜣ zš ꜥ nswt:* 171.
17/4. *jmj-rꜣ šnwtj:* 315, 510. [C]. (Cf. 10/10, 10/13.)
17/5. *jmj-rꜣ kꜣt nbt nt nswt:* 376.
17/6. *wꜥb nswt:* 517. [S].
17/7. *wr* 10 *Šmꜥ:* 90, 95, 123A, 171, 294, 315, 333, 465, 482, 515, 517, 523.
17/8. *mdw rḫjt:* 14, 95, 123A, 171, 515.
17/9. *rḫ nswt:* 523.
17/10. *ḥm-nṯr Mꜣꜥt:* 14, 70, 92, 95, 123A, 161, 163, 171, 220, 244, 294, 309, 315, 465, 482, 516, 523, 544, 564. [S].
17/11. *ḥrj-sštꜣ:* 14, 123A, 257, 376, 482, 517, 523. [S].
17/12. *ḫrj-tp nswt:* 171, 187.
17/13. *zꜣb jmj-rꜣ zš:* 70, 163, 309, 485.
17/14. *zꜣb sḥḏ zš:* 485. [S].

18. Sequences beginning with *RḪ NSWT:*

18/1. *jwn Knmwt:* 350.
18/2. *jmj-rꜣ wpt:* 44, 85, 114, 292 (IV), 383, 457.
18/3. *jmj-rꜣ pr:* 19, 123, 190, 251, 258, 386 (IV), 444 (IV), 492, 493, 518, 550, 568.
18/4. *jmj-rꜣ ḥm-kꜣ:* 11, 104, 123, 251, 424, 444 (IV), 488, 492, 493, 499, 499A, 518, 550, 577.
18/5. *jmj-rꜣ zš ꜥ nswt:* 564. [C]. (Cf. 7/28.)
18/6. *jmj-rꜣ sšr:* 101. [S].
18/7. *jmj-rꜣ šnwtj:* 553. [C]. (Cf. 10/15.)
18/8. *jmj-rꜣ kꜣt nbt nt nswt:* 143 (IV ?).
18/9. *wꜥb nswt:* 5, 10, 21, 25, 40, 66, 71, 115, 190, 218, 233, 251, 254, 258, 267, 277, 290, 332, 355, 386 (IV), 388, 412, 425, 440, 494, 504, 509, 514, 518, 539, 542, 549, 550, 568, 572, 577, 582.
18/10. *wr* 10 *Šmꜥ:* 8, 24, 143 (IV ?), 350, 397, 448.
18/11. *mdw rḫjt:* 350.
18/12. *nst ḫntt:* 8, 187.
18/13. *ḥm-nṯr Mꜣꜥt:* 147, 166, 357. [S].
18/14. *ḥm-nṯr Ḫwfw:* 8, 16, 21, 190, 251, 263, 268A, 277, 317, 355, 386 (IV), 439, 539, 595.
18/15. *ḥm-kꜣ:* 101, 440. [S].
18/16. *ḥrj-sštꜣ:* 16, 40, 115, 257, 277, 332, 391, 416, 417, 474, 520, 523, 568, 581.
18/17. *ḥrj-tp Nḫb:* 492. [C]. (Cf. 25/33, 25/35.)
18/18. *ḥqꜣ ḥt:* 44, 114, 254. [C]. (Cf. 26/27.)
18/19. *ḫntj-š pr-ꜥꜣ:* 372.
18/20. *ḫrp ꜥḥ:* 44 (? Damaged and reading uncertain), 182 (IV). [C]. (Cf. 28/6, 28/9 and 14/5, 23/4.)
18/21. *ḫrp zḥ:* 140, 392, 464. [S].
18/22. *ḫrj-ḥbt:* 182 (IV).
18/23. *ḫrj-tp nswt:* 187, 350, 489.

18/24. *z3b jmj-r3 zš:* 489.
18/25. *z3b ʿḏ-mr:* 187, 350.
18/26. *z3b zš:* 24, 113.
18/27. *z3b sḥḏ zš:* 582.
18/28. *zš:* 448, 514.
18/29. *zš ʿ nswt:* 143 (IV?), 297, 518.
18/30. *smr:* 182 (IV).
18/31. *smr wʿtj:* 182 (IV).
18/32. *sḥḏ ḥm-k3:* 113, 388, 464, 492, 577. [S].
18/33. *sḥḏ ḫntj-š pr-ʿ3:* 398, 539.

19. Sequences beginning with *Ḥ3TJ-ʿ:*

19/1. *jwn Knmwt:* 57, 133, 160, 274, 275, 333, 396. [S].
19/2. *jmj-r3 wpt:* 138, 279, 342, 534 (IV), 556. [S].
19/3. *jmj-r3 pr:* 133, 134. [S].
19/4. *jmj-r3 prwj-ḥḏ:* 32, 57, 146, 158, 160, 202, 212, 229A, 274, 279, 361, 393, 548, 576, 592. [S].
19/5. *jmj-r3 ḫntj-š pr-ʿ:* 15, 83, 110, 131, 134, 177A, 187, 247, 279, 393, 414, 556, 562, 601D. [S].
19/6. *jmj-r3 zš ʿ nswt:* 57, 94, 105, 133, 135, 146, 158, 159, 160, 189, 197, 202, 274, 275, 324, 393, 455, 456, 548, 591.
19/7. *jmj-r3 sšr:* 393. [S].
19/8. *jmj-r3 Šmʿ:* 32, 39, 73A, 81, 106, 110, 131, 133, 134, 135, 137, 187, 202, 212, 279, 323, 345, 395, 493B, 562, 592, 602, 603. [S].
19/9. *jmj-r3 šnwtj:* 32, 57, 133, 134, 146, 158, 160, 197, 202, 212, 274, 279, 361, 393, 408, 548, 576. [S].
19/10. *jmj-r3 k3t nbt nt nswt:* 57, 94, 105, 123A, 135, 146, 155, 158, 159, 160, 189, 197, 260 (IV), 274, 275, 286A–B, 331 (IV), 393, 399 (IV), 455, 456, 548. [S].
19/11. *jrj nfr-ḥ3t:* 105, 133, 167, 202, 246, 279, 285, 361, 396, 408, 422, 548. [S].
19/12. *wr 10 Šmʿ:* 333. [S].
19/13. *mdw rḫjt:* 57, 94, 133, 146, 274, 275, 333, 396, 463, 534 (IV), [S].
19/14. *nst ḫntt:* 146, 333. [S].
19/15. *ḥm-nṯr M3ʿt:* 133, 576. [S].
19/16. *ḥrj-sšt3:* 186, 187, 195, 323. [S].
19/17. *ḥrj-sšt3 pr dw3t:* 105, 133, 167, 187, 195, 197, 202, 249, 414, 534 (IV), 558, 562, 576. [S].
19/18. *ḥrj-tp Nḫb:* 32, 73A, 105, 110, 133, 136, 167, 189, 197, 212, 241 (IV), 246, 345, 414, 422, 479, 548, 576, 602. [S].
19/19. *ḥq3 ḥt:* 32, 81, 83, 106, 110, 131, 177A, 562, 592. [S].
19/20. *ḫrp ʿḥ:* 167, 534 (IV). [S].
19/21. *ḫrp šnḏwt nbt:* 32, 74, 110, 131, 133, 134, 135, 189, 191, 197, 212, 229A, 279, 286A–B, 323, 324, 333, 361, 393, 429, 560, 576, 591, 592. [S].

19/22. *ẖrj-ḥbt:* 15, 32, 39, 68, 81, 105, 106, 111, 131, 132, 133, 134, 136, 160, 167, 177A, 186, 187, 189, 191, 195, 197, 202, 212, 247, 272, 279, 285, 323, 324, 333, 338, 342, 345, 346, 361, 371, 382, 393, 395, 396, 414, 429, 431, 438, 455, 497, 556, 558, 562, 575, 576, 592, 602, 603. [S].
19/23. *ẖrj-ḥbt ḥrj-tp:* 32, 74, 105, 110, 131, 132, 134, 135, 137, 189, 197, 212, 246, 249, 286A–B, 323, 324, 333, 345, 361, 393, 419, 548, 560, 571, 576, 591. [S].
19/24. *ẖrj-tp nswt:* 30, 57, 94, 106, 131, 133, 138, 146, 202, 212, 274, 275, 279, 333, 342, 382, 393, 396, 429, 463, 534 (IV), 602. [S].
19/25. *zꜣ nswt:* 174 (IV), 175 (IV), 260 (IV), 331 (IV), 534 (IV). [V].
19/26. *zꜣb jmj-rꜣ zš:* 133. [S].
19/27. *zꜣb ꜥḏ-mr:* 133, 146, 333. [S].
19/28. *zš:* 133. [S].
19/29. *zš ꜥ nswt:* 131, 133, 576. [S].
19/30. *zš mḏꜣt nṯr:* 32, 105, 110, 133, 160, 167, 189, 197, 246, 249, 323, 361, 393, 497, 548, 560, 562, 571, 576, 592. [S].
19/31. *zš n zꜣ:* 556. [S].
19/32. *smr:* 110, 131, 174 (IV). [S].
19/33. *smr wꜥtj:* 15, 32, 39, 57, 68, 74, 81, 83, 84, 105, 106, 110, 111, 129, 131, 132, 133, 134, 135, 136, 137, 138, 160, 167, 174 (IV), 177A, 186, 187, 189, 191, 195, 197, 202, 212, 229A, 241 (IV), 246, 247, 249, 272, 274, 275, 279, 285, 286A–B, 323, 324, 333, 338, 342, 345, 346, 361, 367, 371, 382, 393, 395, 396, 408, 409, 414, 422, 429, 431, 438, 456, 479, 497, 541, 548, 556, 558, 560, 562, 571, 575, 576, 592, 601D, 602, 603. [S].
19/34. *smr pr:* 133. [S].
19/35. *stm:* 32, 74, 131, 133, 134, 135, 189, 191, 197, 212, 229A, 279, 286A–B, 323, 324, 333, 361, 393, 429, 560, 576, 591, 592. [S].
19/36. *sḏꜣwtj bjtj:* 15, 32, 39, 68, 74, 81, 83, 84, 91 (IV), 106, 110, 129, 132, 133, 134, 135, 136, 138, 146, 160, 177A, 189, 197, 212, 229A, 247, 249, 279, 285, 286A–B, 331 (IV), 345, 361, 367, 370, 371, 382, 395, 396, 408, 409, 429, 431, 463, 471 (IV), 497, 541, 548, 556, 562, 575, 576, 591, 592, 602. [S].
19/37. *špss nswt:* 15, 133, 556. [S].
19/38. *tꜣtj zꜣb ṯꜣtj:* 57, 94, 105, 133, 135, 146, 153, 158, 159, 174 (IV), 184, 189, 197, 202, 249, 274, 275, 324, 331 (IV), 393, 402, 455, 463, 548, 558, 571, 591.

20. Sequences beginning with *ḤM-NṮR MꜣꜥT:*

20/1. *jwn Knmwt:* 171.
20/2. *jmj-rꜣ zš ꜥ nswt:* 171.
20/3. *jmj-rꜣ šnwtj:* 315. [C]. (Cf. 10/10, 10/13, 10/15.)
20/4. *wꜥb nswt:* 115. [C]. (Cf. 14/5.)
20/5. *wr 10 Šmꜥ:* 95.
20/6. *mdw rḫjt:* 171.

20/7. *ḥrj-sštꜣ:* 14, 115, 164, 482, 523.
20/8. *ẖrj-tp nswt:* 171.
20/9. *zꜣb jmj-rꜣ zš:* 309.
20/10. *zš ꜥ nswt:* 77.

21. Sequences beginning with *ḤM-NṮR ḪWFW:*

21/1. *jmj-rꜣ wpt:* 569 (IV).
21/2. *jmj-rꜣ pr:* 190, 251, 258, 386 (IV). [S].
21/3. *jmj-rꜣ ḥm-kꜣ:* 251. [S].
21/4. *wꜥb nswt:* 251, 258, 549.
21/5. *rḫ nswt:* 16, 251, 258, 532, 549.
21/6. *ḥrj-sštꜣ:* 172, 178, 235, 325, 532.
21/7. *smr wꜥtj:* 7 (IV).
21/8. *sḥḏ ḫntj-š pr-ꜥꜣ:* 398.
21/9. *ḫntj-š pr-ꜥꜣ:* 172.

22. Sequences beginning with *ḤM-Kꜣ:*

22/1. *jmj-rꜣ sšr:* 168, 421.
22/2. *ḫrp zḥ:* 168, 421. [S].
22/3. *zš:* 578. [C]. (Cf. 39/1, 39/2.)

23. Sequences beginning with *ḤRJ-SŠTꜣ:*

23/1. *wꜥb nswt:* 40, 332, 517, 528.
23/2. *wr* 10 *Šmꜥ:* 123A, 293 (IV), 517.
23/3. *mdw rḫjt:* 123A.
23/4. *rḫ nswt:* 16, 115 (?), 332, 528, 532.
23/5. *ḥm-nṯr Mꜣꜥt:* 123A, 152.
23/6. *ḥm-nṯr Ḫwfw:* 16, 235.
23/7. *ḫntj-š pr-ꜥꜣ:* 322.
23/8. *zꜣb ꜥḏ-mr:* 293 (IV). [V].
23/9. *zš:* 275A. [S].
23/10. *zš mḏꜣt nṯr:* 293 (IV). [V].

24. Sequences beginning with *ḤRJ-SŠTꜣ PR DWꜣT:*

24/1. *jmj-rꜣ zš ꜥ nswt:* 105, 564.
24/2. *jmj-rꜣ kꜣt nbt nt nswt:* 105.
24/3. *jrj nfr-ḥꜣt:* 583 (IV).
24/4. *ḥrj-sštꜣ:* 109, 564. [S].
24/5. *ḥrj-tp Nḫb:* 105, 300, 418, 564.
24/6. *ḫrp ꜥḥ:* 300, 471 (IV), 559A, 583 (IV).
24/7. *ẖrj-ḥbt:* 300, 564.
24/8. *ẖrj-ḥbt ḥrj-tp:* 249.
24/9. *ẖrj-tp nswt:* 202. [C]. (Cf. 33/7.)
24/10. *zš mḏꜣt nṯr:* 249, 564.

25. Sequences beginning with *ḤRJ-TP NḪB:*

25/1. *jwn Knmwt:* 133. [S].
25/2. *jmj-rꜣ wpt:* 534 (IV).
25/3. *jmj-rꜣ pr:* 133. [S].
25/4. *jmj-rꜣ prwj-ḥḏ:* 212, 592.
25/5. *jmj-rꜣ ḥm-kꜣ:* 492. [S].
25/6. *jmj-rꜣ ḫntj-š pr-ꜥꜣ:* 110, 414. [S].
25/7. *jmj-rꜣ zš ꜥ nswt:* 105, 133, 564.
25/8. *jmj-rꜣ Šmꜥ:* 73A, 133, 592.
25/9. *jmj-rꜣ šnwtj:* 133, 212.
25/10. *jmj-rꜣ kꜣt nbt nt nswt:* 105.
25/11. *jrj nfr-ḥꜣt:* 133, 167, 406, 422, 548, 564, 583 (IV).
25/12. *mdw rḫjt:* 133. [S].
25/13. *ḥm-nṯr Mꜣꜥt:* 133. [S].
25/14. *ḥrj-sštꜣ:* 109, 564. [S].
25/15. *ḥrj-sštꜣ pr dwꜣt:* 109, 133, 167, 197, 300, 414, 418, 534 (IV), 564, 583 (IV).
25/16. *ḥqꜣ ḥt:* 110, 592.
25/17. *ḫrp ꜥḥ:* 109, 126 (IV), 300, 526, 534 (IV), 564, 583 (IV).
25/18. *ḫrp šnḏwt nbt:* 110, 133, 592.
25/19. *ḫrj-ḥbt:* 32, 133, 167, 189, 197, 300, 345, 414, 564, 592, 602.
25/20. *ḫrj-ḥbt ḥrj-tp:* 110.
25/21. *ḫrj-tp nswt:* 133. [S].
25/22. *zꜣ nswt:* 534 (IV). [V].
25/23. *zꜣb jmj-rꜣ zš:* 133. [S].
25/24. *zꜣb ꜥḏ-mr:* 133. [S].
25/25. *zš:* 133. [S].
25/26. *zš ꜥ nswt:* 133. [S].
25/27. *zš mḏꜣt nṯr:* 32, 110, 167, 189, 197, 564, 592.
25/28. *smr:* 110, 126 (IV).
25/29. *smr wꜥtj:* 110, 133, 189, 197, 345, 414, 422, 534 (IV), 592.
25/30. *smr pr:* 133. [S].
25/31. *sḥḏ ḥm-kꜣ:* 492. [S].
25/32. *stm:* 133, 592.
25/33. *sḏꜣwtj bjtj:* 133, 345, 592.
25/34. *špss nswt:* 133. [S].
25/35. *tꜣtj zꜣb ṯꜣtj:* 133.

26. Sequences beginning with *ḤQꜣ ḤT:*

26/1. *jwn Knmwt:* 62, 133, 561. [S].
26/2. *jmj-rꜣ pr:* 133. [S].
26/3. *jmj-rꜣ ḫntj-š pr-ꜥꜣ:* 83, 131, 177A, 181, 196, 247 (? A damaged text reproduced in type only as *ḫrp ḥt*), 562, 563. [S].
26/4. *jmj-rꜣ Šmꜥ:* 81, 133, 192.
26/5. *jmj-rꜣ šnwtj:* 59.

26/6. *jrj nfr-ḥ3t:* 133. [S].
26/7. *wʿb nswt:* 254 (?? Very poor example really based only on a sequence of one title lines. Better disregard.)
26/8. *wr* 10 *Šmʿ:* 9, 62. [S].
26/9. *mdw rḫjt:* 62, 73, 133, 192, 561. [S].
26/10. *nst ḫntt:* 9, 192. [S].
26/11. *ḥm-nṯr M3ʿt:* 133. [S].
26/12. *ḥrj-sšt3 pr dw3t:* 133, 562. [S].
26/13. *ḥrj-tp Nḫb:* 32.
26/14. *ḫrp šndwt nbt:* 192, 324.
26/15. *ẖrj-ḥbt:* 32, 59, 81, 106, 130, 131, 133, 139, 150, 177A, 181, 192, 212, 247 (? cf. 26/3), 324, 335, 432, 438, 497, 562, 563, 590A, 592. [S].
26/16. *ẖrj-ḥbt ḥrj-tp:* 192, 324.
26/17. *ẖrj-tp nswt:* 32, 62, 73, 106, 130, 131, 133, 139, 182, 187, 192, 201, 209, 211, 212, 335, 561. [S].
26/18. *z3b jmj-r3 zš:* 133, 192, 197. [S].
26/19. *z3b ʿḏ-mr:* 62, 192. [S].
26/20. *zš:* 133. [S].
26/21. *zš ʿ nswt:* 131, 133, 197, 201, 432. [S].
26/22. *zš mḏ3t nṯr:* 32, 497, 562, 592. [S].
26/23. *smr:* 110 (? In a list of officials rather than a proper string of titles. Better disregard), 131, 334. [S].
26/24. *smr wʿtj:* 32, 59, 73, 81, 82, 83, 106, 130, 131, 133, 139, 150, 177A, 181, 192, 196, 201, 209, 211, 212, 247 (? cf. 26/3), 324, 335, 336, 432, 438, 497, 560 (? A loose fragment, perhaps not from this tomb), 562, 563, 592. [S].
26/25. *smr pr:* 133. [S].
26/26. *stm:* 192.
26/27. *sḏ3wtj bjtj:* 32, 139, 150, 192, 201, 432, 560 (? cf. 26/24).
26/28. *špss nswt:* 133. [S].

27. Sequences beginning with *ḪNTJ-Š PR-ʿ3:*

27/1. *wʿb nswt:* 16.
27/2. *rḫ nswt:* 16.
27/3. *ḥm-nṯr Ḫwfw:* 16.
27/4. *ḥrj-sšt3:* 16, 172.

28. Sequences beginning with *ḪRP ʿḤ:*

28/1. *jmj-r3 wpt:* 534 (IV).
28/2. *jmj-r3 ḫntj-š pr-ʿ3:* 247 (??? cf. 26/3 and disregard).
28/3. *jmj-r3 zš ʿ nswt:* 564. [C]. (Cf. 7/25, 7/28.)
28/4. *jmj-r3 k3t nbt nt nswt:* 236. [C]. (Cf. 11/24, 11/26.)
28/5. *jrj nfr-ḥ3t:* 406.
28/6. *wʿb nswt:* 252. [S].
28/7. *wr* 10 *Šmʿ:* 473 (IV).
28/8. *rḫ nswt:* 473 (IV), 569 (IV).

28/9. *ḥrj-sštꜣ:* 109, 236, 238, 252, 356, 525, 564. [S].
28/10. *ḥrj-sštꜣ pr dwꜣt:* 109, 203, 215A, 224, 238, 282, 300, 406, 418, 534 (IV), 564, 567 (IV?).
28/11. *ḥrj-tp Nḫb:* 406, 418, 564.
28/12. *ḥqꜣ ḥt:* 44 (?? Sequence based on a restored text. If correct, it must be a case like 3/7.) [V].
28/13. *ḫrp šnḏwt nbt:* 531 (IV). [V].
28/14. *ẖrj-ḥbt:* 247 (??? cf. 28/2), 473 (IV), 564.
28/15. *ẖrj-ḥbt ḥrj-tp:* 30 (IV). [V].
28/16. *zꜣ nswt:* 473 (IV), 531 (IV), 534 (IV). [V].
28/17. *zš mḏꜣt nṯr:* 30 (IV), 564. [C]. (Cf. 41/14.)
28/18. *smr:* 531 (IV). [V].
28/19. *smr wꜥtj:* 247 (??? cf. 28/2). [V].
28/20. *stm:* 531 (IV). [V].

29. Sequence beginning with *ḪRP ZḤ:*

29/1. *jmj-rꜣ ḥm-kꜣ:* 433. [C]. (Cf. 5/1, 5/2, 5/3.)

30. Sequences beginning with *ḪRP ŠNḎWT NBT:*

30/1. *jwn Knmwt:* 133. [S].
30/2. *jmj-rꜣ pr:* 133. [S].
30/3. *jmj-rꜣ prwj-ḥḏ*: 32, 393, 576.
30/4. *jmj-rꜣ ḫntj-š pr-ꜥꜣ:* 131, 393, 414. [S].
30/5. *jmj-rꜣ sšr:* 393. [S].
30/6. *jmj-rꜣ Šmꜥ:* 32, 133, 192.
30/7. *jmj-rꜣ šnwtj:* 32, 393, 576.
30/8. *jmj-rꜣ kꜣt nbt nt nswt:* 286A–B.
30/9. *jrj nfr-ḥꜣt:* 133, 422. [S].
30/10. *mdw rḫjt:* 133, 192. [S].
30/11. *ḥm-nṯr Mꜣꜥt:* 133. [S].
30/12. *ḥrj-sštꜣ:* 323. [S].
30/13. *ḥrj-sštꜣ pr dwꜣt:* 197, 300, 414, 576. [C]. (Cf. 24/8.)
30/14. *ḥrj-tp Nḫb:* 32, 197, 300, 576.
30/15. *ḥqꜣ ḥt:* 32, 131.
30/16. *ḫrp ꜥḥ:* 300. [S].
30/17. *ẖrj-ḥbt:* 32, 131, 133, 189, 191, 197, 300, 323, 393, 414, 429, 576. [S].
30/18. *ẖrj-ḥbt ḥrj-tp:* 286A–B (?? This is a sequence occurring only on the coffin of the sons of *Nḫbw*, and is in flagrant disagreement with the extremely well documented sequences 32/20, 32/30. It may be a mistake.) [V].
30/19. *ḫrj-tp nswt:* 32, 131, 133, 192, 286, 393, 429. [S].
30/20. *zꜣ nswt:* 451 (IV), 531 (IV). [V].
30/21. *zꜣb jmj-rꜣ zš:* 133 [S].
30/22. *zš:* 133. [S].
30/23. *zš ꜥ nswt:* 131, 133. [S].

30/24. *zš mḏꜣt nṯr:* 32, 189, 197, 323, 393, 576. [S].
30/25. *smr:* 131, 451 (IV), 531 (IV). [C]. (Cf. 43/7 and 24/8.)
30/26. *smr wꜥtj:* 32, 74, 131, 133, 135, 189, 191, 197, 228, 286, 286A–B, 323, 393, 414, 422, 429, 545, 576.
30/27. *smr pr:* 133. [S].
30/28. *sḏꜣwtj bjtj:* 32, 74, 286A–B, 591.
30/29. *špss nswt:* 133. [S].

31. Sequences beginning with *ẖRJ-ḤBT:*

31/1. *jwn Knmwt:* 105, 133, 215 (IV), 299, 333, 381.
31/2. *jmj-rꜣ wpt:* 98, 342, 534 (IV), 556.
31/3. *jmj-rꜣ pr:* 133, 134. [S].
31/4. *jmj-rꜣ ḫntj-š pr-ꜥꜣ:* 177A, 185, 187, 247, 556, 563.
31/5. *jmj-rꜣ Šmꜥ:* 39, 81, 133, 603.
31/6. *jmj-rꜣ šnwtj:* 59.
31/7. *jmj-rꜣ kꜣt nbt nt nswt:* 215 (IV), 223.
31/8. *jrj nfr-ḥꜣt:* 154.
31/9. *wr 10 Šmꜥ:* 12, 333, 473 (IV). [C]. (Cf. 15/3.)
31/10. *mdw rḫjt:* 105, 133, 192, 215 (IV), 333, 381.
31/11. *nst ḫntt:* 333. [C]. (Cf. 17/3.)
31/12. *rḫ nswt:* 473 (IV).
31/13. *ḥm-nṯr Mꜣꜥt:* 105, 133, 381. [C]. (Cf. 20/2.)
31/14. *ḥrj-sštꜣ:* 109, 186, 187, 188, 195, 306, 352, 466, 498, 564. [S].
31/15. *ḥrj-sštꜣ pr dwꜣt:* 49, 117, 133, 167, 187, 195, 197, 202, 210, 274, 300, 365, 426, 534 (IV), 562, 576.
31/16. *ḥrj-tp Nḫb:* 197.
31/17. *ḫrp ꜥḥ:* 154, 300, 484 (IV), 534 (IV).
31/18. *ḫrp šnḏwt nbt:* 361 (? Once only. Mistake for *ẖrj-ḥbt ḥrj-tp*, after which it occurs frequently in this tomb? This contradicts one of the better established sequences in our study), 560 (? Once only, as against several occurrences after *ẖrj-ḥbt ḥrj-tp*. See the preceding case.) [V].
31/19. *ẖrj-tp nswt:* 105, 106, 133, 185, 192, 202, 215 (IV), 333, 335, 342, 381, 382.
31/20. *zꜣ nswt:* 534 (IV). [V].
31/21. *zꜣb jmj-rꜣ zš:* 133.
31/22. *zꜣb ꜥḏ-mr:* 199, 333. [C]. (Cf. 36/4.)
31/23. *zš:* 133. [S].
31/24. *zš ꜥ nswt:* 133, 381, 430, 432. [S].
31/25. *zš mḏꜣt nṯr:* 32, 109, 117, 160, 167, 189, 197, 204, 240, 287, 361, 421, 497, 560, 562, 564.
31/26. *zš n zꜣ:* 60, 556, 601D. [S].
31/27. *smr wꜥtj:* 534 (IV), 560 (?? Once only. Mistake for *ẖrj-ḥbt ḥrj-tp* as under 31/18. 44/26 is the best documented sequence in our collection), 603 (? This is certainly very late.) [V].
31/28. *smr pr:* 133, 210. [S].

31/29. *stm:* 361 (?? cf. 31/18), 560 (?? cf. 31/18). [V].
31/30. *špss nswt:* 15, 125, 133, 210, 337, 349A, 556. [S].

32. Sequences beginning with *H̠RJ-ḤBT ḤRJ-TP:*

32/1. *jwn Knmwt:* 133 [S].
32/2. *jmj-rꜣ wpt:* 279. [S].
32/3. *jmj-rꜣ pr:* 133. [S].
32/4. *jmj-rꜣ prwj-ḥd̠:* 27, 32, 279, 393, 548, 576.
32/5. *jmj-rꜣ ḫntj-š pr-ꜥꜣ:* 131, 393. [S].
32/6. *jmj-rꜣ zš ꜥ nswt:* 105, 548.
32/7. *jmj-rꜣ sšr:* 393. [S].
32/8. *jmj-rꜣ Šmꜥ:* 32, 133, 192, 202, 323.
32/9. *jmj-rꜣ šnwtj:* 32, 393, 548, 576.
32/10. *jmj-rꜣ kꜣt nbt nt nswt:* 105, 286A–B, 399 (IV), 548.
32/11. *jrj nfr-ḥꜣt:* 105, 133, 202, 246, 279, 422, 548, 559A (? Partly restored), 583 (IV). [S].
32/12. *mdw rḫjt:* 133, 192. [S].
32/13. *ḥꜣtj-ꜥ:* 399 (IV). [V].
32/14. *ḥm-nt̠r Mꜣꜥt:* 133, 576. [S].
32/15. *ḥrj-sštꜣ:* 323. [S].
32/16. *ḥrj-sštꜣ pr dwꜣt:* 105, 133, 197, 202, 471 (IV), 559A, 576, 583 (IV).
32/17. *ḥrj-tp Nḫb:* 32, 105, 197, 303, 548, 576.
32/18. *ḥqꜣ ḥt:* 32, 110, 131, 592.
32/19. *ḫrp ꜥḥ:* 471 (IV), 559A, 583 (IV). [S].
32/20. *ḫrp šnd̠wt nbt:* 32, 110, 131, 133, 134, 135, 189, 192, 197, 286, 323, 333, 361, 393, 560, 576, 591, 592. [S].
32/21. *h̠rj-ḥbt:* 32, 105, 111, 131, 132, 133, 189, 197, 202, 279, 323, 345, 393, 576, 592. [S].
32/22. *h̠rj-tp nswt:* 32, 131, 133, 192, 202, 279, 286, 393. [S].
32/23. *zꜣb jmj-rꜣ zš:* 133. [S].
32/24. *zš:* 133. [S].
32/25. *zš ꜥ nswt:* 131, 133, 576. [S].
32/26. *zš md̠ꜣt nt̠r:* 30 (IV), 31 (IV), 32, 105, 110, 133, 160, 189, 197, 204, 246, 248 (IV), 249, 303, 323, 361, 393, 548, 560, 571, 576, 592. [S].
32/27. *smr:* 110 (? Based on a list of officials rather than a string), 131. [C]. (Cf. 43/7 and 24/8.)
32/28. *smr wꜥtj:* 27, 32, 74, 105, 110, 111, 131, 132, 133, 135, 137, 189, 197, 202, 246, 279, 286, 286A–B, 303, 323, 345, 393, 422, 471 (IV), 548, 560, 571, 576, 592.
32/29. *smr pr:* 133. [S].
32/30. *stm:* 32, 131, 133, 134, 135, 189, 192, 197, 286, 323, 333, 361, 393, 560, 576, 591, 592. [S].
32/31. *sd̠ꜣwtj bjtj:* 32, 132, 197, 286A–B, 576, 591.
32/32. *špss nswt:* 133. [S].
32/33. *tꜣtj zꜣb t̠ꜣtj:* 248 (IV), 548.

33. Sequences beginning with *ḪRJ-TP NSWT:*

33/1. *jwn Knmwt:* 13, 14, 26, 56, 57, 59, 62, 77, 78, 95, 105, 133, 161, 171, 181, 215 (IV), 273, 274, 275, 281, 294, 315, 333, 350, 363, 381, 394, 396, 402, 467, 470, 480, 481, 482, 495, 500, 505, 516, 523, 560. [S].
33/2. *jmj-rꜣ wpt:* 14, 56, 138, 279, 342, 555, 558.
33/3. *jmj-rꜣ prwj-ḥḏ:* 57, 100, 146, 274, 393, 505.
33/4. *jmj-rꜣ ḥm-kꜣ:* 366. [S].
33/5. *jmj-rꜣ ḫntj-š pr-ꜥꜣ:* 18, 437, 552.
33/6. *jmj-rꜣ zš ꜥ nswt:* 146, 171, 294, 315, 363, 505.
33/7. *jmj-rꜣ Šmꜥ:* 112A, 161, 533.
33/8. *jmj-rꜣ šnwtj:* 13, 57, 78, 112A, 146, 274, 315, 393, 533.
33/9. *jmj-rꜣ kꜣt nbt nt nswt:* 146, 294, 315, 349, 363.
33/10. *wr* 10 *Šmꜥ:* 13, 95, 294, 315, 333, 476 (IV), 482, 505, 523, 559A.
33/11. *mdw rḫjt:* 13, 14, 26, 56, 57, 59, 62, 73, 77, 78, 94, 95, 105, 133, 146, 161, 171, 181, 192, 215 (IV), 273, 274, 275, 281, 294, 315, 333, 350, 363, 381, 394, 396, 402, 467, 470, 480, 481, 482, 495, 500, 505, 516, 523, 534 (IV), 540, 560. [S].
33/12. *nst ḫntt:* 14, 48, 95, 146, 161, 294, 315, 333, 363, 482, 500, 505, 559A.
33/13. *rḫ nswt:* 476 (IV), 523.
33/14. *ḥm-nṯr Mꜣꜥt:* 13, 14, 77, 95, 103, 105, 112, 133, 161, 181, 294, 315, 381, 467, 480, 482, 505, 523.
33/15. *ḥrj-sštꜣ:* 14, 470, 482, 523. [S].
33/16. *ḫrj-ḥbt:* 32, 105, 121, 309, 394.
33/17. *zꜣb jmj-rꜣ zš:* 89, 133, 485.
33/18. *zꜣb ꜥḏ-mr:* 14, 48, 62, 95, 100, 103, 146, 161, 206, 294, 315, 333, 352, 363, 455 (an earlier tomb built by the owner of this one, Lepsius, *Giza*, No. 10), 467, 470, 476 (IV), 482, 485, 500, 505, 558.
33/19. *zꜣb zš:* 558 [C]. (Cf. 37/4 and 35/9.)
33/20. *zꜣb sḥḏ zš:* 415, 485, 558. [S].
33/21. *zš ꜥ nswt:* 77, 79, 89, 127, 131, 133, 181, 201, 381. [S].
33/22. *smr:* 476 (IV). [V].
33/23. *smr pr:* 177, 437. [S].
33/24. *špss nswt:* 177, 306, 437. [S].
33/25. *zš mḏꜣt nṯr:* 32.

34. Sequences beginning with *Zꜣ NSWT:*

34/1. *jwn Knmwt:* 215 (IV), 275, 394. [S].
34/2. *jmj-rꜣ wpt:* 534 (IV).
34/3. *jmj-rꜣ prwj-ḥḏ:* 560. [S].
34/4. *jmj-rꜣ zš ꜥ nswt:* 189, 275, 560. [S].
34/5. *jmj-rꜣ Šmꜥ:* 112, 395. [S].
34/6. *jmj-rꜣ šnwtj:* 560. [S].
34/7. *jmj-rꜣ kꜣt nbt nt nswt:* 64, 182 (IV), 189, 215 (IV), 275, 376, 399 (IV), 530. [S].
34/8. *jrj-pꜥt:* 31 (IV), 471 (IV), 473A (IV). [V].

34/9. *wr* 10 *Šmʿ:* 376, 473 (IV), 473A (IV), 513 (IV), 596. [S].
34/10. *mdw rḫjt:* 215 (IV), 275, 394. [S].
34/11. *nst ḫntt:* 376. [S].
34/12. *rḫ nswt:* 473 (IV), 596. [S].
34/13. *ḥȝtj-ʿ:* 31 (IV), 189, 275, 346, 395, 399 (IV), 450 (IV), 560. [S].
34/14. *ḥm-nṯr Mȝʿt:* 112. [S]
34/15. *ḥrj-sštȝ:* 376. [S].
34/16. *ḥrj-sštȝ pr dwȝt:* 215 (IV), 419, 471 (IV), 484 (IV), 534 (IV). [S].
34/17. *ḥrj-tp Nḫb:* 126 (IV), 189, 303. [S].
34/18. *ḫrp ʿḥ:* 30 (IV), 124 (IV), 471 (IV), 484 (IV), 534 (IV).
34/19. *ḫrp šndwt nbt:* 189, 560. [S].
34/20. *ẖrj-ḥbt:* 30 (IV), 182 (IV), 189, 215 (IV), 309, 346, 394, 395, 473 (IV), 484 (IV), 560. [S].
34/21. *ẖrj-ḥbt ḥrj-tp:* 30 (IV), 91 (IV), 189, 222 (IV), 241 (IV), 248 (IV), 303, 399 (IV), 471 (IV), 560. [S].
34/22. *ẖrj-tp nswt:* 112, 215 (IV), 275, 309, 394. [S].
34/23. *zš mḏȝt nṯr:* 30 (IV), 189, 248 (IV), 303, 560. [S].
34/24. *smr:* 126 (IV), 174 (IV), 182 (IV), 579 (IV).
34/25. *smr wʿtj:* 30 (IV), 64, 112, 174 (IV), 182 (IV), 189, 215 (IV), 275, 303, 346, 395, 419, 450 (IV), 471 (IV), 484 (IV), 530, 534 (IV), 560. [S].
34/26. *stm:* 189, 560. [S].
34/27. *sḏȝwtj bjtj:* 30 (IV), 189, 375 (IV), 395, 450 (IV). [S].
34/28. *tȝtj zȝb ṯȝtj:* 30 (IV), 189, 248 (IV), 275, 471 (IV), 473A (IV), 560. [S].

35. Sequences beginning with *ZȝB JMJ-Rȝ ZŠ:*

35/1. *jmj-rȝ pr:* 13. [C]. (Cf. 3/3.)
35/2. *wʿb nswt:* 115, 256, 517, 528, 582.
35/3. *wr* 10 *Šmʿ:* 517, 544.
35/4. *nst ḫntt:* 48, 156, 517, 544.
35/5. *rḫ nswt:* 115, 315, 417, 528, 582.
35/6. *ḥm-nṯr Mȝʿt:* 55, 70, 115, 118, 163, 298, 495, 544, 582.
35/7. *ḥrj-sštȝ:* 115, 417, 500, 517, 528. [S].
35/8. *ẖrj-ḥbt:* 275A.
35/9. *ẖrj-tp nswt:* 48, 489.
35/10. *zȝb ʿḏ-mr:* 48, 156.
35/11. *zȝb sḥḏ zš:* 115, 118, 485, 548, 582.
35/12. *zš ʿ nswt:* 115, 118.

36. Sequences beginning with *ZȝB ʿḎ-MR:*

36/1. *jwn Knmwt:* 14, 90, 95, 171, 294, 299, 315, 338A, 350, 358, 465, 467, 470, 482, 515, 523, 534 (IV).
36/2. *jmj-rȝ wpt:* 540.
36/3. *jmj-rȝ prwj-ḥḏ:* 100, 232. [C]. (Cf. 4/9, 4/11.)
36/4. *jmj-rȝ zš ʿ nswt:* 171, 505.
36/5. *jmj-rȝ šnwtj:* 279, 315.

36/6. *jmj-rꜣ kꜣt nbt nt nswt:* 88 (IV), 294.
36/7. *wꜥb nswt:* 517. [S].
36/8. *wr 10 Šmꜥ:* 6 (IV), 88 (IV), 90, 95, 123A, 171, 273, 293 (IV), 294, 315, 333, 338A, 465, 476 (IV), 482, 515, 517, 523.
36/9. *mdw rḫjt:* 14, 95, 123A, 171, 350, 467, 470, 515.
36/10. *nst ḫntt:* 13, 14, 45, 48, 59, 90, 95, 123A, 146, 156, 161, 163, 171, 187, 192, 294, 309, 315, 333, 338A, 363, 465, 478, 480, 482, 500, 505, 515, 516, 517, 523, 540, 559A. [S].
36/11. *rḫ nswt:* 476 (IV), 523.
36/12. *ḥm-nṯr Mꜣꜥt:* 13, 14, 95, 103, 123A, 161, 163, 171, 294, 309, 315, 465, 467, 482, 516, 523. [S].
36/13. *ḥrj-sštꜣ:* 3 (IV), 14, 88 (IV), 123A, 356, 470, 482, 517, 523. [S].
36/14. *ḫrp ꜥḥ:* 356. [C]. (Cf. 28/11.)
36/15. *ḫrj-tp nswt:* 171, 187, 350.
36/16. *zꜣb jmj-rꜣ zš:* 133, 163, 309, 485, 517 (? *zꜣb jmj-rꜣ zš* erased and replaced by *zꜣb ꜥḏ-mr*. Sequence follows?)
36/17. *zꜣb zš:* 558. (Cf. 37/4 and 35/10.)
36/18. *zꜣb sḥḏ zš:* 485, 558. [S].
36/19. *zš ꜥ nswt:* 133, 181. [S].
36/20. *zš mḏꜣt nṯr:* 293 (IV).
36/21. *smr pr:* 356. [S].

37. Sequences beginning with *ZꜣB ZŠ:*

37/1. *wꜥb nswt:* 256, 528.
37/2. *rḫ nswt:* 528.
37/3. *ḥrj-sštꜣ:* 528. [S].
37/4. *zꜣb jmj-rꜣ zš:* 256, 528. [S].
37/5. *zꜣb sḥḏ zš:* 256, 528.
37/6. *sḥḏ ḥm-kꜣ:* 113, 479. [S].

38. Sequences beginning with *ZꜣB SḤḎ ZŠ:*

38/1. *jmj-rꜣ pr:* 564, 590. [S].
38/2. *jmj-rꜣ ḥm-kꜣ:* 435. [S].
38/3. *wꜥb nswt:* 115, 256, 528, 582. [S].
38/4. *rḫ nswt:* 115, 435, 528.
38/5. *ḥm-nṯr Mꜣꜥt:* 245. [C]. (Cf. 20/8.)
38/6. *ḥm-kꜣ:* 590. [S].
38/7. *ḥrj-sštꜣ:* 115, 505, 528. [S].
38/8. *zꜣb jmj-rꜣ zš:* 256, 411, 528.
38/9. *zꜣb zš:* 558.
38/10. *zš ꜥ nswt:* 118, 505.
38/11. *zš n zꜣ:* 590. [C]. (Cf. 42/2, 42/9.)

39. Sequences beginning with *ZŠ:*

39/1. *rḫ nswt:* 448.
39/2. *sḥḏ ḥm-kꜣ:* 577. [C]. (Cf. 46/5, 46/6.)

40. Sequences beginning with *ZŠ ꜥ NSWT:*

40/1. *jmj-rꜣ wpt:* 546 (IV). [V].
40/2. *jmj-rꜣ pr:* 134, 564. [S].
40/3. *jmj-rꜣ kꜣt nbt nt nswt:* 143 (IV?). [V].
40/4. *wꜥb nswt:* 115. [S].
40/5. *wr* 10 *Šmꜥ:* 397. [C]. (Cf. 15/1, 15/3, 15/4, 15/12.)
40/6. *rḫ nswt:* 115, 297 (This is the string in which both *zš ꜥ nswt* and *zš ꜥ nswt ḫft-ḥr* occur), 586.
40/7. *ḥm-nṯr Mꜣꜥt:* 495.
40/8. *ḥrj-sštꜣ:* 115 [C]. (Cf. 23/3.)
40/9. *zꜣb jmj-rꜣ zš:* 89, 133, 134, 411, 481, 490A, 495.
40/10. *zꜣb sḥḏ zš:* 115, 411.

41. Sequences beginning with *ZŠ MḎꜣT NṮR:*

41/1. *jwn Knmwt:* 133. [S].
41/2. *jmj-rꜣ zš ꜥ nswt:* 105.
41/3. *jmj-rꜣ Šmꜥ:* 133.
41/4. *jmj-rꜣ kꜣt nbt nt nswt:* 105.
41/5. *jrj nfr-ḥꜣt:* 105, 246.
41/6. *mdw rḫjt:* 133. [S].
41/7. *ḥm-nṯr Mꜣꜥt:* 133. [S].
41/8. *ḥrj-sštꜣ pr dwꜣt:* 105, 197, 562.
41/9. *ḫrj-tp Nḫb:* 105, 197, 303.
41/10. *ḫrj-ḥbt:* 105, 598 (IV).
41/11. *ḫrj-tp nswt:* 133.
41/12. *zꜣb jmj-rꜣ zš*: 133. [S].
41/13. *zš ꜥ nswt:* 133. [S].
41/14. *smr wꜥtj:* 105, 246, 303.
41/15. *tꜣtj zꜣb ṯꜣtj:* 248 (IV). [V].

42. Sequences beginning with *ZŠ N Zꜣ:*

42/1. *jwn Knmwt:* 14. [C]. (Cf. 1/10.)
42/2. *jmj-rꜣ wpt:* 14, 556. [C]. (Cf. 2/8.)
42/3. *jmj-rꜣ pr:* 393.
42/4. *mdw rḫjt:* 14. [C]. (Cf. 16/11.)
42/5. *nst ḫntt:* 14. [C]. (Cf. 17/3.)
42/6. *ḥm-nṯr Mꜣꜥt:* 14. [C]. (Cf. 20/2.)
42/7. *ḥm-kꜣ:* 590. [S].
42/8. *ḥrj-sštꜣ:* 14. [S].
42/9. *ḫrj-tp nswt:* 14. [C]. (Cf. 33/6, 33/16.)
42/10. *zꜣb ꜥḏ-mr:* 14. [C]. (Cf. 36/4.)

43. Sequences beginning with *SMR:*

43/1. *jmj-rꜣ pr:* 61. [S].
43/2. *jmj-rꜣ ḫntj-š pr-ꜥꜣ:* 131. [S].

43/3. *jrj nfr-ḥ3t:* 223, 406, 583 (IV). [C]. (No direct or indirect examples to the contrary. The material as a whole shows, however, that *smr* is likely to be, for purposes of ranking, a variant of *smr wˁtj* throughout the Fifth and Sixth Dynasties. Since in the case of the much better documented *smr wˁtj*, the sequence 44/12 occurs nineteen times and the reverse [13/14] only twice, it is to be expected that the rarer sequence would not be documented for *smr*.)
43/4. *wr* 10 *Šmˁ:* 473 (IV).
43/5. *rḫ nswt:* 318, 473 (IV). [C]. (Cf. 18/18.)
43/6. *ḥrj-sšt3:* 238. [S].
43/7. *ḥrj sšt3 pr dw3t:* 238, 282, 389, 406, 418, 583 (IV). [S].
43/8. *ḥrj-tp Nḫb:* 223, 406, 418, 583 (IV).
43/9. *ḫrp ˁḥ:* 7 (IV), 126 (IV), 238, 268, 282, 406, 418, 441, 473 (IV), 583 (IV). [S].
43/10. *ẖrj-ḥbt:* 131, 182 (IV), 359, 399 (IV), 473 (IV). [S].
43/11. *ẖrj-ḥbt ḥrj-tp:* 583 (IV).
43/12. *ẖrj-tp nswt:* 131, 134, 493A. [S].
43/13. *z3 nswt:* 473 (IV). [V.]
43/14. *zš ˁ nswt:* 131. [S].
43/15. *sḥḏ ḥm-k3:* 62. [S].

44. Sequences beginning with *SMR WˁTJ:*

44/1. *jwn Knmwt:* 62, 133, 160, 215 (IV), 275, 281, 333, 381, 396, 402. [S].
44/2. *jmj-r3 wpt:* 98, 138, 279, 342, 534 (IV), 555, 556.
44/3. *jmj-r3 pr:* 133, 134, 553. [S].
44/4. *jmj-r3 prwj-ḥḏ:* 27, 160, 279, 361, 393, 402, 548, 576.
44/5. *jmj-r3 ḥm-k3:* 366. [S].
44/6. *jmj-r3 ḫntj-š pr-ˁ3:* 15, 83, 131, 134, 177A, 185, 187, 196, 247, 280, 305, 320, 393, 407, 414, 552, 556, 562, 563, 566, 588, 590A, 601D. [S].
44/7. *jmj-r3 zš ˁ nswt:* 105, 160, 402, 564.
44/8. *jmj-r3 sšr:* 393. [S].
44/9. *jmj-r3 Šmˁ:* 39 (? Fluctuates and occurs only once in this position), 81, 112, 133, 202, 603.
44/10. *jmj-r3 šnwtj:* 59, 94A, 160, 361, 393, 548, 553, 576.
44/11. *jmj-r3 k3t nbt nt nswt:* 64, 105, 215 (IV), 236, 275, 530, 564.
44/12. *jrj nfr-ḥ3t:* 105, 133, 142, 154, 167, 202, 223, 225, 246, 279, 285, 300, 361, 401, 408, 422, 434, 548, 564, 583 (IV).
44/13. *wr* 10 *Šmˁ:* 12, 333. [S].
44/14. *mdw rḫjt:* 62, 73, 133, 192, 215 (IV), 275, 281, 333, 381, 396, 402. [S].
44/15. *nst ḫntt:* 333. [S].
44/16. *rḫ nswt:* 553. [C]. (Cf. 18/18.)
44/17. *ḥ3tj-ˁ:* 450 (IV). [V].
44/18. *ḥm-nṯr M3ˁt:* 112, 133, 381. [S].
44/19. *ḥrj-sšt3:* 109, 186, 187, 188, 195, 236, 248 (IV), 323, 399 (IV), 401, 498, 525, 564. [S].

44/20. *ḥrj-sštꜣ pr dwꜣt:* 49, 63, 94A, 105, 109, 133, 167, 187, 195, 197, 202, 203, 215 (IV), 215A, 224, 249, 282, 300, 365, 389, 406, 411, 414, 418, 419, 426, 471 (IV), 534 (IV), 558, 562, 564, 567 (IV?), 576, 583 (IV). [S].
44/21. *ḥrj-tp Nḫb:* 105, 109, 136, 142, 167, 197, 223, 241 (IV), 259, 300, 303, 389, 399 (IV), 418, 426, 479, 522, 526, 548, 564, 583 (IV), 602.
44/22. *ḥqꜣ ḥt:* 83 (? Fluctuates between this position and the more usual 26/24. Mistake?), 110 (?? Not a string of titles but a list of officials in the biography. Better disregard.) [V].
44/23. *ḫrp ʿḥ:* 30 (IV), 31 (IV), 109, 142, 154, 167, 203, 215A, 224, 236, 282, 300, 373, 375 (IV), 389, 399 (IV), 400 (IV), 418, 471 (IV), 512, 522, 525, 526, 531 (IV), 534 (IV), 536 (IV), 559A, 564, 567 (IV?), 583 (IV). [S].
44/24. *ḫrp zḥ:* 525. [S].
44/25. *ḫrp šndwt nbt:* 110, 324, 333, 371 (? Mistake? Cf. 31/18), 531 (IV).
44/26. *ḫrj-ḥbt:* 1, 12, 15, 30 (IV), 32, 39, 49, 59, 60, 65, 68, 81, 86, 94A, 98, 105, 106, 111, 127, 130, 131, 132, 133, 134, 136, 139, 150, 154, 160, 167, 177A, 182 (IV), 185, 186, 187, 188, 189, 191, 192, 195, 197, 202, 210, 212, 215 (IV), 231, 247, 272, 279, 280, 285, 287, 300, 305, 320, 323, 324, 333, 335, 337, 338, 342, 345, 346, 361, 365, 368, 371, 381, 382, 384, 390, 393, 395, 396, 414, 426, 429, 430, 431, 432, 434, 438, 497, 498, 507, 533, 552, 556, 558, 561, 562, 563, 564, 566, 575, 576, 588, 592, 593, 601A, 602. [S].
44/27. *ḫrj-ḥbt ḥrj-tp:* 30 (IV), 249, 324, 333, 583 (IV).
44/28. *ḫrj-tp nswt:* 32, 62, 73, 106, 112, 127, 130, 131, 133, 138, 139, 185, 192, 201, 202, 209, 211, 212, 215 (IV), 275, 279, 281, 286, 296, 333, 335, 341, 342, 366, 381, 382, 393, 396, 402, 429, 552, 555, 602. [S].
44/29. *zꜣ nswt:* 451 (IV), 531 (IV), 534 (IV). [V].
44/30. *zꜣb jmj-rꜣ zš:* 133. [S].
44/31. *zꜣb ʿḏ-mr:* 62, 333. [S].
44/32. *zš:* 133. [S].
44/33. *zš ʿ nswt:* 127, 131, 133, 201, 381, 430, 432. [S].
44/34. *zš mḏꜣt nṯr:* 30 (IV), 32, 110, 160, 167, 189, 197, 249, 287, 323, 361, 393, 497, 562, 564, 571, 576, 592.
44/35. *zš n zꜣ:* 60, 556. [S].
44/36. *smr:* 110 (?? Not in a string but in a list of officials in the biography. Disregard), 531 (IV).
44/37. *smr pr:* 25A, 133, 210. [S].
44/38. *stm:* 333, 361 (? Error? Cf. 44/25), 531 (IV).
44/39. *špss nswt:* 15, 133, 210, 337, 364, 556. [S].

45. Sequences beginning with *SMR PR:*

45/1. *jrj nfr-ḥꜣt:* 360.
45/2. *wʿb nswt:* 233, 332, 360. [S].
45/3. *rḫ nswt:* 233, 332, 360. [C]. (Cf. 18/18.)
45/4. *ḥrj-sštꜣ:* 227, 332, 356, 360, 447A, 550. [S].

45/5. *ḫrp ʿḥ:* 356. [C]. (Cf. 28/14.)

45/6. *špss nswt:* 483 (? No question as to the text, but the sequence is very odd, violating the well attested 50/3. C. de Wit, "Enquête sur le titre de *śmr pr*," *Chronique d'Égypte*, XXXI, 89–104, has given a more complete summary of the uses of this title than we can here, including both combinations with rarer titles and information from tombs that have been left out from the beginning in our study because they contained too little material usable for our purposes.) [V].

46. Sequences beginning with *SḤḎ ḤM-Kꜣ:*

46/1. *jmj-rꜣ pr:* 133, 483.
46/2. *jmj-rꜣ sšr:* 573. [S].
46/3. *ḥm-kꜣ:* 273, 548. [S].
46/4. *ḫrp zḥ:* 483. [S].
46/5. *zꜣb jmj-rꜣ zš:* 197. [C]. (Cf. 35/5.)
46/6. *zꜣb sḥḏ zš:* 197. [C]. (Cf. 38/4.)

47. Sequences beginning with *SḤḎ ḪNTJ-Š PR-ʿꜣ:*

47/1. *wʿb nswt:* 378.
47/2. *rḫ nswt:* 445.
47/3. *ḥm-nṯr Ḫwfw:* 378.
47/4. *smr pr:* 67. [C]. (Cf. 45/2 and 14/15.)

48. Sequences beginning with *STM:*

48/1. *jwn Knmwt:* 133. [S].
48/2. *jmj-rꜣ pr:* 133. [S].
48/3. *jmj-rꜣ prwj-ḥḏ:* 32, 393, 576.
48/4. *jmj-rꜣ ḫntj-š pr-ʿꜣ:* 131, 393, 414. [S].
48/5. *jmj-rꜣ sšr:* 393. [S].
48/6. *jmj-rꜣ Šmʿ:* 32, 133, 192.
48/7. *jmj-rꜣ šnwtj:* 32, 393, 576.
48/8. *jmj-rꜣ kꜣt nbt nt nswt:* 286A–B.
48/9. *jrj nfr-ḥꜣt:* 133, 300, 422. [S].
48/10. *mdw rḫjt:* 133, 192. [S].
48/11. *ḥꜣtj-ʿ:* 571 (?? Mariette's copy shows a string of titles with *stm* written between *jrj-pʿt* and *ḥꜣtj-ʿ*, thus violating sequences 19/35, 51/34, and 32/30, which are among the best documented standard sequences in the collection. One is inclined to suspect a mistake on the part of the ancient scribe.) [V].
48/12. *ḥm-nṯr Mꜣʿt:* 133, 576. [S].
48/13. *ḥrj-sštꜣ:* 323. [S].
48/14. *ḥrj-sštꜣ pr dwꜣt:* 133, 197, 300, 414, 576. [C]. (Cf. 24/8.)
48/15. *ḥrj-tp Nḫb:* 32, 197, 300, 576.
48/16. *ḥqꜣ ḥt:* 32, 110, 131.

48/17. *ḫrp ʿḥ:* 300. [S].
48/18. *ḫrp šndwt nbt:* 32, 74, 110, 131, 133, 134, 135, 189, 191, 192, 197, 202, 212, 228, 229A, 279, 286, 286A–B, 300, 323, 324, 333, 361, 393, 414, 422, 429, 451 (IV), 531 (IV), 545, 548, 560, 571, 576, 591, 592. [S].
48/19. *ḫrj-ḥbt:* 32, 131, 133, 189, 191, 197, 300, 323, 324, 393, 414, 429, 576. [S].
48/20. *ḫrj-ḥbt ḥrj-tp:* 286A–B (?? Mistake? cf. 30/18), 324 (? A late tomb, possibly already First Intermediate), 571 (?? cf. 48/11). [V].
48/21. *ḫrj-tp nswt:* 32, 131, 133, 192, 286, 393, 429. [S].
48/22. *zꜣ nswt:* 451 (IV), 531 (IV). [V].
48/23. *zꜣb jmj-rꜣ zš:* 133. [S].
48/24. *zš:* 133. [S].
48/25. *zš ʿ nswt:* 131, 133, 576. [S].
48/26. *zš mḏꜣt nṯr:* 32, 110, 189, 197, 323, 393, 571, 576. [S].
48/27. *smr:* 110, 131, 451 (IV), 531 (IV). [C]. (Cf. 43/7 and 24/8.)
48/28. *smr wʿtj:* 32, 74, 110, 131, 133, 135, 189, 191, 197, 228, 286A–B, 300, 323, 324, 393, 414, 422, 429, 545, 560, 571, 576.
48/29. *smr pr:* 133. [S].
48/30. *sḏꜣwtj bjtj:* 32, 74, 286A–B, 576, 591.
48/31. *špss nswt:* 133. [S].
48/32. *tꜣtj zꜣb ṯꜣtj:* 571 (?? cf. 48/11). [V].

49. Sequences beginning with *SḎꜣWTJ BJTJ:*

49/1. *jwn Knmwt:* 133, 160, 396. [S].
49/2. *jmj-rꜣ wpt:* 131, 138, 279, 534 (IV), 556. [S].
49/3. *jmj-rꜣ pr:* 133, 134, 553. [S].
49/4. *jmj-rꜣ prwj-ḥḏ:* 146, 160, 279, 361, 393, 548, 576, 592.
49/5. *jmj-rꜣ ḫntj-š pr-ʿꜣ:* 15, 83, 131, 134, 177A, 247, 305, 393, 407, 552, 556, 562, 563, 566, 588. [S].
49/6. *jmj-rꜣ zš ʿ nswt:* 146, 160.
49/7. *jmj-rꜣ ssr:* 393. [S].
49/8. *jmj-rꜣ Šmʿ:* 39, 81, 133, 134, 192, 592, 602.
49/9. *jmj-rꜣ šnwtj:* 133, 134, 146, 160, 361, 393, 548, 553, 576.
49/10. *jmj-rꜣ kꜣt nbt nt nswt:* 146, 160, 260 (IV), 286A–B, 331 (IV).
49/11. *jrj nfr-ḥꜣt:* 133, 279, 285, 361, 396, 408, 548. [S].
49/12. *mdw rḫjt:* 133, 146, 192, 396. [S].
49/13. *nst ḫntt:* 146. [S].
49/14. *rḫ nswt:* 553. [S].
49/15. *ḥꜣtj-ʿ:* 450 (IV). [V].
49/16. *ḥm-nṯr Mꜣʿt:* 133, 576. [S].
49/17. *ḥrj-sštꜣ pr dwꜣt:* 133, 197, 249, 534 (IV), 562, 576. [S].
49/18. *ḥrj-tp Nḫb:* 136, 197, 548, 602.
49/19. *ḥqꜣ ḥt:* 81, 82, 83, 106, 110, 131, 177A, 562, 563, 590A, 592.
49/20. *ḫrp ʿḥ:* 373, 534 (IV). [S].
49/21. (Canceled.)
49/22. *ḫrp šndwt nbt:* 110, 134, 135, 192, 197, 361 (? cf. 31/18), 429, 592.

49/23. *ẖrj-ḥbt:* 15, 32, 39, 68, 81, 106, 111, 131, 132, 133, 134, 136, 139, 150, 160, 177A, 192, 197, 212, 231, 247, 272, 279, 285, 305, 337, 345, 361, 371, 382, 384, 393, 395, 429, 431, 432, 497, 507, 534 (IV), 552, 556, 562, 563, 566, 575, 576, 588, 590A, 592, 593, 602. [S].
49/24. *ẖrj-ḥbt ḥrj-tp:* 134, 135, 192, 212, 249.
49/25. *ẖrj-tp nswt:* 32, 106, 131, 133, 138, 139, 146, 192, 201, 212, 279, 382, 393, 396, 429, 456, 552, 602. [S].
49/26. *zꜣ nswt:* 260 (IV), 331 (IV), 534 (IV). [V].
49/27. *zꜣb jmj-rꜣ zš:* 133. [S].
49/28. *zꜣb ʿḏ-mr:* 133, 146. [S].
49/29. *zš:* 133. [S].
49/30. *zš ʿ nswt:* 131, 133, 201, 432, 576. [S].
49/31. *zš mḏꜣt nṯr:* 32, 110, 160, 189, 197, 249, 361, 393, 497, 562, 576, 592. [S].
49/32. *zš n zꜣ:* 556 [S].
49/33. *smr:* 110, 131. [S].
49/34. *smr wʿtj:* 15, 32, 39, 68, 74, 81, 82, 83, 84, 106, 110, 111, 129, 131, 132, 133, 134, 135, 136, 138, 139, 150, 177A, 192, 197, 201, 212, 213, 222 (IV), 229, 229A, 231, 247, 249, 272, 279, 285, 286A–B, 305, 337, 345, 361, 364, 367, 371, 373, 382, 384, 393, 395, 407, 408, 409, 429, 431, 432, 433, 450 (IV), 497, 507, 534 (IV), 541, 548, 552, 553, 556, 560, 562, 563, 566, 575, 576, 587, 588, 592, 593, 602, 603. [S].
49/35. *smr pr:* 133. [S].
49/36. *stm:* 134, 135, 192, 197, 361 (? cf. 31/18), 429, 592.
49/37. *špss nswt:* 15, 133, 337, 364, 556. [S].
49/38. *tꜣtj zꜣb ṯꜣtj:* 260 (IV). [V].

50. Sequences beginning with *ŠPSS NSWT:*

50/1. *jmj-rꜣ pr:* 133. [S].
50/2. *zš:* 133. [S].
50/3. *smr pr:* 18, 47, 60, 86, 98, 133, 149, 177, 183, 183A, 210, 273A, 449, 507. [S].

51. Sequences beginning with *TꜣTJ ZꜣB ṮꜣTJ:*

51/1. *jwn Knmwt:* 13, 57, 133, 160, 274, 275, 315, 505. [S].
51/2. *jmj-rꜣ wpt:* 279, 534 (IV). [S].
51/3. *jmj-rꜣ pr:* 133. [S].
51/4. *jmj-rꜣ prwj-ḥḏ:* 57, 146, 158, 160, 162, 202, 229A, 274, 279, 393, 505, 548, 560. [S].
51/5. *jmj-rꜣ ḫntj-š pr-ʿꜣ:* 279, 393. [S].
51/6. *jmj-rꜣ zš ʿ nswt:* 13, 27, 57, 62, 105, 133, 135, 146, 158, 159, 160, 162, 189, 197, 202, 229A, 274, 275, 315, 324, 333, 340, 393, 455, 456, 505, 548, 560, 590, 591, 602. [S].
51/7. *jmj-rꜣ sšr:* 393. [S].
51/8. *jmj-rꜣ Šmʿ:* 133, 279, 602. [S].

51/9. *jmj-rꜣ šnwtj:* 13, 57, 77, 133, 146, 158, 160, 162, 197, 202, 274, 279, 315, 393, 548, 560. [S].
51/10. *jmj-rꜣ kꜣt nbt nt nswt:* 57, 105, 146, 158, 159, 160, 167, 189, 197, 223, 246, 260 (IV), 274, 275, 315, 331 (IV), 393, 399 (IV), 455, 456, 505, 548, 590. [S].
51/11. *jrj nfr-ḥꜣt:* 105, 133, 279. [S].
51/12. *wr* 10 *Šmꜥ:* 13, 315, 473A (IV), 505. [S].
51/13. *mdw rḫjt:* 13, 57, 133, 146, 160, 274, 275, 505, 534 (IV). [S].
51/14. *nst ḫntt:* 146, 315 (? Restoration, cf. 1/5), 505. [S].
51/15. *ḥꜣtj-ꜥ:* 91 (IV), 160, 229A, 279, 399 (IV), 534 (IV), 560, 602.
51/16. *ḥm-nṯr Mꜣꜥt:* 13, 133, 315, 505, 576. [S].
51/17. (Canceled.)
51/18. *ḥrj-sštꜣ:* 399 (IV).
51/19. *ḥrj-sštꜣ pr dwꜣt:* 105, 133, 197, 471 (IV), 534 (IV), 558. [S].
51/20. *ḥrj-tp Nḫb:* 105, 197, 399 (IV), 602.
51/21. *ḫrp ꜥḥ:* 399 (IV), 471 (IV), 534 (IV).
51/22. *ḫrp šnḏwt nbt:* 135, 189, 197, 229A, 279, 393, 560, 591. [S].
51/23. *ẖrj-ḥbt:* 105, 133, 160, 189, 197, 223, 279, 393, 455, 558, 560, 602. [S].
51/24. *ẖrj-ḥbt ḥrj-tp:* 105, 135, 189, 197, 399 (IV), 471 (IV), 560, 571, 591.
51/25. *ẖrj-tp nswt:* 13, 57, 133, 146, 274, 275, 279, 393, 456, 505, 534 (IV), 602. [S].
51/26. *zꜣ nswt:* 260 (IV), 331 (IV), 471 (IV), 534 (IV). [V].
51/27. *zꜣb jmj-rꜣ zš:* 133. [S].
51/28. *zꜣb ꜥḏ-mr:* 133, 146, 505. [S].
51/29. *zš:* 133. [S].
51/30. *zš ꜥ nswt:* 133, 576. [S].
51/31. *zš mḏꜣt nṯr:* 105, 160, 189, 197, 249, 393, 560, 571. [S].
51/32. *smr wꜥtj:* 105, 133, 135, 160, 189, 197, 229A, 275, 279, 393, 399 (IV), 471 (IV), 558, 560, 571, 602. [S].
51/33. *smr pr:* 133. [S].
51/34. *stm:* 135, 189, 197, 229A, 279, 393, 560, 591. [S].
51/35. *sḏꜣwtj bjtj:* 30 (IV), 91 (IV), 133, 135, 146, 160, 197, 229A, 279, 331 (IV), 456, 591, 602. [S].
51/36. *špss nswt:* 133. [S].

From this data it is a relatively easy matter to construct the charts of standard sequences given on pages 199–201. Because of the uncertainties already mentioned that are inherent in poorly documented sequences whose reverse does not occur, it seemed safest to begin by drawing up a chart of those standard sequences that are documented most frequently. Then a less well attested group would be worked in. In this manner, in the case of an indirect contradiction such as is pointed out in the above list in the remarks under [C], in other words, a contradiction which only implied that one of the two possibilities must be excluded from the chart, the better attested one was always given preference. In the case of a direct contradiction, one that can be easily determined from the list just given by checking whether the reverse of the sequence in question also is attested, neither sequence is, of course, admitted to the chart.

In view of the differing frequency with which various titles and groups of titles occur, it is not astonishing to find that some uncontradicted sequences admitted to the chart are attested much less frequently than some fluctuating ones that cannot be admitted and will be discussed in the next chapter. Nor should one expect to find that in the case of such variations the number of occurrences should be about the same each way. In general, the proportion attested for each will correspond roughly to the length of time that it was in use, and a case such as 19/38 *vs.* 51/15 is not unusual.

This brings us back again to the question of the reliability of the chart of standard sequences. If a sequence can occur some ten times as frequently as its reverse, just what is the likelihood that a sequence neither directly or indirectly contradicted in our documentation actually was valid only for a portion of the period during which the ranking system was in force? We can hardly go into a statistical discussion of the matter, and it would, I think, hardly repay the trouble. The sequences 7/16 and 7/27, both attested six times, are the best documented sequences not directly contradicted in the collection for which it must be assumed on the basis of an indirect contradiction that the reverse of these sequences was also in use at some time. This gives us a reasonable limit for safe procedure. The chances are that an uncontradicted sequence attested at least ten times will have been valid throughout the period under consideration; if the reverse had been in use, an attestation would be expected.

Our chart has, however, to fulfil two purposes. First of all, to show what sequences seem in the opinion of the writer to have actually remained unaltered, and, second, to eliminate from our discussion of the variable sequences those for which no fluctuation can be detected at present. It seemed advisable to present three charts, the first giving the standard sequences attested at least thirty times, another for those occurring ten times or more, and finally one giving the entire group. The reader can check the reliability of those occurring in the last chart by comparison with the detailed source list and by seeing to what extent it agrees with the general pattern. Some poorly attested sequences are, of course, absolutely certain because they involve the terminal titles in a long chain the individual links of which are well documented. Such sequences are inevitably included in the charts of the better attested sequences. It would be impossible to keep them out.

The charts as actually presented call for a few remarks. For reasons of space it was necessary to abbreviate the titles. A list of the abbreviations is given, and I hope that it will not occasion too great an inconvenience on the part of the reader. It became clear from a study of its behavior that the title *smr* is, for purposes of ranking, a variant of the title *smr wꜥtj*, at least during the Fifth and Sixth Dynasties. It seems most commonly, but by no means exclusively, documented in the earlier part of the Old Kingdom. In any case, it has not been entered separately.

The titles were originally selected on the basis of the frequency of their occurrence in the total collection; the rankability of such occurrences was not checked in advance as it would have involved a considerable amount of labor that would hardly repay itself except in the form of a certain symmetry of presentation. An advantage of this process is that at least a few of the titles usually held by dependents of the great officials who built the major tombs from which the bulk of our data is drawn have been included. A disadvantage is that the title *sḥḏ ḫntj-š pr-ꜥꜣ* has had to be omitted from the chart of standard sequences. While it occurs in rankable context with other titles, it is always in a variable sequence.

An apology is probably in order for the confusing appearance of the chart. It is to be read in the same fashion as the charts given for individual tombs in chapter ii. The standard sequences follow the lines from top to bottom. As usual, changes in direction are permissible at the circles. The main difference is that fluctuations are not indicated. Any sequence of titles not involving reading *up* a line is permissible, but if it involves the linking of two titles not connected by a line, it is a variable one that probably did not remain in use throughout the later Old Kingdom.

The charts indicate both the groups of titles that apparently always followed each other in the same sequence such as *zꜣb ꜥḏ-mr*, *nst ḫntt*, *ḥm-nṯr Mꜣꜥt*, and were probably felt to belong together by the ancient Egyptians, and the limits within which these groups fluctuated. It is the latter that cause most of the complexity in the charts.

In concluding this chapter, two matters still have to be treated. First, we present a list of those charts which give the 51 common titles *only* in the standard sequences and no others. All the information they contain as to the ranking of these titles is included in the charts on pages 199–201. For the purposes of the next chapter, they need not be discussed. Most of them do contain other titles than the very common ones, and some of them may occur in sequences characteristic only for a limited period. We shall return to a few of them later. The charts that have been exhausted for the time being are:

1, 3, 25A, 47, 60, 61, 63, 65, 68, 73, 79, 80, 84, 92, 101, 125, 127, 129, 130, 145, 147, 149, 166, 177, 183, 183A, 186, 188, 196, 209, 211, 220, 222, 227, 229, 231, 244, 252, 262, 268, 272, 273A, 281, 288, 296, 306, 320, 329, 334, 336, 337, 338, 340, 341, 346, 349A, 357, 359, 364, 366, 367, 368, 370, 371, 373, 375, 384, 390, 392, 396, 400, 404, 407, 409, 415, 430, 431, 438, 441, 447, 449, 464, 466, 475, 477, 478, 493A, 493B, 498, 502A, 507, 512, 513, 516, 525, 541, 561, 566, 573, 575, 579, 587, 588, 593, 601A, 601D.

More interesting, if also more troublesome, than these is the group of tombs containing violations of the standard sequences. They have to be analyzed under several headings. First we give a complete list:

26, 30, 31, 44, 95, 143, 167, 174, 175, 182, 215, 248, 260, 286A–B, 293, 307, 324, 331, 358, 361, 399, 450, 467, 471, 473, 473A, 476, 483, 531, 534, 536, 546, 560, 571, 601.

Of these the following can be easily and convincingly explained as the result of simple error:

[44] Sequences 28/12 and 18/20 (the latter not a direct violation) seem to be the result of an incorrect restoration on the part of the author of a damaged title beginning with *ḫrp*. On reconsideration, *ḫrp ʿpr* would be more likely than *ḫrp ʿḥ*.

[95] The sequence *jwn Knmwt*, *mdw rḫjt* is found on an offering slab which also reverses the sequence *nst ḫntt*, *wr* 10 *Šmʿ* attested five times in the mastaba proper. The chances are that this is a carelessly made object.

[358] This document has *wr* 10 *Šmʿ* followed at a considerable distance by *smr*. In view of the archaizing nature of this text, which is full of odd writings of well known titles and many that seem to be the product of the scribe's fertile imagination, one wonders whether this text has really any value whatsoever for our purposes.

[361] and [560] Both of these, in one case each, have *ẖrj-ḥbt* before *stm*, instead of *ẖrj-ḥbt ḥrj-tp*, which one would expect and which is well attested in these two tombs also.

These cases seemed to be pretty obvious, and with the exception of [358] it seemed to be safe to continue to use them for the consideration of the varying title sequences in the next chapter.

The next group to be considered might also be the result of error. The violation in each case consists of a simple inversion of the sequence of adjoining titles within well documented groups that very commonly occur together in the strings. We have the following cases:

[26, 215, 467] These reverse the sequence *mdw rḫjt*, *jwn Knmwt*, but, unlike the situation in [95], it is not quite so evident that the scribe made a

CHART I

Standard Title Sequences Documented Thirty Times or More

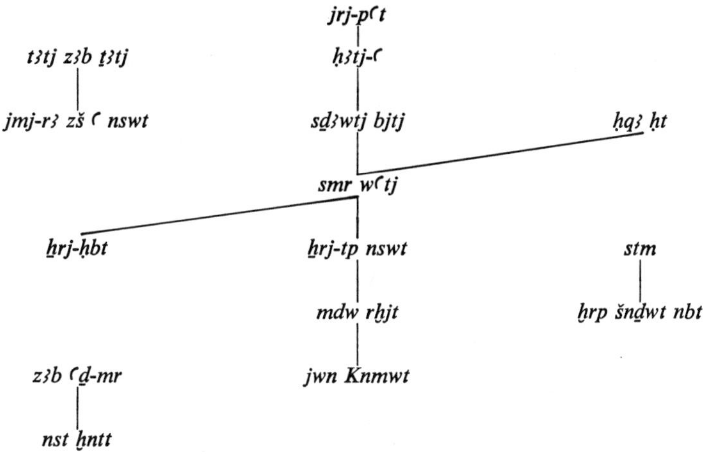

KEY TO ABBREVIATIONS
(IN THE ORDER OF THE EGYPTIAN ALPHABET)

JK	*jwn Knmwt*	*ḤTN*	*ḥrj-tp Nḫb*
WN	*wꜥb nswt*	*Ḫꜥ*	*ḫrp ꜥḥ*
WMŠ	*wr* 10 *Šmꜥ*	*ḪZ*	*ḫrp zḥ*
MW	*jmj-rꜣ wpt*	*ḪŠP*	*ḫntj-š pr-ꜥꜣ*
MP	*jmj-rꜣ pr*	*ḪŠN*	*ḫrp šnḏwt* (*nbt*)
MPḤ	*jmj-rꜣ prwj-ḥḏ*	*ẖḤ*	*ẖrj-ḥbt*
MR	*mdw rḫjt*	*ẖḤḤT*	*ẖrj-ḥbt ḥrj-tp*
MḤK	*jmj-rꜣ ḥm-kꜣ*	*ẖTN*	*ẖrj-tp nswt*
MḪŠP	*jmj-rꜣ ḫntj-š pr-ꜥꜣ*	*ZꜥM*	*zꜣb ꜥḏ-mr*
MZꜥN	*jmj-rꜣ zš ꜥ nswt*	*ZꜥN*	*zš ꜥ nswt* (*ḫft-ḥr*)
MSr	*jmj-rꜣ sšr*	*ZMN*	*zš mḏꜣt nṯr*
MŠꜥ	*jmj-rꜣ Šmꜥ*	*ZMZ*	*zꜣb jmj-rꜣ zš*
MŠn	*jmj-rꜣ šnwtj*	*ZN*	*zꜣ nswt* (*smsw*)
MKNN	*jmj-rꜣ kꜣt nbt nt nswt*	*ZZš*	*zꜣb zš*
NḪ	(*nj*) *nst ḫntt*	*ZSZ*	*zꜣb sḥḏ zš*
RP	*jrj-pꜥt*	*Zš*	*zš*
RNḤ	*jrj nfr-ḥꜣt*	*ZšZ*	*zš n zꜣ*
RḪN	*jrj-ḫt nswt* (*rḫ nswt*)	*SW*	*smr* (*wꜥtj*)
Ḥꜥ	*ḥꜣtj-ꜥ*	*SB*	*sḏꜣwtj bjtj*
ḤNM	*ḥm-nṯr Mꜣꜥt*	*SP*	*smr pr*
ḤNḪ	*ḥm-nṯr Ḫwfw*	*Sm*	*stm*
ḤK	*ḥm-kꜣ*	*SḤK*	*sḥḏ ḥm-kꜣ*
ḤS	*ḥrj-sštꜣ*	*SḪŠP*	*sḥḏ ḫntj-š pr-ꜥꜣ*
ḤSPD	*ḥrj-sštꜣ pr dwꜣt*	*ŠN*	*špss nswt*
ḤqḤ	*ḥqꜣ ḥt*	*TZṮ*	*tꜣtj zꜣb ṯꜣtj*

CHART II

STANDARD TITLE SEQUENCES DOCUMENTED TEN TIMES OR MORE

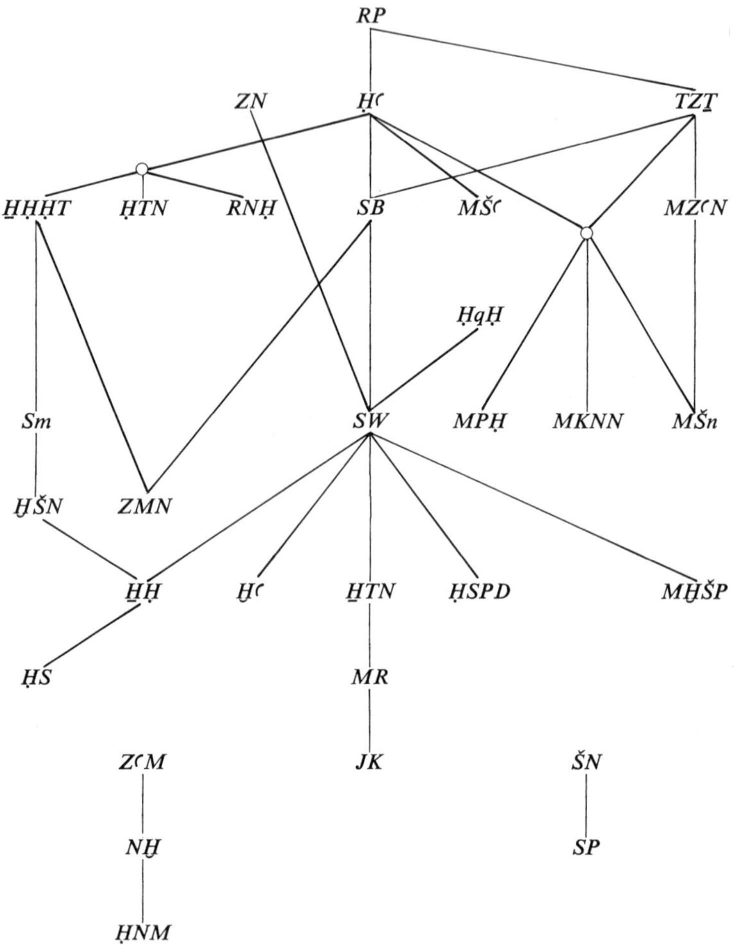

CHART III
Standard Title Sequences—Complete Series

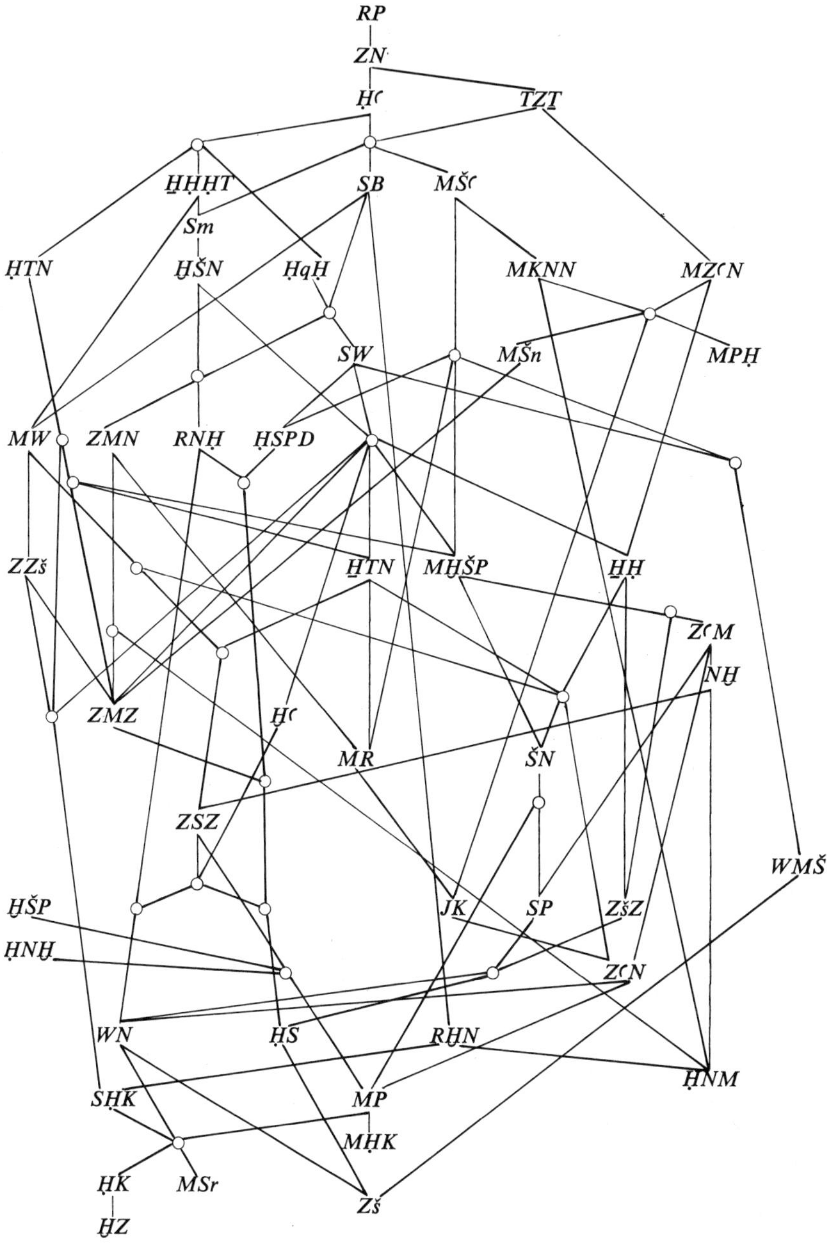

mistake, and the sequences are well documented on the walls of the mastabas. In the cases of [26] and [215] a dating to the early Fifth Dynasty would be possible, and the latter has been marked as such in the list of sequences, but [467] is almost certainly not. It seemed best, therefore, to retain the group for further consideration.

[483] This reverses *špss nswt, smr pr*. The text is well attested and cannot be rejected out of hand.

[286A–B] These write *stm, ḫrp šnḏwt nbt, ẖrj-ḥbt ḥrj-tp*, instead of the very common standard sequence.

In all these cases, though the sequences involved were not admitted to the standard sequence chart, as they seemed to be quite unusual, the divergence still did not seem sufficiently strong to warrant the decision to exclude these charts completely from the treatment of the variable sequences, which would be tantamount to dating them either to the Fourth and early Fifth Dynasties or to a period after the end of the Old Kingdom. Such datings could be possible, but the evidence seemed too slim. [26] was, however, removed since, aside from its one violation, it contained nothing but standard sequences.

The violation in [167] has already been discussed under 3/7. Since it is a servant's titles that are involved, there again seemed no reason to exclude this chart from discussion in the next chapter, particularly since neither an early nor a late date seems at all probable. For the same reason, [571] has been retained, despite the fact that it contains an exceedingly serious, and for the time being, inexplicable anomaly discussed under 48/11.

There remain two groups of charts showing more serious violations, reversals of titles over a considerable range in the standard sequences or misplacements of such exceedingly well attested sequences as *smr wʿtj, ẖrj-ḥbt*. The greater part of these charts clearly dates from the Fourth or early Fifth Dynasties; a few appear to be quite late. The violating sequences will be given below, and a comparison with the standard sequence charts will enable the reader to judge the seriousness of the violation.

[30] *ḫrp ʿḥ, ẖrj-ḥbt ḥrj-tp.*

[31] *nsw-bjt Ḫʿfrʿ zȝ.f n ẖt.f smsw, jrj-pʿt.*

[143] *zš ʿ nswt, jmj-rȝ kȝt nbt nt nswt.* (The standard sequence here is not too well documented, so this case is probably rather doubtful.)

[174] *ḥȝtj-ʿ, zȝ nswt n ẖt.f.*

[175] *ḥȝtj-ʿ, . . . , zȝ nswt n ẖt.f.*

[182] *wr* 10 *Šmʿ, rḫ nswt, . . . , smr wʿtj.*

[248] *jrj-pʿt, . . . , zš mḏȝt nṯr, tȝtj zȝb ṯȝtj.*

[260] *sḏꜣwtj bjtj, tꜣtj zꜣb ṯꜣtj.*
[293] *ḫrj-sštꜣ, zꜣb ꜥḏ-mr, . . . , zš mḏꜣt nṯr.* Also *zꜣ nswt* at the end of a string composed of relatively uncommon titles.
[307] *wr* 10 *Šmꜥ, . . . , ḥqꜣ ḥt.*
[331] *sḏꜣwtj bjtj, . . . , jmj-rꜣ kꜣt nbt nt nswt, zꜣ nswt n ẖt.f.*
[399] *zꜣ nswt, ẖrj-ḥbt ḥrj-tp, ḥꜣtj-ꜥ.*
[450] *smr wꜥtj, ḥꜣtj-ꜥ.*
[451] *stm, ḫrp šnḏwt, smr, zꜣ nswt.*
[471] *jrj-pꜥt, tꜣtj zꜣb ṯꜣtj, zꜣ nswt n ẖt.f.*
zꜣ nswt n ẖt.f, jrj-pꜥt, etc.
[473] *ḫrp ꜥḥ, zꜣ nswt n ẖt.f, ẖrj-ḥbt.*
[473A] *zꜣ nswt n ẖt.f, jrj-pꜥt.*
[476] *ẖrj-tp nswt, smr.*
[531] *smr wꜥtj, ḫrp ꜥḥ, stm, ḫrp šnḏwt, zꜣ nswt; ḫrp šnḏwt, smr.*
[534] *ḥꜣtj-ꜥ, zꜣ Snfrw, ḫrp ꜥḥ, . . . , zꜣ nswt.*
sḏꜣwtj bjtj, . . . , ẖrj-ḥbt, . . . , zꜣ nswt, smr wꜥtj, ḫrp ꜥḥ, . . . , zꜣ nswt. (Incidentally, one of the few early tombs with long usable strings of titles, resulting in even worse confusion than usual in tombs of this period.)
[536] *mdw rḫjt, smr.*
[546] *zš ꜥ nswt, jmj-rꜣ wpt.*

These are early cases. There are two which seem to be late:

[324] *stm, smr wꜥtj, ẖrj-ḥbt ḥrj-tp.*
[603] *ẖrj-ḥbt, smr wꜥtj.*

In these sequences, dots indicate one or more titles in the charts that have been omitted.

It will be seen that most of these violations of the standard sequence charts are quite serious; furthermore, I have been unable to detect any pattern in them.

We can now draw our first chronological conclusions. It must be stressed again that the chronological explanation of the varying title sequences is a working hypothesis. On the basis of that hypothesis reasonably secure archeological datings have been used to sort out characteristics that might be chronologically valid—in this case title sequences that are not documented after the early Fifth or before the end of the Sixth Dynasties.

To my mind, the evidence thus far adduced seems to indicate that a chart of ranked titles containing serious violations of the standard ranking charts is a reasonable indication of a date either before the early-middle Fifth Dynasties or after the end of the Sixth.

The limits can be drawn somewhat more exactly by examining the dates given in the previous chapter. The tombs just listed as being early range from the reign of Khufu to that of Sahure [471]. Among the tombs that agree with the standard ranking chart, [105] is definitely dated to the reign of Neferirkare, and others, such as [146] and [300], are not likely to be much later. I feel reasonably safe, therefore, in asserting that the early tombs just listed are all to be dated before about the middle of the reign of Neferirkare.

Only two charts that might be later than the Old Kingdom disagree with the standard sequences. Since [602] can be dated with some assurance to the end of the Eighth Dynasty, it seems likely that they are to be assigned at least to the Ninth.

While a serious violation of the standard ranking sequences seems to indicate a date before Neferirkare or after the end of the Old Kingdom, the reverse is not true. The ranking system obviously neither developed instantaneously, nor did it disappear completely at the end of the Old Kingdom. And while the system was gradually being developed, the strings of titles as written, though showing some uncertainties and confusion, were not utterly chaotic and reflect the developing system of standard ranking sequences to a greater or lesser degree. As a result, tombs such as [262], which dates from the middle of the Fourth Dynasty, or [323], which is certainly later than [324], do not violate the standard sequences.

There seems to be little point in preparing a list of such early or late tombs that have not yet been excluded. The interested reader can derive one from the datings in chapter iii. Some of these tombs have already been excluded because they contained few rankable titles, or only standard sequences, and thus contain data inadequate for dating by titles. In the next chapter we shall attempt to determine the title sequences characteristic for various periods during the range of time from Neferirkare to the end of the Eighth Dynasty. It will be interesting to see if those charts that probably are to be dated outside these limits agree or disagree with the sequences valid within them.

V

THE VARIABLE SEQUENCES

*

Before presenting the variable sequences of the 50 commonest titles, we must present the data on which our conclusions will be based. The amount of material contained in the charts has been considerably reduced by the elimination of the less commonly attested titles and the discarding of those charts which are of no use for our purpose. The remaining titles will be presented in the form of title sequences rather than charts, and the titles themselves will be abbreviated according to the system used in the charts of standard sequences in chapter iv (cf. p. 199); this will add a certain element of inconvenience but saves a considerable amount of space.

Titles are only included if they are attested in a rankable context. Any others will be ignored.

[5] *RḪN, WN.*
[6] *ZʿM, WMŠ.*
JK, ḤK.
[7] *ḤNḪ, SW, Ḫʿ.*
[8] *RḪN, WMŠ, NḪ.*
RḪN, ḤNḪ.
[9] *ḤqḤ, WMŠ, NḪ.*
[10] *RḪN, WN.*
[11] *RḪN, MḤK.*
[12] *SW, H̱Ḥ, WMŠ.*
[13] *TZṮ, MZʿN, H̱TN, MR, JK, ḤNM.*
MŠʿ, MR, ...
. . . , MR, MŠn.
. . . , MR, WMŠ.
ZʿM, NḪ.
ZʿM, ḤNM.
ZMZ, MP.
MSr, ḤK.
[14] *ZšZ, H̱TN, ZʿM, NḪ, MR, JK, ḤNM, ḤS.*
. . . , H̱TN, MW.

[15] *Ḥʿ, SB, SW, MḪŠP, H̱Ḥ, ŠN.*

[16] *ḪŠP, WN, ḤS, ḤNḪ, RḪN* and *WN, RḪN, ḤS,* . . . .

[18] *ŠN, SP.*
H̱TN, MḪŠP.

[19] *RḪN, MP.*

[21] *RḪN, WN, ḤNḪ.*

[22] *WN, RḪN.*

[24] *RḪN, ZZš.*
RḪN, WMŠ.

[25] *RḪN, WN* and *WN, RḪN.*

[27] *TZṮ, MZʿN.*
ḪḤḪT, SW, MPḤ.

[32] *RP, ḪḤḪT, Sm, ḪŠN, MŠʿ, MŠn, MPḤ, ḤqḤ, SB, SW, H̱TN, H̱Ḥ, ZMN.*
Ḥʿ, ḪḤḪT, ...
. . . , *ḤqḤ, ḤTN, H̱Ḥ,* . . . .

[36] *MḪŠP, ZʿM.*
WN, ḤS.
WN, ḤNḪ.

[39] *Ḥʿ, SB, MŠʿ, SW, H̱Ḥ* and . . . , *SB, SW, H̱Ḥ, MŠʿ.* (The titles are of *Sꜣbnj.*)

[40] *RḪN, ḤS, WN.*

[44] *RḪN, MW, ḤqḤ.* (The reading of *ḫrp ʿḥ* has been rejected; cf. above, p. 198.)

[45] *ZʿM, NḪ.*
WMŠ, ḤNM.

[48] *ZMZ, H̱TN, ZʿM, NḪ.*
MW, H̱TN, ...

[49] *SW, H̱Ḥ, ḤSPD.*

[55] *ZMZ, ḤNM.*

[56] *H̱TN, MR, JK.*
H̱TN, MW.

[57] *RP, Ḥʿ, TZṮ, MZʿN, MKNN, H̱TN, MR, JK, MŠn.*
. . . , *Ḥʿ, SW.*
. . . , *H̱TN, MPḤ.*

[59] *ḤqḤ, SW, H̱Ḥ, MŠn.*
H̱TN, MR, JK.
ZʿM, NḪ.

[62] *TZṮ, MZʿN.*
SW, H̱TN, MR, JK.
. . . , *H̱TN, ZʿM.*
ḤqḤ, H̱TN.
ḤqḤ, WMŠ.
SW, SḤK.

[64] *ZN, SW, MKNN.*

[66] *RḪN, WN.*

[67] *SḪŠP, SP.*

[70] *WMŠ, NḪ, ZMZ, ḤNM.*

[71] *RḪN, WN.*

[73A] *RP, SW.*
RP, TZṮ.
Ḥʿ, ḤTN, MŠʿ.

[74] *Ḥʿ, Sm, ḪŠN, SB, SW.*
Ḥʿ, H̱ḤḤT, SW.

[75] *WN, ḤS.*

[77] *H̱TN, MR, JK, ḤNM, ZʿN.*

[78] *TZṮ, MŠn.*
H̱TN, MŠn.
H̱TN, MR, JK.

[81] *Ḥʿ, MŠʿ, SB, ḤqḤ, SW, H̱Ḥ* and . . . , *SB, ḤqḤ, SW, H̱Ḥ, MŠʿ.*

[82] *SB, ḤqḤ, SW.*

[83] *Ḥʿ, SB, ḤqḤ, SW, MḪŠP.*

[85] *RḪN, MW.*

[86] *ŠN, SP.*
SW, H̱Ḥ.
MḪŠP, H̱TN.

[88] *ZʿM, WMŠ, ḤS.*
ZʿM, MKNN.

[89] *H̱TN, ZʿN, ZMZ.*

[90] *ZʿM, NḪ, JK, WMŠ.*

[91] *RP, ZN, H̱ḤḤT.*
TZṮ, Ḥʿ, SB.

[94] *RP, Ḥʿ, TZṮ, MKNN, H̱TN, MR.*
. . . , *TZṮ, MZʿN.*
JK, ḤNM.

[94A] *SW, MŠn.*
SW, H̱Ḥ.
SW, ḤSPD.

[95] *H̱TN, ZʿM, NḪ, JK, ḤNM, WMŠ* and . . . *WMŠ, NḪ* (once).
MR, JK, ... (The sequence *jwn Knmwt*, *mdw rḫjt* has been corrected. Cf. above, p. 198.)

[98] *SW, H̱Ḥ, MW.*
ŠN, SP.

[100] *H̱TN, ZʿM, MPḤ.*

[103] *H̱TN, ZʿM, ḤNM.*

[104] *RḪN, MḤK.*

[105] *Ḥʿ, TZṮ, H̱ḤḤT, ZMN, SW, RNḤ, H̱Ḥ.*
. . . , *RNḤ, ḤSPD, ḤTN, MZʿN* and . . . , *MKNN, MZʿN.*
H̱TN, MR, JK, H̱Ḥ and . . . , *H̱Ḥ, H̱TN, MR, JK*, ...
. . . , *JK, ḤNM.*

[106] *Ḥʿ, MŠʿ, SB, ḤqḤ, SW, H̱Ḥ, H̱TN.*

[109] SW, ḤTN, Ḫʿ, ḤSPD, ḤS.
H̱Ḥ, ZMN.
H̱Ḥ, ḤS.
[110] Ḥʿ, MŠʿ, ḤTN, H̱ḤḤT, SW, ZMN.
. . . , ḤTN, MḪŠP.
SB, SW, ...
Sm, SW, ...
. . . , SW, ḪŠN.
[111] Ḥʿ, SW, H̱Ḥ.
SB, SW, ...
H̱ḤḤT, SW, ...
[112] ZN, SW, MŠʿ, H̱TN, ḤMN.
[112A] H̱TN, MŠʿ, MŠn.
[113] RḪN, ZZš, SḤK.
[114] RḪN, ḤqḤ.
RḪN, MW.
[115] ZMZ, ZʿN, ZSZ, RḪN, WN, ḤS (once . . . , ḤS, RḪN. Error?)
ZMZ, ḤNM, WN, ...
[117] H̱Ḥ, ḤSPD.
H̱Ḥ, ZMN.
[118] ZMZ, ḤNM.
ZMZ, ZSZ, ZʿN.
[121] H̱TN, H̱Ḥ.
[123] RḪN, MP, MḤK.
[123A] Ḥʿ, MKNN.
ZʿM, NḪ, ḤS, WMŠ, MR, ḤNM.
[124] WN, RḪN.
[126] ZN, ḤTN, SW, Ḫʿ.
[128] WMŠ, RḪN.
[131] Ḥʿ, MŠʿ, H̱ḤḤT, Sm, ḪŠN, ḤqḤ, SW, H̱TN, ZʿN.
. . . , SW, MḪŠP, H̱Ḥ.
SB, MW, ḤqḤ, ...
[132] RP, Ḥʿ, H̱ḤḤT, SB, SW, H̱Ḥ.
[133] RP, Ḥʿ, ḤTN, TZṮ, MZʿN, SB, MŠn, ZʿM, ZʿN, ZMZ.
. . . , Ḥʿ, H̱ḤḤT, Sm, ḪŠN, SW, H̱Ḥ, MŠʿ, H̱TN, MR, JK, ḤNM.
. . . , ḤTN, Sm, ...
. . . , SB, SW, ...
. . . , SW, RNḤ.
. . . , ḤTN, ZʿN, ...
ḤqḤ, SW, ...
. . . , H̱ḤḤT, ZMN, MŠʿ, ...
. . . , H̱Ḥ, ḤSPD.
. . . , H̱Ḥ, ŠN, SP.
. . . , ŠN, Zš.
. . . , ŠN, MP.
SḤK, MP.

[134] *Ḥʿ, SB, MŠʿ, H̱ḤḤT, Sm, ḪŠN.*
. . . , MŠʿ, MŠn.
. . . , MŠʿ, SW, H̱Ḥ, MP.
. . . , SW, MḪŠP.
. . . , SW, H̱TN.
ZʿN, MP.
ZʿN, ZMZ.
[135] *RP, Ḥʿ, TZT̠, MZʿN, SB, H̱ḤḤT, Sm, ḪŠN, SW.*
. . . , Ḥʿ, MŠʿ, SW.
. . . , MŠʿ, MKNN.
[136] *Ḥʿ, SB, SW, H̱Ḥ.*
. . . , SW, ḤTN.
[137] *Ḥʿ, MŠʿ, H̱ḤḤT, SW.*
[138] *Ḥʿ, SB, SW, H̱TN, MW.*
[139] *ḤqḤ, SB, SW, H̱TN.*
. . . , SW, H̱Ḥ.
[140] *WN, MḤK.*
RḪN, ḪZ.
[142] *SW, RNḤ, ḤTN.*
SW, Ḫʿ.
[146] *Ḥʿ, TZT̠, SB, H̱TN, MR, MKNN, MZʿN.*
. . . , H̱TN, ZʿM, NḪ.
. . . , H̱TN, MŠn, MPḤ.
[150] *ḤqḤ, SB, SW, H̱Ḥ.*
[152] *ḤS, ḤNM.*
[153] *RP, Ḥʿ, TZT̠.*
[154] *SW, H̱Ḥ, RNḤ, Ḫʿ.*
[155] *Ḥʿ, MKNN.*
MP, ZšZ.
[156] *ZMZ, ZʿM, NḪ.*
[158] *RP, Ḥʿ, TZT̠, MZʿN, MKNN, MŠn, MPḤ.*
[159] *RP, Ḥʿ, TZT̠, MZʿN, MKNN.*
[160] *RP, TZT̠, Ḥʿ, SB, MKNN, MZʿN, JK, MŠn, MPḤ.*
. . . , Ḥʿ, SW, MZʿN, ...
. . . , TZT̠, MR, JK, ...
. . . , MZʿN, H̱Ḥ, ZMN.
H̱ḤḤT, ZMN.
H̱TN, MR, ...
[161] *H̱TN, MR, JK, ZʿM, NḪ, ḤNM.*
H̱TN, MŠʿ.
MSr, ḤK.
[162] *TZT̠, MŠn, MPḤ.*
TZT̠, MZʿN.
[163] *ZʿM, NḪ, ZMZ, ḤNM.*
[164] *ḤNM, ḤS.*

[167] *TZṮ, MKNN.*
Ḥʿ, SW, ḤTN, RNḤ, H̱Ḥ, ḤSPD.
. . . , *SW, Ḫʿ.*
. . . , *H̱Ḥ, ZMN.*
MP, ḤqḤ. (*sic*! cf. above, p. 170).
(The data is certainly incomplete.)
[168] *ḤK, MSr.*
ḤK, ḪZ.
[170] *RNḤ, SW.*
RNḤ, SP.
[171] *ZʿM, NḪ, WMŠ, ḤNM, H̱TN, MR, MZʿN, JK.*
[172] *WN, ḤNḪ, ḪŠP, ḤS.*
[177A] *Ḥʿ, SB, ḤqḤ, SW, H̱Ḥ, MḪŠP.*
[178] *ḤNḪ, ḤS.*
[181] *ZʿM, ZʿN.*
H̱TN, ZʿN.
H̱TN, MR, JK, ḤNM.
[184] *RP, Ḥʿ, TZṮ.*
[185] *MKNN, ḤqḤ, SW, H̱Ḥ, MḪŠP, H̱TN.*
[187] *Ḥʿ, MŠʿ, SW, H̱Ḥ, MḪŠP.*
. . . , *H̱Ḥ, ḤS.*
. . . , *H̱Ḥ, ḤSPD.*
ḤqḤ, H̱TN.
WMŠ, RḪN, ZʿM, NḪ, H̱TN.
[189] *RP, Ḥʿ, TZṮ, MZʿN, H̱ḤḤT, Sm, ḪŠN, SW, H̱Ḥ, ZMN.*
ZN, Ḥʿ, ...
. . . , *Ḥʿ, ḤTN, SW,* . . . .
. . . , *Ḥʿ, SB, ZMN.*
. . . , *MZʿN, MKNN.*
[190] *RḪN, WN, ḤNḪ, MP.*
[191] *Ḥʿ, Sm, ḪŠN, SW, H̱Ḥ.*
[192] *ḤqḤ, SB, H̱ḤḤT, Sm, ḪŠN, MŠʿ, H̱TN, MR.*
ḤqḤ, ZMZ.
ḤqḤ, ZʿM, NḪ.
. . . , *SB, SW, H̱Ḥ, H̱TN,* . . . .
[193] *WN, ḤNḪ.*
[195] *Ḥʿ, SW, H̱Ḥ, ḤS.*
. . . , *H̱Ḥ, ḤSPD.*
[197] *RP, Ḥʿ, TZṮ, MKNN, MZʿN, H̱ḤḤT, SB, Sm, ḪŠN, SW, H̱Ḥ, ZMN, ḤTN, ḤSPD* and . . . , *ḪŠN, ḤTN, SW, H̱Ḥ, ZMN, ḤSPD.*
. . . , *MZʿN, MŠn.*
SḤK, ZSZ.
SḤK, ZMZ.
ḤqḤ, ZMZ.
ḤqḤ, ZʿN.
ZšZ, ḤK. (The reverse also occurs but is probably the domestic usage

of the title referred to in chap. ii and similar to the usage of *ḥqꜣ ḥt* discussed in chap. iv under 3/7.)

[198] *WMŠ, ZMZ.*
[199] *WN, RẖN.*
[201] *ḤqḤ, SB, SW, ẖTN, ZꜥN.*
[202] *RP, Ḥꜥ, TZṮ, MZꜥN, MŠn, MPḤ.*
RP, Ḥꜥ, SW, ẖḤ, ḤSPD, ẖTN.
ẖḤḤT, SW, ...
. . . , SW, MŠꜥ.
. . . , SW, RNḤ.
Sm, ẖSN.
(Only a small part of the texts in this tomb has been available.)
[203] *SW, ẖꜥ, ḤSPD.*
[204] *ẖḤ, ZMN.*
ẖḤḤT, ZMN.
[206] *ẖTN, ZꜥM.*
[207] *WN, MP, MSr.*
[210] *SW, ẖḤ, ŠN, SP.*
MW, ŠN, ...
ẖḤ, ḤSPD.
[212] *Ḥꜥ, MŠꜥ, ḤTN, MŠn, MPḤ.*
Ḥꜥ, Sm, ẖŠN.
. . . , MŠꜥ, SB, SW, ẖTN.
. . . , SB, ẖḤḤT.
ḤqḤ, SW, ...
. . . , SW, ẖḤ.
[213] *MŠꜥ, SB, SW.*
[215] *ZN, SW, ẖḤ, MKNN, ẖTN, MR, JK.* (*jwn Knmwt, mdw rẖjt* corrected. Cf. p. 198.)
. . . , SW, ḤSPD.
[215A] *SW, ẖꜥ, ḤSPD.*
[218] *RẖN, WN.*
[223] *RP, ZN.*
TZṮ, ẖḤ, MKNN.
SW, RNḤ, ḤTN.
[224] *SW, ẖꜥ, ḤSPD.*
[225] *SW, RNḤ.*
[228] *Sm, ẖŠN, SW.*
[229A] *RP, TZṮ, MZꜥN, Ḥꜥ, Sm, ẖŠN.*
. . . , Ḥꜥ, SB, SW.
. . . , Ḥꜥ, MPḤ.
[232] *ZꜥM, MPḤ.*
[233] *SP, RẖN, WN.*
[235] *WN, ḤNẖ, ḤS* and . . . , *ḤS, ḤNẖ.*
[236] *SW, ẖꜥ, MKNN, ḤS.*

[238] *SW, Ḫʿ, ḤS.*
. . . , Ḫʿ, ḤSPD.
[240] *H̱Ḥ, ZMN.*
[241] *RP, ZN, H̱ḤḤT.*
RP, H̱Ḥ.
RP, TZṮ.
Ḥʿ, SW, ḤTN.
[242] *WN, SḤK.*
[243] *WN, RḪN.*
[245] *WN, ḤS.*
ZSZ, ḤNM.
[246] *Ḥʿ, H̱ḤḤT, ZMN, SW, RNḤ.* (Something is wrong here.  Read: *SW, RNḤ*, and new string *Ḥʿ, ḤTN*? Accidentally run together?)
TZṮ, MKNN.
Ḥʿ, ḤTN.
[247] *Ḥʿ, SB, SW, MḪŠP, H̱Ḥ* and . . . , *SW, H̱Ḥ, MḪŠP.*
ḤqḤ, SW, ... (? Reading uncertain; cf. above, p. 181.)
[249] *RP, Ḥʿ, TZṮ, SB, SW, ḤSPD, H̱ḤḤT, ZMN.*
(Only this one string of titles available in my notes. This is certainly far from complete.)
[250] *WMŠ, RḪN.*
[251] *ḤNḪ, RḪN, WN, MP, MḤK* and . . . , *WN, RḪN*, . . . and . . . , *WN, ḤNḪ, MP*, ...
[254] *RḪN, ḤqḤ, WN.*
[256] *ZZš, ZSZ, ZMZ, WM.*
[257] *WMŠ, NḪ, ḤS.*
RḪN, ḤS.
[258] *ḤNḪ, RḪN, WN, MP* and . . . , *WN, RḪN*, ...
[259] *SW, ḤTN.*
[263] *RḪN, ḤNḪ.*
[267] *RḪN, WN.*
[268A] *RḪN, ḤNḪ.*
[273] *H̱TN, MR, JK.*
ZʿM, WMŠ.
SḤK, ḤK.
[274] *RP, Ḥʿ, TZṮ, MZʿN, MKNN, H̱TN, MR, JK, MŠn, MPḤ* and . . . , *MKNN, MZʿN*, ...
. . . , Ḥʿ, SW.
MŠʿ, MŠn.
H̱Ḥ, ḤSPD.
[275] *ZN, Ḥʿ, TZṮ, SW, MKNN, H̱TN, MR, JK.*
. . . , TZṮ, MZʿN, H̱TN, ...
ḤK, MSr.
ḤK, ḪZ.
ḤK, Zš.

[275A] *ḤS, Zš.*
ZMZ, H̱Ḥ.
[277] *RḪN, ḤNḪ.*
RḪN, WN, ḤS.
[279] *RP, TZṮ, Ḥʿ, SB, SW, H̱TN, MW.*
RP, H̱ḤḤT, SW, ...
. . . , Ḥʿ, MḪŠP.
. . . , Ḥʿ, MŠn.
ZʿM, MŠn.
. . . , Ḥʿ, MŠʿ.
. . . , Ḥʿ, Sm, ḪŠN.
. . . , SW, MPḤ.
. . . , SW, H̱Ḥ.
. . . , SW, RNḤ.
[280] *SW, MḪŠP, H̱Ḥ.*
[282] *SW, Ḫʿ, ḤSPD.*
SḤK, Zš, ḤK.
[285] *RP, Ḥʿ, SB, SW, RNḤ.*
. . . , SW, H̱Ḥ.
[286] *H̱ḤḤT, Sm, ḪŠN, SW, H̱TN.*
MKNN, SW, ...
[286A–B] *Ḥʿ, H̱ḤḤT, Sm, ḪŠN, SB, MKNN, SW.* (The sequence *stm, ḫrp šnḏwt nbt, ẖrj-ḥbt ḥrj-tp* has been corrected. Cf. above, p. 202.)
[287] *SW, H̱Ḥ, ZMN.*
[290] *RḪN, WN.*
[292] *RḪN, MW.*
[294] *H̱TN, MR, ZʿM, NḪ, JK, WMŠ, ḤNM* and *. . . , ZʿM, JK, WMŠ, NḪ, ḤNM.*
. . . , MR, MZʿN, WMŠ, ...
. . . , ZʿM, MKNN, NḪ, . . . and *. . . , ZʿM, NḪ, MKNN, . . .* (position of *nst ḫntt* fluctuates).
[297] *ZʿN* (two varieties, cf. p. 164), *RḪN.*
[298] *ZMZ, ḤNM.*
[299] *H̱Ḥ, ZʿM, JK.*
[300] *Sm, ḪŠN, ḤSPD, ḤTN, Ḫʿ* and *. . . , ḪŠN, ḤTN, Ḫʿ, ḤSPD.*
Sm, SW, ḤTN, ...
. . . , SW, ḤSPD, ...
. . . , SW, RNḤ.
. . . , ḤTN, H̱Ḥ, ḤSPD. (*Ḥrj-sštꜣ pr dwꜣt* fluctuates here.)
[303] *RP, ZN, H̱ḤḤT, ZMN, SW, ḤTN.*
[305] *SB, SW, MḪŠP, H̱Ḥ.*
[309] *ZʿM, NḪ, ḤNM, ZMZ.*
[311] *RP, ZN, H̱TN, H̱Ḥ.*
[313] *WMŠ, RḪN.*

[315] *TZṮ, MZʿN, MKNN, MŠn.*
. . . , *MZʿN, JK, ḤNM, MŠn.*
. . . , *JK, WMŠ.*
MŠʿ, H̱TN, ZʿM, NḪ, JK, ...
. . . , *H̱TN, MR, MZʿN,* . . . .
ZMZ, RḪN.
. . . , *WMŠ, NḪ.* (?? Very doubtful. Last title damaged and only the *nst* visible. If correct, *nst ḫntt* would fluctuate in this tomb. But how else to fill the lacuna?)

[317] *RḪN, ḤNḪ.*

[318] *SW, RḪN.*

[322] *WN, ḤS, ḪŠP.*

[323] *Ḥʿ, H̱ḤḤT, Sm, ḪŠN, SW, ZMN.*
Ḥʿ, MŠʿ, SW, ...
. . . , *SW, H̱Ḥ.*
. . . , *SW, ḤS.*

[325] *ḤNḪ, ḤS.*

[332] *SP, ḤS, WN, RḪN* and *SP, WN, ḤS* and *RḪN, WN, ḤS.* (A bad case of fluctuation.)

[333]. *TZṮ, MZʿN.*
RP, Ḥʿ, SW, H̱Ḥ, H̱TN, MR, JK, ZʿM, NḪ, WMŠ.
. . . , *SW, H̱ḤḤT, Sm, ḪŠN.*

[335] *ḤqḤ, SW, H̱Ḥ, H̱TN.*

[338A] *ZʿM, WMŠ, NḪ, JK.*

[342] *RP, Ḥʿ, SW, H̱Ḥ, H̱TN, MW.*

[345] *Ḥʿ, MŠʿ, SB, SW, H̱Ḥ.*
Ḥʿ, H̱ḤḤT, SW, ...
Ḥʿ, ḤTN. SB, ... (The title *ḤTN* occurs in two strings in this tomb. They are (omitting the titles not discussed here): *Ḥʿ, ḤTN, SW, H̱Ḥ* and *Ḥʿ, SW, H̱Ḥ, ḤTN, SB, SW, H̱Ḥ.* Something is wrong with the second; one of the *SW, H̱Ḥ* sequences must be removed or emended. The choice was made on the basis of the first string. Could a sequence *Ḥʿ, H̱ḤḤT, ḤTN, SB,* etc. have been intended? It seems safer not to carry emendation that far.)

[349] *H̱TN, MKNN.*
MŠn, MPḤ.

[350] *RḪN, WMŠ, ZʿM, H̱TN, MR, JK.*

[351] *WMŠ, RḪN.*

[352] *H̱TN, ZʿM.*
H̱Ḥ, ḤS.

[355] *RḪN, WN, ḤNḪ.*

[356] *MḪŠP, SP, Ḫʿ, ḤS.*
ZʿM, SP, ...

[360] *SP, RNḤ, WN, RḪN.*
. . . , *RNḤ, ḤS.*

[361] *RP, Ḥʿ, SB, SW, RNḤ, MPḤ, MŠn, H̱Ḥ, ZMN.*
. . . , Ḥʿ, H̱ḤḤT, Sm, ḪSN.
. . . , H̱ḤḤT, ZMN.
(The sequence *ẖrj-ḥbt, stm* which occurs once has been taken to be an error for *ẖrj-ḥbt ḥrj-tp, stm*. Cf. above, p. 198.)

[363] *H̱TN, MKNN, MZʿN.*
H̱TN, MR, JK, ZʿM, NḪ.

[365] *SW, H̱Ḥ, ḤSPD.*

[372] *RḪN, ḤSP.*

[376] *ZN, WMŠ, NḪ, MKNN, ḤS.*

[378] *SḪŠP, WN, ḤNḪ* and *WN, ḤNḪ, SḪŠP.*

[381] *SW, H̱Ḥ, H̱TN, MR, JK, ḤNM.*
. . . , JK, ZʿN (? Partly restored.)

[382] *Ḥʿ, SB, SW, H̱Ḥ, H̱TN.*

[383] *RḪN, MW.*

[386] *RḪN, WN, ḤNḪ, MP.*
RP, ZN.

[388] *RḪN, WN.*
RḪN, SḤK.

[389] *SW, ḤTN.*
SW, Ḫʿ.
SW, ḤSPD.

[391] *RḪN, ḤS.*

[393] *RP, Ḥʿ, TZT̠, H̱ḤḤT, Sm, ḪŠN, SW, H̱TN, MPḤ, MŠn.*
. . . , TZT̠, MKNN, H̱TN, ...
. . . , TZT̠, MZʿN.
SB, SW, ...
. . . , SW, ZMN.
. . . , SW, H̱Ḥ.
. . . , SW, MSr.
ZšZ, MP.
. . . , SW, MḪŠP, MPḤ, ...

[394] *ZN, H̱TN, MR, JK, H̱Ḥ.*

[395] *RP, Ḥʿ, MŠʿ, SW, H̱Ḥ.*
ZN, Ḥʿ, ...
. . . , Ḥʿ, SB, SW, ...

[397] *RḪN, WMŠ.*
ZʿN, WMŠ.

[398] *WN, ḤNḪ, SḪŠP.*
RḪN, SḪŠP.

[401] *SW, RNḤ, ḤS.*

[402] *RP, Ḥʿ, TZT̠.*
SW, H̱TN, MR, JK.
SW, MZʿN, MPḤ.
MKNN, MŠn.

[406] *SW, Ḫʿ, ḤTN, RNḤ.*
. . . , Ḫʿ, ḤSPD.
[408] *RP, Ḥʿ, SB, SW, RNḤ.*
RP, MPḤ.
Ḥʿ, MŠn.
[411] *RNḤ, SW, ḤSPD.*
ZʿN, ZSZ, ZMZ.
[412] *RḪN, WN.*
[414] *Ḥʿ, ḤTN, SW, H̱Ḥ.*
Sm, ḪŠN, SW, ...
. . . , SW, ḤSPD.
. . . , SW, MḪŠP.
[416] *RḪN, ḤS.*
[417] *ZMZ, RḪN, ḤS.*
[418] *SW, Ḫʿ, ḤSPD, ḤTN* and *. . . , Ḫʿ, ḤTN, ḤSPD.*
[419] *Ḥʿ, H̱Ḥ[ḤT?].*
ZN, SW, ḤSPD.
MZʿN, SW, ...
[421] *H̱Ḥ, ZMN.*
ḤK, MSr.
ḤK, ḪZ.
[422] *Ḥʿ, ḤTN, SW, RNḤ.*
Sm, ḪŠN, SW, ...
H̱ḤḤT, SW, ...
[424] *RḪN, MḤK.*
[425] *RḪN, WN.*
[426] *SW, H̱Ḥ, ḤSPD.*
SW, ḤTN.
[428] *WN, RḪN.*
[429] *Ḥʿ, SB, Sm, ḪŠN, SW, H̱Ḥ.*
. . . , SW, H̱TN.
[432] *ḤqḤ, SB, SW, H̱Ḥ, ZʿN.*
[433] *ḪZ, MḤK.*
SB, SW.
[434] *SW, RNḤ.*
SW, H̱Ḥ.
[435] *ZSZ, MḤK, RḪN.*
[437] *H̱TN, MḪŠP, ŠN.*
. . . , MḪŠP, SP.
[439] *RḪN, ḤNḪ.*
[440] *RḪN, WN, ḤK.*
[444] *RḪN, MP, MḤK.*
[445] *SḪŠP, RḪN.*
[448] *WMŠ, Zš, RḪN* and *RḪN, WMŠ, ...*
[452] *WN, ZMZ.*
WN, ZZš.

[455] *RP, Ḥʿ, TZT̠, MKNN, MZʿN, H̱Ḥ* and . . . , *MZʿN, MKNN*, ...
H̱TN, ZʿM.
[456] *RP, Ḥʿ, MKNN, MZʿN*.
RP, TZT̠, MKNN, ...
. . . , *Ḥʿ, SW*.
[457] *RḪN, MW*.
[458] *WN, RḪN*.
[463] *Ḥʿ, TZT̠, SB, H̱TN*.
Ḥʿ, MR.
MKNN, ḤS.
[465] *ZʿM, WMŠ, NḪ, ḤNM* and . . . , *NḪ, WMŠ*, ...
. . . , *NḪ, JK*.
MR, JK.
MZʿN, MŠn.
[467] *H̱TN, ZʿM, MR, JK, ḤNM*. (*Jwn Knmwt, mdw rḫjt* corrected. Cf. above, p. 198.)
[470] *H̱TN, ZʿM, MR, JK, ḤS*
[474] *RḪN, ḤS*.
[479] *Ḥʿ, SW, ḤTN*.
ZZš, SḤK.
MP, SḤK.
[480] *H̱TN, MR, JK, ḤNM*.
ZʿM, NḪ.
[481] *H̱TN, MR, JK*.
ZʿN, ZMZ.
[482] *H̱TN, ZʿM, JK, NḪ, WMŠ, ḤNM, ḤS*.
H̱TN, MR, JK, ...
[483] *ŠN, SP*. (Inverted order corrected. Cf. above, p. 202.)
SḤK, MP, ḪZ.
[484] *RP, ZN, ḤSPD*.
. . . , *ZN, SW*.
. . . , *ZN, H̱Ḥ, Ḫʿ*. (Reading of last title uncertain.)
[485] *H̱TN, ZʿM, ZMZ, ZSZ*.
NḪ, ZMZ, ...
[486] *WN, RḪN*.
[488] *RḪN, MḤK*.
[489] *WMŠ, RḪN, ZMZ, H̱TN*.
[490A] *ZʿN, ZMZ*.
[492] *RḪN, ḤTN, MḤK, SḤK*.
RḪN, MP.
WN, MḤK, ...
[493] *RḪN, MP*.
RḪN, MḤK.
[494] *RḪN, WN*.
[495] *ZʿN, ZMZ, ḤNM*.
H̱TN, MR, JK.

[497] *Ḥ‘, SB, SW, H̱Ḥ, ZMN.*
ḤqḤ, SW, ...
[499] *RH̱N, MḤK.*
[499A] *RH̱N, MḤK.*
[500] *H̱TN, MR, JK, Z‘M, NH̱.*
ZMZ, ḤS.
[501] *WN, ḤNH̱.*
[502] *WN, ḤNH̱.*
[504] *RH̱N, WN.*
[505] *TZṮ, MKNN, H̱TN, MR, WMŠ, JK, ḤNM.*
MŠ‘, H̱TN, ...
. . . , H̱TN, Z‘M, NH̱.
. . . , Z‘M, MZ‘N.
. . . , H̱TN, MPḤ.
. . . , MR, MZ‘N.
ZSZ, ḤS.
ZSZ, Z‘N.
[509] *RH̱N, WN.*
[510] *NH̱, MŠn.*
[511] *WMŠ, WN.*
[514] *RH̱N, WN, Zš.*
[515] *Z‘M, NH̱, WMŠ, MR, JK.*
[517] *Z‘M, NH̱, ḤS, WN, WMŠ.*
ZMZ, NH̱, ...
Z‘M, ZMZ, ... (? *Zꜣb jmj-rꜣ zš* was erased and replaced by *zꜣb ‘ḏ-mr*. Does the sequence follow?)
[518] *RH̱N, MP, MḤK, WN.*
RH̱N, Z‘N.
[520] *RH̱N, ḤS.*
WN, ḤS.
[522] *SW, H̱‘.*
SW, ḤTN.
[523] *H̱TN, MR, JK, RH̱N, ḤS.* (Once . . . *ḤS, RH̱N.*)
. . . , MR, WMŠ, ḤNM.
Z‘M, NH̱, WMŠ, ...
. . . , NH̱, JK, ...
. . . , JK, WMŠ, . . . and . . . *WMŠ, JK, ...*
[526] *SW, ḤTN, H̱‘.*
[528] *ZZš, ZSZ, ZMZ, ḤS, WN, RH̱N.*
[530] *ZN, SW, MKNN.*
[532] *WMŠ, NH̱.*
WMŠ, RH̱N.
ḤNH̱, ḤS, RH̱N.
[533] *H̱TN, MŠ‘, MŠn.*
SW, H̱Ḥ.

[539] *RḪN, WN, SḪŠP.*
. . . , WN, ḤNḪ.
[540] *H̱TN, MR.*
ZʿM, NḪ, MW.
[542] *RḪN, WN.*
[543] *WMŠ, MW, WN.*
WMŠ, RḪN.
[543A] *MW, RḪN.*
WMŠ, RḪN.
[544] *ZMZ, WMŠ, NḪ, ḤNM.*
[545] *Sm, H̱ŠN, SW.*
[548] *RP, Ḥʿ, H̱ḤḤT, TZṮ, MZʿN, MŠn, MPḤ.*
. . . , Ḥʿ, SB, SW, ḤTN, RNḤ.
. . . , H̱ḤḤT, SW, ...
. . . , H̱ḤḤT, ZMN.
. . . , SW, MŠn, MPḤ.
. . . , MZʿN, MKNN.
Sm, H̱ŠN.
ZMZ, ZSZ.
SḤK, ḤK.
[549] *ḤNḪ, RḪN, WN.*
[550] *WN, RḪN, MP* and *RḪN, WN, ...*
RḪN, MḤK.
SP, ḤS.
[552] *SB, SW, H̱TN, MḪŠP.*
. . . , SW, H̱Ḥ.
[553] *SB, SW, MP, RḪN, MŠn.*
[555] *SW, H̱TN, MW.*
[556] *Ḥʿ, SB, SW, H̱Ḥ, MḪŠP, ZšZ, MW.*
. . . , MḪŠP, ŠN.
[558] *Ḥʿ, TZṮ, SW, ḤSPD.*
. . . , SW, H̱Ḥ.
H̱TN, MW, ZʿM, ZSZ, ZZš.
[559A] *H̱ḤḤT, RNḤ, ḤSPD, H̱ʿ.* (? *jrj nfr-ḥꜣt* partly restored.)
SW, H̱ʿ.
MR, JK.
ZʿM, NḪ.
H̱TN, NḪ.
H̱TN, WMŠ.
[560] *RP, ZN, TZṮ, MZʿN, MŠn, MPḤ, H̱ḤḤT, Sm, H̱ŠN.*
. . . , TZṮ, Ḥʿ, SW.
ḤqḤ, SB, SW. (The *ḥqꜣ ḥt* is on a piece found loose that may not belong to this tomb.)
. . . , Sm, SW.
. . . , MPḤ, H̱Ḥ, ZMN.
. . . , H̱ḤḤT, ZMN.

(The sequence *ẖrj-ḥbt*, *stm* which occurs once has been taken to be an error for *ẖrj-ḥbt ḥrj-tp*, *stm*, which is much better attested. Cf. above, p. 198.)

[562] *RP, Ḥʿ, MŠʿ, SB, ḤqḤ, SW, MḪŠP, H̱Ḥ, ZMN, ḤSPD.*
[563] *SB, ḤqḤ, SW, H̱Ḥ, MḪŠP.*
[564] *SW, ḤTN, RNḤ, Ḫʿ, ḤSPD, H̱Ḥ, ZMN* and . . . , *RNḤ, ḤTN*, . . . and . . . , *ḤSPD, ḤTN.*
SW, MKNN, MZʿN.
. . . , *ḤSPD, MZʿN.*
RḪN, MZʿN.
. . . , *H̱Ḥ, ḤS.*
NḪ, ḤNM.
ZʿN, MP.
ZSZ, MP.
[567] *SW, Ḫʿ, ḤSPD.*
[568] *RḪN, MP.*
RḪN, WN.
RḪN, ḤS.
[569] *Ḫʿ, RḪN.*
ḤNḪ, MW.
[570] *WMŠ, MW, RḪN.*
[571] *RP, Sm* (!), *Ḥʿ, TZṮ, H̱ḤḤT, SW, ZMN.* (Certainly wrong position of *stm*, but how to correct? Cf. above, p. 202.)
Sm, ḪŠN.
[572] *RḪN, WN.*
[576] *RP, Ḥʿ, H̱ḤḤT, Sm, SB, SW, ZMN.*
. . . , *Sm, ḪŠN, SW*, ...
. . . , *ḪŠN, ḤTN.*
. . . , *SW, MŠn.*
. . . , *SW, H̱Ḥ, ḤSPD.*
. . . , *SW, MPḤ.*
. . . , *SW, ZʿN.*
. . . , *SW, ḤNM.*
TZṮ, ZʿN.
TZṮ, ḤNM.
[577] *RḪN, WN, MḤK.*
RḪN, SḤK.
Zš, SḤK.
[578] *WMŠ, NḪ.*
ḤK, Zš.
[581] *WMŠ, RḪN, ḤS.*
[582] *ZMZ, RḪN, ZSZ, WN.*
ZMZ, ḤNM.
[583] *SW, ḤTN, ḤSPD, RNḤ, Ḫʿ.*
SW, H̱ḤḤT, ḤSPD.
[586] *ZʿN, RḪN.*

[590] *TZṮ, MKNN, MZʿN.*
ZSZ, MP, ZšZ, ḤK.
[590A] *SB, ḤqḤ, H̱Ḥ.*
SW, MḪŠP.
[591] *RP, Ḥʿ, TZṮ, MZʿN, H̱ḤḤT, Sm, ḪŠN, SB.*
[592] *RP, Ḥʿ, SB, MŠʿ, ḤqḤ, SW, H̱Ḥ, Z̄MN.*
ḤTN, SB, ...
H̱ḤḤT, ḤqḤ, ...
H̱ḤḤT, Sm, ḪŠN.
. . . , MŠʿ, Sm, ...
. . . , MŠʿ, MPḤ.
MŠn, MPḤ.
[595] *RḪN, ḤNḪ.*
[596] *Z̄N, WMŠ, RḪN.*
[598] *ZMN, H̱Ḥ.*
[600] *WN, RḪN.*
[602] *RP, TZṮ, MZʿN, Ḥʿ, SB, MŠʿ, SW, ḤTN, H̱Ḥ.*
. . . , SW, H̱TN.

This completes the presentation of the material on which we shall base our conclusions. It should be relatively easy for the reader to convert the sequences given here into ranking charts; three dots indicate the omission of portions of a sequence given elsewhere in the entry.

The material in the individual tombs can often be considerably simplified and expanded by the addition of data from the chart of standard sequences given in the last chapter. *All such additions of data will be taken for granted in the following discussion and not mentioned specifically.* The standard sequences that are only documented once have to be treated with a certain amount of care. In the reconstruction of the title sequences characteristic for the various periods, three of the standard sequences attested only once turned out to be spurious. They are: *zš md͟ꜣt nṯr, mdw rḫjt; zš md͟ꜣt nṯr, ḥm-nṯr Mꜣʿt; jmj-rꜣ šnwtj, zꜣb jmj-rꜣ zš.* They were abandoned with no great qualms.

The material just presented had next to be sorted into groups on the basis of their differing title sequences. The ranking charts with relatively numerous titles and long sequences were studied first, and from them were selected the largest group possible, every one of which had at least one title sequence conflicting with all the others. There would then have to have been at least as many periods characterized by different ranking patterns as there were charts in the initial group. These base charts were roughly arranged in chronological sequence, insofar as the data in chapter iii permitted. The remaining material was then searched for charts with characteristics conflicting with all but one of the base charts, either differing title sequences or chronological conflicts between the date of the base chart and the tomb in question, if there was some independent evidence for it. Ranking sequences from charts that could in this way definitely be linked with one of the base charts were added to the master chart being constructed for each period.

As more tombs were assigned to the various periods, it became possible to establish their chronological limits more exactly and to determine their relative sequence; more precise datings and the growth of the master charts also made it possible to assign charts that could not be worked in at first. It goes without saying that charts for which a date before Neferirkare or after the end of the Old Kingdom was suspected were used only with caution and excluded from consideration as base charts. Theoretically it was possible that, as the title sequences for the different periods were worked out, some charts could clearly not be assigned to any of the nine developed from the base charts, and that other periods would have to be set up. Fortunately this did not happen in practice.

Ideally, the end product of this work would be a series of diagrams giving all 50 titles in a straight sequence. In practice, of course, the data was not adequate. By no means all the titles are documented in any period; and while the charts given at the end could be considerably expanded by the addition of information from the standard sequence chart, it was decided to restrict such additions to the straightening out of the sequences of titles actually documented in the period. No great stress should be placed on the presence or absence of a title or group of titles in any one chart. The documentation is really not sufficient for that purpose. Only in the case of the group of titles containing *ẖntj-š* did the evidence seem sufficient to permit use of the argument from silence; our conclusions will be given in the next chapter.

One major obstacle in the way of obtaining a simple, rectilinear ranking chart for a period is the fluctuation of titles found in some tombs. In a few cases it seemed reasonably safe to treat the fluctuation as a simple error; in most cases it had to be retained. Virtually all the fluctuations in the final charts are found in the same form in individual tombs. In a few cases, however, it seemed justifiable to expand slightly the range of a fluctuation already documented for a period, or to introduce a fluctuation of similar titles of almost identical rank, such as *jmj-rꜣ šnwtj* and *jmj-rꜣ prwj-ḥḏ*. In dealing with a chart containing a fluctuation, it seemed best to consider it for inclusion only in those periods in which a similar fluctuation was already documented or, if not, in which the titles concerned had closely similar rank. In actual practice the problem was only acute for our first period, which is what one would expect.

The charts for the nine periods are given below, pages 231 ff. They use the same conventions as the ranking charts given previously. Accompanying each are given the numbers of the tombs that could be assigned with reasonable certainty to the period, and on which the ranking chart for the period is based. There are in all 135 of these. In addition, some others could be shown by their title sequences to belong to none of the nine periods and could be assigned with some degree of certainty either to the time before Neferirkare or after the end of the Old Kingdom. A very much larger number of tombs did not contain enough characteristic title sequences to permit assignment to a specific period. The data they contained could not, therefore, be used in setting up the charts for the periods. However, the range for dating these tombs could be restricted quite considerably by the title sequences; and this information could be valuable for the historical reconstructions with which we propose to conclude our discussion. A list was therefore prepared of all tombs whose dating could be limited by the title sequences and added at the end of the chapter.

A warning is called for here. The method followed—unfortunately it seems to be the only one possible for handling the material—is very susceptible to errors which, instead of canceling themselves out, have ever increasing repercussions. The author can hardly flatter himself that he has worked without error; and in addition, one is, of course, helpless when faced by an undetected or unsuspected error in the source. Eventually, considerable changes may be necessary in the details of the various title-sequence periods.

In order to enable the reader to check the work, we will present the tombs assigned to the various periods in the order in which they were dated. Insofar as the assignment was made on the basis of information given in chapter iii and the title sequences given earlier in this chapter, no further comment will be given than the period to which it was assigned. If other decisions are involved, or if the addition of the tomb has implications for the sequence and delimitation of the periods, a brief discussion will be added. Reference to the standard sequence charts will make it easier to follow the details.

The sequence of the periods was only very vaguely evident at the beginning of the work. For simplicity's sake, however, they will be referred to from the beginning by the designations given after the order was finally determined. The periods are indicated by a Roman numeral for the dynasty and a letter. Since the introduction of the system of ranking is somewhat later than the beginning of the Fifth

Dynasty, it seemed best not to use the designation V A. Our first period is, therefore, V B. The last period in the Fifth Dynasty extends into the Sixth. It has been numbered V D/VI A, but V D will usually be used alone as being sufficiently clear. It is quite possible that the system of ranking titles extended into the First Intermediate Period. No attempt was, however, made to collect material for that period or to sort out those of our tombs that turned out to belong to it into groups. Our last period is VI G, which extends into the Eighth Dynasty.

We first list our nine base charts in their final order. The date as known at the beginning (see chap. iii) is given in parentheses.

V B:	[105]	(Neferirkare)
V C:	[505]	(mid-V or later)
V D:	[13 + 161]	(Djedkare–Unis. These two tombs are part of the same large mastaba complex and appear to have been built at the same time. It seemed justifiable, therefore, to conflate the titles of the two.)
VI B:	[197]	(Teti)
VI C:	[135]	(Pepi I or later)
VI D:	[32]	(Early Pepi II)
VI E:	[133]	(Early—middle Pepi II)
VI F:	[171]	(Sixth Dynasty?)
VI G:	[560]	(Pepi II, second half)

To these base charts the others were then added. The sequence was rather vague at the beginning but soon became much clearer through the addition of better dated tombs. The list follows:

[564]	V C	This restricts the period to the later Fifth Dynasty.
[279]	VI F	The inclusion of the titles in the pyramid temple of Pepi II places this period in the second half of the reign of that king.
[602]	VI G	The Koptos Decrees date from the Eighth Dynasty. VI G therefore follows VI F.
[110]	VI C	The reign of Mernere falls at least partly within VI C. This tomb contains the sequence *stm*, *smr wꜥtj*, *ẖrp snḏwt nbt*, which is unique for an Old Kingdom tomb, occurring otherwise only in [324], which is certainly from the First Intermediate, and conflicting with all the base charts. Since the titles and sequences involved are common, it seemed safe to treat this as a mistake.
[160]	V C	This fixes the position of V C between V B and V D.
[592]	VI F	
[202]	VI E	This is a rather later date than one would have expected a priori, but note that [57] seems to have to be assigned to VI C.
[562]	VI C	
[361]	VI F	

[192]	VI E	
[591]	VI D	
[212]	VI C	This is the father of [133] and helps to establish the approximate interval between VI C and VI E.
[548]	V D	This period now extends into the reign of Teti.
[146]	V B	
[315]	V B	This shows that the first period extended from the time of Neferirkare into the reign of Djedkare and allows us to add all the tombs known to date from that time.
[223]	V B	
[376]	V B	
[164]	V B	
[112]	V C	This period must certainly extend into the reign of Unis.
[249]	V C	In all probability the string of titles I have from this tomb belonged to the original owner rather than the usurper.
[106]	VI C	Period VI B would also be possible, but seems unlikely since the tomb belonged to either the father or the son of [192]. The relationship is now settled.
[246]	VI E	Title sequence as emended.
[111]	V D	This places the limit between V C and V D into the reign of Unis.
[187]	VI B	This period extended into the reign of Mernere, where the border between this period and VI C must be placed.
[153]	VI B	
[300]	V B	
[134]	VI F	Period VI G would also be possible but seems unlikely since the tomb belonged to the brother of [133] and the son of [212].
[132]	VI D	This fits in very nicely with the genealogy, according to which the tomb belongs to the son of [212] and elder brother of [133] and [134]. The title sequences fit no other period.
[81]	VI C	The title *jmj-rꜣ Šmꜥ* fluctuates and once occurs below *ẖrj-ḥbt*. In that position it would fit nowhere. The chances are that this fluctuation is a mistake.
[286]	VI B	
[421]	VI B	
[168]	VI C	Shares tomb complex with the preceding, but apparently later. The common titles alone would not permit an exact dating. Conflict in the ranking of the priestly titles. See next chapter.
[62]	V D	The father of [187]. According to the biography found in this tomb, *Jzj* lived until the reign of Teti and according to the editors there is no possibility that Pepi I was ever mentioned in it. This would agree with our dating. Unfortunately, in the corridor of this tomb there appears to be a person named *Ppjj-snb*. The name could, of course, have been added later, which would hardly be unparalleled. The publication does not permit one to check.

[294]	V B	
[455]	V B	This period must thus have lasted at least until the sixteenth year of Djedkare.*
[456]	V C	
[170]	VI B	Periods VI C–D would also be possible, and the choice is largely based on the unexpectedly late date for this tomb. Cf. Smith, *HESP*, p. 196.
[167]	V D	
[112A]	V D	
[177A]	VI B	
[131]	VI C	
[14]	VI E	Period VI G might also be possible, but would separate it even further from [12].
[57]	VI C	
[39]	VI F	The position of *jmj-rꜣ Šmꜥ* fluctuates between that characteristic for VI E and VI F. The tomb probably dates from the latter, the decorator being confused by the recent change. Incidentally, this helps to fix the relative order of Periods VI D and E.
[563]	VI B	
[74]	VI D	
[258]	V B	
[142]	V C	
[64]	V C	Built at the same time as the preceding.
[530]	V C	Younger contemporary of [315]. Same titles as [64].
[185]	VI B	
[189]	VI C	The son of [197]. The interval required between the two seems a bit too long. Fitting this tomb into Period VI B would, however, not only require a fluctuation of *jmj-rꜣ zš ꜥ nswt* and *jmj-rꜣ kꜣt nbt nt nswt*, which would not be too bothersome, but also wide fluctuation of some of the less common titles, such as *ḥrj wrw*, which we are not considering at the moment. An interval of thirty years between the building of the main tomb and the annex is not, however, impossible.
[363]	V B	
[282]	V B	This rests on the identification of *Nn-ḫft-kꜣj* with the official of that name in the pyramid temple of Sahure.
[303]	V B	
[518]	V C	
[118]	V C	
[140]	V D	
[229A]	VI G	

* This is hardly the place to enter into the vexed question of annual vs. biennial count during the Old Kingdom. But the twentieth numbering of Djedkare is known (Borchardt, "*Ḫnt-kꜣw.s*, die Stammutter der 5ten Dynastie," *ASAE*, XXXVIII, 210) and would hardly fit the 28 years given him by the Turin Papyrus if the biennial count were valid.

[297]	V B	
[532]	V D	This tomb was built by the grandson of the owner of a tomb which precedes Period V B. We thus have a means for estimating the length of V B and the still uncertain reign of Neuserre which is entirely contained within that period.
[44]	VI C	
[25]	V B	If correctly dated by the excavator to precede Unis.
[393]	VI B	Period VI C is also possible but seems excessively late.
[528]	VI D	Period VI G is also possible but seems to be excluded by the archeological data.
[558]	VI E	
[559A]	V B	Period V D would also be possible but seems to be stretching the limits of archeological probabilities.
[158]	V B	Dated on assumption that Mariette's guess has some validity. V D would also be possible. In any case, this does not involve any changes in the ranking pattern for the period.
[159]	V B	See preceding.
[582]	VI G	
[492]	VI C	
[16]	VI E	
[254]	V C	Period VI C might also be possible but seems unlikely in view of the fact that this was the first mastaba to be built in this part of the cemetery. A considerable number of large mastabas were built around it later.
[114]	V C	
[251]	VI D	Considering that the tomb turns out to be somewhat later than expected, this would seem to be more probable than VI E.
[517]	VI C	This large false-door is hardly likely to be as late as VI G, whose title sequences would also fit.
[350]	VI G	
[482]	V B	
[115]	V B	Involves slight extension of the range of fluctuation of *wʿb nswt*.
[411]	VI B	
[48]	V D	
[345]	VI D	
[136]	VI G	
[485]	V C	Period V B seems too early.
[163]	V C	
[8]	VI G	
[88]	V B	
[128]	V B	
[250]	V B	Few titles and could well be earlier.
[457]	V C	
[479]	V D	
[543]	V B	

[543A]	V B	
[274]	VI B	Note that *jmj-rꜣ kꜣt nbt nt nswt* and *jmj-rꜣ zš ꜥ nswt* fluctuate here and compare under [189] above.
[360]	VI E	
[402]	V D	
[590]	V C	If halfway contemporary with the *Snḏm-jb* to whose *ḏt* he belonged.
[332]	V D	The fluctuating titles in this tomb fit smoothly only here.
[550]	V D	The father of the preceding. V B would also be possible, but the interval seems a bit too large.
[418]	V C	The fluctuation of *ḥrj-tp Nḫb* fits more smoothly into V C than V B, which is also possible.
[426]	V D	Period V B would also be possible, but the adjustment of the fluctuating titles would be troublesome.
[444]	V B	Few titles and could be earlier.
[567]	V B	As preceding.
[523]	VI E	Period V B is also possible, but the fluctuating titles would not fit smoothly.
[406]	V D	If of Fifth Dynasty date.
[155]	V C	
[263]	V C	
[448]	VI D	
[95]	VI C	
[493]	V D	
[109]	V C	
[515]	VI F	
[544]	VI G	Assuming with Junker that a date at the beginning of the Sixth Dynasty is excluded.
[570]	V B	If the identity of names remarked on in chapter iii is valid.
[154]	VI G	Few titles and could, of course, be First Intermediate.
[500]	VI D	Period V D also possible, and the choice was based mostly on Mariette's estimate.
[458]	VI E	*Wꜥb nswt* and *rḫ nswt* are here separated by several priesthoods. Since these two titles follow each other in that order without fluctuating only in Period VI E, it seems the most probable choice. In all the other periods in which this sequence of the two titles is possible, they fluctuate and are thus not likely to have been separated in rank by any considerable number of titles.
[486]	VI E	As above.
[600]	VI E	As above.
[66]	V B	
[100]	VI C	
[309]	VI B	
[77]	VI C	This tomb belongs to the father of [495] if we accept Reisner's genealogy. [77] could be VI B, C or G. [495] could be VI D

or E. All things considered, VI C for [77] and VI D for his son seems the likeliest combination.

[495] VI D See preceding.

[no number] The decree of Teti (*Urkunden*, I, 208) has the sequence *sḏ3wtj bjtj, jmj-r3 Šmʿ*, which dates that document to V D.

At this point, tossing a coin would seem to be the only means left for deciding the relative merits of the dating possibilities of the remaining tombs, so it is wiser to stop here.

In addition to the tombs listed at the end of the preceding chapter as belonging either to the periods before or after the range of time being discussed here, some others also fall outside the limits of the nine periods and are listed below. Most of them have title sequences conflicting with those of all the periods that would seem at all probable. However, this seemed to be as good an occasion as any to eliminate those tombs that quite evidently fall outside the limits, even though there are no obvious conflicting title sequences. These are tombs with very few of the common titles to begin with. They are marked: (date only). In almost all cases the basis for the dating is given in chapter iii. A few have been added because they are closely linked to others that are certainly either too early or too late.

The following precede Neferirkare: [6] (date only), [7] (date only), [21], [91], [123A] (this confirms Borchardt's dating as against my own estimate in chapter iii), [126] (date only), [215], [241] (date only), [292], [386], [484] (date only), [489], [569] (date only), [583], [598] (date only). To these can be added the following tombs with standard sequences only: [3], [222], [262], [375], [400], [513]. The dating is obviously not based on the titles.

The following follow the end of the Old Kingdom: [275A], [286A–B] (so it seems unlikely that these are actually the sons of *Nḫbw*; they could, of course, be descendants), [287] (date only), [323] (cf. [324]), [333], [435], [533] (he is certainly not the son of *Mrrw-k3*), [553], [576] (note that it would be very unusual for the holder of so many exalted titles to have such a tiny tomb fitted in between earlier ones during the Old Kingdom, so it is not astonishing that the title sequences fit nowhere).

This is the material on which our analysis of the differing title sequences is based. The chronological hypothesis for explaining the different title sequences has been applied constantly. Very few tombs were assigned to one period or another without some idea as to the likely range, and quite a number of tombs have been assigned to a period solely on the basis of a previously known exact dating. The results obtained seem to the writer to be reasonably consistent and as close to proof of the hypothesis as can be expected considering the nature of the materials one must work with. Particularly the second process would be expected to have caused considerable trouble if the hypothesis were not valid. In the following pages we shall use the datings obtained in this chapter as the basis of our discussion. I hope that enough material has been presented to enable the reader to form an independent judgment.

We have given the ranking charts for the nine periods on pages 231–239. The approximate range of time covered by these periods is indicated at the head of each chart. Let us attempt to establish the duration of the periods a little more exactly.

Period V B begins in the reign of Neferirkare [105] and lasts until approximately the sixteenth year of Djedkare [455]. *Jj-mrjj* [21], who is described as a priest of Neferirkare in his son's tomb but not in his own, built his mastaba before the beginning of Period V B. It is thus possible, though by no means certain, that Period V B began after the middle of the relatively short reign of Neferirkare.* Tomb [532] was decorated for *Kꜣ-n-nswt* II by his son after his death. The tomb of *Kꜣ-n-nswt* I, the father of [532], antedates Period V B. Since [532] is dated to Period V D, we have at the utmost 60 years for Periods V B and C. We can show that Periods V C, D, and VI B must each have lasted about a generation. Taking about 20 years for V C, we have about 40 for V B. The Turin Papyrus gives Menkauhor 8 years. This leaves about 16 years for Neferefre and Neuserre.

Period V C lasted approximately 20 years, or from the sixteenth year of Djedkare to around the tenth of Unis. *Snḏm-jb Jntj* was buried in V B, his son *Snḏm-jb Mḥj* [456] in V C, his younger son *Ḫnm-ntj* [402] in V D, and his grandson *Nḫbw* [286] built his tomb in VI B. The elder *Ptḥ-ḥtp* [160] erected his mastaba in Period V C, and the joint tomb of his son and grandson [13 + 161] was built in the following period. A generation would seem to be appropriate for each of these periods, say 20 years for V C and 30 each for V D and VI B. The Turin Papyrus (cols. 3, 11, 24–25) gives Djedkare and Unis 28 and 30 years, respectively. The reign of Teti is lost. The highest date known for Pepi I is the twenty-fifth numbering (*Urkunden*, I, 95). Combining all this, we have Period V D lasting from the tenth year of Unis to about the tenth of Teti, which would be near the end of his reign. Period VI B lasted from the tenth year of Teti, through the reign of Pepi I of at least 25 years, and into the short reign of Mernere.

The remaining five periods all partly or entirely lie within the 94 years that Pepi II reigned. They would average about 20 years each,

* *Ḥꜣt-zp* 5 in the Annals, *Urkunden*, I, 248. Count probably biennial.

PERIOD V B

NEFERIRKARE TO DJEDKARE

SOURCES: 25, 66, 88, 105, 115, 128, 146, 158, 159, 164, 223, 250, 258, 282, 294, 297, 300, 303, 315, 363, 376, 444, 455, 482, 543, 543A, 559A, 567, 570.

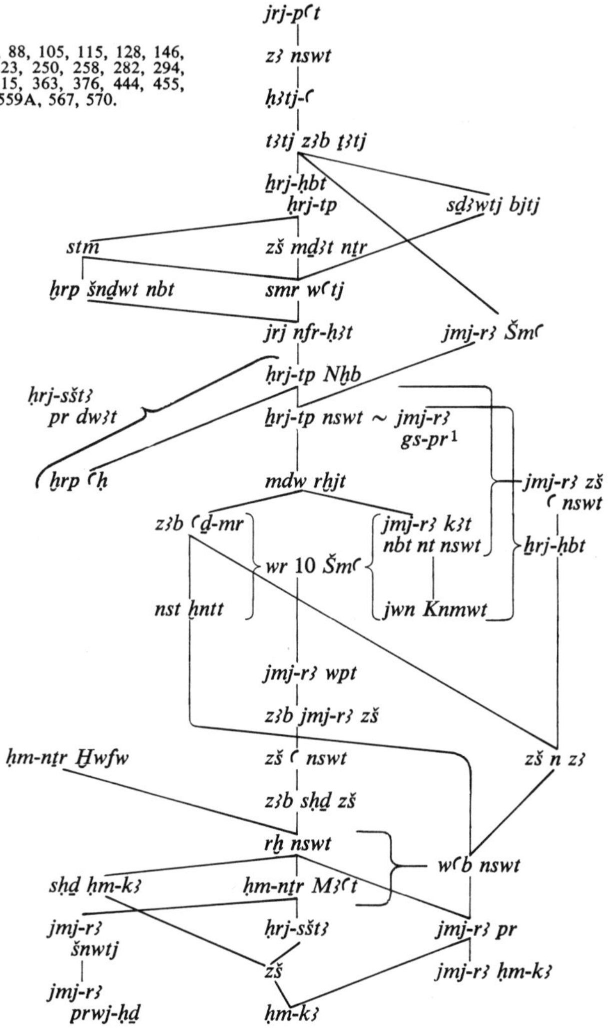

[1] For *jmj-rꜣ gs pr* in this and the following charts see the Appendix to chapter v.

PERIOD V C
Djedkare to Unis

SOURCES: 64, 109, 112, 114, 118, 142, 155, 160, 163, 249, 254, 263, 418, 456, 457, 485, 505, 518, 530, 564, 590.

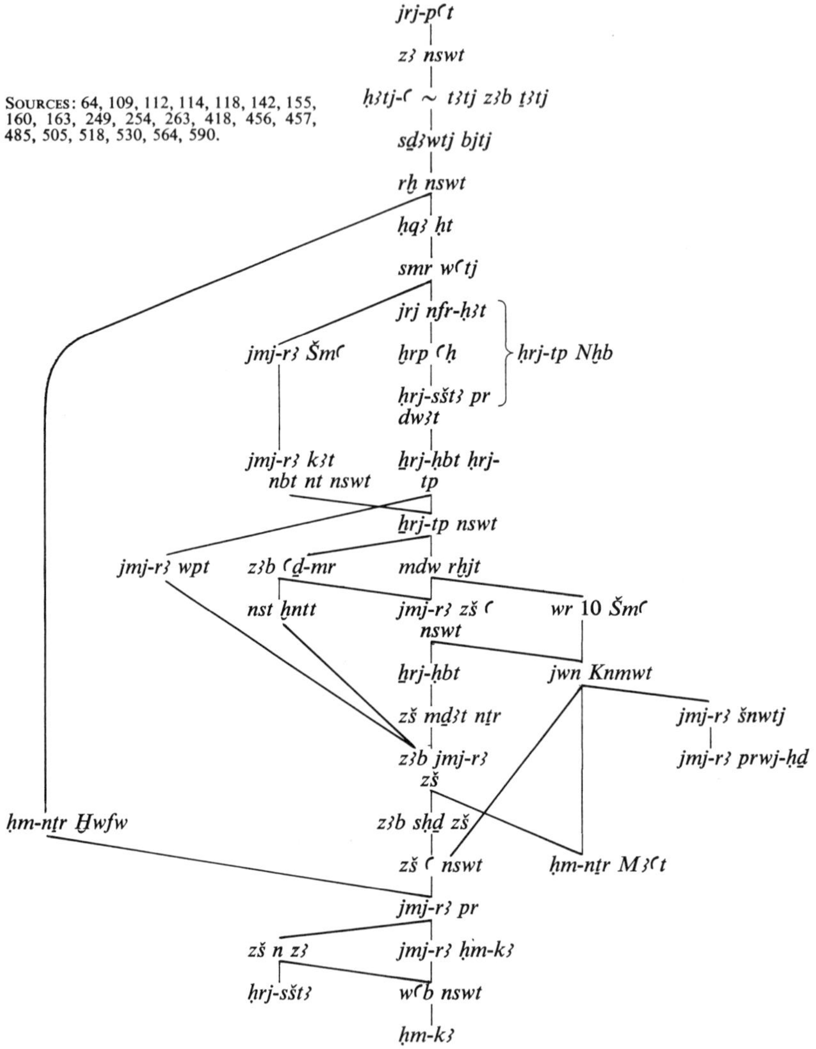

PERIOD V D/VI A
UNIS TO TETI

SOURCES: 13, 48, 62, 111, 112A, 140, 161, 167, 332, 402, 406, 426, 479, 493, 532, 548, 550, *Urkunden*, I, 208.

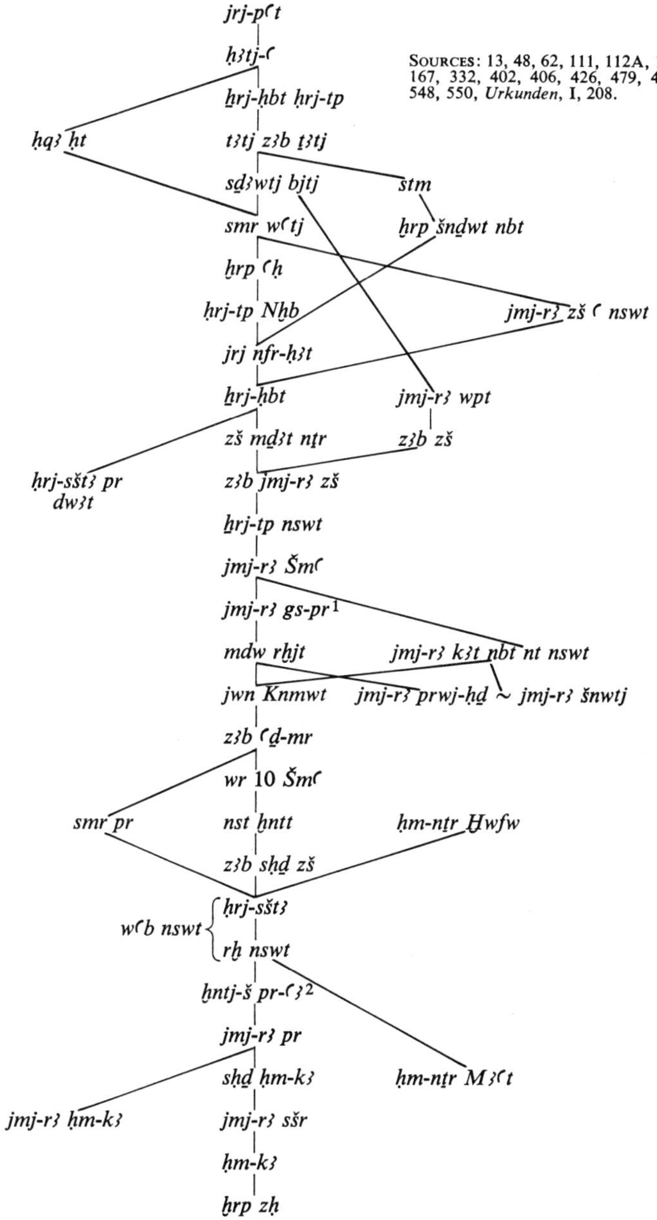

[2] Added from the conclusions in chapter vi, page 273.

PERIOD VI B
Teti to Mernere

Sources: 153, 170, 177A, 185, 187, 197, 274, 286, 309, 393, 411, 421, 563.

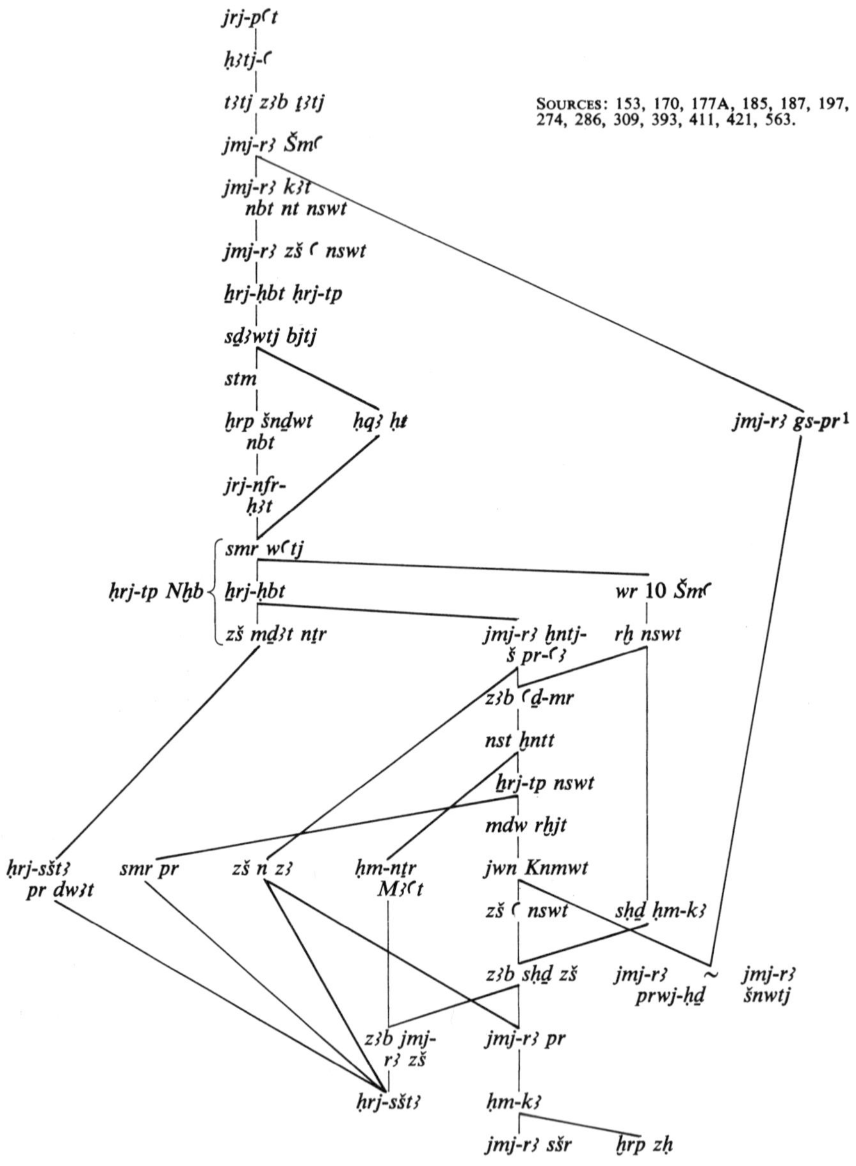

PERIOD VI C
Mernere to Early Pepi II

Sources: 44, 57, 77, 81, 95, 100, 106, 110, 131, 135, 168, 189, 212, 492, 517, 562.

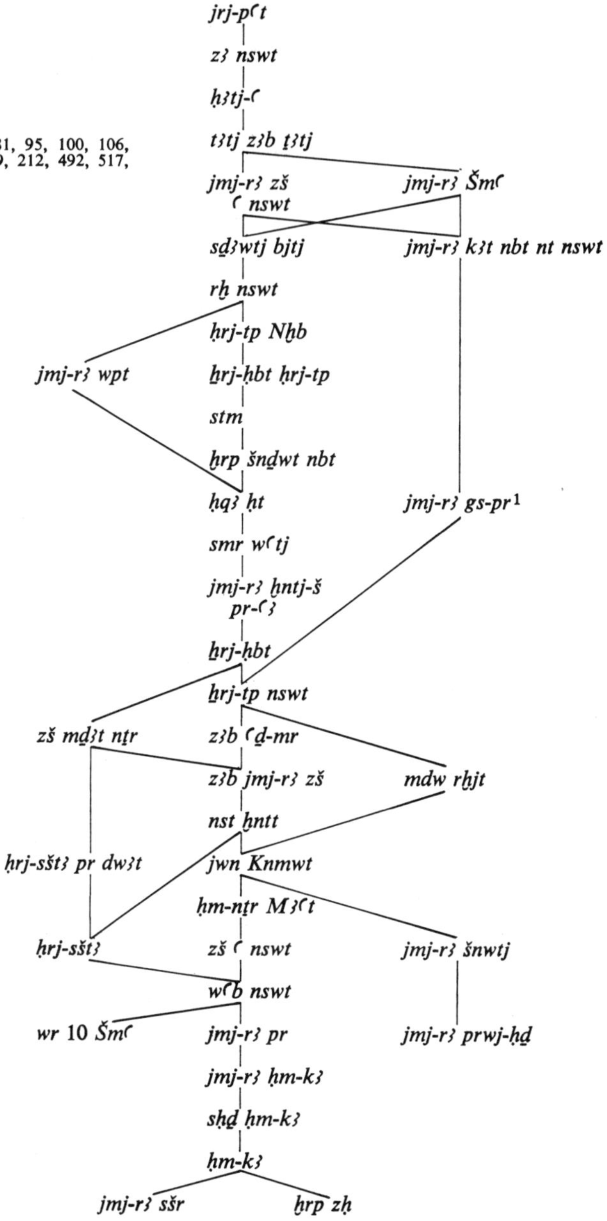

PERIOD VI D
Early to Middle Pepi II

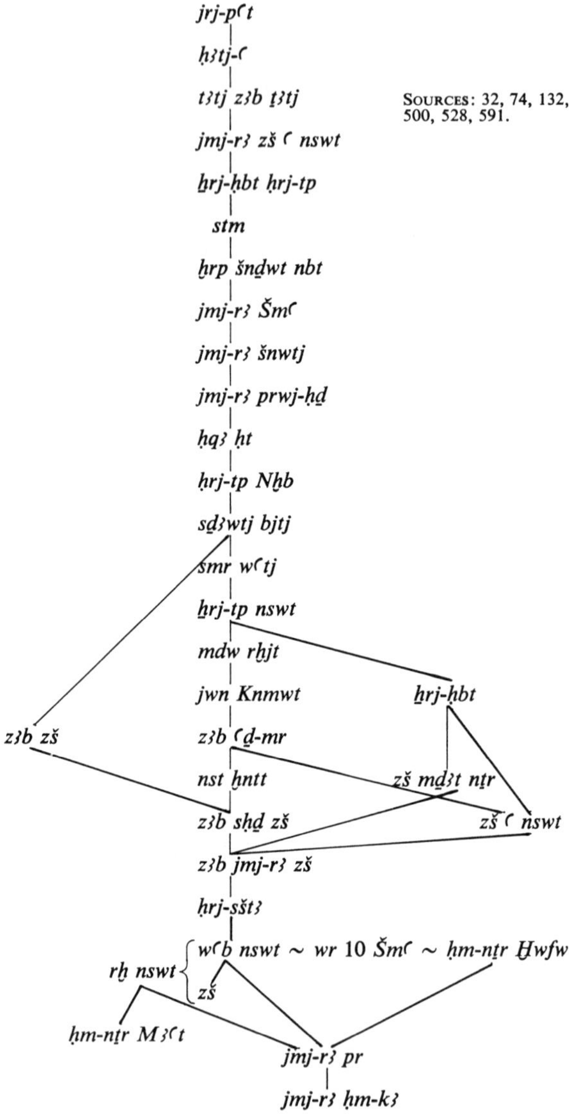

Sources: 32, 74, 132, 251, 345, 448, 495, 500, 528, 591.

PERIOD VI E
Middle Pepi II

Sources: 14, 16, 133, 192, 202, 246, 360, 458, 486, 523, 558, 600.

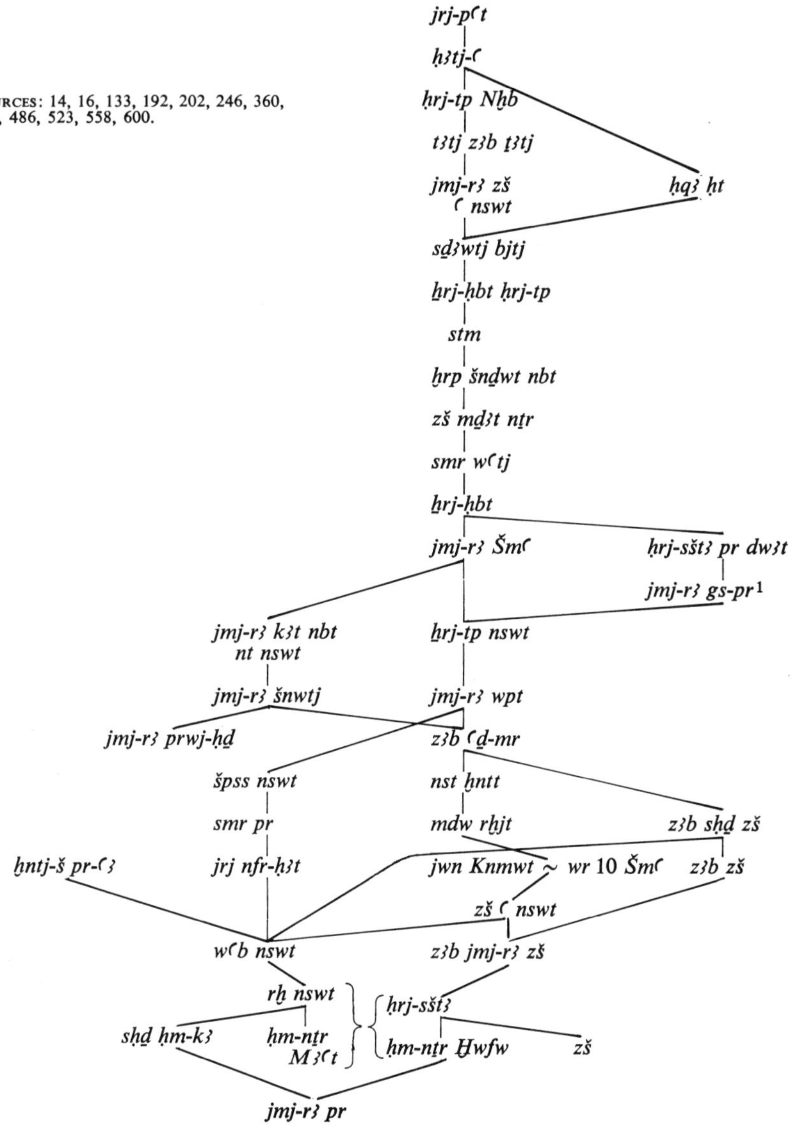

PERIOD VI F
Middle to Late Pepi II

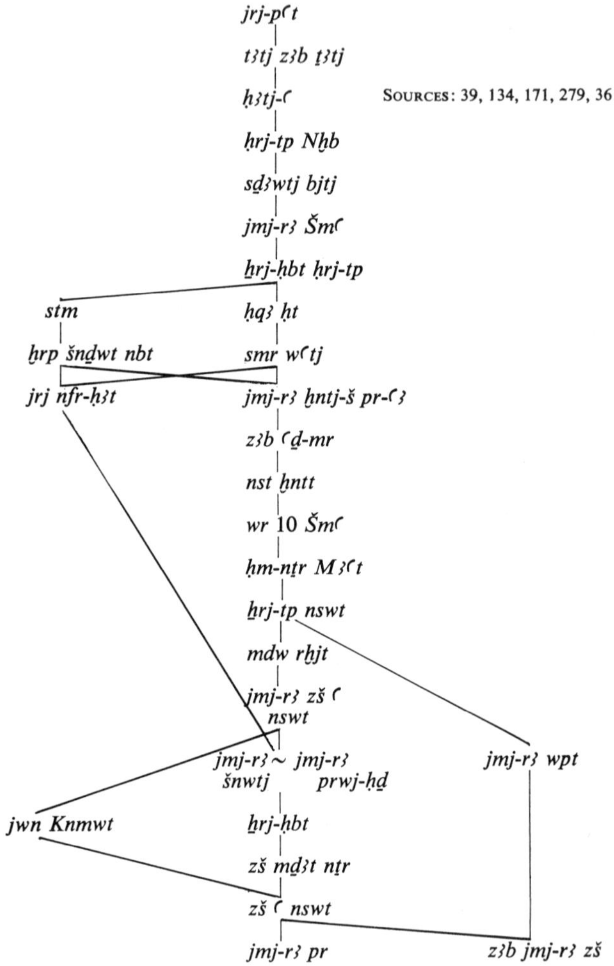

Sources: 39, 134, 171, 279, 361, 515, 592.

PERIOD VI G
Late Pepi II to End of Eighth Dynasty

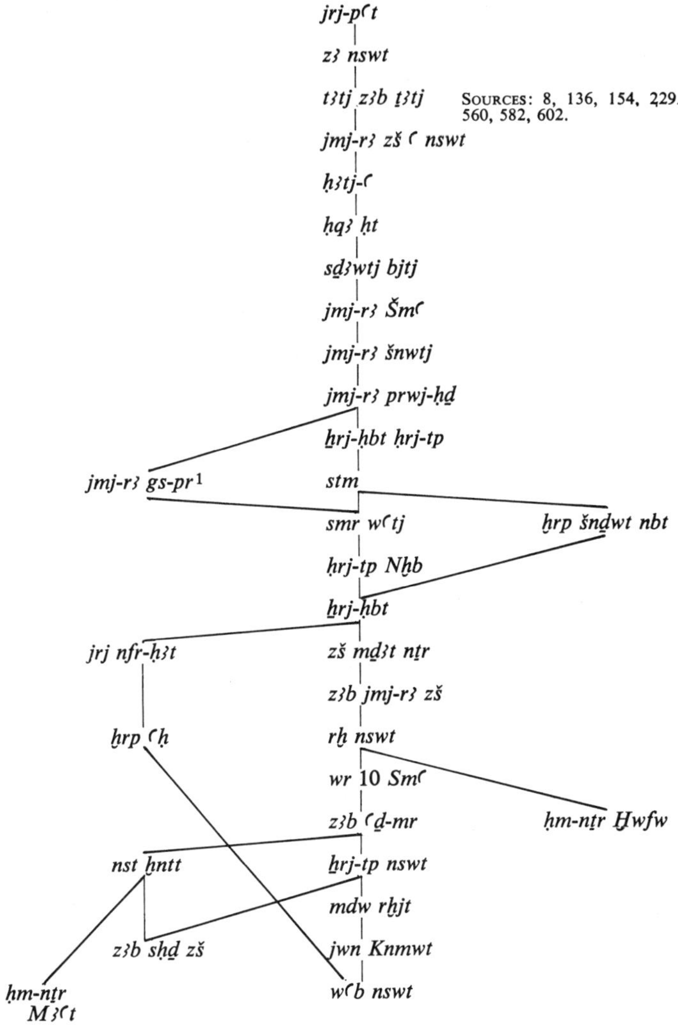

Sources: 8, 136, 154, 229A, 350, 544, 560, 582, 602.

with the exception of the last two, which included the end of the Old Kingdom. These shorter periods fit the genealogical indications that we have. *N-ʿnḫ-Ppjj* [212] and his three sons, all named *Ppjj-ʿnḫ*, built their tombs in periods VI C, D, E, and F, respectively. The nomarch *Jbj* [32] had his tomb cut in VI D. His son died (apparently rather unexpectedly, since he had prepared no tomb for himself) two periods later. The decoration of the pyramid temple of Pepi II was completed around the middle of his reign [279] and falls in Period VI F. We thus obtain the approximations of Table I.

TABLE I

Period	Begins		Ends		Duration
V B . . .	End Neferirkare		Djedkare yr.	16	40 yrs.
V C . . .	Djedkare yr.	16	Unis	10	20
V D/VI A . .	Unis	10	Teti	10	30
VI B . . .	Teti	10	Mernere		30
VI C . . .	Mernere		Pepi II	15	20
VI D . . .	Pepi II	15	Pepi II	35	20
VI E . . .	Pepi II	35	Pepi II	55	20
VI F . . .	Pepi II	55	Pepi II	85	30
VI G . . .	Pepi II	85	End Eighth Dyn.		?

To conclude the chapter, we will present a list of the remaining tombs given at the beginning of this chapter. They could not be dated to a specific period either on the basis of their title sequences or the data given in chapter iii or both. However, their title sequences and whatever other information is known about them do permit one, in most cases, to limit the range of periods to which the tombs could conceivably be assigned. The possibilities for dating that are still left after consideration of the conclusions of this chapter are given after the number of each entry. The list follows:

[5] V D, VI B–D, F–G.
[9] V B–D, VI, B, G.
[10] V B–D, VI B–D, F–G.
[11] V B–D, VI B.
[12] V B–D, VI B–E.
[15] VI C–D, F–G.
[18] VI D–E.
[19] V C–D, VI B–G.
[22] VI D–E.
[24] V C, VI C.
[27] VI B–C, E–F.
[36] VI B, E–G.
[40] VI B–C, F–G.
[45] V B–D (also VI B, D–G?).
[49] V D, VI B–G.
[55] VI D–E.
[56] VI B, D–F.
[59] VI B–C, E.
[67] V D, VI B–G.
[70] V B–C.
[71] V B–D, VI B–D, F–G.
[73A] VI E–F.
[75] VI B, E–G.
[78] VI B–C, E–F.

[82] VI C, F.
[83] VI C, F.
[85] VI B–C, F.
[86] VI E–G.
[89] VI B, D–F.
[90] V B, VI C, E.
[94] VI B–E.
[94A] VI B–C, E–F.
[98] VI D–G.
[103] V B–D (also VI C–E?).
[104] V B (or earlier?).
[113] VI B–C, F.
[117] VI C–D, F–G.
[121] VI D, F (or First Intermediate).
[123] V B–D, VI B–G.
[124] V B, D, VI D–E.
[137] VI B–C, F–G.
[138] VI B, D–F.
[139] VI D–E, G.
[150] VI D–E, G.
[152] V C–D, VI C–E, G.
[156] V D, VI G.
[162] V B–D, VI B–G (probably not the latter part of the range).
[172] VI B, F–G.
[178] VI B–C, F–G.
[181] V B–D, VI B–E, G.
[184] VI C–E.
[190] VI B–D, F–G.
[191] VI B–G.
[193] VI B–G.
[195] VI B–G.
[198] V B–C, VI B, E–F.
[199] V B, D, VI D–E.
[201] VI D–E, G.
[203] V B–C.
[204] V C–D, VI B–D, F–G.
[206] V B–D, VI C–E.
[207] VI B–G.
[210] VI B–G.
[213] VI B–D.
[215A] V B–D, VI B–G.
[218] V D, VI B–D, F–G.
[224] V C–D, VI B–G.
[225] VI C–G.
[228] V B, D, VI B–G.
[232] V D, VI B–C, F.
[233] V B, D, VI D.
[235] VI B, G.
[236] V B–D, VI C, E–F.
[238] V B–D, VI B–G.
[240] V C–D, VI B–D, F–G.
[242] V B–D, VI C–G.
[243] V B, D, VI D–E.
[245] V B–D, VI B, E, G.
[247] VI D, G.
[256] VI B, D, F.
[257] VI B, G.
[259] V B–D, VI B, G.
[267] V B–C.
[268A] V C, VI, B–G.
[273] VI C–F.
[275] VI C, E.
[277] VI B, F–G.
[280] VI C–D, F–G.
[285] VI E–G.
[290] V B–D, VI B–C, F–G.
[298] V B–C.
[299] VI B–C, E, G.
[305] VI C–D, F–G.
[311] V B–C, VI D, F.
[313] V B, D, VI B, D–F.
[317] VI B–G.
[318] V B, D, VI B, D–G.
[322] VI B, E–G.
[325] VI B–C, F–G.
[335] VI B–C, E. G.
[338A] V B–C.
[342] VI B, E.
[349] V B, D, VI E–F.
[351] V B, D, VI B, D–F.
[352] V C–D, VI C–E.
[355] VI B–D, F–G.
[356] V D, VI B.
[365] VI B–G.
[372] V B–D.
[378] VI B–G.
[381] VI B–C, E, G.
[382] VI C, E, G.
[383] V C, VI B–C.

[388] VI B–D, F–G.
[389] V B–D, VI B, G.
[391] V B–C, VI B–C, E–G.
[394] VI D, F.
[395] VI B–D, F–G.
[397] VI C–D.
[398] VI B–G.
[401] VI C–G.
[408] VI C–G.
[412] V D, VI B–D, F–G.
[414] VI C–F.
[416] V B–C, VI B–C, E–G.
[417] V B, VI E, G.
[419] VI B–E, G.
[422] VI C–F.
[424] V C–D, VI B–G.
[425] V B–D, VI B–D, F–G.
[428] V B, D, VI D–E.
[429] VI B–C, E–G.
[432] VI D–E, G.
[433] VI B, D–G.
[434] VI C–G.
[437] VI D–E.
[439] V C, VI B–G.
[440] V D, VI B–D, F–G.
[445] VI B–G.
[452] VI E–F.
[463] VI B–E.
[465] V B–C, VI F.
[467] VI C, E.
[470] VI C, E.
[474] VI B–C, E–G.
[480] V D, VI B–E, G.
[481] VI B, D–F.
[483] VI B, D–G.
[488] V B–D, VI B–G.
[490A] VI B, D–F.
[494] V D, VI B–D, F–G.
[497] VI B–D, F–G.
[499] V D, VI B–G.
[499A] VI B–G.
[501] VI B–G.
[502] VI B–G.
[504] V B–D, VI B–D, F–G.
[509] V B (also V C–D, VI B–D, F–G?).
[510] V B–D (also VI B–C, F?).
[511] V D, VI B, D–G.
[514] V B–D, VI B–D, F–G.
[520] VI B, E–G.
[522] V B–D.
[526] V B–C (also VI B?).
[539] VI B–D, F–G.
[540] VI B, D, F.
[542] V B–D, VI B–D.
[545] V D, VI B–G.
[549] V B–D, VI B–D, F.
[552] VI D–E (or First Intermediate?).
[555] VI B, D–F.
[556] VI B, D–E, G.
[568] V B–C, VI B–C, F–G.
[571] VI B–D.
[572] V B–D, VI B–D, F–G.
[577] V D, VI C–D, F–G.
[578] V C–D, VI B, G.
[581] V B, VI B, E–F.
[586] V B, D, VI D–E.
[590A] VI B–C, F.
[595] V C, VI B–G.
[596] V B, D, VI B, D–F.

Unfortunately, in the majority of cases, the study of the titles has not produced any great improvement over the datings proposed in chapter iii. Most of the tombs are small and have only a very few titles. Most of them could undoubtedly be dated to much closer limits if we only knew more of the title sequences characteristic for each period. The range of periods given here usually extends somewhat beyond the limits suggested in chapter iii. It seemed wiser to be somewhat on the cautious side in stating that a tomb could not be assigned to a specific period. Not all the cases in which a tomb might possibly have to be assigned to the First Intermediate Period were marked; compare the archeological discussion for each tomb. A sufficiently large number of tombs has, however, been restricted to a relatively short range of periods, and this can be of help in our discussion in the next chapter.

APPENDIX: *JMJ-RȜ GS-PR*

After the manuscript was finished, it seemed desirable to add the ranking of the title *jmj-rȝ gs-pr* to the ranking charts. It does not occur as commonly as the titles discussed so far, but seemed to be useful for dating certain tombs that the writer intended to discuss in a future study. The treatment of this one title is more appropriate in the framework of this study than in an article basically devoted to other matters.

The method used is that which is also used in the next chapter for establishing the ranking of less common titles. First we present the sequences in which the title occurs, as at the beginning of chapter v (*jmj-rȝ gs-pr* will be abbreviated *MGP*). Each entry contains the number of the tomb (in brackets) and the dating as far as it is known. In this case, since this Appendix was written after the completion of the remainder of the work, the datings are taken from the Appendix to chapter vi. The ranking of *MGP* from tombs of known date has then been added to the ranking charts (it is marked with a raised [1]). Wherever possible, this information was then used to date other tombs, but in this case it was only possible to restrict the possible range of dates, and no new exact datings were obtained. First we give the data:

[13] (V D): *MŠʿ, MGP, MR.*
[57] (VI C): *MKNN, MGP, H̱TN.*
[133] (VI E): *MGP, H̱TN.*
[146] (V B): *SB, MGP, H̱TN, MR* and *SB, H̱TN, MGP, MR.*
MGP, MŠn, MPḤ.
[150] (VI D–E, G): *ḤqH̱, SB, MGP, SW, H̱Ḥ* and *SW, MGP, H̱Ḥ.*
[161] (V D): *H̱TN, MŠʿ, MGP.*
[201] (VI D–E, G): *ḤqH̱, SB, MGP, SW, H̱TN, ZʿN.*
[202] (VI E): *SW, H̱Ḥ, ḤSPD, MGP, H̱TN.*
[229A] (VI G): *MPḤ, MGP.*
[231] (Pepi II): *SB, MGP, SW.*
[274] (VI B): *MŠʿ, MGP, MŠn, MPḤ.*
[363] (V B): *H̱TN, MGP, ZʿM.*
[381A] (Pepi I or later): *SB, MGP.*
[431] (Pepi I or later): *SW, H̱Ḥ, MGP.*
[432] (VI D–E, G): *ḤqH̱, SB, MGP, SW, H̱Ḥ, ZʿN.*

[497] (VI B–D, F–G): *Ḥꜥ, SB, MGP, SW, ẖḤ, ZMN.*
[560] (VI G): *ḤqḤ, SB, MGP, SW.*

These are all the cases in our collection in which *jmj-rꜣ gs-pr* occurs in a rankable sequence. The material does not suffice to give exact datings in those cases where they were not known before, but the range of possibilities could be significantly reduced in the following cases:

[150] VI D, G.
[201] VI D, G.
[231] VI C–D, F–G.
[431] VI B–F.
[432] VI D, G.

As in the case of several other titles that are not well documented, we were not able to determine the ranking of this title in all periods.

VI

ROYAL PRIESTS AND NOMARCHS

*

The titles discussed in the preceding chapter were chosen on the basis of their frequent occurrence, and as such were the best for establishing the existence and basic characteristics of the nine periods. Most of them, however, are not the kind of titles that would permit historical conclusions to be drawn from them. In this chapter we propose to remedy that omission by discussing two groups of titles: the priesthoods of the kings and at the pyramids, and some of the titles connected with the administration of Upper Egypt. Titles belonging to the former group are relatively easy to identify, and for that reason we have treated them rather fully. Our knowledge of the details of the administration of Egypt is still quite limited. For the discussion of the titles connected with the provincial administration, therefore, we have restricted ourselves to a survey of the cemeteries of Upper Egypt and a discussion of the relatively common titles in whose case there seems little doubt that they refer to the administration of the province, such as *ḥrj-tp ꜥꜣ n spt*. In the case of persons buried at Memphis, only those have been considered where a title contains a geographical indication. In the case of the vast number of other titles whose functions might possibly involve the government of the provinces, I have preferred to avoid what would be a very complex, and, I fear, rather inconclusive discussion by leaving them out completely.

The priesthoods in general were rather neglected in the discussion of chapter v, and we will present first a brief survey of the titles of the high priests of Ptah at Memphis. This will serve as a background for the treatment of the royal priesthoods. My collection only contains those of the high priests of Ptah for whom adequate ranking charts could be established. The discussion, therefore, does not pretend to give a complete survey of the history of this office during the Old Kingdom, nor is the documentation adequate for following the priesthood in question through the nine periods. However, some of these high priests had a considerable number of characteristic titles, and three of them could be dated to a specific period—which unfortunately does not seem to be possible in the case of the high priests of Heliopolis whose tombs were excavated by Daressy: [191], [381], [429], [430]. We shall begin by discussing the titles of the three high priests of Ptah who can be dated exactly: [164], [421], [422]. Naturally, we shall not list all the titles they held, only those that seem to be connected with the office and recur regularly. In order to enable the reader to place these titles in context, the common titles in these tombs will also be listed, and we shall add (in brackets) a few titles from the ranking chart for the period in question.

PERIOD V B [164]

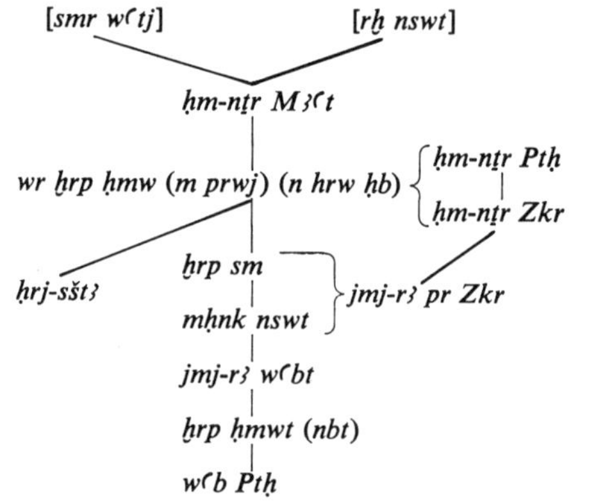

PERIOD VI B [421]

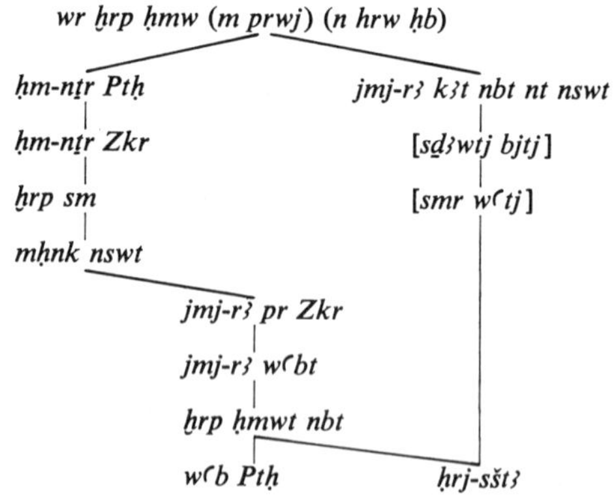

PERIOD VI C [168]

wr ḫrp ḥmw (m prwj hrw n ḥb)

ḥm-nṯr Ptḥ

ḥm-nṯr Zkr

ḫrp sm

mḥnk nswt

wʿb Ptḥ

jmj-rꜣ pr Zkr

jmj-rꜣ wʿbt

ḫrp ḥmwt nbt

The last has no titles to link this sequence with the charts of chapter v. Examination will show that the titles characteristic for the high priest of Ptah change their relative ranking only slightly in the three periods for which we have detailed evidence. The position of the whole group has, however, changed quite considerably in the Sixth Dynasty. In Period V B the priestly titles rank near the bottom of the chart. In the Sixth Dynasty, a common title for the high priest, *wr ḫrp ḥmw*, has been advanced to a position near the top of the chart. Whether the other titles followed is not clear. We shall see that this development parallels the treatment of the royal priesthoods, which are much better documented. The development is not identical, however, and should not be stressed too much.

The remaining charts of priests of Ptah do not contain enough titles to add anything to the picture. *Sꜣbw Ṯtj* [422] (Periods VI C–F) has the title *wr ḫrp ḥmw* again ranking below *smr wʿtj*; since the tomb cannot be dated precisely, we can only suggest that the change took place around the middle of the Sixth Dynasty. *Wꜣš-Ptḥ* [104] has *rḫ nswt* fluctuating with *ḥm-nṯr Ptḥ*, which contradicts the sequence given above for Period V B and suggests that the tomb is probably earlier. The other tombs, [35B], [226], [304], [380], [417A], [420], have only short extracts from the group of titles given above. They could fit equally well in any period, and nothing can be added to the information given about them in chapter iii.

We now proceed to the priesthoods of the kings of the Old Kingdom, their pyramids, and of the solar temples erected in the Memphite necropolis by them. Because of the inherent interest of these titles and the element of dating they contained, it seemed convenient to collect as completely as possible all occurrences of titles connected with such institutions and a few others compounded with the names of kings.

The material is presented in the tables and lists of references. We hope that it will be useful. It includes all occurrences of all the titles in our collection, whether they are recorded in a rankable context or not.* In our discussion of the ranking of these priesthoods we shall, however, as before, restrict our attention in most cases to the better documented offices.

For reasons of space, the kings of the Old Kingdom whose priesthoods are referred to in contemporary documents have been abbreviated in the headings and references to the tables given below and in the lists given later in this chapter by means of the following key. The Roman numeral refers to the dynasty, the Arabic to the reign.

Snefru	IV 1	Neferefre	V 4
Khufu	IV 2	Neuserre	V 5
Djedefre	IV 3	Menkauhor	V 6
Khafre	IV 4	Djedkare Izezi	V 7
Menkaure	IV 5	Unis	V 8
Shepseskaf	IV 6	Teti	VI 1
Userkaf	V 1	Merire Pepi I	VI 2
Sahure	V 2	Mernere	VI 3
Neferirkare	V 3	Neferkare Pepi II	VI 4

Inspection of the tables shows that the structure of the priesthood and administration of a royal funerary establishment was quite complex; I would venture to state the unsupported impression that it was considerably more so than that of any other god. However, since I have made no attempt to collect the rarer titles connected with the cults of such gods with any approach to exhaustiveness, this statement can be no more than an impression and it seems futile to attempt to document it.

It is also clear that the structure of the priesthoods at the various pyramids changed both from pyramid to pyramid and with the passage of time. A study of this structure is not one of the purposes of this study; we will therefore restrict ourselves to an analysis of the better documented titles in the general framework of the ranking system. From this point of view common titles found used at many pyramids are of greater interest than the title peculiar to the cult of only one king.

A detailed study of the material (and a reassessment of it in the light of the datings proposed here) would be a valuable study but goes beyond the limits of our subject.†

* Publications reaching Chicago after July, 1958 could not be utilized, and it is inevitable that much was simply overlooked.

† I do not flatter myself that I have not overlooked any references. Helck, *Untersuchungen*, pp. 128–30, treats the subject rather briefly. A paper by Kaiser, "Zu den Sonnenheiligtümern der 5. Dynastie," *MDIAAK*, XIV, 104–16, surveys the material for the solar

References for Table I:

1. V 2: 486.
   V 3: 487, 523.
   V 4: 487.
   V 5: 95, 173, 454, 487, 523, 526, 528, 540A, 582.
   V 6: 173, 482, 500A.
   V 7: 14, 243A, 447, 482, 517, 519.
   V 8: 14, 86, 168, 343, 558.
   VI 1: 437.
   VI 2: 189, 273A, 365.
2. V 3: 564.
3. IV 4: 48.
   V 3: 226.
   V 4: 93.
   V 5: 288.
   V 6: 93, 255.
   V 7: 170, 447A.
   V 8: 18, 183B, 320, 421.
   VI 1: 61A, 168, 364, 389A, 393, 421.
   VI 3: 58.
   VI 4: 32, 592 (two persons).
4. VI 2: 562.
   VI 3: 562.
   VI 4: 493A, 562.

   NOTE: One wonders whether this title, *sḥḏ*, is not a mistake for the following, *sḥḏ ḥm-nṯr*. In [562] these titles occur once each, and together, and contrast with several occurrences of the more usual title.

5. IV 2: 9.
   IV 5: 48, 319.
   V 5: 13.

---

temples. His information is not complete, however, and he spoils his conclusions by relying on royal names and temples in titles as an index for exact dating. Like Helck (cf. chap. iii, pp. 8–9), he also believes that priesthoods at the solar temples cease to occur after Menkauhor. His n. 4 on p. 106, which is intended to explain away the obvious exception of [421] remains to me utterly unconvincing. Cf. Porter and Moss, *Topographical Bibliography*, III, 109, for the stela he refers to, which actually does come from Mariette E 1/2 (*not* 12). The inscription containing the priesthoods at the solar temples also contains the cartouche of Teti; this is not the only reason for not taking it to be a mechanical, unthinking copy of a text of the middle Fifth Dynasty.

After I had completed this manuscript, Helck, "Bemerkungen zu den Pyramidenstädten im Alten Reich," *MDIAAK*, XV, 91–111, arrived in Chicago. I cannot discuss it here, but feel it necessary to state that, in addition to many other points where I disagree, his datings are based to such an extent on the use of royal priesthoods as an index for exact dating that for this reason alone I must reject his conclusions as to the history and development of the royal cults almost *in toto*. I hope to discuss the subject more adequately elsewhere.

TABLE I

Offices at the Royal Pyramid

Title	Kings																	
	Dynasty IV						Dynasty V								Dynasty VI			
	1	2	3	4	5	6	1	2	3	4	5	6	7	8	1	2	3	4
1. *ḥm-nṯr*								1	2	1	9	3	6	5	1	3		
2. *jmj-rꜣ ḥm-nṯr nw* . .									1									
3. *jmj-ḫt ḥm-nṯr* . . .				1					1	1	1	2	2	4	6		1	3
4. *sḥḏ*																1	1	2
5. *sḥḏ ḥm-nṯr*		1			2						1	2	2	5	12	12	6	10
6. *wꜥb*	1			1	1		4	5	2		4	1	1	1				
7. *jmj-rꜣ wꜥb*				1														
8. *jmj-rꜣ wꜥb ḫꜣstjw* (?) .					1													
9. *jmj-ḫt n wꜥb* . . .							1											
10. *sḥḏ wꜥb*	1	7		4	1		3	1			1							
11. *wꜥb nswt*		2																
12. *ḫrp wꜥb nswt* . . .		1																
13. *wꜥb* 200																2	1	2
14. *ḫntj-š*														3	10	12		2
15. *jmj-rꜣ ḫntj-š* . . .															1	1		
16. *jmj-rꜣ wpt ḫntj-š* . .														1	2	1		
17. *sḥḏ ḫntj-š*														1				
18. *jmj-rꜣ*	4	3		8	2	1			1		1							
19. *jmj-rꜣ njwt*		2			1				1		2	2	2	1	1	2		1
20. *jmj-rꜣ ꜥḥ*				1														
21. *jmj-rꜣ wpt*														1		1		1
22. *jmj-rꜣ wpt nswt*. . .																1		
23. *jmj-rꜣ wpt ḥtpt-nṯr* . .																		1
24. *jmj-rꜣ njwwt mꜣwt nt* .													1					
25. *jmj-rꜣ zš n*		1																
26. *jmj-rꜣ*  *nt*.		1																
27. *jmj-rꜣ šnꜥ*																	1	
28. *jmj-rꜣ ḏꜣt*					1													
29. *ḥm-kꜣ*														1				
30. *jmj-rꜣ ḥm-kꜣ* . . .			1															
31. *ḫrp m zꜣ*				2														
32. *zš n zꜣ*															1	1		
33. *mtj n zꜣ*				1											2		2	1
34. *ḥqꜣ ḥt*				1												3	1	2
35. *ḥrj sštꜣ*				1	3													
36. *zꜣb ḥrj sštꜣ*				1														
37. *ꜥḏ-mr Ṯn rsj* . . .				1														
38. *rḫ nswt*				1														1
39. *zš n ꜥ nswt m sḏꜣwt nbt ntt m*							1											
40. *smsw hꜣjt*		2		1	1								1					
41. *sḥḏ n ḥs*							1											
42. *jmj-rꜣ rwd* (?) . . .		1		1														

V 6: 13, 161.
V 7: 13, 161.
V 8: 14A, 183B, 249, 320, 390.
VI 1: 94, 168A, 189, 190A, 197, 202, 246, 273, 274, 364, 393, 548.
VI 2: 83, 110, 130A, 189, 202, 225, 358B, 393, 395, 414, 562, 576.
VI 3: 83, 110, 225, 395, 556, 562.
VI 4: 83, 84, 229A, 358B, 366A, 371, 382, 409, 562, 592.
6. IV I: 559.
IV 4: 559.
IV 5: 559.
V 1: 35B, 540B, 559, 581.
V 2: 282, 452, 462, 523, 559.
V 3: 357, 517.
V 5: 227, 517, 523, 528.
V 6: 447.
V 7: 436.
V 8: 284.
7. IV 4: 292.
8. IV 5: 97.
9. V 1: 215A.
10. IV 1: 448.
IV 2: 8, 33, 55, 77, 153A, 203A, 544.
IV 4: 77, 318, 362, 495.
IV 5: 179A.
V 1: 146, 236, 282.
V 2: 123A.
V 5: 161.
11. IV 2: 254, 494A.
12. IV 2: 207A.
13. VI 2: 149, 393.
VI 3: 15.
VI 4: 587, 592.
14. V 8: 343, 390, 601A.
VI 1: 94, 117, 189, 190A, 197, 231A, 273, 274, 365, 389A.
VI 2: 1, 18, 77, 131, 149, 210, 349A, 414, 495, 552, 566, 576.
VI 4: 136, 592.
15. VI 1: 190A.
VI 2: 247A.
16. V 8: 86.
VI 1: 190A (two persons).
VI 2: 430A.
17. V 8: 507.
18. IV 1: 338A, 534, 581 (two persons).
IV 2: 10, 263, 452A.
IV 4: 257, 269A (two persons), 313, 508, 511 (?), 574 (two persons).
IV 5: 24, 257.

IV 6: 243B.
V 3: 564.
V 5: 564.
19. IV 2: 495, 509.
IV 5: 495.
V 3: 153A.
V 5: 13, 161.
V 6: 13, 161.
V 7: 13, 161.
V 8: 390.
VI 1: 548.
VI 2: 136, 560.
VI 4: 560.
20. IV 4: 292.
21. V 8: 507.
VI 2: 64A.
VI 4: 32.
22. VI 2: 280.
23. VI 4: 84.
24. V 7: 544.
25. IV 2: 11.
26. IV 2: 327.
27. VI 3: 590A.
28. IV 5: 459.
29. V 8: 390.
30. IV 3: 424.
31. IV 4: 292, 574.
32. VI 1: 284.
VI 2: 393.
33. IV 4: 37A.
VI 1: 35A, 553.
VI 3: 110, 136.
VI 4: 84.
34. IV 4: 37A.
VI 2: 81, 177A, 431.
VI 3: 177A.
VI 4: 32, 81.
35. IV 4: 574.
IV 5: 24, 124, 459.
36. IV 4: 292.
37. IV 4: 292.
38. IV 4: 292.
VI 4: 84.
39. V 1: 215A.
40. IV 2: 494A, 601.
IV 4: 550.

IV 5: 268B.
V 7: 167A.
41. V 1: 242.
42. IV 2: 570A.
IV 4: 570A.

NOTE: This title comes from an excessively poorly published text. The word transcribed *rwd* is written , , and . An emendation of some sort is called for; the one given I owe to Fischer.

TABLE II

OFFICES CONNECTED WITH THE NAMES OF THE KINGS

Title	Kings																	
	Dynasty IV						Dynasty V								Dynasty VI			
	1	2	3	4	5	6	1	2	3	4	5	6	7	8	1	2	3	4
1. *ḥm-nṯr* (king)	7	41	3	17	13		11	17	14	2	9							
2. *ḥm-nṯr* (Horus-name)	2	8		1					1									
3. *ḥm-nṯr* (Two-Ladies-title). . .		4		1														
4. *ḥm-nṯr* (gold monogram) . . .	1	3																
5. *ḥm-nṯr* (king) *m* (pyramid) . .							1											
6. *ḫrp ḥm-nṯr* (king)	1																	
7. *sḥḏ ḥm-nṯr* (king)		1			1													
8. *sḥḏ ḥm-nṯr ḥt-kꜣ* (king) . . .																3		
9. *wꜥb* (king)			1	1				1										
10. *ḥqꜣ ḥt-nṯr nt* (king)	1																	
11. *ḥqꜣ ḥt* (king)		2											1			2		
12. *ḥqꜣ ḥt dwꜣt* (?) (king)		1																
13. *zš n sḏꜣwt nt ḥt* (king)					1													
14. *ḥtj* (Horus-name)			1															
15. *jmj-rꜣ sḫwt* (king)		1																

References for Table II:

1. IV 1: 116, 502A, 511A, 529A, 534, 538, 569A.
IV 2: 7, 8, 16, 21, 36, 104, 172, 178, 182, 190, 193, 235, 251, 258, 263,

268A, 277, 317, 325, 355, 375 (?), 377, 378, 386, 398, 404, 436A, 439, 441, 457, 491, 501, 502, 532 (two persons), 539, 549, 559, 569, 577, 595.
IV 3: 126, 317, 441.
IV 4: 42, 116, 199, 252, 261, 264, 267, 292, 313, 316, 317, 318, 460, 492, 523, 550, 574.
IV 5: 24, 97, 118, 140, 199, 267, 384A, 388, 391, 464, 546A, 599 (two persons).
V 1: 157, 215A, 242, 245, 358A, 406, 452, 454, 457, 540B, 559.
V 2: 21, 40, 66, 95, 123A, 161A, 239, 256, 258, 290, 360, 458, 486, 491, 523, 583A, 600.
V 3: 21, 66, 118, 215A (two persons), 258, 360, 454, 462, 469, 491, 523, 528, 583A.
V 4: 242, 360.
V 5: 40, 66, 114, 258, 332, 360, 469, 583A, 594.

2. IV 1: 502A, 534.
IV 2: 172, 178, 251, 322, 325, 378, 501, 539.
IV 4: 550.
V 3: 582.

3. IV 2: 172, 251, 377, 539.
IV 4: 550.

4. IV 1: 376.
IV 2: 172, 325, 376.

5. V 1: 157.

6. IV 1: 534.

7. IV 2: 10.
IV 5: 319.

8. VI 2: 69, 196, 490A. Note that in these three cases the king is simply called *Ppjj*, which is ambiguous, but is more likely to refer to the first.

9. IV 3: 512.
IV 4: 550.
V 2: 528.

10. IV 1: *Mṯn, Urkunden*, I, 7.

11. IV 2: 230, 412.
V 7: 327.
VI 2: 192, 561.

12. IV 2: 487A.

13. IV 5: 24.

14. IV 3: 476.

15. IV 2: 327.

References for Table III:

1. V 1: 452, 559 (two persons).
V 3: 118, 288, 529.
V 5: 152, 227, 523.

TABLE III

OFFICES AT THE ROYAL SOLAR TEMPLES

TITLES	KINGS					
	Dynasty V					
	1	2	3	4	5	6
1. *ḥm-nṯr*	3		3		3	
2. *ḥm-nṯr Rꜥ m*	18	2	13		8	1
3. *ḥm-nṯr Rꜥ Ḥtḥr m*	2		11			
4. *ḥm-nṯr Rꜥ-Ḥr-ꜣḫtj m*			1			
5. *ḥm-nṯr Ḥr*	1					
6. *jmj-ḫt ḥm-nṯr*					1	
7. *jmj-ḫt ḥm-nṯr Rꜥ m*			1			2
8. *sḥḏ ḥm-nṯr Rꜥ m*			1			
9. *wꜥb*					1	
10. *wꜥb Rꜥ m*	1		1			
11. *sḥḏ wꜥb*	1					
12. *sḥḏ wꜥb Rꜥ m*	1					
13. *jmj-rꜣ*		1	1	1	1	
14. *jmj-rꜣ pr-šnꜥ*	2		1			
15. *jmj-rꜣ ḫt-šmꜥ*	1					
16. *sḥḏ pr-šnꜥ*					1	
17. *zš n ꜥ nswt m sḏꜣwt nbt ntt m* . .	1					
18. *ḥrj sštꜣ Rꜥ m*			1			

2. V 1: 35B, 95, 113A, 147, 157, 164, 239, 245, 256, 421, 454, 458, 486, 523, 540B, 581, 600, 601C.
   V 2: 102A, 564.
   V 3: 88A, 113A, 164, 256, 454, 462, 475, 487, 523, 529, 564, 578, 582.
   V 5: 40, 164, 277, 332, 357, 421, 582, 640A.
   V 6: 332.
3. V 1: 215A (two persons).
   V 3: 66, 115, 152, 215A (two persons), 236, 243, 360, 469, 517, 528.
4. V 3: 421.
5. V 1: 559.
6. V 5: 288.

7. V 3: 226.
   V 6: 93, 255.
8. V 3: 564.
9. V 5: 451A.
10. V 1: 282.
    V 2: 565.
11. V 1: 406.
12. V 1: 236.
13. V 2: 564.
    V 3: 564.
    V 4: 564.
    V 5: 564.
14. V 1: 105A, 219.
    V 3: 601B.
15. V 1: 253A.
16. V 5: 451B.
17. V 1: 215A.
18. V 3: 166.

TABLE IV

OFFICES AT THE *MRT* OF THE KING AND THE *ḪNT* OF THE PYRAMID

TITLE	KINGS																	
	Dynasty IV						Dynasty V								Dynasty VI			
	1	2	3	4	5	6	1	2	3	4	5	6	7	8	1	2	3	4
1. *ḥm-nṯr mrt* (king)							1											
2. *ḥm-nṯr Ḥtḥr mrt* (king)												1						
3. *ḥm-nṯr*  *mrt* (king) . . .																1		
4. *jmj-ḫt ḥm-nṯr mrt* (king) . . .															1			
5. *sḥḏ ḥm-nṯr mrt* (king)																1		
6. *sḥḏ ḥm-nṯr Ḥtḥr mrt* (king) . .								1						1				
7. *wʿb nswt mrt* (king)							1											
8. *ḥm-nṯr ḫnt* (pyramid)	1	2																
9. *ḥm-nṯr Ḥtḥr ḫnt* (pyramid) . . .							1											

References for Table IV:

1. V 1: 406.
2. V 6: 580.
3. VI 2: 64A.

4. VI 1: 190A.
5. VI 2: 414.
6. V 2: 256.
   V 8: 558.
7. V 1: 157.
8. IV 1: 293.
   IV 2: 230, 327.
9. V 1: 406.

It will be convenient to begin our discussion with the titles connected with the kings from Unis to Pepi II. Their usage can be described quite simply. The following statements are, therefore, intended to cover not only the commoner priesthoods but also the rarer offices. Further references than those given in the notes to the tables seemed unnecessary.

1. The earliest securely dated occurrence of a priesthood in this group is [249] from Period V C (time of Unis). They continue well beyond the end of the Old Kingdom, for instance [364], [553].

2. Without exception, all titles in this group outrank whatever titles they may be combined with in a string, including the very highest such as *jrj-pʿt* and *zȝ nswt*. The earliest securely dated ranked occurrence is [548] in Period V D (time of Teti).

3. No priesthoods (*ḥm-nṯr*, *wʿb*) of any of the *names* of the kings in this group occur. Priests and officials are always stated to be priests or officials of the pyramid or other institution of the king in question.

4. Priesthoods at two or more different pyramids *never* occur in the same string of titles. Two (but apparently never more) different offices at the same institution are, however, found in the same string of titles, though not very frequently. The complete list follows:

[32]	(VI D)	*jmj-ḫt ḥm-nṯr*, *jmj-rȝ wpt* at the Pyramid of	Pepi II
[136]	(VI G)	*ḫntj-š*, *zš n zȝ*	Pepi II
[183B]		*jmj-ḫt*, *sḥḏ ḥm-nṯr*	Unis
[189]	(VI C)	*sḥḏ ḥm-nṯr*, *ḫntj-š*	Teti
[197]	(VI B), [273], [274] (VI B): same as [189]		
[343]		*ḥm-nṯr*, *ḫntj-š*	Unis
[364]	(X!)	*sḥḏ ḥm-nṯr*, *jmj-ḫt ḥm-nṯr*	Teti
[389A]		*jmj-ḫt ḥm-nṯr*, *ḫntj-š*	Teti
[390]		*ḫntj-š*, *ḥm-kȝ*	Unis
[548]	(V D)	*jmj-rȝ njwt*, *sḥḏ ḥm-nṯr*	Teti

The figures in parentheses give the dates where known. No information useful for dating can be drawn from the material given above. As far as it goes, the ranking is quite uniform, with the one exception of a tomb quite securely dated to the Tenth Dynasty.*

5. It is uncommon for persons with priesthoods of kings in this group to have in addition priesthoods of earlier kings. There are three exceptions, [14], [77], [495], with a fourth [421] holding priesthoods at the pyramids of Unis and Teti and at the same time at the solar temples of Userkaf, Neferirkare, and Neuserre. In contrast, seventeen persons have priesthoods at two or more pyramids within the group, with the titles, of course, carefully listed in separate strings.†

We will reserve a discussion of the implications of these facts for our concluding chapter. Here I will only state that to my mind the second point implies the fourth. Since this class of titles was intended to outrank everything, placing priesthoods of two different kings in the same string and thus assigning one of them a rank superior to that of the other was to be avoided at all costs.

The offices and priesthoods of the kings before Unis cannot be dealt with so briefly. We will have to present the data in full and will restrict ourselves to those kinds of priesthood that are attested at least fifteen times in the aggregate. The presentation will be in the same form as that at the beginning of the last chapter, with the rankings presented in the form of title sequences. To save space, we shall have to burden the reader with more abbreviations. We give below a list of the classes of priesthood that will be discussed:

At the pyramid temples:

ḥm-nṯr	*ḤN Pyr*
jmj-ḫt ḥm-nṯr	*MḪḤN Pyr*
sḥḏ ḥm-nṯr	*SḤN Pyr*
wʿb	*Wb Pyr*
sḥḏ wʿb	*SWb Pyr*
jmj-rꜣ	*M Pyr*
jmj-rꜣ njwt	*MN Pyr*

Priests of the kings' cartouches:

ḥm-nṯr	*ḤN*

At the royal solar temples:

ḥm-nṯr	*ḤN ST*
ḥm-nṯr (Rʿ)	*ḤN (R) ST*
ḥm-nṯr (Ḥtḥr)	*ḤN (H) ST*

* Edel writes me that the sequence *jmj-ḫt ḥm-nṯr, sḥḏ ḥm-nṯr* at the pyramid of Pepi II occurs in unpublished material at Aswan.

† Clédat, "Deux monuments nouveaux de Tell el-Maskhoutah," *Recueil de Travaux*, XXXII, 40–41 publishes in addition a cylinder seal with titles at the pyramids of Djedkare, Pepi I, and Mernere.

These abbreviations are followed by the indication of the king concerned by means of the Roman and Arabic numerals given earlier in this chapter (p. 248). Thus *ḤN* (*RH*) *ST V* 3 means *ḥm-nṯr Rʿ Ḥtḥr m St-jb-Rʿ*; *ḤN IV* 2 reads *ḥm-nṯr Ḫwfw* and will here be used in preference to the *ḤNḪ* of the preceding pages.

The sources will be quoted by their numbers in brackets, as usual, followed by an indication of date in parentheses. Where possible, the conclusions of chapter v will be used. Otherwise we give approximations and refer the reader to chapter iii. The terms "Early" and "Late" will be used for tombs outside the range of the nine periods.

We will not give here a complete listing of all occurrences of the classes of titles listed above. If the title occurs only in unrankable context, it will be left out. Whenever possible, we will include enough of the common titles in the sequences to enable the reader to place them in the context of the results of the preceding chapter. If one of the priesthoods occurs in rankable context but none of the other titles belongs to the group of 50 common ones, we will indicate by a dash (—) that a title precedes or follows. If the priesthood of some other god occurs in the sequences, it will be indicated by *ḥm-nṯr* or *wʿb* or other title, as the case may be, with the name of the god omitted, as that does not concern us here. The title will *not* be abbreviated. We now present the data. It should go without saying that the rankings in the tombs marked "Early" or Fourth Dynasty should not be relied on.

[7] (Khafre): *ḤN* IV 2, *SW*.
[8] (VI G): *SWb Pyr* IV 2, *RḪN*, *ḤN* IV 2.
[9] (V B–D, VI B, G): *SḤN Pyr* IV 2, *ḤqḤ*, *WMŠ*, *NḪ*.
[10] (V B–D, VI B–D, F–G): —, *M Pyr* IV 2.
[13] (V D): *MN Pyr* V 7, *SḤN Pyr* V 7.
MN Pyr V 6, *SḤN Pyr* V 6.
MN Pyr V 5, *SḤN Pyr* V 5.
MN Pyr V 7, *TZṮ*.
[14] (VI E): *ḤN Pyr* V 8, *ZʿM*.
ḤN Pyr V 7, *ḪTN*.
[16] (VI E): *WN*, *ḤS*, *ḤN* IV 2.
[21] (Early): *RḪN*, *WN*, *ḤN* IV 2, —.
[24] (V C, VI C): —, *ḤN* IV 5.
[33] (VI): *SWb Pyr* IV 2, —.
[35B] (V or later): *ḤN* (*R*) *ST* V 1, *Wb Pyr* V 1.
[36] (VI B, E–G): *WN*, *ḤN* IV 2.
[40] (VI B–C, F–G): *ḤN* V 5, *RḪN*, *ḤS*, *WN*, *ḤN* V 2.
[42] (Mid-V or later): *ḤN* IV 4, *RḪN*.
[48] (V D): *SḤN Pyr* IV 5, *ḪTN*.
MḪḤN Pyr IV 4, —.

[55] (VI D–E): *SWb Pyr* IV 2, *ZMZ*, *ḤNM*.
[66] (V B): *RḪN* (?), *ḤN* (*RH*) *ST* V 3, *ḤN* V 3, *ḤN V* 2, *ḤN* V 5.
[93] (Menkauhor or later): *MḪḤN Pyr* V 4, *MḪḤN Pyr* V 6, *ḤS*.
[95] (VI C): —, *ḤN* V 2, *WN*.
[97] (Date?): *WN*, *ḤN* IV 5.
[102A] (Sahure or later): *ḤN* (*R*) *ST* V 2, *WN*.
[104] (Early): *RḪN*, *ḥm-nṯr*, *ḤN* IV 2, *MḤK*.
[115] (V B): *ZSZ*, *ḤNM* (*ḥm-nṯr*!), *ḤN* (*RH*) *ST* V 3, *WN*, *ḤS*.
[116] (End V—VI): *WN*, *ḥm-nṯr*, *ḤN* IV 1, *ḤN* IV 4.
[118] (V C): *ḤN ST* V 3, *ḤN* V 3, *ZMZ*, *ḤNM*.
ḥm-nṯr, *ḤN* IV 5, *ZMZ*.
[123A] (Early): —, *ḤN* V 2, *SWb Pyr* V 2.
[126] (Early): *ZN*, *ḤN* IV 3.
[140] (V D): *WN*, *ḤN* IV 5, *MḤK*.
[146] (V B): *ḥm-nṯr*, *Zʿ M*, *NḪ*, *SWb Pyr* V 1.
[147] (VI ?): *RḪN*, *ḤN* (*R*) *ST* V 1, *ḤNM*.
[152] (V C–D, VI C–E, G): *ḤS*, *ḤNM*, *ḤN* (*RH*) *ST* V 3.
WN, *ḤN ST* V 5.
[157] (Userkaf or later): *ḤN* (*R*) *ST* V 1, *ḥm-nṯr*, *ḤN* V 1 (*m Pyr* V 1).
[161] (V D): *MN Pyr* V 7, *SḤN Pyr* V 7, *ḪTN*.
MN Pyr V 6, *SḤN Pyr* V 6.
MN Pyr V 5, *SWb Pyr* V 5, *Zʿ M*.
[164] (V B): *ḤN* (*R*) *ST* V 1, *ḤN* (*R*) *ST* V 5, *wr ḫrp ḥmw*, *ḤS*.
ḥm-nṯr, *ḤM* (*R*) *ST* V 3, *ḥm-nṯr*, *wr ḫrp ḥmw*.
[170] (VI B): *MḪḤN Pyr* V 7, *RNḤ*, *SW*.
[172] (VI B, F–G): *WN*, *ḤN* IV 2, *ḪŠP*, *ḤS*.
[173] (VI): *ḤN Pyr* V 5, *ḤqḤ*.
ḤN Pyr V 6, *ḤqḤ*.
[178] (VI B–C, F–G): *ḤN* IV 2, *ḤS*.
[182] (Early): *wr mꜣ Jwnw*, *ḤN* IV 2.
[190] (VI B–D, F–G): *RḪN*, *WN*, *ḤN* IV 2, *MP*.
[193] (VI B–G): *WN*, *ḤN* IV 2.
[199] (V B, D, VI D–E): *ḤN* IV 4, *ḤN* IV 5, *WN*, *RḪN*.
[226] (Neferirkare or later): *RNḤ*, *MḪḤN Pyr* V 3, *ḥm-nṯr*.
[227] (Neuserre or later): —, *ḤN ST* V 5, *Wb Pyr* V 5.
[235] (VI B, G): *WN*, *ḤN* IV 2.
[236] (V B–D, VI C, E–F): *SW*, *MKNN*, *SWb Pyr* V 1, *ḤN* (*RH*) *ST* V 3, *ḤS*.
[239] (Sahure or later): —, *ḤN* V 2.
ḤN (*R*) *ST* V 1, *WN*.
[242] (V B–D, VI C–G): *ḤN* V 4, *ḤN* V 1 (and vice versa).
[243] (V B, D, VI D–E): *ḤN* (*RH*) *ST* V 3, *WN*, *RḪN*.
[245] (V B–D, VI B, E, G): *WN*, *ḤN* V 1, *ḤS*.
ḤN (*R*) *ST* V 1, *ḤS*.
[251] (VI D): *ḤN* IV 2, *RḪN* and *WN*, *ḤN* IV 2 (for fluctuations see chap. v).

[252] (Mid-V or later): *Ḫʿ, WN, ḤN* IV 4.
[255] (Menkauhor or later): *MḪḤN Pyr* V 6, *ḤS.*
[256] (VI B, D, F): *ZSZ, ZMZ, ḤN* V 2.
ZMZ, ḤN (*R*) *ST* V 3, *ḤN* (*R*) *ST* V 1.
[257] (VI B G): *WMŠ, NḪ, M Pyr* IV 4, *ḤS.*
M Pyr IV 5, *ḤS.*
[258] (V B): *ḤN* IV 2, *ḤN* V 3, *RḪN.*
ḤN V 2, *RḪN.*
ḤN V 5, *WN.*
[261] (Date?): —, *ḤN* IV 4, —.
[263] (V C): *RḪN, ḤN* IV 2.
RḪN, M Pyr IV 2.
[267] (V B–C): *RḪN, WN, ḤN* IV 4, *ḤN* IV 5.
[268A] (V C, VI B–G): *RḪN, ḤN* IV 2.
[269A] (V or later): *RḪN, M Pyr* IV 4.
WMŠ, M Pyr IV 4.
[277] (VI B, F–G): *RḪN, ḤN* IV 2, *ḤN* (*R*) *ST* V 5.
[282] (V B): *ḤSPD, SWb Pyr* V 1.
Wb Pyr V 2, —.
[288] (Neuserre or later): *RNḤ, MḪḤN Pyr* V 5.
ḪN (*R*) *ST* V 3, *ḤS.*
[290] (V B–D, VI B–C, F–G): *RḪN, WN, ḤN* V 2.
[313] (V B, D, VI B, D–F): *WMŠ, M Pyr* IV 4, *ḤN* IV 4.
[316] (Early V): *ḤN* IV 5, *RḪN.*
[317] (VI B–G): *RḪN, ḤN* IV 2, *ḤN* IV 4.
[318] (V B, D, VI B, D–G): *SW, SWb Pyr* IV 4, *ḤN* IV 4.
SWb Pyr IV 4, *RḪN.*
[325] (VI B–C, F–G): *ḤN* IV 2, *ḤS.*
[332] (V D): *WN, ḤN* (*R*) *ST* V 5, *ḤN* (*R*) *ST* V 6, *ḤN* V 5.
[338A] (V B–C): *ZʿM, WMŠ, M Pyr* IV 1.
[355] (VI B–D, F–G): *RḪN, WN, ḤN* IV 2.
[357] (Neuserre or later): *ḤN* (*R*) *ST* V 5, *ḤS.*
[358A] (V or VI): *WN, ḤN* V 1.
[360] (VI E): *RNḤ, ḤN* V 2, *WN, ḤN* V 5, *RḪN.*
ḤN (*RH*) *ST* V 3, *ḤN* V 2, *ḤN* V 3, *ḤN* V 4, *ḤN* V 5, *RḪN.*
[362] (V or later): *RḪN, SWb Pyr* IV 4.
[375] (Later IV): *ḤN* IV 2 (? in Daressy's copy only.), *RP, TZṮ.*
[377] (End V or later): *ḤN* IV 2, —.
[378] (VI B–G): *WN, ḤN* IV 2.
[386] (Early): *RḪN, WN, ḤN* IV 2, *MP.*
[388] (VI B–D, F–G): *RḪN, WN, ḤN* IV 5.
[391] (V B–C, VI B–C, E–G): —, *ḤN* IV 5, *RḪN.*
[398] (VI B–G): *WN, ḤN* IV 2, *SḪŠP.*
[406] (V D): —, *ḤN* V 1.
[421] (VI B): *MḪḤN Pyr* V 8, *wr ḫrp ḥmw, ḤN* (*R*) *ST* V 1, *ḤN* (*R*) *ST* V 5.

MḪḤN Pyr VI 1, *wr ḫrp ḥmw*, *ḤN* (*Rʿ Ḥr-ȝḫtj*) *ST* V 3, *ḥm-nṯr*.

Note also the similar ranking of the numerous other *ḥm-nṯr*'s in this tomb. This is the only case in which the relative ranking of a title in the later group and in the earlier group can be determined directly, though the earlier ones are rather priesthoods at solar temples than at pyramids.

[436] (Djedkare): —, *Wb Pyr* V 7.
[439] (V C, VI B–G): *RḪN*, *ḤN* IV 2.
[441] (Mid-VI or later): —, *ḤN* IV 2.
ḤN IV 3, *ḥm-nṯr*, *SW*.
[447A] (End V or later): *MḪḤN Pyr* V 7, —.
[448] (VI D): *SWb Pyr* IV 1, *WMŠ*.
[452] (VI E–F): *ḥm-nṯr*, *WN*, *ḤN* V 1, *ZZš*.
ḤN ST V 1, *WN*, *ḤN* V 1, *ZZš*.
Wb Pyr V 2, *ZZš*.
[454] (Neuserre or later): *ZMZ*, *ḤN* (*R*) *ST* V 1, *ḤN* V 1, *ḤN* (*R*) *ST* V 3, *ḤN* V 3, *ḤN Pyr* V 5.
[458] (VI E): *WN*, *ḤN* V 2, *ḤN* (*R*) *ST* V 1, *RḪN*.
[460] (Mid-V or later): *RḪN*, *ḤN* IV 4.
[462] See [528].
[465] (VI): *WN*, *ḤN* IV 5.
[469] (Neuserre or later): *WN*, *ḤN* V 3.
[482] (V B): *ZʿM*, *ḤN Pyr* V 7, *ZšZ*, *ḤS*.
ZʿM, *ḤN Pyr* V 6, *ḤS*.
[486] (VI E): *WN*, *ḤN* V 2, *ḤN* (*R*) *ST* V 1, *RḪN*.
ḤN Pyr V 2, —.
[487] (Neuserre or later): *ḤN Pyr* V 3, *ḤS*.
[492] (VI C): *WN*, *ḤN* IV 4, *MḤK*.
[495] (VI D): *MN Pyr* IV 2, *ZʿN*.
MN Pyr IV 5, *ZʿN*.
SWb Pyr IV 4, *ZʿN*.
[501] (VI B–G): *WN*, *ḤN* IV 2, —.
[502] (VI B–D): *WN*, *ḤN* IV 2.
[502A] (Mid-V or later): —, *ḤN* IV 1.
[508] (Mid-V or later?): *M Pyr* IV 4, *ḤK*.
[509] (V B?): *RḪN*, *MN Pyr* IV 2, *WN*.
[511] (V D, VI B, D–G): *WMŠ*, *M Pyr* IV 4, *WN*.
[517] (VI C): *ZʿM*, *Wb Pyr* V 5.
ḤN (*RH*) *ST* V 3, *Wb Pyr* V 3, *ḤS*, *WN*, *ḤN Pyr* V 7, *WMŠ*.
[519] (Djedkare or later): —, *ḤN Pyr* V 7, *ḤS*.
[523] (VI E): *ḤN* V 2, *ḤN* IV 4.
ḤN V 2, —, *Wb Pyr* V 2.
ḤN (*R*) *ST* V 1, *ḤN Pyr* V 5, *ḤS*.
ḤN (*R*) *ST* V 3, *ḤN Pyr* V 3, *ḤS*.
ḤN ST V 5, *Wb Pyr* V 5, *ḤN* V 3, *WN*.

[528] (VI D): *ḤN* (*RH*) *ST* V 3, *ḤN* V 3, *ḤN Pyr* V 5, *RḪN*.
—, *ḤN* V 3, *Wb Pyr* V 2, *RḪN*.
Wb Pyr V 5, *RḪN*.

[529] (Mid-V or later): *ḤS*, *ḤN ST* V 3.

[532] (V D): *ḤN* IV 2, *ḤS*.

[534] (Early): *SB*, *H̱Ḥ*, *ZN*, *M Pyr* IV 1, *ZN*, *SW*.
ḤN IV 1, —.
Note that this is a quite early tomb; the ranking is still completely confused.

[538] (Date?): *ḤN* IV 1, *WN*.

[539] (VI B–D, F–G): *RḪN*, *WN*, *ḤN* IV 2.

[540B] (V or later): *ḤN* (*R*) *ST* V 1, *ḤN* V 1.
—, *Wb Pyr* V 1.

[549] (V B–D, VI B–D, F): *ḤN* IV 2, *RḪN*, *WN*.

[550] (V D): *WN*, *ḤN* IV 4, *MP*.
SP, *ḤN* V 5.

[559] (Mid-V): —, *ḤN* (*Ḥr*) *ST* V 1, *ḤS*, *ḤN* V 1, *ḥm-nṯr*, *ḤN* IV 5.
Wb Pyr V 2, *ḤS*, etc.
Wb Pyr IV 1, —.
ḤN IV 2, —.
Wb Pyr IV 4, —.
Wb Pyr IV 5, —.
Note also a *ḥm-nṯr* above *ḥrj-sštꜣ* parallel to the titles at the solar temples.

[564] (V C): *ḤN* (*R*) *ST* V 2, *ḤS*.
ḤN (*R*) *ST* V 3, *RḪN*, *SW*, —, *ḥm-nṯr*, *H̱Ḥ*, *ZMN*, *ḥm-nṯr* (different gods, of course).
ḤN (*R*) *ST* V 3, *RḪN*, *SW*, *MKNN*, *M Pyr* V 3.
—, *M Pyr* V 5.

[569] (Early): *ḤN* IV 2, *MW*, *ḥm-nṯr*.

[569A] (Date?): *RḪN*, *ḤN* IV 1.

[574] (Date?): —, *ḤN* IV 4, — *RḪN*.
M Pyr IV 4, *ḤS*.
M Pyr IV 4, *RḪN*.

[578] (V C–D, VI B, G): —, *ḤN* (*R*) *ST* V 3.

[581] (V B, VI B, E–F): *ḤN* (*R*) *ST* V 1, *Wb Pyr* V 1, —.
WMŠ, *RḪN*, *M Pyr* IV 1.

[582] (VI G): *ZSZ*, *ḤN* (*R*) *ST* V 3, *ḥm-nṯr*, *ḤN* (*R*) *ST* V 5.
ḤN Pyr V 5, *ḤN* (*R*) *ST* V 5.

[583A] (Neuserre or later): *ḤN* V 2, *ḤN* V 3.
ḤN V 5, *ḤN* (*RH*) *ST* [. . .].

[594] (End V or later): *ḤN* V 5, *ḤS*.

[595] (V C, VI B–G): *RḪN*, *ḤN* IV 2.

[600] (VI E): *WN*, *ḤN* V 2, *ḤN* (*R*) *ST* V 1, *RḪN*.

[601B] (V or later): *ḤM* (*R*) *ST* V 1, [. . .] *Pyr* V 1.

I regret that the last few pages look rather like something from a chemical formulary. It will be evident, however, upon study of the foregoing data that the treatment of the titles of the priests of the kings before Unis differs in every point from those of the later group of kings.

First of all, the kinds of priesthoods found differ. For the kings from Snefru to Neferefre, *ḥm-nṯr* of the king is the commonest title by far, with *ḥm-nṯr* of the pyramid occurring only sporadically. In the case of Neuserre, the two are about equally divided. For Menkauhor and Djedkare only *ḥm-nṯr* of the pyramid are found. The specific distribution is interesting. We give the results in Table V.

TABLE V

Kings	Priests of King	Range of Well Dated Examples	Priests of Pyramid	Range of Well Dated Examples
Snefru to Neferefre	Very common, 125 cases	Early to VI G	Rare; 9 cases in all	V C to VI E
Neuserre . . .	9 cases	V B to VI E; slight trend to Fifth Dynasty	11 cases	V C to VI G; slight trend to Sixth Dynasty
Menkauhor and Djedkare . .	. . . . . .	. . . . . .	18 cases	V B to VI E

That some sort of change in the structure of the royal priesthoods took place with Neuserre has long been noticed.* We see now, however, that the change did not take place during the reign of Neuserre, but rather at a later date, at which time the cult of that king was partially adapted to that of his successors. This adaptation took place more rarely in the case of his predecessors, whose cult tended to retain the structure which had already become well established; however it did occur, and not only in the case of Sahure and his successors, as Helck seems to think, but as far back as Khufu.

With the data given above, we can now trace the change in greater detail. In the course of the reigns of Menkauhor or Djedkare, the funerary cult of the reigning monarch, and possibly his immediate predecessor, was altered. Presumably the change took place in the time of Djedkare, since he was the first king of the Fifth Dynasty not to build a solar temple, which indicates that some change must have taken place in the royal cult. The office of *ḥm-nṯr* of the king was

* Helck, *Untersuchungen*, p. 128, is a recent statement.

replaced by that of his pyramid. The significance of this change, I must confess, escapes me at the moment. I presume that it is connected with the trend also reflected by the personification of the pyramids from the Fifth Dynasty onward* and the use of the name of the pyramid instead of the name of the king in describing relationship to the monarch.†

In the course of Period V C the new style of priesthood was extended by the creation on a regular basis of similar offices in the cult of King Neuserre; in the well established cults of his predecessors, however, such offices were created or filled only sporadically, it seems. Indeed, the documentation is so poor that one might suspect the nine cases that occur to be mostly errors on the part of scribes accidentally bringing the priesthoods of the older kings in line with the titles customary for the cults of the reigning dynasty. But there is no way of telling.

The change first took place, as we have seen, late in Period V B, presumably in the reign of Djedkare. The extension to earlier cults began in Period V C, whether in the reign of Djedkare or that of Unis cannot be determined as yet. It seems better to reserve the remainder of this discussion until we have examined the ranking of the priesthoods of the kings before Unis. It will give us a sounder basis for making a decision.

Before proceeding to the next point, I would like to tie up a few loose ends. The discussion in the last few paragraphs is based only on the relatively common titles selected a few pages back. Since the problem was one of form rather than rank, those cases in which the titles are not rankable, and thus are not given in the list of sequences, were also considered. The references can be found in the complete table of priesthoods. The discussion in the next few pages involves ranking and will be based only on the sequences given earlier in this chapter.

The tomb of *Kꜣ-m-rḥw*, [526], contains the title *ḥm-nṯr Mn-swt-Nwsrrꜥ*. Its dating was uncertain, with both Periods V B and V C seeming equally probable. I think that on the basis of the parallelism with the earlier kings we can eliminate V B as a possibility and assign it to Period V C. This gives us the earliest dated example for this

* Discussed at great length by Wilke, "Zur Personifikation von Pyramiden," *ZÄS*, LXX, 56–83, and briefly by Gardiner, "An Unexplained Passage in the Inscription of Weni," *JEA*, XLI, 121.

† For instance *Jdwt*, the wife of Teti and mother of Pepi I, Firth and Gunn, *Teti Pyramid Cemeteries*, pl. 55; the wives of Pepi I, *Urkunden*, I, 117; the wives of Pepi II, Jéquier, *La pyramide d'Oudjebten*, pp. 15, 21, Jéquier, *Les pyramides des reines Neit at Apouit*, pp. 4 42, 53. All cases seem to date from the Sixth Dynasty, as far as I can tell, but the documentation above is not intended to be exhaustive.

priesthood in the case of Neuserre. It contains no titles that would involve a change in the ranking charts for the period as presented in the last chapter. In addition, the range for dating the following tombs can be narrowed down somewhat:

[9]	V C–D, VI B, G.
[93]	V C or later.
[226]	V C or later.
[288]	V C or later.
[454]	V C or later.
[487]	V C or later.
[540A]	V C or later.

Unlike the priesthoods of Unis and later kings, there appears to be no compunction about placing the priesthoods at the institutions of different kings of the earlier group into the same string, and this practice is continued until the end of the Old Kingdom; at the same time priesthoods at more than one institution of the same king (for we must include here the solar temples erected by the first six kings of the Fifth Dynasty), or several titles at the same institution occur so frequently in the same string that it seemed pointless to repeat the documentation here.

Before continuing with a discussion of the ranking of these titles, I would like to point out that according to the data presented above, and in contrast to the opinions of Helck and Kaiser, the priesthoods at the solar temples of the Fifth Dynasty appear to continue to a point late in the Old Kingdom. It may be presumed that the cult also continued. Priesthoods at the solar temples are documented in Period VI E in the following cases: [360], [458], [486], [523], [600]. In Period VI G they occur in [582]. They occur as early as Period V B ([66], [115], [164]) and there seems to be no reason for supposing that the temples were not built by the kings to whom they are ascribed.*

The most radical difference between the priesthoods of the kings before Unis and those after is the difference in rank. Where the priesthoods of the later monarchs outrank all other titles, those of the earlier group are, in general, as a cursory inspection of the ranking sequences will show, of relatively low rank, tending to cluster in the vicinity of such titles as *rḫ nswt*, *wʿb nswt*, and *ḥrj-sštꜣ*—a position approximately similar to that of the priests of other, more heavenly gods. Could the change from *ḥm-nṯr* of the king to *ḥm-nṯr* of the pyramid, in other words

* The recent excavations at *Nḫn-Rʿ* have shown that there are serious problems involved in the dating of the building and rebuilding of various portions of these structures. Cf. Ricke, *ASAE*, LIV, 75 ff. and 305 ff. These, however, are questions of much smaller divisions of time than in our scheme of periods and hardly concern us here.

a conscious break from a form of title indicating a parallelism with the cults of the gods, though it took place in Period V B, be the first step in the process which led to the drastic change in rank in Period V C or D? We will now proceed to examine the ranking of the priesthoods of the kings before Unis in greater detail.

The charts on pages 268–270 present the facts we could elucidate about the ranking of the priesthoods. There were thirty-seven accurately dated tombs in the list presented earlier in this chapter, and the charts are largely based on them. As an inspection will show, the relative ranking of the priesthoods being discussed changed little, and the titles tended to appear in similar positions in the main ranking charts, enough of whose titles have been included in the brief charts given here to enable the reader to locate the priesthoods on the charts in chapter v. When this is combined with the inadequate documentation (we have been able to obtain nothing even approaching a complete analysis of the titles listed in the sequences given earlier in this chapter, and for Period VI F there is no securely dated material to begin with), the reader will understand that it has been virtually impossible to assign tombs of uncertain date to one or another of the periods on the basis of the ranking of the royal priesthoods. There was only one exception, tomb [267], which could be assigned to Period V B.

The charts follow the usual conventions. The kings for whom the various priesthoods given in the charts are actually documented in the dated cases are listed in the notes. Owing to the poor documentation, our conclusions must inevitably remain rather uncertain; I should therefore like to stress again that the main point being made here, that the priesthoods of the kings preceding Unis generally had a low rank, whereas those of Unis and his successors were always ranked above anything else, does not depend only on the material used for the charts but is also supported by the whole mass of less securely dated material presented earlier. It is hoped that the details in the charts, uncertain as they may be, will help us to follow the changes that took place in greater detail.

The development of the titles at the royal funerary establishments seems to have been approximately as follows:

1. In Period V B, probably in the reign of Djedkare (the first half), the new *ḥm-nṯr* of the pyramid was introduced for the cult of the reigning monarch and his predecessor. The title still was ranked relatively low, but ranked higher than the older *ḥm-nṯr* of the king still being used for the cults of Neuserre and his predecessors. It is possible that the new titles also came into use for the earlier cults at this time—our documentation is hardly so extensive that this possibility can be

PERIOD V B

SOURCES: 66, 115, 146, 164, 258, 267, 282, 482, 509.

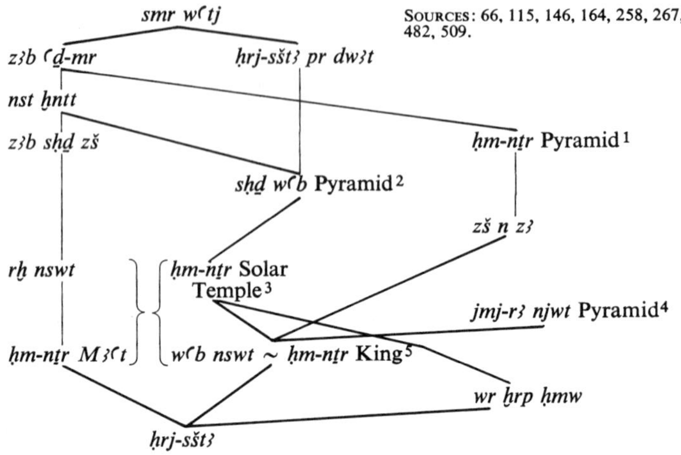

[1] Menkauhor, Djedkare.
[2] Userkaf.
[3] Userkaf, Neferirkare, Neuserre.
[4] Khufu (?).
[5] Khufu, Sahure Neferirkare, Neuserre.

PERIOD V C

SOURCES: 118, 263, 564.

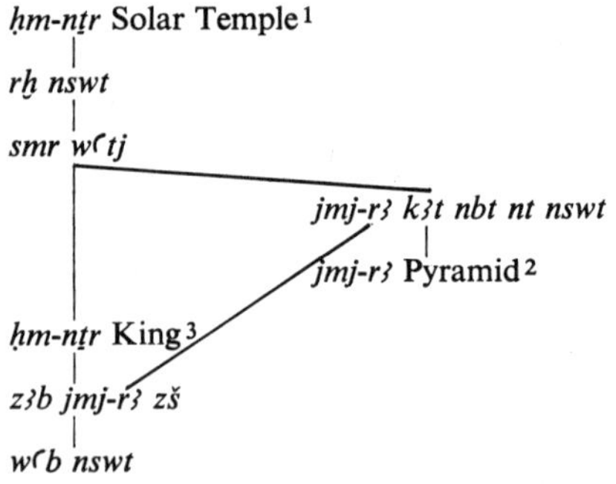

[1] Sahure, Neferirkare.
[2] Khufu, Neferirkare, Neuserre.
[3] Khufu, Menkaure, Neferirkare.

PERIOD V D

SOURCES: 13, 48, 140, 161, 332, 406, 532, 550.

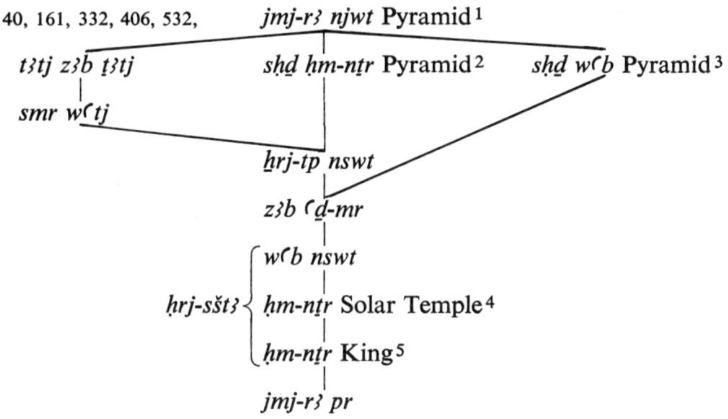

[1] Neuserre, Menkauhor, Djedkare.
[2] Menkaure, Neuserre, Menkauhor, Djedkare.
[3] Neuserre.
[4] Neuserre, Menkauhor.
[5] Khufu, Khafre, Menkaure, Userkaf, Neuserre.

PERIOD VI B

SOURCES: 170, 421.

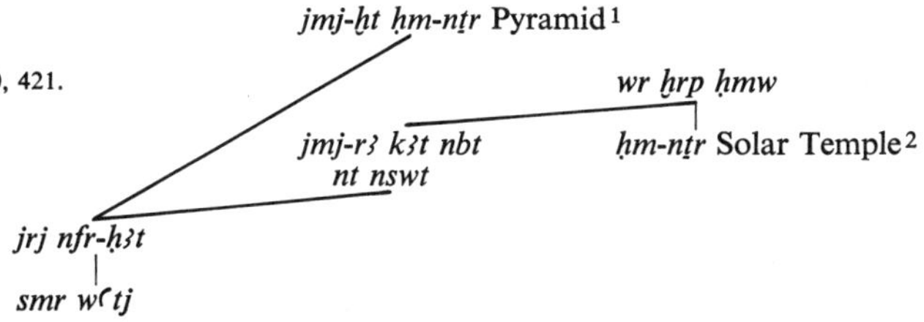

[1] Djedkare. [2] Userkaf, Neferirkare, Neuserre.

PERIOD VI C

SOURCES: 95, 492, 517.

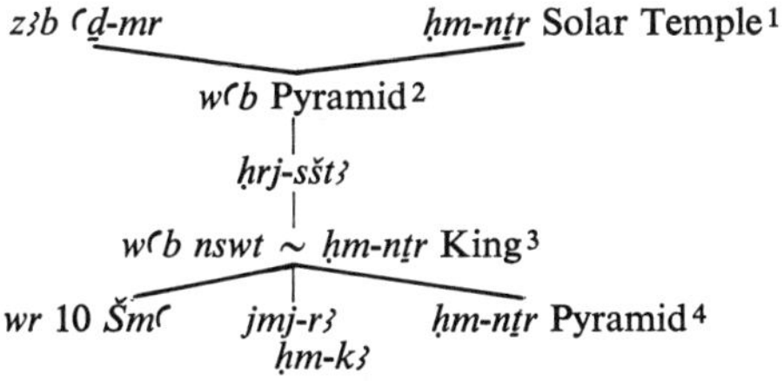

[1] Neferirkare. [2] Neferirkare, Neuserre. [3] Khafre, Sahure. [4] Djedkare.

PERIOD VI D

SOURCES: 251, 448, 495, 528.

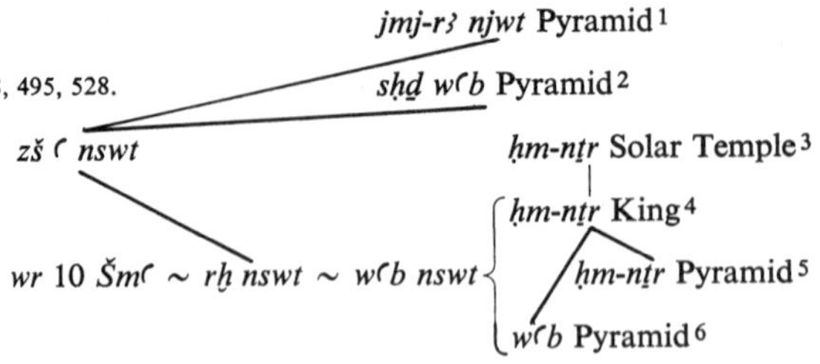

[1] Khufu, Menkaure.
[2] Snefru, Khafre.
[3] Neferirkare.
[4] Khufu, Neferirkare.
[5] Neuserre.
[6] Sahure, Neuserre.

PERIOD VI E

SOURCES: 14, 16, 360, 458, 486, 523, 600.

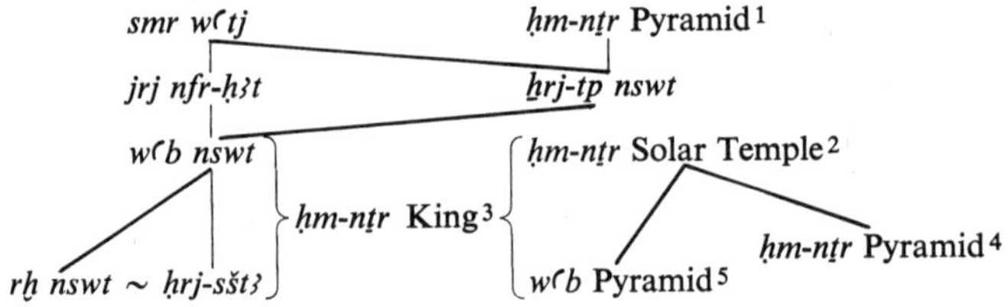

[1] Djedkare.
[2] Userkaf, Neferirkare, Neuserre.
[3] Khufu, Khafre, Sahure, Neferirkare, Neferefre, Neuserre.
[4] Neferirkare, Neuserre.
[5] Sahure, Neuserre.

PERIOD VI G

SOURCES: 8, 582.

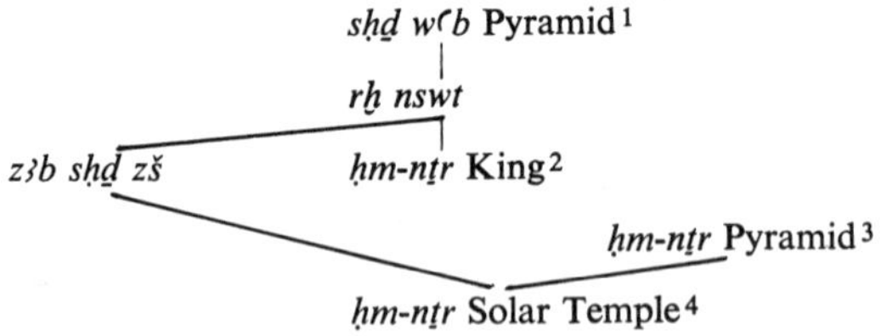

[1] Khufu. [2] Khufu. [3] Neuserre. [4] Neferirkare, Neuserre.

rejected out of hand—but they first appear in the next period ([526], [564]).

2. In Period V C, the chart, unfortunately particularly poorly documented, seems to show a very definite trend towards raising the rank of some of the priesthoods. Since the reign of Unis began in this period, it is only natural to connect this trend with the drastic change in the ranking of his own priesthoods that presumably took place about this time. Since the only case of a priesthood of Unis from this period [249] cannot be ranked with the incomplete data available to me from this tomb, it must remain uncertain whether the change in rank was already accomplished in Period V C, the earlier part of the reign of Unis, or whether it did not take place until the latter half of his reign in Period V D, for which the new ranking is documented. In view of the general upward trend already noted for this period, I would, however, tend to date the change to V C.

The new-style priesthoods were certainly extended to the cults of Neuserre and earlier kings by this period; I would guess still in the reign of Djedkare. Unfortunately no *rankable* occurrence of a *ḥm-nṯr* of a pyramid before Unis can be dated to this period, so that we cannot say to what extent they were influenced by the new rank of the *ḥm-nṯr*'s of the pyramid of Unis.

3. In Period V D/VI A the picture is a little clearer. At least some of the priesthoods of Neuserre, Menkauhor, and Djedkare have been adapted to the new pattern and outrank the title of vizier. As far as the documentation goes, only high-ranking titles are found for Menkauhor and Djedkare, the immediate predecessors of the reigning king, but for Neuserre the low ranking *ḥm-nṯr* of the king is also found. Possibly at this time the new priesthoods at the pyramid were all given high rank, regardless of the king concerned, while the old-style priesthoods of Neuserre (and the earlier kings) continued to be ranked rather low. It should be noted that the partial rise of these latter titles in V C was abandoned in V D, and they returned to the general vicinity of *wꜥb nswt*.

4. The data for Period VI B is particularly inadequate, but it seems to show that the priesthoods at the pyramid of Djedkare still held high rank. As the Sixth Dynasty advanced into Period VI C, however, the rank of the *ḥm-nṯr* of the pyramid of Djedkare was reduced to the general level of the priesthoods of the kings of the Fourth and Fifth Dynasties. Period VI E, which is relatively well documented, shows that even at this late date the priest at the pyramid of Djedkare was ranked rather higher than the priests at the pyramids of the earlier kings of the Fifth Dynasty. Incidentally, this is the only clear case of

similar titles at different establishments having a noticeably different rank. A priori, I would have expected such a phenomenon to have occurred more frequently, and it seems just possible that the case of tomb [360] could be due in part to such a differential ranking and not entirely the result of the fluctuation of *wꜥb nswt* at this period. The data is, however, completely inadequate to answer the question, and one can say little more than that in all other cases the grouping together of such similar titles was the most plausible, if not the only possible ranking.

For the purposes of our concluding chapter we shall take the following analysis of the facts as our point of departure:

Reign of Djedkare: introduction of the *ḥm-nṯr* of the royal pyramid.
Reign of Unis: change in the rank of officials bearing the new titles.
Reign of Mernere or early Pepi II: reduction of the rank of the *ḥm-nṯr* of the pyramids of the predecessors of Unis.

If this analysis is correct, the dates of the following tombs could be limited still further on the basis of high (above *ḥqꜣ ḥt*, *smr wꜥtj*) or low rank of *ḥm-nṯr*'s at the pyramids of Neuserre or earlier kings:

[9]	V C–D, VI B.
[173]	V D, VI B.
[288]	VI C–G.
[454]	VI C–G.

The occurrence of the (unique) title *jmj-rꜣ ḥmw-nṯr nw Bꜣ-Nfrjrkꜣrꜥ* in the tomb of *Ṯjj* [564] Period V C, in a low-ranking position warns us, however, that the *ḥm-nṯr* of the pyramids of kings *before* Neuserre are particularly poorly attested. There is no guarantee that the development outlined above, with those titles first rising in the time of Unis and then losing rank ever actually took place.

The argument from silence is a particularly dangerous one to use. The group of titles containing the element *ḫntj-š* is, however, sufficiently well attested that its use seems possible. It is hardly a new observation on my part that these titles seem to occur for the first time in the course of the Fifth Dynasty.* In view of the abundant documentation of these titles, it seemed worthwhile to try to establish the date of their introduction a little more precisely. The references for the various kinds of *ḫntj-š* at the pyramids are given in Table I in this chapter. They occur at the pyramids of the kings from Unis to Pepi II and are first documented in Period VI B ([197], [274]), though some uncertain cases

* Helck, *Untersuchungen*, pp. 107–8 is a recent treatment of these titles. The problem of the significance of these titles seems to me to be still far from solution, but this is not the place to attempt to solve it.

may be older. The various *ḫntj-š* not attached to a pyramid occur in the following tombs:

5, 15, 16, 18, 25A, 35A, 36, 37, 67, 76, 83, 84, 86, 110, 124, 125, 131, 134, 149, 172, 177A, 185, 187, 188, 195, 196, 203B, 247, 273, 273A, 277, 279, 280, 295, 305, 320, 322, 343, 347, 355, 356, 361, 365, 372, 378, 391, 393, 398, 403, 407, 413, 414, 416, 430A, 437, 443, 445, 449, 483, 501, 502, 539, 540B, 548, 552, 556, 557, 562, 563, 566, 581, 588, 590A, 601D.

The earliest securely dated examples are [548] and [372]. The former is definitely from V D, the latter cannot be later. In Period VI B we have [177A], [185], [187], [393], [563]. It might seem, therefore, that these titles made their first appearance in Period V D, perhaps under Unis, in which case this new department of the administration of royal domains and pyramid temples would have been instituted at about the same time as the change in ranking that we have just discussed.*

The following tombs can be dated more closely by the use of this observation:

[37] V D or later.
[124] V D, VI D–E.
[125] V D or later.
[295] V D or later.
[372] V D. This tomb is exactly dated and adds the sequence *rḫ nswt*, *ḫntj-š pr-ˁꜣ* to the chart for Period V D.
[391] VI B–C, E–G.
[416] VI B–C, E–G.
[443] V D or later.
[540B] V D or later.
[581] VI B, E–F.

* It should be noted, however, that the fragment from the Abusir Papyri reproduced by Borchardt, "*Ḫnt-kꜣw.ś*, die Stammutter der 5ten Dynastie," *ASAE*, vol. XXXVIII, pl. 29, as from the reign of Djedkare and thus not later than Period V C, shows the expression *ḫntj-š* in parallelism with *ḥm-nṯr*. It is thus possible that the title was introduced at that time. After all, one must allow a certain amount of time to pass between the introduction of a new title, as contrasted with a change in ranking patterns, and the first appearance of that title in a tomb.

Helck, "Bemerkungen zu den Pyramidenstädten im Alten Reich," *MDIAAK*, XV, 98, refers to the unpublished tomb of a *Kꜣ-m-wˁb* at Saqqara. He was a *sḥḏ ḫntj-š*, and, according to Helck, the tomb is dated to the fourth numbering of Neferirkare. This would be by far the earliest occurrence of such a title. I have asked Helck for further information, and he informs me:

> Das Grab . . . stammt wohl aus den Grabungen Selim Hassans. Die Datierung ist in der Tat nicht sicher. . . . Der Architrav beginnt mit "rnpt-sp 4" und dann folgen Titel, eingeleitet mit einem Amt bei der Pyramide (!) *Ḫˁ-bꜣ-Nfr-ỉr-kꜣ-Rˁ*.

It does not seem to me to follow that the dating refers to the reign of Neferirkare, and the location in the Unis-causeway area might militate against such an early date. Until more information becomes available, it seems wiser to ignore this example.

We now continue with a brief survey of some of the more obvious titles used in the provincial administration of Upper Egypt during the Fifth and Sixth Dynasties. Two titles connected with Upper Egypt have already been discussed. Of these the title *wr* 10 *Šmʿ* hardly seems to have indicated a practical function during the time we are studying—or perhaps it would be wiser to be more cautious: the title appears to be a part of the exceedingly common cluster of titles including *ẖrj-tp nswt* and *zꜣb ʿd-mr* and occurs quite frequently in the tombs of persons living at the capital who appear to have had no other connection with Upper Egypt. It is, of course, quite possible that they were members of a central board or group of councils supervising the administration of Upper Egypt from the capital and it is best not to be too dogmatic.

The other title is that of *jmj-rꜣ Šmʿ*. Unlike the former, it is a title of relatively high rank, outranking *sḏꜣwtj bjtj* in some periods. The usage of this title has been studied in detail by Kees and Goedicke, and there is no need to add anything to their discussion.* It is clear that the title was usually functional, *Wnj* [110] for instance exercising control over all of Upper Egypt. As late as the Koptos Decrees [602] we find clear cases of the bearer of the title exercising control of all twenty-two nomes, but it is equally clear that in other cases the title implied control over only a limited portion of Upper Egypt, according to Goedicke one of the three parts into which Upper Egypt was divided. The changes in the rank of this title can be followed in the charts in chapter v. The statement of Kees that *Rʿ-špss* [315] is the oldest known holder of the title is supported by our conclusions, which date his tomb into the first half of the reign of Djedkare in Period V B. However, it now seems likely that *Kꜣj* [505] and *Wnjs-ʿnḫ* [112] held this office in Period V C before *ꜣḫt-ḥtp* [13] and *Ptḥ-ḥtp* [161] in Period V D. But this is a minor point.

It is evident that the administration of Upper Egypt must have been of considerable complexity and involved many different kinds of officials, not all of which can be easily identified by the translation of the titles. We will restrict our attention to the titles found in the tombs of the nomarchs in Upper Egypt (it should be borne in mind, however, that every owner of a decorated tomb in Upper Egypt is not by that fact automatically to be considered a nomarch), to which can be added the tombs in the Memphite area in which similar titles are found. In the latter case, however, we need consider only those cases in which the function is specifically stated to have been exercised in the provinces.

* Kees, "Beiträge zur altägyptischen Provinzialverwaltung und der Geschichte des Feudalismus," *Nachr. Gött.*, Phil.-hist. Klasse, 1932, pp. 85–115; Goedicke, "Zu *ỉmj-rꜣ šmʿ* und *tp-šmʿ* im Alten Reich," *MIOF*, IV, 1–10.

Thus *Nswt-nfr* [292] at Giza states that he was *jmj-rꜣ wpt* in the eighth and tenth nomes of Upper Egypt. It does not follow that every holder of the title *jmj-rꜣ wpt* can be considered to have been a provincial administrator; the existence of such titles as *jmj-rꜣ wpt pr-ꜥꜣ*, *nt ꜥš*, *ḥtp-nṯr*, and at various pyramids, to give just a few examples,* shows that this does not follow.

The titles of the nomarchs fall into two groups. In general, persons with titles from one group do not hold titles in the other. The first is exemplified by the titles of *Nswt-nfr* [292], who was *jmj-rꜣ* of the *mnww*, *nswtjw*, *wpt*, *sšm-tꜣ*, and *ḥqꜣ ḥt-ꜥꜣt* in the eighth and tenth nomes of Upper Egypt or *Srf-kꜣ* [457] who was *jmj-rꜣ wpwt*, *jmj-rꜣ mnww*, *sšm-tꜣ*, and *jmj-rꜣ njwwt mꜣwt* in the fifteenth nome. The second group is very common in the Sixth Dynasty and comprises such titles as *jmj-rꜣ Šmꜥ*, *ḥrj-tp ꜥꜣ n spt*, or of a specific nome and *jmj-rꜣ ḥm-nṯr* (not of a specific god). The titles were recently discussed by Helck, who analyzes their development in some detail.† It is clear that the second group occurs, in general, at a later date than the first, but, as we shall show, the change occurred gradually, rather than at one time throughout Upper Egypt. As in the case of the priesthoods, we shall present the data in some detail. The presentation will be in the usual form of sequences, with a selection of the common titles treated previously for comparison. We select for discussion five titles from the first group and three from the second, which will be abbreviated as follows:

GROUP I:	*jmj-rꜣ wpt*	*MW*
	jmj-rꜣ mnww	*MMn*
	jmj-rꜣ njwwt mꜣwt	*MNM*
	jmj-rꜣ nswtjw	*MNst*
	sšm-tꜣ	*SšT*
GROUP II:	*jmj-rꜣ ḥm-nṯr*	*MḤN*
	jmj-rꜣ Šmꜥ	*MŠꜥ*
	ḥrj-tp ꜥꜣ (n spt)	*ḤTpꜥ(S)*

These titles will be listed whether they occur in rankable context or not. If the nome is added to the title, it will be indicated by the addition of its number in the canonic order in Roman numerals. Thus *ḤTpꜥ II* would be the *ḥrj-tp ꜥꜣ* of the nome of Edfu. The material is presented in geographic order from south to north. The numbers of all tombs at

* The examples are taken from the index of titles, Junker, *Giza*, XII, 167, and the table of royal priesthoods given earlier in this chapter.

† *Untersuchungen*, pp. 81–91, 125–27. I doubt that too much stress can be placed on the absence of the title *jmj-rꜣ ḥm-nṯr* in the tombs of some of the earlier nomarchs of the second group, as Helck does. There are really not enough cases to prove anything.

Upper Egyptian sites for which the collection contains ranking charts will be given, and if it contains "no titles" of the group listed above, the fact will be noted. The list follows. The date of the tomb is given in parentheses after the number.

1. ASWAN:

[39] (VI F): *MŠʿ*, *SW* and *H̱Ḥ*, *MŠʿ* (the latter perhaps an error; see p. 226).
[136] (VI G): no titles.
[345] (VI D): *Ḥʿ*, *MŠʿ*, *SB*.
[367] (Mernere to early Pepi II): no titles.
[373A] (Date? Possibly relatively early.): *SšT*, *RḪN*.
[384] (VI): no titles.
[433] (VI): no titles.
[575] (Mernere to early Pepi II): no titles.

It should be noted that none of the titles usually connected with the administration of a nome occurs at Aswan except in the case of [373A], which is a graffito. The titles held by the owners of these tombs tend to indicate conduct of foreign relations and expeditions rather than the local administration of Aswan, which is also supported by the descriptions of the careers of those officials as recorded in their biographies. Their activities ranged from Byblos to Punt and Nubia; the description of these tombs as belonging to nomarchs seems inappropriate.*

2. EDFU:

[62] (V D): *H̱TN*, *ḤTpʿS*.
[187] (VI B): *Ḥʿ*, *MŠʿ*, *SW*, *H̱Ḥ*, *ḤTpʿS*.
H̱Tpʿ II.
MḤN.
[344] (Pepi II or later): no titles.
[369] (VI or later): no titles.

3. EL-KAB:

[229] (Pepi I or later): no titles.
[593] (End VI—First Intermediate): *H̱Ḥ*, *MḤN*.

4. THEBES:

[59] (VI B–C, E): *H̱Ḥ*, *ḤTpʿS*.
[112A] (V D): *H̱TN*, *MŠʿ*.

5. KOPTOS:

[602] (VI G): *SB*, *MŠʿ*, *SW*, *H̱Ḥ*, *MḤN*.
[603] (Late): *SW*, *MŠʿ*, *MḤN* and *MḤN*, *MŠʿ*.

* In the meantime, Edel has written me that the title *ḥrj-tp ʿꜣ* does occur in recently discovered texts from Aswan.

6. DENDERA:

[34] (Date?): no titles.
[81] (VI C): *Ḥʿ, MŠʿ, SB, H̱Ḥ, ḤTpʿS.*
[82] (VI C, F): *ḤTpʿS.*
[177A] (VI B): no titles.
[272] (Pepi I or later): *Ḥʿ, MḤN, SW. ḤTpʿS.*
[563] (VI B): *H̱Ḥ, ḤTpʿS.*

7. EL-QASR WA'S-SAIYAD:

[83] (VI C, F): *MH̱ŠP, ḤTpʿS.*
[562] (VI C): *Ḥʿ, MŠʿ, SB, ḤTpʿS, SW, MḤN* and *SW, ḤTpʿS, H̱Ḥ* and *H̱Ḥ, ḤSPD, ḤTpʿS.*

8. ABYDOS:

[27] (VI B–C, E–F): no titles.
[73A] (VI E–F): *ḤTN, MŠʿ.*
[110] (VI C): *Ḥʿ, MŠʿ, ḤTN.*
[135] (VI C): *Ḥʿ, MŠʿ, SW.*
[137] (VI B–C, F–G): *Ḥʿ, MŠʿ, H̱ḤḤT.*
[225] (VI C–G): no titles.
[273A] (Pepi I or later): no titles.
[296] (VI?): no titles.
[366] (Pepi II): no titles.
[472] (VI?): no titles.
[591] (VI D): no titles.

Some of the persons marked "no titles" did hold titles that may have reflected a minor post in the provincial administration, but it is astonishing that in this cemetery, the major cemetery of the Thinite Nome, nobody who could be considered to have been a nomarch was ever buried. This is all the more surprising since the nomarchs of the nome are well attested both at Deir el-Gebrawi (Twelfth Nome) and at Memphis (for the latter see Fischer, "Four Provincial Administrators at the Memphite Cemeteries," *JAOS*, LXXIV, 26–34). As is pointed out by Fischer, pp. 32–33, Abydos seems to have been the center of the administration of Upper Egypt and retained close links with the capital, which were reinforced by the close relationship of the local family of magnates to the Sixth Dynasty.

9. HAGARSA:

[524] (V?): *WN, MNst.*

10. AKHMIM:

[85] (VI B–C, F): *RH̱N, MW.*

[129] (VI or later): *SW*, *MḤN*.
H̱Ḥ, *ḤTpʿ* IX.
[138] (VI B, D–F): *H̱TN*, *MW*.
[340] (VI or later): *Ḥʿ*, *MḤN*.
[341] (VI or later): no titles.
[342] (VI B, E): *Ḥʿ*, *MMn*, *MNM*, *SW*, *H̱TN*, *MW*.
[396] (VI or later): *SB*, *MḤN*, *ḤTpʿ* IX, *H̱TN*.
[498] (VI or later): no titles.
[541] (VI or later): *SW*, *MḤN*, *ḤTpʿ* IX.
[554] (VI or later): no titles.
[555] (VI B, D–F): *H̱TN*, *MW*.

11. HEMAMIA:

[543] (V B): *WMŠ*, *MW*, *MMn*.
MW, *WN*.
[543A] (V B): *MW*, *RḪN*.
MMn.
MNst.

12. DEIR EL-GEBRAWI:

[32] (VI D): *ḪŠN*, *MŠʿ*, *MŠn*, *SW*, *ḤTpʿ* VIII, *ḤTpʿ* XII and *ḤTpʿ* VIII, *ḤTpʿ* XII, *MŠʿ*.
[323] (Late): *Ḥʿ*, *MŠʿ*, *SW*, *ḤS*, *ḤTpʿ* XII.
[324] (Late): *H̱Ḥ*, *ḤTpʿ* XII.
[333] (Late): *H̱Ḥ*, *ḤTpʿ* XII.
[592] (VI F): *SB*, *MŠʿ*, *ḤTpʿ* VIII, *ḤTpʿ* XII, *ḤqḤ*, *H̱Ḥ* and *H̱Ḥ*, *ḤTpʿ* VIII, *ḤTpʿ* XII.

13. DARA:

[338] (End VI or later): *SW*, *MḤN*, *H̱Ḥ*.

14. MEIR and QOSEIR EL-AMARNA:

[132] (VI D): *H̱Ḥ*, *MḤN*.
[133] (VI E): *H̱Ḥ*, *MŠʿ*, *H̱TN*, *MḤN*.
[134] (VI F): *SB*, *MŠʿ*, *SW*, *ḤTpʿ* XIII + XIV.
SW, *H̱Ḥ*, *MḤN*.
[177] (VI): no titles.
[212] (VI C): *Ḥʿ*, *MŠʿ*, *SB*, *H̱Ḥ*, *MḤN*.
[213] (VI C if same as last): *H̱Ḥ*, *MḤN*.

15. SHEIKH ATIYA:

[278] (VI?): *WN*, *MḤN*.

16. SHEIKH SAID:

[106] (VI C): *Ḥʿ*, *MŠʿ*, *SW*, *ḤTpʿ* XV.

[114] (V C): *RḪN*, *MW* (XV), *SšT* (XV).
MNM (XV).
[192] (VI E): *ḪŠN*, *MŠ*ʿ, *ẖTN*, *MNM*. (Note titles from both groups.)
[457] (V C): *RḪN*, *MW*.
MMn.
SšT XV.
MNM.
[561] (Pepi I or later): *MNM*.

17. ZAWIYET EL-MAIYITIN:

[69] (Pepi I or later): no titles.
[122] (VI?): *MW*.
MMn.
MNst.
SšT XVI.
[196] (Pepi I or later): no titles.
[211] (Pepi I or later): no titles.
[383] (V C, VI B–C): *RḪN*, *MW* (XVI), *SšT* (XVI), *MḤN* (XVI). (Note titles from both groups.)
[490A] (Pepi I or later): no titles.

18. TIHNA:

[237] (Early, V B): *RḪN*, *MNM* and *MNM*, *RḪN*.
[397] (VI C–D): no titles.

Some of the tombs at Tihna are the earliest inscribed tombs known from Upper Egypt. Our [237] is one of them. The title *jmj-rꜣ njwwt mꜣwt* alone, however, does not suffice to make him a nomarch. To judge from the texts in his tomb, he rather seems to have been the head of a wealthy local family with some administrative, and, in particular, priestly functions.

19. KOM EL-AHMAR SAWARIS:

[131] (VI C): *Ḥ*ʿ, *MŠ*ʿ, *ẖḤḤT*.
SB, *MW*, *ḤqḤ*.

20. DESHASHA:

[44] (VI C): *RḪN*, *MW*, *MMn nswt*, *SšT*.
MMn nswt, *ḤqḤ*.
[73] (VI D or later): *MR*, *MMn nswt*. (Conflicts with above.)

21. SEDMENT:

[188] (Late VI): no titles.
[281] (VI): no titles.

None of the titles in these two tombs could be connected with the nome administration.

22. MEMPHIS:

Here, of course, we list only those tombs containing titles clearly stated to be connected with the administration of a nome. The examples have been discussed much more fully than we can here by Fischer in the article already mentioned above.

[264] (Probably Early or V B if correctly identified by Fischer): *RḪN*, *MW* VIII.
[292] (Early): *MMn* (VIII), *MNst* (VIII), *MW* (VIII).
MW (X), *MMn* (X), *MNst* (X).
Note the fluctuating ranking, which one would expect in a tomb as early as this one.
[293] (Early): *MW* V, VI and VII.
[370] (Pepi II): *Ḥʿ*, *ḤTpʿ* VIII.
[371] (Pepi II): *MḤN*, *ḤTpʿ* VIII.
[556] (VI B, D–E, G): *H̱Ḥ*, *ḤTpʿ* VIII, *MḤN*.

The designation "no titles" refers, of course, only to the eight titles given at the head of the list. In most of the tombs some titles are found that can be connected with the administration of the nome; but there is no reason to think that the persons holding them ever headed the administration.

On the next pages, we present a series of ranking charts for the titles in the provincial administration. They were drawn up in the usual fashion from the securely dated examples. One tomb, number [342], could be dated to Period VI B on the basis of the ranking of the provincial titles. Tomb [338] was relegated to the First Intermediate Period. In a few other cases it would have been possible to eliminate several periods, but since for many of them the First Intermediate Period, for which we have no charts, is to be considered a very likely possibility, it hardly seemed worthwhile to prepare a detailed listing. Indeed, if [342] had not contained titles from the earlier group, it would hardly have seemed justifiable to exclude a dating in the First Intermediate Period as a possibility. In view of the extremely uncertain dating of the cemetery at Akhmim, it seemed best not to include the data from [342] in the ranking chart for Period V B in chapter v. We have, however, done so here.

One could hardly claim that these sequences were extravagantly well documented, and our conclusions must, of course, remain relatively uncertain as a result.

First of all, it is clear that the two groups of titles cannot be rigidly separated. The older group occurs from the period preceding V B to VI E, the younger group (in Upper Egyptian tombs) from V D to VI G and into the First Intermediate Period. That the two groups cannot be rigidly separated is also clear in the case of the few tombs (from Middle Egypt) that have some titles from each. This is only to be expected. *Jmj-rꜣ Šmꜥ* was certainly introduced in Period V B, and there is no inherent reason that it should have been grouped with *ḥrj-tp ꜥꜣ* when that title was first introduced in V D. Actually it is the title *ḥrj-tp ꜥꜣ* that is diagnostic for the later group of titles. The appearance of this title reflects a fundamental change in the administration of Upper Egypt and the culmination of a trend that appears to have brought about the introduction of the title *jmj-rꜣ Šmꜥ* a generation earlier.

It is customary to call the holders of titles in the first group nomarchs. In the strict sense of the word that is, I think, unwarranted. Helck has already recognized that they actually are officials who have gathered in one hand the administration of several local offices that were originally administered as separate branches of a centralized government.* This is borne out by several other facts. We have already pointed out above that an *jmj-rꜣ wpt* could also be concerned with other sections of the administration than nomes. The same holds true for *jmj-rꜣ njwwt mꜣwt*, which can be used to refer to an official of a pyramid temple.† The existence of the title *jmj-rꜣ sšm-tꜣ* of a nome shows that there could be more than one *sšm-tꜣ* to a nome; translating the title as "nomarch" seems therefore to me to be unjustified. Incidentally, such passages as *Urkunden*, I, 280, in the address of the rescript of Pepi II show that in the Sixth Dynasty there could be more than one *ḥrj-tp* to a nome. It is only the *ḥrj-tp ꜥꜣ* who seems in all cases to be an official actually heading the administration of a nome; only this title should therefore be translated "nomarch."

To return to the older group of titles, we can posit an original administration of Upper Egypt divided into several branches, each centrally administered and with its representative(s) in the nome. However, by the beginning of the Fifth Dynasty we see clearly that certain individuals already held titles from all the important branches of the local administration. The organization was evidently changing from one based on different fields of administration, such as the fortresses or the *nswtjw* (whatever that class of persons may have been) to one based on geographical divisions. It was this development, to my mind, that brought about the creation of the office of *jmj-rꜣ Šmꜥ*, a governor controlling a geographical area administered by officials in charge of each nome. The latter were thus, for all practical purposes, nomarchs, but instead of holding a distinctive title they simply were the local representatives of each branch of the administration in their

* *Untersuchungen*, p 81. † See title No. 24 in Table I of this chapter.

PERIOD V B

SOURCES: 543, 543A.

wr 10 *Šmꜥ*

jmj-rꜣ wpt

rḫ nswt ~ *wꜥb nswt*   *jmj-rꜣ mnww*

PERIOD V C

SOURCES: 114, 457.

rḫ nswt

jmj-rꜣ wpt

sšm-tꜣ

PERIOD V D

SOURCES: 62, 112A.

ẖrj-tp nswt

ḥrj-tp ꜥꜣ   *jmj-rꜣ Šmꜥ*

PERIOD VI B

SOURCES: 187, 342, 563.

ḥꜣtj-ꜥ

jmj-rꜣ mnww

jmj-rꜣ Šmꜥ

jmj-rꜣ njwwt mꜣwt

smr wꜥtj

ẖrj-ḥbt

ḥrj-tp ꜥꜣ   *ẖrj-tp nswt*

mj-rꜣ wpt

PERIOD VI C

SOURCES: 44, 81, 106, 110, 131, 135, 212, 213, 562.

ḥꜣtj-ꜥ

jmj-rꜣ Šmꜥ

sḏꜣwtj bjtj

jmj-rꜣ wpt

jmj-rꜣ mnww nswt

sšm-tꜣ

ḥqꜣ ḥt

smr wꜥtj

ẖrj-ḥbt   } *ḥrj-tp ꜥꜣ*

jmj-rꜣ ḥm-nṯr   *ḥrj-sštꜣ pr dwꜣt*

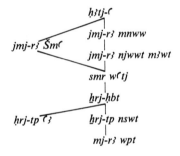

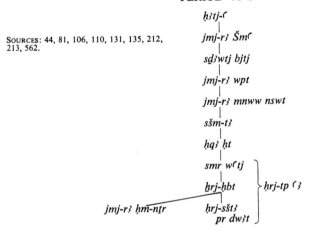

PERIOD VI D

ḥꜣtj-ʿ
|
ḫrp šndwt nbt
|
jmj-rꜣ Šmʿ ⎫
|
jmj-rꜣ šnwtj ⎪
|
sḏꜣwtj bjtj ⎬ *ḥrj-tp ʿꜣ*
|
smr wʿtj ⎭
|
ḫrj-ḥbt
|
jmj-rꜣ ḥm-nṯr

Sources: 32, 132, 345.

PERIOD VI E

smr wʿtj
|
ḫrj-ḥbt
|
jmj-rꜣ Šmʿ
|
ẖrj-tp nswt
|
jmj-rꜣ ḥm-nṯr — *jmj-rꜣ njwwt mꜣwt*

Sources: 133, 192.

PERIOD VI F

sḏꜣwtj bjtj
|
jmj-rꜣ Šmʿ
|
ḥqꜣ ḥt ⎫
|
smr wʿtj ⎬ *ḥrj-tp ʿꜣ*
|
ḫrj-ḥbt ⎭
|
jmj-rꜣ ḥm-nṯr

Sources: 39, 134, 592.

PERIOD VI G

sḏꜣwtj bjtj
|
jmj-rꜣ Šmʿ
|
smr wʿtj
|
ḫrj-ḥbt
|
jmj-rꜣ ḥm-nṯr

Source: 602.

nome. The titles of these provincial governors were of low rank and the title *jmj-r3 Šmʿ* also was not too high at the beginning. With the passage of time and the growing independence of the provincial authorities, both tend to rise in rank, with *jmj-r3 Šmʿ* staying slightly ahead.

TABLE VI

Place	Period										
	Early	V B	V C	V D	VI B	VI C	VI D	VI E	VI F	VI G	Late
Aswan	I(?)						II		II		
Edfu				II	II						
El-Kab											II
Thebes				II				II			
Koptos	I									II	II
Dendera	I				II	II			II		
El-Qasr wa's-Saiyad	I(?)					II			II		
Abydos	I					II	II		II	II	
Hagarsa		I(?)									
Akhmim					I						II
Hemamia	I	I									
Deir el-Gebrawi							II		II		
Dara											II
Meir						II	II	II	II		
Sheikh Atiya											II
Sheikh Said			I		I	II		I/II			
Zawiyet el-Maiyitin			I		I(?)						
Tihna	I										
Kom el-Ahmar						I/II					
Deshasha						I	I				

In Period V D, we find for the first time a new title, the *ḥrj-tp ʿ3* of a nome. This is a formal recognition on the part of the central government of the new state of affairs. As we stated above, the two kinds of provincial administration persisted side by side for a considerable time. If we make a table of the occurrences of titles from the two groups in the various nomes at various times, we can see the course of the change more clearly. Table VI is based on the data just presented and on the securely dated examples. A Roman I or II indicates from which group titles are found in each period. If titles from both groups occur, we write I/II and do this also in the case of tombs containing titles from both groups. In view of the structure of the table, it hardly seemed necessary to repeat the references. Titles are entered under the place at which they occur, with offices in the Thinite Nome being entered under Abydos, this being the main cemetery of the nome. Material of uncertain date is entered under the earliest possibility for Group I, the latest for Group II.

The evidence is undoubtedly not as clear or as copious as one could wish, but I think it emerges quite clearly from this chart that the change from the older style of provincial title to the newer proceeded from south to north with the passage of time. We can, I think, distinguish three areas: the southernmost one, in which the new titles were introduced in Period V D; a central district, in which they do not appear until Period VI C; and a northern one, in which the older group seems to have continued in use, though occasionally mixed with the title *jmj-r3 Šmʿ* from the younger one, until the end of the Old Kingdom. We have indicated on the chart by heavy ruling the points at which the changes took place. Evidently, too much stress should not be placed on the details in view of the rather limited quantity of data at our disposal. The triple division of Upper Egypt thus obtained calls to mind the three districts of Upper Egypt pointed out by Goedicke.* The agreement is not perfect, our border line being in each case one nome farther south than his. But this may well be the fault of our own inadequate documentation. A detailed study of the provincial titles alone might easily improve the picture, but in the framework of this study it was hardly feasible to attempt to analyze more than the commonest titles in tombs presenting at least a certain minimum of rankable title sequences.

We began with the statement that in Period V D, about the time of Teti, it was felt necessary to formalize the status of the growing class of nomarchs by creating a new title. We see now that this was instituted at first only for those parts of Egypt farthest from the capital and thus least amenable to a centralized administration, where the need for a governor responsible for all branches of administration and able to act with a certain amount of autonomy would be felt most acutely. It was apparently deemed advisable to keep up the pretense of centralized

* "Zu *imj-r3 šmʿ* und *tp-šmʿ* im Alten Reich," *MIOF*, IV, 7–9.

control—or possibly even the reality—in the more northerly nomes. Eventually, perhaps as a result of the marriage of Pepi I into a family of magnates from Abydos, the administrators of the central nomes of Upper Egypt were also enabled to acquire a more independent position, while in the areas nearest the capital, the centralized administration was maintained.

The increasing area (and presumably influence and power) of the newer nomarchies is reflected in the ranking of the titles. When introduced, the title *ḥrj-tp ꜥꜣ* ranked below the older titles. The bearers of this new title did, however, have a much higher rank than that customary for provincial administrators of the older type; this was obtained by granting them, as a general rule, titles of the order of *ḥꜣtj-ꜥ* and *jrj-pꜥt*. They were also quite frequently appointed *jmj-rꜣ Šmꜥ*. The possibly fictitious nature of the retention of the older, more centralized system in the northern nomes is underlined by the fact that this practice is soon followed by the administrators of these nomes who still held titles of the older group. Thus [342] in Akhmim in Period VI B is *jrj-pꜥt* and *tꜣtj zꜣb ṯꜣtj*, and in the northernmost group of nomes similar high-ranking titles are documented from Period VI C onward.

With the increasing power of the nomarchs, the titles concerned began to rise. The reader can follow the progression in our charts. The high point was reached in Period VI D, at which time the rank of *ḥrj-tp ꜥꜣ*, which seems to have caused the scribes some trouble to judge by the not uncommon fluctuation of this title within one tomb, is even found on occasion to exceed that of *jmj-rꜣ Šmꜥ*, a rather anomalous situation. Apparently things had gone a bit too far, or perhaps there was reassertion of the central authority; in any case, in Period VI E the rank of the titles is suddenly lowered quite drastically. They soon resume their rise, however, but on a more modest scale. The Koptos Decrees [602] show that the central government still had a considerable amount of control over Upper Egyptian affairs at the end of the Eighth Dynasty, though it certainly had to take cognizance of the desires of the local magnates.

Appendix: List of Dated Tombs

We present here a complete list of all the tombs which could be dated within reasonably close limits. The list gives the number of the tomb, the name of the owner, and the date. If a tomb has been assigned in chapter v to one of the nine periods or to the early or late period, it is marked simply by giving the period indication. If the assignment to the early or late periods is the result of a violation of the standard sequences, the dating is also marked: (viol.). If the dating is based also on the results of chapter vi, we use the appropriate indications: (priest), (*ḫntj-š*), or (nomes). Tombs are also included if a reasonably close dating was possible on the basis of the facts adduced in chapter iii, even if they did not contain enough characteristic title sequences to permit a dating on the basis of the titles. In that case the dating is in terms of dynasties and reigns. When it was not possible to assign a tomb to a definite period, it was only included if the data was adequate to permit a dating to a restricted range of time. The elimination of one or two periods leaving still a range of four or five scattered datings equally probable hardly seemed to warrant inclusion here. Of course, the overwhelming majority of tombs originally discarded because they contained only uncommon titles or standard title sequences have not been listed here. In a few cases the dating obtained differs markedly from that given in chapter iii; we will comment briefly on them.

[3]	*ꜣḫj*	Menkaure (chap. iii).
[6]	*ꜣḫt-ḥtp*	Early (chap. iii).
[7]	*ꜣḫt-ḥtp*	Khafre (chap. iii).
[8]	*ꜣḫt-ḥtp*	VI G.
[9]	*ꜣḫt-ḥtp*	V C to VI B (priest).
[13]	*ꜣḫt-ḥtp*	V D.
[14]	*ꜣḫt-ḥtp*	VI E.
[16]	*Jꜣzn*	VI E. Our dating here is considerably later than that proposed by Reisner, but the archeological data seemed to indicate that his date was too early; there was no way of predicting that it would come out as late as it did.
[18]	*Jjj*	VI D to VI E.
[21]	*Jj-mrjj*	Early, probably Neferirkare. This dating is somewhat earlier than expected. I had proposed, in agreement with Reisner (who, incidentally does not state his reasons), a dating in the time of Neuserre. This was in part due to the fact that his brother-in-law [66] had a tomb that was certainly to be dated at least to that period (in its final form) and that from Lepsius' plans I had the impression that the two had been planned as a unit. I have inquired from Dr. W. S. Smith in Boston, who informs me that there can be no question that the complex chapels around the original mastabas of *Jj-mrjj* and *Jtj* [66] were planned and built as a unit. It is, of course, still possible to explain the ten years' difference in dating that we obtained by assuming that some time intervened between the building and decoration of the chapel of [66].

[22]	*Jj-mrjj*	VI D to VI E.
[24]	*Jj-nfrt*	V C or VI C.
[25]	*Jj-kꜣ*	V B.
[26]	*Jj-ḏfꜣ*	Early (? viol.); early Fifth Dynasty seems most probable.
[29]	*Jwnw*	Khufu (chap. iii).
[30]	*Jwn-Mn*	Early (viol.); probably end Fourth (chap. iii).
[31]	*Jwn-Rꜥ*	Early (viol.); probably end Fourth (chap. iii).
[32]	*Jbj*	VI D.
[38]	*Jnj*	Khufu (chap. iii).
[39]	*Jn-jt.f* and *Sꜣbnj*	VI F.
[44]	*Jntj*	VI C.
[48]	*Jr.n-ꜣḫt*	V D.
[55]	*Jḥꜣ*	VI D to VI E. A little later than suggested in chap. iii.
[57]	*Jḥj*	VI C. Rather later than I supposed. The relative order of the mastabas in this portion of the Unis cemetery is maintained, but the construction seems to have covered a much longer span of time than I had guessed. Of course, there is nothing in the published data that would not permit a later date.
[61]	*Jḫj*	Pepi II, around the thirty-third numbering (chap. iii).
[62]	*Jzj*	V D. A bit earlier than supposed. This has already been discussed in chap. v.
[64]	*Jzzj-ꜥnḫ*	V C. Reign of Djedkare.
[66]	*Jtj*	V B. Reign of Neuserre.
[70]	*Jtj-sn*	V B to V C.
[73]	*Jttj: Šdw*	VI D to VI F (nomes). He was a son of [44], which sets the lower limit.
[73A]	*Jdj*	VI E to VI F.
[74]	*Jdj: Tp-m-kꜣw*	VI D.
[77]	*Jdw*	VI C.
[81]	*Jdw*	VI C.
[82]	*Jdw*	VI C or VI F.
[83]	*Jdw: Snnj*	VI C or VI F.
[86]	*ꜥnḫj*	VI E to VI G.
[88]	*ꜥnḫ-jr.s*	V B if not early.
[91]	*ꜥnḫ-m-ꜥ-Rꜥ*	Early; probably end Fourth (chap. iii).
[95]	*ꜥnḫ-m-ꜥ-kꜣj*	VI C.
[99]	*ꜥnḫ-ḥꜣ.f*	Khafre (chap. iii).
[100]	*ꜥnḫ-ḥꜣ.f: Qꜣr*	VI C.
[103]	*Wꜣš-Ptḥ*	V B to V D. Possibly later.
[104]	*Wꜣš-Ptḥ*	Early; probably end Fourth or early Fifth Dynasties.
[105]	*Wꜣš-Ptḥ: Jzj*	V B. Reign of Neferirkare.

[106]	*Wjw: Jjjw*	VI C.
[108]	*Wp-m-nfrt*	Khufu (chap. iii).
[109]	*Wp-m-nfrt: Wp*	V C.
[110]	*Wnj*	VI C. Reign of Mernere.
[111]	King *Wnjs*	V D. Reign of Unis.
[112]	*Wnjs-ʿnḫ*	V C. This fits the date assigned to it in chap. iii, but the tomb of *Jḥj* [57] was built against it after a greater lapse of time than we had supposed.
[112A]	*Wnjs-ʿnḫ*	V D. Hardly the same person as the above.
[114]	*Wr-jr.n.j*	V C.
[115]	*Wr-jr.n-Ptḥ*	V B.
[118]	*Wr-ḫww*	V C.
[121]	*Wḥꜣ*	VI D or VI F (if not First Intermediate).
[123A]	*Wsrkꜣf-ʿnḫ*	Early; reign of Sahure. Our judgment was badly at fault here in accepting the identification of the owner of this tomb with the person of the same name in the mortuary temple of Neuserre. Borchardt's early dating on the basis of the odd plan of that temple is obviously correct. It is of some interest to note that a king of Egypt allowed the existence of an older tomb of a private individual on the site chosen for his pyramid to influence the plan.
[126]	*Bꜣ-kꜣ*	Early; probably end Fourth (chap. iii).
[128]	*Bb-jb*	V B.
[131]	*Ppij-ʿnḫ: Ḫwj*	VI C.
[132]	*Ppjj-ʿnḫ*	VI D.
[133]	*Ppjj-ʿnḫ ḥrj-jb*	VI E.
[134]	*Ppjj-ʿnḫ: Ḫnj km*	VI F.
[135]	*Ppjj-nḫt*	VI C.
[136]	*Ppjj-nḫt: Ḥqꜣ-jb*	VI G.
[138]	*Ppjj-snb: Sn-jfd*	VI B. This depends on our rather shaky conclusions about the date at which the provincial titles changed. It usually seemed safer not to use them to date tombs for which no other indication of date was available—particularly if the First Intermediate Period is also a possibility for dating. We have here allowed ourselves to be swayed by the name—a most risky proceeding. Periods VI D to VI F are also possible.
[140]	*Pn-mrw*	V D.
[142]	*Pr-nb*	V C. Thus decorated a little later than the tomb of his father.
[143]	*Pr-sn*	Early (viol.); probably early Fifth (chap. iii).
[144]	*Pr-sn*	Sahure (chap. iii).

[146]	*Pḥ.n-w-kꜣ*	V B.
[153]	*Ptḥ-mr-Mrjjrꜥ*	VI B. The twenty-first numbering (year?) of Pepi I (chap. iii).
[154]	*Ptḥ-m-ḥꜣt*	VI G.
[155]	*Ptḥ-nb-nfrt*	V C.
[156]	*Ptḥ-ḥtp*	V D or VI G.
[157]	*Ptḥ-ḥtp*	Userkaf (chap. iii).
[158]	*Ptḥ-ḥtp*	V B (?).
[159]	*Ptḥ-ḥtp dšr*	V B (?).
[160]	*Ptḥ-ḥtp*	V C.
[161]	*Ptḥ-ḥtp*	V D.
[163]	*Ptḥ-ḥtp*	V C (?).
[164]	*Ptḥ-špss*	V B. Reign of Neuserre.
[167]	*Ptḥ-špss*	V D.
[168]	*Ptḥ-špss*	VI C (priest of Ptah).
[170]	*Mꜣ-nfr*	VI B.
[171]	*Mꜣ-nfr*	VI F.
[173]	*Mn-ꜥnḫ*	V D to VI B (priest).
[174]	*Mn-ḫꜥ.f*	Early (viol.); probably Khafre to Menkaure (chap. iii).
[175]	*Mn-ḏd.f*	Early (viol.); probably Menkaure (chap. iii).
[177A]	*Mn-ꜥnḫ-Ppjj*	VI B. The statement originally made by Petrie, and repeated by Fischer in "Four Provincial Administrators at the Memphite Cemeteries," *JAOS*, LXXIV, 33, n. 61, that the name indicates a dating at least to the reign of Pepi II because the name is identical with the name of the pyramid of that monarch, does not seem to me to be tenable. It rests on the unproved assumption that the name was given with the name of a pyramid in mind. To my knowledge, it would be a unique case of a person named after a pyramid; the argument could just as well be turned into its opposite—the identity of the name with that of the pyramid of Pepi II indicates an earlier date.
[180]	*Mrjj*	Mid-Fourth (chap. iii).
[182]	*Mr-jb*	Early (viol.); probably early Fifth (chap. iii).
[184]	*Mrjjrꜥ-jꜣm*	VI C to VI E.
[185]	*Mrjjrꜥ-ꜥnḫ*	VI B.
[187]	*Mrjjrꜥ-nfr: Qꜣr*	VI B. Reign of Mernere.
[189]	*Mrjj-Ttj*	VI C.
[192]	*Mrw: Bbj*	VI E. Thus clearly the son of [106].
[197]	*Mrrw-kꜣ*	VI B. Probably still reign of Teti.
[202]	*Mḥw*	VI E. Again somewhat later than expected. See above under [57].
[203]	*Ms-zꜣ*	V B to V C.

[203B] *Mṯṯj*	Teti (chap. iii).
[212] *N-ꜥnḫ-Ppjj: Sbk-ḥtp: Ḥpj km*	VI C.
[213] *N-ꜥnḫ-Ppjj km*	VI C (if same person as the last).
[215] *N-ꜥnḫ-Rꜥ*	Early (viol. and by other sequences); probably early Fifth (chap. iii).
[221] *N-ꜥnḫ-Sḫmt*	Sahure (chap. iii).
[222] *N-wsr-Rꜥ*	End Fourth (chap. iii).
[223] King *N-wsr-Rꜥ*	V B. Reign of Neuserre.
[229A] *N-ḥb-sd-Nfrkꜣrꜥ*	VI G.
[235] *N-sw-sꜥnḫ*	VI B or VI G.
[237] *N-kꜣ-ꜥnḫ*	Userkaf or at most a few reigns later (chap. iii).
[241] *N-kꜣw-Rꜥ*	End Fourth (chap. iii).
[246] *Nb-*[. . .]	VI E.
[247] *Nbj*	VI D or VI G.
[248] *Nb-m-ꜣḫt*	Early (viol.); probably end Fourth (chap. iii).
[249] *Nb-kꜣw-ḥr*	V C. Considering the early date, it seems likely that the string of titles on which the dating was based goes back to the original decoration for the first owner of this mastaba [14A] rather than the man who usurped. In the absence of a detailed publication, however, it is impossible to tell for sure.
[250] *Nfr*	Early or V B; probably early Fifth (chap. iii).
[251] *Nfr*	VI D. The date is somewhat later than expected, but hardly catastrophically so.
[254] *Nfrj*	V C.
[257] *Nfr-jḥj*	VI B or VI G.
[258] *Nfr-bꜣw-Ptḥ*	V B. Reign of Neuserre? The later dating proposed in ch. iii depended entirely on the excessively late date proposed for his father. See [21].
[260] *Nfr-mꜣꜥt*	Early (viol.); probably early Fourth (chap. iii).
[262] *Nfr-mꜣꜥt*	Khafre to Menkaure (chap. iii).
[263] *Nfrt-nswt*	V C.
[267] *Nfr-ḥr-n-Ptḥ: Ffj*	V C (priest).
[274] *Nfr-ssm-Rꜥ: Ššj*	VI B.
[275] *Nfr-ssm-Sšꜣt: Ḫnw*	VI C or VI E.
[275A] *Nfr-ssm-Sšꜣt: Sꜥnḫ-Ptḥ-Ppjj: Ššj*	Late.
[279] King *Nfr-kꜣ-Rꜥ: Ppjj* II	VI F.
[282] *Nn-ḫft-kꜣj*	V B.
[285] *Nḥrj*	VI E to VI G.
[286] *Nḫbw*	VI B. Reign of Pepi I.

[286A–B]	*Ptḥ-mr-ꜥnḫ-Ppjj* *Sꜣbw-Ptḥ: Jbbj*	Late (viol. and disagrees with the sequences). These individuals cannot be the sons of [286], who had the same names, unless we assume that the scribe made a serious error in the inscriptions on the coffin—which might not be too unlikely in view of the uncertain ownership and other problems raised by the texts. If the texts are correct, they would have to be at least the great-grandchildren of [286].
[287]	*Nḫtj*	Tenth Dynasty (chap. iii).
[292]	*Nswt-nfr*	Early; presumably early Fifth.
[293]	*Nṯr-ꜥpr.f*	Early (viol.); presumably Fourth (chap. iii).
[294]	*Nṯr-wsr*	V B. Presumably the father of [315] rather than his son. Date approximately Menkauhor or early Djedkare.
[297]	*Rꜥ-wr*	V B.
[298]	*Rꜥ-wr*	V B to V C. Reign of Djedkare or early Unis (chap. iii).
[300]	*Rꜥ-wr*	V B. Reign of Neferirkare or slightly later (chap. iii).
[303]	*Rꜥ-m-kꜣj*	V B. The presence of the name *Jzzj* without a cartouche in one of his estate-names would suggest a date near the end of this period, perhaps before the accession of Djedkare.
[307]	*Rꜥ-ḥtp*	Early (viol.); presumably early Fourth (chap. iii).
[309]	*Rꜥ-ḥtp*	VI B.
[315]	*Rꜥ-špss*	V B. Reign of Djedkare.
[323]	*Hnqw: H̱ttj*	Late. Cf. [324].
[324]	*Hnqw: Jj-*[. . .]*f*	Late (viol.); this tomb is earlier than [323].
[331]	*Ḥm-Jwnw*	Early (viol.); reign of Khufu (chap. iii).
[332]	*Ḥmw*	V D.
[333]	*Ḥm-Rꜥ: Jzj*	Late (viol.); contemporary with [324].
[338]	*Ḥnnj*	Late (nomes).
[338A]	*Ḥn-kꜣ*	V B to V C.
[342]	*Ḥrwj*	VI B (nomes).
[345]	*Ḥr-ḫw.f*	VI D.
[350]	*Ḥknj-H̱nmw*	VI G.
[356]	*Ḥtp.n-Ptḥ*	V D to VI B.
[360]	*Ḫꜥ-bꜣw-Ptḥ*	VI E.
[361]	*Ḫꜥ-bꜣw-H̱nmw: Bjw*	VI F.
[363]	*Ḫꜥ-mrr-Ptḥ*	V B.
[364]	*Ḫwj*	Tenth Dynasty (chap. iii).
[367]	*Ḫwj*	Mernere to early Pepi II (chap. iii).
[372]	*Ḫwfw-ꜥnḫ*	V D (*ḫntj-š*).
[375]	*Ḫwfw-ḫꜥ.f*	Mid-Fourth to end Fourth (chap. iii).
[376]	*Ḫwfw-ḫꜥ.f*	V B. Reign of Neuserre.

[383]	*Ḫw-ns*	V C or VI B to VI C.
[386]	*Ḫmt.nw*	Early; presumably end Fourth (chap. iii).
[393]	*Ḫntj-kȝ: Jḫḫj*	VI B. Reign of Pepi I.
[394]	*Ḫnt-kȝw-Ḥr*	VI D or VI F.
[397]	*H̱nw-kȝ*	VI C to VI D.
[399]	*H̱nmw-bȝ.f*	Early (viol.); presumably early Fifth (chap. iii).
[400]	*H̱nmw-bȝ.f*	End Fourth to early Fifth (chap. iii).
[402]	*H̱nm-ntj*	V D. Reign of Teti.
[406]	*H̱nmw-ḥtp*	V D.
[411]	*Zwf*	VI B.
[415]	*Zzj*	Pepi I (chap. iii).
[418]	*Zṯw*	V C.
[421]	*Sȝbw: Jbbj*	VI B. Reign of Teti.
[426]	*Sʿnḫw-Ptḥ*	V D.
[435]	*Smȝ-ʿnḫ*	Late.
[436]	*Smnḫw-Ptḥ: Jtwš*	Djedkare (chap. iii).
[437]	*Smdntj* (?)	VI D to VI E.
[444]	*Snbw-kȝ*	Early Fifth (chap. iii).
[448]	*Snfrw-ḥtp*	VI D.
[450]	*Snfrw-ḫʿ.f*	Early (viol.); presumably end Fourth to early Fifth (chap. iii).
[451]	*Snfrw-snb*	Early (viol.); presumably mid-Fourth to early Fifth (chap. iii).
[452]	*Snnw-ʿnḫ*	VI E to VI F.
[455]	*Snḏm-jb: Jntj*	V B. Reign of Djedkare around the sixteenth numbering (chap. iii).
[456]	*Snḏm-jb: Mḥj*	V C. Reign of Unis.
[457]	*Srf-kȝ*	V C. Thus somewhat later than Davies' date.
[458]	*Sr-nfr*	VI E.
[462]	*Sḥtpw*	VI D. Cf. [528].
[465]	*Sḫm-ʿnḫ-Ptḥ*	V B to V C, or VI F.
[467]	*Sḫm-kȝ*	VI C or VI E.
[470]	*Sḫm-kȝ*	VI C or VI E.
[471]	*Sḫm-kȝRʿ*	Early (viol.); reign of Sahure (chap. iii).
[473]	*Sšȝt-ḥtp: Htj*	Early (viol.); presumably early Fifth (chap. iii).
[473A]	. . .	Early (viol.); the father of [473] (chap. iii).
[476]	*Sšm-nfr*	Early (viol.); presumably Sahure (chap. iii).
[477]	*Sšm-nfr*	About time of Neuserre (chap. iii).
[478]	*Sšm-nfr*	Early Djedkare (chap. iii).
[479]	*Sšm-nfr*	V D.
[482]	*Sšm-nfr: Ḥbȝ*	V B. Time of Djedkare.
[484]	*St-kȝ*	Middle to end Fourth (chap. iii).
[485]	*Stj-kȝj*	V C.
[486]	*Sdȝwg*	VI E.
[489]	*Špsj*	Early; probably early Fifth.
[491]	*Špsskȝf-ʿnḫ*	Early Fifth. The tomb of the father of [21]. Since

we have dated the latter to the reign of Neferirkare, the date of this tomb will have to be adjusted somewhat. In the tomb of his grandson [258], *Špssk3f-ʿnḫ* is a priest of Neferirkare, so he probably lived into that reign.

[492]	*Špssk3f-ʿnḫ*	VI C.
[493]	*Špssk3f-ʿnḫ*	V D.
[495]	*Q3r: Mrjjrʿ-nfr*	VI D.
[500]	*Qd-ns*	VI D.
[505]	*K3j*	V C.
[509]	*K3-jrw-Ḫwfw*	V B, but only on the assumption that it is not a later insertion into the mastaba of *Pr-sn* [143]. Otherwise there would be several possibilities, ranging as far as VI G. Probably best to ignore this.
[513]	*K3-wʿb*	Mid-Fourth (chap. iii).
[515]	*K3-pw-Jnpw*	VI F.
[517]	*K3-pw-Ptḥ*	VI C.
[518]	*K3-pw-nswt: K3j*	V C. Our date is, if anything, even later in the Fifth Dynasty than Junker's, which reinforces his argument that *K3-pw-nswt* is to be dated considerably later than the *J3btjt* whose priest he was and whose chapel he rebuilt.
[521]	*K3-m-ʿḥ*	Khufu (chap. iii).
[523]	*K3-m-nfrt*	VI E.
[526]	*K3-m-rḥw*	V C.
[528]	*K3-m-snw*	VI D. This evidently confirms Kees's dating of the mastaba as opposed to that of Firth, by which I allowed myself to be unduly influenced in chap. iii.
[530]	*K3-m-ṯnnt*	V C. Reign of Djedkare.
[531]	*K3-n-nswt*	Early (viol.); early Fifth, presumably Sahure or Neferirkare.
[532]	*K3-n-nswt*	V D. This is the tomb of the son of the last, built posthumously. A date in the reign of Unis would seem to be the latest possibility.
[533]	*K3-nbw.f*	Late.
[534]	*K3-nfr*	Early (viol.); Djedefre to Khafre (chap. iii).
[535]	*K3-nfr*	Mid-Fourth (chap. iii).
[536]	*K3-nfr*	Early (viol.); early Fifth (chap. iii).
[543]	*K3-ḫnt*	V B. The son of the next. My date in chap. iii, which is little more than a rough estimate, is evidently a bit too late. Approximately time of Menkauhor or Djedkare.
[543A]	*K3-ḫnt*	V B. The father of the above. About the time of Neuserre.

[544]	*Kꜣ-ḫr-Ptḥ: Ftk-tꜣ*	VI G.
[546]	*Kꜣ-sḏꜣ*	Early (viol.). The titles ranked are actually the ones in the tomb of his father *Kꜣ-nfr* [536] and belong to the early Fifth. His own tomb would be somewhat later, around the middle of the Fifth Dynasty.
[548]	*Kꜣ-gm-nj*	V D. Reign of Teti.
[550]	*Kꜣ-dwꜣ*	V D.
[552]	*Gm.n.j*	VI D to VI E (if not First Intermediate).
[553]	*Gm.n.j-m-ḥꜣt*	Tenth Dynasty (chap. iii).
[558]	*Tp-m-ꜥnḫ*	VI E.
[559A]	*Tp-m-ꜥnḫ*	V B.
[560]	*Ttj*	VI G.
[562]	*Ṯꜣwtj*	VI C.
[563]	*Ṯꜣwtj: Rsj*	VI B.
[564]	*Ṯjj*	V C.
[567]	*Ṯntj*	V B (if not earlier).
[569]	*Ṯntj*	Fourth Dynasty (? chap. iii). The title sequences would fit V B.
[570]	*Ṯntj*	V B.
[575]	*Ṯtj*	Mernere to early Pepi II (chap. iii).
[576]	*Ṯtw*	Late.
[582]	*Dwꜣ-ḥp*	VI G.
[583]	*Dbḥ-n*	Menkaure (chap. iii).
[590]	*Ḏꜣtj*	V C.
[591]	*Ḏꜥw*	VI D.
[592]	*Ḏꜥw: Šmꜣj*	VI F.
[598]	. . .	Mid-Fourth to late Fourth (chap. iii).
[600]	. . .	VI E.
[601D]	Decree of Pepi II from the Valley Temple of Menkaure: dated to the thirty-fifth numbering.	
[602]	Koptos Decrees	VI G. End of the Eighth Dynasty.
[603]	Expedition of *Ṯꜣwtj Jqr* to Wadi Hammamat: Late (viol.).	

This list contains 255 sources, of which 42 were dated within narrow limits in chapter iii; these datings are not new. The other 213 are based at least partly on the ranking patterns. In the overwhelming majority of cases, the tombs could be grouped by characteristic title sequences in such a fashion as not to conflict with the range of time permitted by archeological criteria. The few cases of discrepancy appear largely to be the result of faulty archeological judgments on the part of the author; he hopes that enough material has been presented here to enable the reader to form his own opinion as to the validity of the use of title sequences as an index for dating.

VII

CONCLUSIONS

*

The various changes discussed in the preceding chapters were presented outside their historical context. In this concluding chapter we will attempt to remedy the omission and will begin by gathering the pertinent data into a single list. For period headings we have, for the first time in this study, employed absolute dates. They are based on the chronology given at the end of chapter v; the assumption that Period VI G also lasted about thirty years, until the end of the Eighth Dynasty; a similar estimate for the length of the reigns of Userkaf, Sahure, and Neferirkare before the introduction of the ranking system;* and an approximate date of 2250 B.C. for the end of the Eighth Dynasty.†

2520–2490

Userkaf: Founds the Fifth Dynasty.
Introduces the official cult of Re.‡
Builds the first royal solar temple.

(In this period we begin to detect the first traces of the accumulation of power in the hands of provincial magnates in Upper Egypt.)

2490–2450

Neferirkare: Issues the first standardized system of ranking titles in place of the rather informal, haphazard system that appears to have prevailed before.

* Taking the reign of Userkaf as about seven years, that of Sahure as fourteen and allowing about ten years to the reign of Neferirkare until the introduction of the ranking system. Cf. *Urkunden*, I, 242, 246, 248.

† This leaves about a century for the period before the rise of Thebes. Henry Fischer informs me that in his unpublished thesis *Dendereh in the Old Kingdom and Its Aftermath*, p. 372, he has concluded that a minimum of six successive overseers of priests were to be dated between the end of the Sixth Dynasty and the beginning of Theban expansion. This would result in about the span of time used in our estimate. It must be remembered, of course, that Period VI G extended into what is usually called the Eighth Dynasty (Koptos Decrees). We thus prefer the older estimate for the length of the First Intermediate Period rather than that proposed, among others, by Stock, *Die Erste Zwischenzeit Ägyptens*, pp. 91 ff.

‡ Compare the enormous donation of land to Re made by Userkaf, Baer, "A Note on Egyptian Units of Area in the Old Kingdom," *JNES*, XV, 117.

Neuserre (?):	Osiris appears for the first time in the funerary invocation formulas.*
Djedkare:	Ceases to build royal solar temples. Changes organization of priesthoods at the royal pyramid temples from priest of king to priest of the pyramid. Introduces office of overseer of Upper Egypt.
2450–2430	
Djedkare:	Changes the ranking system for the first time since its introduction; henceforth it is changed by every king except Pepi I. Extends the new-style royal priesthoods sporadically to the cults of his predecessors. Possibly introduces the type of domain administrator known as *ḫntj-š*.
Unis:	Founds the Sixth Dynasty. Drastically changes the rank of the new-style priesthoods at his pyramid so as to outrank all other titles. The corresponding change in the priesthoods of his predecessors was probably not made until the next period.
2430–2400	
Unis:	Inscribes pyramid texts for the first time on the walls of the chambers and passages of his pyramid.
Teti:	Reorganizes the administration of the southernmost part of Upper Egypt by placing the entire administration of a nome (for the first time officially) in the hands of one person. The remainder of Upper Egypt is still ruled (at least in theory) by a centralized administration.
2400–2370	
Pepi I:	Forms a close dynastic alliance with a prominent Upper Egyptian family, which upon his death and during the minority of his sons practically rules the country.
2370–2350	
Mernere and Pepi II:	The country is ruled by a regency. The rank of the priesthoods of Fifth Dynasty kings is reduced. Decentralized administration is extended to the central portion of Upper Egypt, probably for the benefit of the

* The following tombs from Period V B contain invocation formulas with the name of Osiris: [115], [164], [294], [363], [455], [482]. Of these [164] can be dated to the reign of Neuserre and [294, 482] to the reign of Djedkare. None antedates Neuserre. Osiris occurs on an unpublished fragment from the mortuary temple of Djedkare, to my knowledge the earliest example of this god on a royal monument.

uncles of the young king. Titles typical of the newer form of administration appear in the northern part of Upper Egypt but never completely replace the older ones.

2350–2330

Pepi II: The titles of the Upper Egyptian nomarchs rise to their highest ranking.

2330–2310

Pepi II: A sudden drop in the ranking of the titles of the nomarchs. Does it reflect a reassertion of central authority? The family of the mother of Pepi II continues to hold high office. [229A].

2280–2250

Pepi II: His long reign finally comes to an end.

(The Koptos Decrees [602] show that the ephemeral kings at the end of the Old Kingdom still retained some measure of control over Upper Egypt, though this was becoming increasingly dependent on the co-operation of the powerful local families.)

2250–2150

(Presumably at some point within this period the standardized system of ranking titles collapsed.)

The reader will notice that the Sixth Dynasty has here been begun with Unis rather than the more traditional Teti. The suggestion was, to my knowledge, first made by Lauer on the basis of blocks from the pyramid of Djedkare that were found reused in the casing of the pyramid of Unis.* He also points out that Unis was the first king to inscribe Pyramid Texts in his pyramid. This suggestion can now be considerably strengthened. It was in the reign of Unis that the ranking of the priests of the king's pyramid was changed radically; it is quite possible that there is some connection between this and the appearance of the Pyramid Texts. In Period VI C the rank of the priesthoods at the pyramids of the kings of the Fifth Dynasty was again reduced, but the priesthoods at the pyramid of Unis retained their high rank together with those of the later kings. This seems to indicate that Unis was felt to belong with the kings of the reigning dynasty, and would support Lauer's suggestion.

In 1952, Ahmed Fakhry conducted excavations at the Haram el-Shauwaf in the course of which certain facts appeared that might have

* Lauer, "Fouilles du Service des Antiquités à Saqqarah," *ASAE*, XXXIX, 454.

a bearing on the question. The excavation was largely devoted to the queen's pyramid which turned out to have an unusually large and complex plan. Though it was badly destroyed, enough remained of its relief decoration to show that the scenes had been secondarily altered: stereotyped texts above the queen's figure had been erased and replaced by vultures and other royal insignia.* It is tempting to connect this with the change in dynasty just proposed. The unusual position enjoyed by this lady (whose name unfortunately was not recovered) recalls that of Queen *Ḫnt-kꜣw.s*, who apparently formed the link between the Fourth and Fifth Dynasties. The nature of the link in this case, if any, remains obscure; it does not seem likely that she would have remarried after the death of Djedkare, who reigned for twenty-eight years and can hardly have been a young man when he died. Did she attempt to rule the country by herself, only to be replaced by the founder of the new dynasty? This might explain the secondary alterations in the reliefs of her temple and probably agrees better with the noticeable lack of respect shown by Unis for the monument of his predecessor than assuming she married Unis. I recall seeing a column built into the walls of the Unis Causeway that in form, size, and workmanship could well have come from this queen's temple, in which case Unis would have showed no more respect for her pyramid than for her husband's.

Let us now return to the beginning of the Fifth Dynasty. It is difficult nowadays to conceive the intellectual frame of mind that accompanied the rise of the official cult of Re at the beginning of the Fifth Dynasty. The author has no particular preferences and is averse to rummaging in the Pyramid Texts for data to fit a theory. A remark of Kees's in regard to the Heliopolitan system of gods is pertinent here. He refers to, "eine für die heliopolitanische Geisteswelt sehr bezeichnende bürokratische Abstimmung."† This should not be stressed too heavily, but there does seem to be a parallelism between the attitude referred to here and the mentality out of which the organized system of ranking titles must have arisen.

We should not underestimate the intellectual feat which that system involved. As our survey of the material has shown, the titles in tombs previous to Neferirkare were not arranged completely chaotically. The uncertainties were great, fluctuations were common and the order frequently violated the standard sequence chart of later times. But still, there is a considerable amount of consistency even in the early tombs. The important point, though, is that there is no evidence for a really

* I owe this information to the kindness of Dr. Fakhry, under whose supervision I worked while on a Fulbright grant in Egypt.

† *Der Götterglaube im alten Ägypten*, p. 240.

well developed system of ranking the titles. They were arranged more or less according to rank, with many exceptions, presumably pretty much as seemed best to the scribe decorating the tomb. As a result, it was impossible to detect any system underlying the rankings even in those tombs of the period that showed internally consistent rankings. Contemporary tombs might have a completely different system of ranking and all the indications are that individual ideas were given free rein.* I rather suspect that nobody really had any definite ideas as to the proper ranking of titles, except a vague one that a title such as *jrj-pꜥt* was a high-ranking one and therefore most appropriately written at the head of a column of titles.

The introduction of a standardized system of ranking the titles in the reign of Neferirkare involved the gathering, ordering, and systematization of an enormous number of titles. The common ones discussed in this study are only a small fraction of the total, and no matter how carelessly the work was done in practice (and the great amount of fluctuation in Period V B does indicate a certain lack of perfection), a considerable amount of thinking about the structure and formalization of an extremely large and complex state must have been done.

It is only to be expected that the introduction of this organization comes at a time at which the administration of Egypt was finally divorced from the family of the king and his household.† The development is of the kind that one would expect to accompany the rise of an independent civil service and of families of powerful officials. I presume that this new class soon became too independent for the comfort of the king.

In any case, the available evidence seems to indicate an attempt on the part of the king to restore the central position of the monarchy, beginning about the time of Djedkare. Ricke believes that the reintroduction of older elements in the royal funerary cult that had been displaced in the earlier Fifth Dynasty by the cult of Re can be detected in the plans of the royal mortuary temples from Djedkare onward.‡ Royal solar temples were no longer built. One suspects that the change in the royal priesthoods that was introduced at this time was connected somehow with this attempted restoration of the central position of the king, but it is only with the change of the rank of these priesthoods in the next reign that the purpose behind the changes becomes clear.

One should, of course, not underestimate the position of the king

* Compare, for instance, the titles of *Jwn-Mn* [30], *Jwn-Rꜥ* [31], *Nb-m-ꜣḫt* [248], and *Sḫm-kꜣ-Rꜥ* [471], all sons of Khafre; there are many other examples.

† Helck, *Untersuchungen*, p. 58.

‡ *Bemerkungen zur ägyptischen Baukunst des Alten Reiches*, II, 83 ff.

even at the time when the cult of Re was at its height. Three incidents reported of King Neferirkare indicate that he possessed in the minds of the Egyptians an aura and majesty almost inconceivable to us. *Rˁ-wr* [300] (*Urkunden*, I, 232) was accidentally struck on his foot by the king's scepter in the course of a ceremony. The results (only magical, or perhaps also due to the intervention of the bodyguard?) would have been dreadful if his majesty had not apologized—in any case, the event was deemed worthy of commemoration. On two occasions, Neferirkare suggested as a special mark of favor, which was duly recorded in the tombs of the persons concerned, that *Wꜣš-Ptḥ* [105] (*Urkunden*, I, 41) and *Ptḥ-špss* [164] (*Urkunden*, I, 53) kiss his foot rather than the dust in front of it.

But all this could not conceal the fact that officialdom was quietly amassing more and more power. The increasing size and complexity of their tombs indicates it, as does the steadily increasing size of the funerary domains and the fact that these tombs no longer cluster so closely around the royal pyramid as they had in the past. This became particularly noticeable when Djedkare moved his pyramid to South Saqqara and the high officials of his reign did not follow.

I have the impression that Djedkare attempted to battle this trend, probably not very successfully. Aside from changes on the theological plane, practical changes were also made. The new office of overseer of Upper Egypt was perhaps introduced in an attempt to get better control over the officials in Upper Egypt who by then were already firmly entrenched in decentralized, local office. Djedkare wrote enthusiastic, laudatory letters to his viziers *Rˁ-špss* [315] and *Snḏm-jb Jntj* [455], both in Period V B. One gets from them the impression that he was attempting to bind the most important figures of the administration to himself by feelings of personal loyalty. Openly he was successful; whether officialdom actually became more complaisant, we cannot tell. In any case, Djedkare seems soon afterward to have decided that a complete reorganization of the administration was the only solution to the difficulties. Just possibly the introduction of the *ḫntj-š* into the administration of public domains at this time was also part of the reorganization. Unfortunately the significance of this cannot be understood until we can get a better idea of the meaning of the term. Djedkare's reign and the Fifth Dynasty ended about ten years later. Successful or not, the reorganization of the administration that he carried out was considered a good model to follow and was repeated at regular intervals throughout the rest of the Old Kingdom.

Unis seems to have been faced by the same problems. On the theological plane he attempted to solve them by the drastic change in the rank of his priests. Teti found it necessary to recognize formally the growing autonomy of the provincial governors in the extreme south of Egypt. Could the favor shown the new class of nomarchs, reflected also by the extremely high titles they held and the fact that viziers now came to be chosen from among the provincial magnates,* be an attempt to create a counterbalance to the powerful metropolitan bureaucracy at Memphis? It seems probable, since the Sixth Dynasty apparently found it to its interest to cultivate the nomarchs of Upper Egypt; the marriage of Pepi I and the resulting extension of local autonomy seem to be an indication of this. If so, the kings of the Sixth Dynasty, in their attempt to defend themselves against uncongenial forces at Memphis only succeeded in sowing the seeds of the eventual destruction of the Old Kingdom.

* In this context too much stress should not be placed on such statements as that of *Mrjjrʿ-nfr Qȝr* [187] (*Urkunden*, I, 254) that he was sent by Mernere to be nomarch of Edfu. He was in all probability a son or descendant of *Jzj* [62] who had been nomarch before him. That he was sent to be educated at Memphis means nothing in this regard. He could still have been a representative of the hereditary provincial nobility.

BIBLIOGRAPHY

*

ABU-BAKR, ABDEL MONEIM. *Excavations at Giza 1949–1950.* Cairo, 1953.

ALLEN, T. G. *A Handbook of the Egyptian Collection.* Chicago Art Institute. Chicago, 1923.

ALLIOT, MAURICE. *Rapport sur les fouilles de Tell Edfou.* (*FIFAO*, Vol. X, Part 2.) Cairo, 1935.

"Archaeological News," *Archaeology*, VI (1953), 185.

BADAWI, A. M. "Denkmäler aus Saḳḳarah, II," *ASAE*, XL (1941), 573–80.

BAER, KLAUS. "A Note on Egyptian Units of Area in the Old Kingdom," *JNES*, XV (1956), 113–17.

BALCZ, HEINRICH. "Zur Datierung der Mastaba des *Snofru-ỉni-ỉštef* in Dahsûr," *ZÄS*, LXVII (1931), 9–15.

BARSANTI, ALEXANDRE. "Fouilles autour de la pyramide d'Ounas," *ASAE*, I (1900), 150–60.

———. "Rapport sur la fouille de Dahchour," *ASAE*, III (1902), 198–205.

BERGMANN, ERNST VON. "Inschriftliche Denkmäler der Sammlung ägyptischer Alterthümer des Österr. Kaiserhauses," *Recueil de Travaux*, VII (1886), 177–96.

BISSING, F. W. VON. *Die Mastaba des Gem-ni-kai*, 2 vols. Berlin, 1905–11.

———. "Les tombeaux d'Assouan," *ASAE*, XV (1915), 1–14.

BISSON DE LA ROQUE, FERNAND. *Rapport sur les fouilles d'Abou-Roasch* (*1922–1923*). (*FIFAO*, Vol. I, Part 3.) Cairo, 1924.

———. *Rapport sur les fouilles d'Abou-Roasch* (*1924*). (*FIFAO*, Vol. II, Part 1.) Cairo, 1925.

BLACKMAN, A. M. *The Rock Tombs of Meir.* 6 vols. London, 1914–53.

BOESER, P. A. A. *Beschreibung der aegyptischen Sammlung des Niederländischen Reichsmuseums der Altertümer in Leiden.* The Hague, 1905.

BORCHARDT, LUDWIG. *Denkmäler des Alten Reiches*, Vol. I. ("Catalogue général des antiquités égyptiennes du Musée du Caire," Vol. XCVII.) Berlin, 1937.

This volume contains Nos. 1295–1541. The projected second volume has not yet appeared.

———. *Das Grabdenkmal des Königs Ne-user-Reʿ.* ("7. Wissenschaftliche Veröffentlichung der Deutschen Orient-Gesellschaft.") Leipzig, 1907.

———. *Das Grabdenkmal des Königs Śaꜣḥu-Reʿ.* 3 vols. ("14. [und] 26. Wissenschaftliche Veröffentlichung der Deutschen Orient-Gesellschaft.") Leipzig, 1910–13.

———. "*Ḫnt-kꜣw'ś*, die Stammutter der 5ten Dynastie," *ASAE*, XXXVIII (1938), 209–16.

———. "Ein Königserlass aus Dahschur," *ZÄS*, XLII (1905), 1–11.

———. "Ein Rechnungsbuch des königlichen Hofes aus dem Alten Reiche," *Aegyptiaca: Festschrift für Georg Ebers*, pp. 8–15.

Borchardt, Ludwig. *Statuen und Statuetten von Königen und Privatleuten*, Vol. I. (Catalogue général des antiquités égyptiennes du Musée du Caire, Vol. LIII.) Berlin, 1911.

Brodrick, Mary, and Morton, A. A. "The Tomb of Pepi Ankh (Khua) near Sharuna," *PSBA*, XXI (1899), 26–33.

Capart, Jean. *L'art égyptien: Choix de documents*. 4 vols. Brussels, 1922–47.

———. *Documents pour servir à l'étude de l'art égyptien*. 2 vols. Paris, 1927–31.

———. "Pour reconstituer la biographie de Itoush," *Chronique d'Égypte*, XIV (1939), 339–40.

———. *Une rue de tombeaux à Saqqarah*. 2 vols. Brussels, 1907.

Černý, Jaroslav. "Consanguineous Marriages in Pharaonic Egypt," *JEA*, XL (1954), 23–29.

Chaban, Mohammed, "Sur une nécropole de la VIe Dynastie, à Koçeir el-Amarna," *ASAE*, III (1902), 250–53.

Chassinat, E. G. "À propos d'une tête en grès rouge du roi Didoufre," *Monuments Piot*, XXV (1921–22), 53–75.

Cooney, J. D. "Three Egyptian Families of the Old Kingdom," *Brooklyn Museum Bulletin*, XIII, No. 3 (1952), 1–18.

———. "The Wooden Statues Made for an Official of King Unas," *Brooklyn Museum Bulletin*, XV, No. 1 (1953), 1–25.

Dam, C. H. "The Tomb Chapel of Ra-ka-pou," *The University of Pennsylvania Museum Journal*, XVIII (1927), 188–200.

Daressy, Georges. "Inscription du mastaba de Pepi-Nefer à Edfou," *ASAE*, XVII (1917), 130–40.

———. "Le mastaba de Khâ-f-Khoufou à Gizeh," *ASAE*, XVI (1916), 257–67.

———. "Le mastaba de Mera," *Mémoires de l'Institut Égyptien*, III (1898), 521–71.

———. "La nécropole des grands prêtres d'Héliopolis sous l'Ancien Empire," *ASAE*, XVI (1916), 193–212.

Davies, Norman de G. *The Mastaba of Ptahhetep and Akhethetep at Saqqarah*. 2 vols. London, 1900–1901.

———. *The Rock Tombs of Deir el-Gebrâwi*. 2 vols. London, 1902.

———. *The Rock Tombs of Sheikh Saïd*. London, 1901.

———. "The Work of the Robb de Peyster Tytus Memorial Fund at Thebes," *BMMA*, XIII (1918), Supplement, 14–23.

Dennis, J. T. "New Officials of the IVth to Vth Dynasties," *PSBA*, XXVII (1905), 32–34.

Dittmann, K. H. "Zum Titel ," *ZÄS*, LXXVII (1942), 7–12.

Drioton, Étienne. "Description sommaire des chapelles funéraires de la VIe Dynastie récemment découverts derrière le mastaba de Mérérouka à Saqqarah," *ASAE*, XLIII (1943), 487–514.

Duell, Prentice, *et al. The Mastaba of Mereruka*. 2 vols. Chicago, 1938.

Dunham, Dows, "The Biographical Inscriptions of Nekhebu in Boston and Cairo," *JEA*, XXIV (1938), 1–8.

Dunham, Dows. "A 'Palimpsest' on an Egyptian Mastaba Wall," *AJA*, XXXIX (1935), 300–309.

———. "Some Old Kingdom Tomb Reliefs," *BMFA*, XXVII (1929), 36–37.

Edel, Elmar. *Altägyptische Grammatik*, Vol. I. ("Analecta Orientalia," Vol. XXXIV.) Rome, 1955.

———. "Inschriften des Alten Reiches, I," *ZÄS*, LXXIX (1954), 11–17.

———. "Inschriften des Alten Reiches, II," *MIOF*, I (1953), 210–26.

———. "Ein 'Vorsteher der Farafra-Oase' im Alten Reich?" *ZÄS*, LXXXI (1956), 67–68.

Épron, Lucienne, and Wild, Henri. *Le Tombeau de Ti*. 2 fascicules. Cairo, 1939–53.

Erman, Adolf, and Grapow, Hermann. *Wörterbuch der ägyptischen Sprache*. 6 vols. Leipzig, 1925–50.

Erman, Adolf, and Ranke, Hermann. *Ägypten und ägyptisches Leben im Altertum*. 2d ed. Tübingen, 1923.

Fakhry, Ahmed. "The Excavation of Snefru's Monuments at Dahshur: Second Preliminary Report," *ASAE*, LII (1954), 563–94.

———. *Sept tombeaux à l'est de la Grande Pyramide de Guizeh*. Cairo, 1935.

———. "Stela of the Boat-Captain Inikaf," *ASAE*, XXXVIII (1938), 35–46.

"The False Door of Ptah-Arit," *University of Pennsylvania Museum Bulletin*, II (1930), 57–59.

Firth, C. M., and Gunn, Battiscombe. *Teti Pyramid Cemeteries*. 2 vols. Cairo, 1926.

Fischer, H. G. "Four Provincial Administrators at the Memphite Cemeteries," *JAOS*, LXXIV (1954), 26–34.

Fisher, C. F. "The Harvard University–Museum of Fine Arts Egyptian Expedition," *BMFA*, XI (1913), 19–22.

———. *The Minor Cemetery at Giza*. Philadelphia, 1924.

Fraser, George. "The Early Tombs at Tehneh," *ASAE*, III (1902), 67–76, 121–30.

Gardiner, A. H. *Ancient Egyptian Onomastica*. 3 vols. London, 1947.

———. "An Unexplained Passage in the Inscription of Weni," *JEA*, XLI (1955), 121.

Garnot, J. S.-F. "Les Mastabas," *Fouilles Franco-Polonaises*, I (Cairo, 1937), 25–58.

Gauthier, Henri. "Deux noveaux princes de l'Ancien Empire à Guizeh," *ASAE*, XXII (1922), 205–7.

———. *Le livre des rois*. 5 vols. Cairo, 1907–17.

Goedicke, Hans, "A Deification of a Private Person in the Old Kingdom," *JEA*, XLI (1955), 31–33.

———. "Zu *ỉmj-rꜣ šmꜥ* und *tp-šmꜥ* im Alten Reich," *MIOF*, IV (1950), 1–10.

Grdseloff, Bernhard, "Deux inscriptions juridiques de l'Ancien Empire," *ASAE*, XLII (1943), 25–70.

———. "Notes sur deux monuments inédits de l'Ancien Empire," *ASAE*, XLII (1943), 107–25.

GRDSELOFF, BERNHARD. "Nouvelles données concernant la tente de purification," *ASAE*, LI (1951), 129–42.

GRIFFITH, F. LL. "Notes on a Tour in Upper Egypt," *PSBA*, XI (1888), 228–34.

HAAB, FRANÇOIS (ed.). *Encyclopédie photographique de l'art*. Paris, 1936——.

HALL, H. R. *Hieroglyphic Texts from Egyptian Stelae, etc., in the British Museum*, Vol. VI. London, 1922.

HASSAN, SELIM. *Excavations at Giza*. Vol. I, Oxford, 1932; Vols. II–VIII, Cairo, 1936–53.

———. "Excavations at Saqqara (1937–1938)," *ASAE*, XXXVIII (1938), 503–22.

HAYES, W. C. "Royal Decrees from the Temple of Min at Coptus," *JEA*, XXXII (1946), 3–23.

———. *The Scepter of Egypt*. New York, 1953——.

HELCK, WOLFGANG. *Untersuchungen zu den Beamtentiteln des äegyptischen Alten Reiches*. Glückstadt, 1954.

HOELSCHER, UVO. *Das Grabdenkmal des Königs Chephren*. Leipzig, 1912.

HUSSEIN, A. M. "The Reparation of the Mastaba of Meḥu at Saqqara (1940)," *ASAE*, XLII (1943), 417–45.

JAMES, T. G. H. *The Mastaba of Khentika Called Ikhekhi*. London, 1953.

JÉQUIER, GUSTAVE. *Le monument funéraire de Pepi II*. 3 vols. Cairo, 1936–40.

———. *La pyramide d'Oudjebten*. Cairo, 1928.

———. *Les pyramides des reines Neit et Apouit*. Cairo, 1933.

———. *Tombeaux de particuliers contemporains de Pepi II*. Cairo, 1929.

———. "Tombes de particuliers de l'époque de Pepi II," *ASAE*, XXXV (1935), 132–59.

JUNKER, HERMANN. *Giza*. 12 vols. Vienna, 1929–55.

———. "Die Stele des Hofarztes *'Irj*," *ZÄS*, LXIII (1928), 53–70.

———. "Weta und das Lederkunsthandwerk im Alten Reich," *Österreichische Akademie der Wissenschaften, Sitzungsberichte*, Phil-hist. Klasse, CCXXXI, No. 1 (1957).

———. "Zu den Titeln des ," *ASAE*, XLIX (1949), 207–15.

KAISER, WERNER. "Zu den Sonnenheiligtümern der 5. Dynastie," *MDIAAK*, XIV (1956), 104–16.

KAMAL, AHMED. "Fouilles à Dara et à Qoçéîr el-Amarna," *ASAE*, XII (1912), 128–42.

———. "Notes prises aux cours des inspections," *ASAE*, IX (1908), 85–91.

KEES, HERMANN. "Beiträge zur altägyptischen Provinzialverwaltung und der Geschichte des Feudalismus," *Nachrichten von der Gesellschaft der Wissenschaften zu Göttingen*, phil-hist. Klasse, 1932, 85–115.

———. "Beiträge zur Geschichte des Vezirats im Alten Reich," *Nachrichten von der Gesellschaft der Wissenschaften zu Göttingen*, phil.-hist. Klasse, N.F. IV, No. 2 (1940), 39–54.

———. "Eine Familie königlicher Maurermeister aus dem Anfang der 6. Dynastie," *WZKM*, LIV (1957), 91–100.

———. *Der Götterglaube im alten Ägypten*. 2d ed. Berlin, 1956.

KOEFOED-PETERSEN, OTTO. *Recueil des inscriptions hiéroglyphiques de la Glyptothèque Ny Carlsberg*. Brussels, 1936.

LABIB HABACHI, "A Group of Unpublished Old and Middle Kingdom Graffiti on Elephantine," *WZKM*, LIV (1957), 55–71.

LAUER, J.-P. "Fouilles du Service des Antiquités à Saqqarah," *ASAE*, XXXIX (1939), 447–67.

LECLANT, JEAN. "Compte-rendu des fouilles et travaux menés en Égypte durant les campagnes 1948–1950," *Orientalia*, N.S. XIX (1950), 360–73, 489–501.

LEGRAIN, GEORGES. "Notes archéologiques prises au Gebel Abou Fodah," *ASAE*, I (1900), 3–14.

LEPSIUS, K. R. *Auswahl der wichtigsten Urkunden des aegyptischen Alterthums*. Leipzig, 1842.

———. *Denkmäler aus Äegypten und Äthiopien*. 12 vols., Berlin, 1849–56.

———. ———. *Ergänzungsband*. Leipzig, 1913.

———. ———. *Text*. 5 vols. Leipzig, 1897–1913.

LUTZ, H. F. *Egyptian Statues and Statuettes in the Museum of Anthropology of the University of California*. Leipzig, 1930.

———. *Egyptian Tomb Steles and Offering Stones of the Museum of Anthropology and Ethnology of the University of California*. Leipzig, 1927.

LYTHGOE, A. M. *The Tomb of Perneb*. New York, 1916.

MACRAMALLAH, R. N. *Le Mastaba d'Idout*. Cairo, 1935.

MARIETTE, AUGUSTE. *Abydos*, 2 vols. Paris, 1869–80.

———. *Catalogue général des monuments d'Abydos*. Paris, 1880.

———. *Les mastabas de l'Ancien Empire*. Paris, 1889.

MASPERO, G. C. C. *Le Musée Égyptien*. 3 vols. Cairo, 1890–1915.

———. "Trois années de fouilles dans les tombeaux de Thèbes et de Memphis," *MMAFC*, I (1884), 133–242.

MOGENSEN, M. P. *Inscriptions hiéroglyphiques du Musée National de Copenhague*. Copenhagen, 1918.

———. *Le mastaba égyptien de la Glyptothèque Ny Carlsberg*. Copenhagen, 1921.

MOHR, H. T. *The Maṣṭaba of Hetep-her-akhti*. Leiden, 1943.

MONTET, PIERRE. *Abou-Roach*. Paris, 1946.

———. "Les tombeaux dits de Kasr-el-Sayad," *Kemi*, VI (1936), 81–129.

MORET, ALEXANDRE. "Une nouvelle disposition testamentaire de l'Ancien Empire égyptien," *CRAIBL* (1914), 539–46.

MORET, ALEXANDRE, and LEFEBVRE, GUSTAVE. "Un nouvel acte de fondation à Tehneh," *Revue égyptologique*, N.S., I (1919), 30–38.

MORGAN, J. J. M. DE. *Catalogue des monuments et inscriptions de l'Égypte antique*. 3 vols. Vienna, 1894–1909.

———. "Découverte du mastaba de Ptah-chepsés dans la nécropole d'Abou-Sir," *Revue archéologique*, ser. 3, XXIV (1894), 18–33.

———. *Fouilles à Dahchour*. 2 vols. Vienna, 1895–1903.

MURRAY, M. A. *Index of Names and Titles of the Old Kingdom*. London, 1908.

———. *Saqqara Mastabas*. 2 vols. London, 1905–37.

MURRAY, M. A. "Some Fresh Inscriptions," *Ancient Egypt*, IV (1917), 62–68.

MURRAY, M. A. and PETRIE, HILDA. *Seven Memphite Tomb Chapels*. London, 1952.

NEWBERRY, P. E. "The Inscribed Tombs of Ekhmîm," *LAAA*, IV (1912), 99–120.

———. "A Sixth Dynasty Tomb at Thebes," *ASAE*, IV (1903), 97–100.

———. "Three Old Kingdom Travellers to Byblos and Pwenet," *JEA*, XXIV (1938), 182–84.

NIMS, C. F. "Some Notes on the Family of Mereruka," *JAOS*, LVIII (1938), 638–47.

PETRIE, W. M. F. *Athribis*. London, 1908.

———. *Dendereh*. 2 vols. London, 1900.

———. *Deshasheh*. London, 1898.

———. *Gizeh and Rifeh*. London, 1907.

———. *Medum*. London, 1892.

———. *Meydum and Memphis (III)*. London, 1910.

———. *Sedment*. London, 1924.

PETRIE, W. M. F., and MACKAY, E. J. H. *Bahrein and Hemamieh*. London, 1929.

PIRENNE, JACQUES. *Histoire des institutions et du droit privé de l'Ancienne Égypte*. 3 vols. Brussels, 1932–35.

PIRIE, A. A., and PAGET, R. F. E. *The Tomb of Ptah-hetep*. London, 1898.

PORTER, BERTHA, and MOSS, R. L. B. *Topographical Bibliography of Ancient Egyptian Hieroglyphic Texts, Reliefs and Paintings*. 7 vols. Oxford, 1927–51.

QUIBELL, J. E. *Excavations at Saqqara*. 6 vols. Cairo, 1907–23.

QUIBELL, J. E., and HAYTER, A. G. K. *Teti Pyramid, North Side*. Cairo, 1927.

RANKE, HERMANN. *Die ägyptischen Personennamen*. 2 vols. Hamburg, 1932–52.

"Recent Discoveries at the Giza Pyramids," *BMFA*, XXIII (1925), 12–14.

REID, R. W. *Illustrated Catalogue of the Anthropological Museum, Marischal College, University of Aberdeen*. Aberdeen, 1912.

REISNER, G. A. *The Development of the Egyptian Tomb down to the Accession of Cheops*. Cambridge, Mass., 1936.

———. "Excavations in Egypt and Ethiopia 1922–1925," *BMFA*, XXIII (1925), 17–29.

———. "A Family of Royal Estate Stewards of Dynasty V," *BMFA*, XXXVII (1939), 29–35.

———. *A History of the Giza Necropolis*, Vol. I. Cambridge, Mass., 1942.

———. "Nefertkauw, the Eldest Daughter of Sneferuw," *ZÄS*, LXIV (1929), 97–99.

———. "New Acquisitions of the Egyptian Department," *BMFA*, XI (1913), 53–66.

———. "Report on the Egyptian Expedition During 1934–35," *BMFA*, XXXIII (1935), 69–77.

———. "The Servants of the *Ka*," *BMFA*, XXXII (1934), 1–12.

REISNER, G. A. "The Tomb of Meresankh, a Great-Granddaughter of Queen Hetepheres I and Sneferuw," *BMFA*, XXV (1927), 61–78.

REISNER, G. A., and FISHER, C. S. "Preliminary Report on the Work of the Harvard–Boston Expedition in 1911–13," *ASAE*, XIII (1913), 227–52.

REISNER, G. A., and SMITH, W. S. *A History of the Giza Necropolis*, Vol. II. Cambridge, Mass., 1955.

RICKE, HERBERT. *Bemerkungen zur ägyptischen Baukunst des Alten Reiches*. 2 vols. Zürich, 1944–50.

———. "Erster Grabungsbericht über das Sonnenheiligtum des Königs Userkaf bei Abusir," *ASAE*, LIV (1956), 75–82.

———. "Zweiter Grabungsbericht über das Sonnenheiligtum des Königs Userkaf bei Abusir," *ASAE*, LIV (1956), 305–16.

ROUGÉ, EMMANUEL DE. *Inscriptions hiéroglyphiques copiés en Égypte*. Paris, 1877–79.

R[OWE], L. E. "Two Mastaba Chambers," *BMFA*, VIII (1910), 19–20.

SAAD, ZAKI. "A Preliminary Report on the Excavations at Saqqara, 1939–1940," *ASAE*, XL (1941), 675–714.

———. "Preliminary Report on the Excavations of the Department of Antiquities at Saqqara, 1942–1943," *ASAE*, XLIII (1943), 449–86.

———. "Preliminary Report on the Royal Excavations at Saqqara," *Supplément aux ASAE*, Cahier No. 3 (1947), pp. 55–103.

SCHÄFER, HEINRICH. *Aegyptische Inschriften aus den Königlichen Museen zu Berlin*. Leipzig, 1913–24.

———. *Priestergräber und andere Grabfunde vom Ende des Alten Reiches bis zur Griechischen Zeit vom Totentempel des Ne-user-Rê*. ("8. Wissenschaftliche Veröffentlichung der Deutschen Orient-Gesellschaft.") Leipzig, 1908.

SCHOTT, SIEGFRIED, "Zur Krönungstitulatur der Pyramidenzeit," *Nachrichten der Akademie der Wissenschaften in Göttingen*, phil.-hist. Klasse, No. 4 (1956), pp. 55–79.

SCOTT-MONCRIEFF, P. D. *Hieroglyphic Texts from Egyptian Stelae, etc., in the British Museum*. Vol. I. London, 1911.

SEATTLE ART MUSEUM. *Handbook*. Seattle, 1951.

SETHE, K. H. *Urkunden des Alten Reiches*. 2d ed. Leipzig, 1932–33.

SMITH, W. S. *A History of Egyptian Sculpture and Painting in the Old Kingdom*. 2d ed. London, 1949.

———. "Inscriptional Evidence for the History of the Fourth Dynasty," *JNES*, XI (1952), 113–28.

———. "The Origin of Some Unidentified Old Kingdom Reliefs," *AJA*, XLVI (1942), 509–31.

———. "Topography of the Old Kingdom Cemetery at Saqqarah" (in Reisner, *The Development of the Egyptian Tomb*, pp. 390–411).

SMOLENSKI, THADÉE. "Le Tombeau d'un prince de la VIe Dynastie à Charouna," *ASAE*, VIII (1907), 149–53.

SPELEERS, LOUIS, *Recueil des inscriptions égyptiennes des Musées Royaux du Cinquantenaire à Bruxelles*. Brussels, 1923.

Spiegelberg, Wilhelm, and Pörtner, Balthasar. *Aegyptische Grabsteine und Denksteine aus Süddeutschen Sammlungen.* 3 vols. Strasbourg, 1902–6.

Steindorff, Georg. *Das Grab des Ti.* Leipzig, 1913.

Stock, Hanns. *Die erste Zwischenzeit Ägyptens.* Rome, 1949.

Vandier, Jacques. *Manuel d'archéologie égyptienne.* Paris, 1952——.

Varille, Alexandre. *La Tombe de Ni-ankh-Pepi à Zâouiyet el Mayetîn.* Cairo, 1938.

Weil, Arthur. *Die Veziere des Pharaonenreiches.* Strasbourg, 1908.

Weill, Raymond. *Des monuments et de l'histoire des IIe et IIIe Dynasties égyptiennes.* Paris, 1908.

Wiedemann, Alfred and Pörtner, Balthasar. *Aegyptische Grabreliefs aus der Grossherzoglichen Altertümer-Sammlung zu Karlsruhe.* Strasbourg, 1906.

Wilke, Carl. "Zur Personifikation von Pyramiden," *ZÄS*, LXX (1934), 56–83.

Williams, C. L. R. *The Decoration of the Tomb of Per-nēb.* New York, 1932.

Wit, Constant de. "Enquête sur le titre de *śmr pr*," *Chronique d'Égypte*, XXXI (1956), 89–104.

Wreszinski, Walter. *Aegyptische Inschriften aus dem K. K. Hofmuseum in Wien.* Leipzig, 1906.

———. *Atlas zur altägyptischen Kulturgeschichte.* Vol. III. Leipzig, 1936.

Zayed, Abd el Hamid. "Réflexions sur une statue de 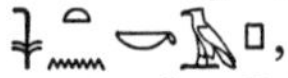, menuisier et constructeur de la fin de l'Ancien Empire," *Trois études d'égyptologie* (Cairo, 1956), pp. 1–11.